Honoré de Balzac, Clara Bell, Jno. Rudd, George Saintsbury

**The Deputy for Arcis - Part II**

And, The middle Classes

Honoré de Balzac, Clara Bell, Jno. Rudd, George Saintsbury

**The Deputy for Arcis - Part II**
*And, The middle Classes*

ISBN/EAN: 9783337061197

Printed in Europe, USA, Canada, Australia, Japan

Cover: Foto ©ninafisch / pixelio.de

More available books at **www.hansebooks.com**

H. DE BALZAC

# THE
# DEPUTY FOR ARCIS
PART II

AND

# THE MIDDLE CLASSES

TRANSLATED BY

JNO. RUDD, B.A., and CLARA BELL

WITH A PREFACE BY

GEORGE SAINTSBURY

PHILADELPHIA
THE GEBBIE PUBLISHING CO., Ltd.
1899

# CONTENTS

|  | PAGE |
|---|---|
| *PREFACE* . . . . . . . . . . | ix |
| *THE DEPUTY FOR ARCIS* | |
|     PART II . . . . . . . . . . | 1 |
| *THE MIDDLE CLASSES* . . . . . . . | 48 |

# LIST OF ILLUSTRATIONS

CAST OF BALZAC'S HAND . . . . . . *Frontispiece.*
    *Reproduced by kind permission of M. le Vicomte de Spoelberch de Lovenjoul.*

                                                                      PAGE

"EH, WELL, YES, I LOVE YOU," SAID HE . . . . . 105
    *Drawn by D. Murray-Smith.*

IT WERE USELESS TO PAINT A BALL OF THIS KIND . . . 143
    *Drawn by W. Boucher.*

"BUT DOES MADEMOISELLE REALLY SUIT ME?" REPLIED LA PEYRADE . . . . . . . . . . 268
    *Drawn by J. Ayton Symington.*

"BUT LOOK AT THE DOCTOR," SHE CRIED . . . . . 425
    *Drawn by F. C. Tilney.*

# PREFACE.

"LE DÉPUTÉ D'ARCIS," like the still less generally known "Les Petits Bourgeois," stands on a rather different footing from the rest of Balzac's work. Both were posthumous, and both, having been left unfinished, were completed by the author's friend, Charles Rabou. Rabou is not much known nowadays as a man of letters; he must not be confused with the writer Hippolyte Babou, the friend of Baudelaire, the reputed inventor of the title "Fleurs du Mal," and the author of some very acute articles in the great collection of Crepet's "Poètes Français." But he figures pretty frequently in association of one kind or another with Balzac, and would appear to have been thoroughly imbued with the scheme and spirit of the Comédie. At the same time, it does not appear that even the indefatigable and most competent M. de Lovenjoul is perfectly certain where Balzac's labors end and those of Rabou begin.

It would seem, however (and certainly internal evidence has nothing to say on the other side), that the severance, or rather the junction, must have taken place somewhere about the point where, after the introduction of Maxime de Trailles, the interest suddenly shifts altogether from the folk of Arcis and the conduct of their election to the hitherto unknown Comte de Sallenauve. It would, no doubt, be possible, and even easy, to discover in Balzac's undoubted work—for instance, in "Le Curé de Village" and "Illusions Perdues"—instances of shiftings of interest nearly as abrupt and of changes in the main centre of the story nearly as decided. Nor is it possible, considering the weakness of constructive finish which always marked Balzac, to rule out offhand the substitution, after an unusually lively and business-like beginning, of the nearly always frigid scheme of letters, topped up with a conclusion in which, with very doubtful art, as many personages of the Comédie, and even direct references to as many of its books as possible, are dragged in. But it is as nearly as possible certain that he would never have left things in such a condition, and I do not even think that he would ever have arranged them in quite the same state, even as an experiment.

The book belongs to the Champenois or Arcis-sur-Aube series, which is so brilliantly followed by "Une Ténébreuse Affaire." It is curious and worth notice, as showing the conscientious fashion in which Balzac always set about his mature work, that though his provincial stories are taken from parts of France widely distant from one another, the selection is by no means haphazard, and arranges itself with ease into groups corresponding to certain haunts or sojourns of the author. There is the Loire group, furnished by his youthful remembrances of Tours and Saumur, and by later ones down to the Breton coast. There is the group of which Alençon and the Breton-Norman frontiers are the field, and the scenery of which was furnished by early visits of which we know little, but the fact of the existence of which is of the first importance, as having given birth to the "Chouans," and so to the whole Comédie in a way. There is the Angoumois-Limousin group, for which he informed himself during his frequent visits to the Carraud family. And lastly, there is one of rather wider extent, and not connected with so definite a centre, but including the Morvan, Upper Burgundy, and part of Champagne, which seems to have been commended to him by his stay at Saché and other places. This was his latest set of studies, and to this "Le Député d'Arcis" of course belongs. To round off the subject, it is noteworthy that no part of the coast except a little in the north, with the remarkable exceptions of the scenes of "La Recherche de l'Absolu" and one or two others; nothing in the greater part of Brittany and Normandy; nothing in Guienne, Gascony, Languedoc, Provence, or Dauphiné, seems to have attracted him. Yet some of these scenes—and with some of them he had meddled in the Days of Ignorance—are the most tempting of any in France to the romancer, and his abstention from them is one of the clearest proofs of his resolve to speak only of that he did know.

The certainly genuine part of the present book is, as certainly, not below anything save his very best work. It belongs, indeed, to the more minute and "meticulous" part of that work, not to the bolder and more ambitious side. There is no Goriot, no Eugénie Grandet, not even any Corentin or Vautrin, hardly so much as a Rastignac about it. But the good little people of Arcis-sur-Aube are represented "in their natural," as Balzac's great compatriot would have said, with extraordinary felicity and force. The electoral meeting in Madame Marions' house is certainly one of the best things in the whole Comédie for completeness within its own limits, and none of the personages, official or other, can be said to suffer from that touch of exaggeration which, to some tastes, interferes with the more celebrated and perhaps more generally attractive delineations of Parisian journalism in "Illusions Perdues" and similar books. In fact, in what he wrote of "Le Député d'Arcis," Balzac seems to have had personal knowledge to go upon, without any personal grievances to revenge or any personal crazes to enforce. The latter, it is true, often prompted his sublimest work; but the former frequently helped to produce his least successful. In "Le Député d'Arcis" he is at the happy mean. It is not necessary to give an elaborate bibliography of it; for, as has been said, only the "Election" part is certainly Balzac's. This appeared in a newspaper, "L'Union Monarchique," for April and May 1847.

**G. S.**

# PREFACE.

The least known of Balzac's works is undoubtedly "Les Petits Bourgeois;" it was not published until 1854, more than three years after his death, being the last, with the exception of a few minor pieces, to reach the public. It is believed that Charles Rabou—who finished "Le Député d'Arcis"—completed this. Much of it seems quite foreign to Balzac's style, particularly the often long drawn-out dialogues; much of which must be that of another hand. Then the abrupt breaks, though Balzac was not by any means free from this vice, give a further tendency to this opinion.

It will be noted that, in a sense, he clears the stage of a number of his characters—Corentin, Popinot, *et al.;* the former of whom resigns his bâton to his successor, and the latter, one of his pet goody characters, being found decently interred, though honored still. Lousteau, after a long rest, is again shown in his great forte of "turning an honest dollar" in connection with the despised press, in the sale of the "Écho de la Bièvre." Cérizet, first met with in "Illusions Perdues," comes more fully on the scene than in any other volume—the same villain still. The spy, Dutocq, who was the cause of Rabourdin's downfall in "Les Employés," drops out without his meed of poetical justice. To give Balzac his proper due, it must be said that he seldom controverts the happenings of real life to attain the "married and live-happy-ever-after style" of the usual novel.

In "Les Petits Bourgeois" several new characters appear, perhaps the three most notable ones being Madame Cardinal, Louis-Jérôme Thuillier (only slightly mentioned in "Les Employés"), and Mademoiselle Marie-Jeanne-Brigitte Thuillier; of the first we would have wished to see more; the second is a careful study of the clerk-beau arrived at middle age; while the last mentioned is a clean, delightful sketch—perhaps a little harsh at times—of the old maid who has "made her way." One finds in Brigitte traces of Cousin Bette, without her evil mind, and of Mademoiselle Cormon in "Les Rivalités."

"Les Petits Bourgeois" has little of history to record. As said it was not published until 1854, although Balzac says of it, in March, 1844: "I may tell you that my work called 'Les Petits Bourgeois,' owing to much difficulty of construction, requires a full month of labor; still it is entirely written." In October, 1846, he says again: "It is to these scruples that the delay which has injured some of my works is due; for example: 'Les Paysans,' which has been nearly completed for a long time, and 'Les Petits Bourgeois,' which has been in type at the printery for quite eighteen months."

Now this seems strange in view of the fact that Balzac always needed money. In other of these prefaces it has been shown what "finished" and "completed" often meant. It was this that caused the trouble between himself and the publisher of "Le Lys dans la Vallée," his leaving it in an incomplete state after it was "finished." In the case of the present volume, neither the MS. nor proofs were ever seen by anybody. It really first came out in the "Pays," in the Autumn of the year mentioned.

PUBLISHER'S EDITOR.

# THE DEPUTY FOR ARCIS.

## PART II.

When Vautrin had mentioned Bixiou as the recruiting-sergeant of his company, this was what he had meant by calling him her "client." Unless one has never read Molière's "Avare," he cannot but be aware of Maître Simon, who ever stands as a screen between the usurer's traffic and the arm of the law.

Now, Master Bixiou, whose extremely free-and-easy life frequently compelled him to have recourse to his credit, had, through an intermediary, found himself in business relations with Jacqueline Collin; and by his monkey-skill in worming out mysteries, especially such as might interest himself, in spite of the queer disguises in which she involved herself, he had succeeded in getting face to face with his creditor. Then, one day, being quite unable to meet a bill which would fall due on the morrow, he had boldly attacked the ogress, to work the miracle of extracting a renewal on favorable terms. The woman liked a man of spirit, and, like all wild beasts, she had her intervals of ruth. It need hardly be said that Bixiou had done his utmost to propitiate her; he was witty under his reverses, full of dazzling paradoxes and theories of jovial immorality, which so effectually bewildered the moneylender, that not only did she renew the bill, but she had even lent him a further sum; and this sum, to crown the marvel, he had actually repaid her.

Hence, between the artist and the "matrimonial agent" there arose a certain friendly feeling. Bixiou, not knowing whom the terrible creature was with whom he rubbed shoulders, flattered himself that it was his cleverness that made her laugh, and now and then, when he was at his wits' end, enabled him to soften her to the extent of a few napoleons; he did not know that he was the dog of the raree show in the lion's den; and that this woman, in whose past life there had been incidents *à la* Brinvilliers, was not incapable of making him pay with his life for his insolent familiarity, to say nothing of the interest on her loans.

Meanwhile, and pending this fatal termination which was not very probable, Jacqueline Collin did not hesitate to employ this jovial gossip in the ferreting he practiced so successfully; indeed, she not infrequently gave him, without his knowning it, a part to play in the shady imbroglios that were the occupation of her life.

In the affair of Luigia, the caricaturist was wonderfully useful; through him she could insure publicity for the rumor of Count Halphertius' appearance on the Parisian horizon, his passion for the singer, and the immense sums he was prepared to put down in her behalf.

On the 21st, at seven o'clock precisely, all the guests, of whom Desroches had given Bixiou the list, and Desroches himself, were assembled in the drawing-room in the Rue de Provence when the negro announced Sir Francis Drake and Count Halphertius, who had insisted on not being named first.

As he glanced at the assembled circle, Vautrin was annoyed to perceive that his aunt's habits and instincts had proved stronger than his special and express injunctions, and a sort of turban, green and yellow, would have put him seriously out of temper, but that the skill she had shown in carrying out all his other wishes won forgiveness for her head-dress. As for Luigia, dressed, as usual, in black, having had the wisdom to refuse the assistance of a hairdresser who had vainly attempted to reduce what he had called the disorder of her hair, she was supremely beautiful; and an air of melancholic gravity stamped on all her person compelled a feeling of respect, which surprised these men, to whom Bixiou had spoken of her as awaiting their verdict.

The only person who was specially introduced to Vautrin was Desroches, whom Bixiou brought up to him with this jovially emphatic formula—

"Maître Desroches, the most intelligent attorney of modern times."

As to Sir Francis Drake, if he seemed a shade less scornful than he had intended to be of the influence of journalism as affecting the supply of capital, it was because he happened to be acquainted with Félicien Vernou and Lousteau, two writers for the journalistic press, with whom he shook hands warmly.

Before dinner was announced, Count Halphertius thought it his part to make a little speech; and after a few minutes' conversation with Signora Luigia, to whom he had good taste enough not to speak till he had been in the room a short while, he ostensibly addressed Madame de Saint-Estève, but loud enough to be heard by all who were present.

"My dear madame," said he to his aunt, "you are really a wonderful woman. The first time I find myself in a Paris drawing-room, and you make me to meet all that is most distinguished in literature, in arts, and in the world of business. I, what am only a northern barbarian, though my country has its famous men—Linnæus, Berzelius, the great Thorvaldsen, Tegner, Franzen, Geier, and our charming novelist, Frédérica Bremer—I am here astonished and timid, and I do not know how to say to you that I am so extraordinary obliged."

"Well, through Bernadotte,"* said the lady, whose erudition took her so far as that, "France and Sweden clasped hands."

"It is quite certain," said Vautrin, "that our beloved sovereign Charles XIV.——"

* Jean-Baptiste-Jules Bernadotte, a French general raised to the Swedish throne, 1812.

He was interrupted by a butler, who threw open the doors and announced dinner.

Madame de Saint-Estève took Vautrin's arm, and whispered as they went—

"Don't you think it all very well done?"

"Yes," said Jacques Collin, "it is very well gotten up. Nothing is wrong but your diabolical parrot-colored turban, which startled me a good deal."

"No, no," said Jacqueline, "with my Javanese phiz" (she was born, in fact, in Java) "something Oriental carries it off."

The dinner was not, on the whole, particularly lively. The Human Comedy has more than once had occasion to include a picture of the cheerful race who were here present in force, under the brilliant light of the *triclinium;* but then they had not been muzzled as they were at this banquet. Bixiou, as a message from Madame de Saint-Estève, had particularly impressed on all the guests that they were to say nothing that could distress the chaste ears of the pious Italian. So these men, forced to be cautious, all men of wit and feeling—more or less, as a famous critic said, had lost their spirit; and falling back on the dinner, which was excellent, they murmured in undertones, or reduced the conversation to commonplace remarks. In short, they ate and they drank under protest, so to speak; but they did not really dine.

Bixiou, to whom such a state of things was quite unendurable, was bent on making some break in this monotony. The intimacy between a foreign nobleman and their hostess had given him food for thought; he had also been struck by a certain inefficiency in the Amphitryon; and he had said to himself that a genuine nobleman would at a smaller cost have succeeded in putting some life into the party. So, in order to feel his way, it occurred to him to test the count by speaking of Sweden, and at the beginning of the second course he asked him all across the table—

"Monsieur le Comte, you are too young, I imagine, to

have known Gustavus III., whom Scribe and Auber have set in an opera, and who in France has given his glorious name to a *galop*."

"I beg your pardon," replied Vautrin, seizing the opportunity thus offered to him; "I am very nearly sixty, which would make me thirteen in 1792, when our beloved sovereign was killed by the assassin Anckastroem; so I can remember those times."

Having said this, by the help of a volume called "Caractères et Anecdotes de la cour de Suède" (published by Arthus Bertrand in 1808 without the author's name), which he had picked up at a bookstall since his incarnation as a Swede, Vautrin was in a position to defy pitfalls. He improved the occasion; like a speaker who only waits to be started on a familiar text to display his powers to the best advantage, no sooner was the tap turned on than he flowed with such erudition and pertinence on all the great men of his country, gave so many circumstantial details, related so many curious and secret facts, especially with regard to the famous *Coup d'État*, by which Gustavus III. emancipated the crown in 1772; in short, was so precise and so interesting that, as they rose from table, Émile Blondet said to Bixiou—

"I was like you—a foreign count, introduced by this matchmonger, at first struck me as suspicious. But not only was the dinner really princely; this man knows his Swedish Court in a way that is not to be obtained from books. He is undoubtedly a man of good family; and if only I had time, I could make a very interesting pamphlet out of all he has told us. But the diva is about to sign her agreement."

"He is a very cunning fox," said Desroches to Bixiou as they came to the drawing-room. "He must be enormously rich; he paid the Englishman a hundred thousand crowns down in bank-bills on the spot; and when I wanted to insert a rather stringent clause in the agreement as to the payment of the lady's salary—for Sir Francis Drake has not a reputation for paying 'on the tail,' as Léon de Lora would say—our gentleman would allow no written expression of distrust—whence I conclude that the fair Italian keeps him at arm's length, and that he is not sorry to have some hold over her through arrears of pay."

"And your fees," said Bixiou. "Did he happen to mention them? I told old Saint-Estève that she must not expect a man of your consequence to put himself out of the way for soup and beef—that they must be flavored with mint-sauce."

"Here you are!" said Desroches, taking out of his pocket a gold box, oval in shape, and very handsomely chased. "Just now, while I was reading the indentures, I had laid my snuff-box of Irish horn—worth about ten francs perhaps—on the table by my side. Our friend interrupted me to ask for a pinch. When I had done reading and wanted it, in the place of my box, which had vanished, I found this gem."

"Your 'uncle,'" said Bixiou, "would lend you three or four hundred francs on it, which would mean a value of about a thousand."

"As I protested against such an exchange," Desroches went on, "'I am the gainer by it,' says he. 'I have a relic of the Napoleon of attorneys.'"

"Mighty genteel!" said Bixiou, "and please God and the old woman I will cultivate his acquaintance. I say, supposing I were to sketch him in an early number of the 'Charivari'?"

"First we must find out whether he has enough French wit in him to be pleased to see himself caricatured."

At this moment a chord on the piano announced that the Signora Luigia was about to face the enemy. She sang the "Willow Song" with a depth of expression which touched her audience, though the trial was held by an areopagus who was digesting a dinner of no sparing character.

The song ended, Vernou and Lousteau, going up to Sir Francis Drake, said, with an assumption of indignation as flattering to his skill as to his hopes as a manager—

"What a mean wretch you must be to have secured such an artist for fifty thousand francs—a mere song!"

Luigia then sang an air from "Nina," by Paesiello, and in this light and vivacious character revealed a gift of impersonation at least equal to her talent as a singer.

"She startled me!" said the old aunt to Vautrin. "I fancied I saw Peyrade's daughter."*

What crowned Luigia's success, and recommended her especially to her reporters, was her modesty—a sort of ignorance of her wonderful gifts in the midst of the praises that were showered on her. This little crowd of journalists, accustomed to the extravagant vanity and insolent assumption of the smallest stage queens, could not get over the humility and artlessness of this Empress of Song, who seemed quite surprised at the effect she had produced.

A few words skillfully whispered at parting to each of these great men, and a card left at their lodgings next day by Count Halphertius, secured for his protege, at any rate for the moment, a chorus of admiration which would echo across the channel, and be almost as good as a brilliant debut at the Italian opera house in Paris.

Some days before Luigia's journey, the Boulogne boat carried another person of this drama to England.

As soon as he had ascertained where he could find Sallenauve, to give him the information he thought so urgent, Jacques Bricheteau abandoned the idea of writing him. He thought it simpler and safer to go and see him.

On reaching London, the traveler was somewhat surprised to learn that Hanwell was one of the most famous lunatic asylums in the three kingdoms. If he had but remembered the apprehensions his friend had felt at the state of Marie-Gaston's brain, he would have guessed the truth; but he was quite at sea when he was further informed that this asylum,

* See "The Harlot's Progress."

maintained by the taxes, was open only to mad people of the lower classes, and not to paying patients.

Hanwell is a large building of not unhandsome appearance; the front, nine hundred and ninety-six feet in length, is broken by three octagonal towers, three stories high—one at each end, and one in the middle; the monotony is thus relieved, though the melancholy purpose of the building necessitated a very moderate use of ornament.

The asylum is pleasantly situated at the foot of a hill on the borders of Jersey (*sic*)* and Middlesex. The extensive grounds, gardens, and farms lie between the Uxbridge road, the river Brent, and the Grand Junction canal; nine hundred patients can be accommodated and treated there. As it is well known that manual labor is one of the most valuable elements of the cure, the house contains workshops for carpentry, smiths' work, painting, glazing, and brushmaking; cotton is spun, shoes, baskets, strawberry pottles, and straw hats are made, and other light work for women. The finer qualities of work are sold to visitors in a bazaar, and bring in a considerable profit.

Such patients as are incapable of learning a trade work in the garden and farm, which supply many of the wants of the establishment; bread and ale are made on the premises; all the necessary linen is made up and washed by means of a steam engine, which also heats every part of the building. A chapel with a fine organ, a library, and a concert-room—the salutary effect of music on the patients being amply proved—show that, hand in hand with intelligent care given to physical suffering, the needs of the spiritual and intellectual man are not neglected.

Finally, as Lord Lewin had told Sallenauve in his letter, the superintendent and director was Dr. Ellis, a distinguished physician to whom we owe a valuable treatise on the develop-

* This curious mistake seems to have arisen from the proximity of Osterley Park, Lord Jersey's residence.

ment and therapeutics of mental disease. In his treatment of these maladies this learned man does not despise the aid of phrenology.

On being shown into the doctor's room, the organist asked him whether a Frenchman named Sallenauve were not staying for a time at Hanwell. Here, again, Bricheteau paid the penalty of his neglected and shabby appearance; without vouchsafing any inquiries or explanations, Dr. Ellis shortly replied that he had never even heard Monsieur de Sallenauve's name. This, after all, was very probable; so Jacques Bricheteau withdrew, much disappointed; and fancying that Madame de l'Estorade had misread, or he himself had mistaken, the name of Hanwell, he spent some days in running about the county of Middlesex visiting every spot of which the name ending in *ell* invited his attention.

All his inquiries having resulted in nothing, as he rarely allowed his persevering and resourceful spirit to be beaten in anything he undertook, Jacques Bricheteau resolved to make another attempt on Hanwell by letter, thinking, very rightly, that a letter sometimes got in where a man was barred out. In point of fact, on the evening of the day when he posted his letter he received a reply from Sallenauve, inviting him to call at the asylum, where he was promised a most cordial welcome.

Dr. Ellis' conduct was accounted for when Jacques Bricheteau learned the extent of the disaster that had befallen Marie-Gaston. Discretion is, of course, one of the most indispensable virtues in the head of an asylum for the insane; since every day, by his position, he becomes the depository of secrets which affect the honor of whole families.

When Bricheteau arrived at the asylum, and was introduced by Sallenauve as his friend, he was heartily welcomed. Dr. Ellis made every apology; and having on various occasions in the course of his practice found really wonderful benefit derived from music, he said that he regarded the organist's arrival as quite a godsend, since his great musical talent might be of immense use as a means toward effecting the cure of the patient.

Since leaving Ville-d'Avray, Marie-Gaston's state had unfortunately become seriously complicated. Until he reached England he had been comparatively cheerful and docile to Lord Lewin's advice; they might have been supposed to be friends traveling together for pleasure. But when, instead of embarking at once for South America, Lord Lewin, under the pretext of business to transact in the neighborhood of London, proposed to Marie-Gaston to accompany him, the madman began to suspect some snare into which he had been wheedled. He allowed himself, nevertheless, to be driven to Hanwell, represented by Lord Lewin as one of the royal residences; he had not even resisted when invited to cross the threshold of his prison; but once in the presence of Dr. Ellis, who had been forewarned by a letter from Lord Lewin, a sort of instinct, of which the insane are very capable, seemed to tell the unhappy man that his freedom was in danger.

"I do not like that man's face," he said aloud to Lord Lewin. "Let us go."

The doctor had tried to laugh off the remark; but Marie-Gaston, getting more and more excited, exclaimed:

"Hold your tongue! Your laughter is intolerable. You look just like an executioner."

And it is possible that the deep attention with which mad doctors must study the countenance of a patient, added to the stern fixed gaze by which they are often compelled to control a maniac, may at last give their features an expression of inquisitorial scrutiny. This, no doubt, has a highly irritating effect on the overstrung nervous sensibilities of the unhappy creatures brought within their ken.

"You will not deprive me, I hope," said the doctor, "of the pleasure of keeping you and my friend Lord Lewin to dinner?"

"I! Dine with you?" cried Marie-Gaston vehemently. "What—that you may poison me!"

"Well, but poison is just what you want, surely?" said Lord Lewin quickly. "Were you not talking the other day of a dose of prussic acid?"

Lord Lewin was not, as might perhaps be supposed, merely rash in making this pointed speech; he had studied mad persons, and he discerned that a deeply hostile aversion for the doctor was seething in Marie-Gaston's mind; so, being strong and active, he intended to divert on himself the storm that was about to burst. It fell out as he had expected.

"Vile scoundrel!" cried Marie-Gaston, seizing him by the throat, "you are in collusion with the other, and selling my secrets!"

It was with some difficulty, and the help of two warders, that Lord Lewin had shaken off his desperate clutch; the poor man had developed raving mania.

The paroxysm, after lasting some days, had yielded to care and treatment; the patient was now gentle and quiet, and showed some hopeful symptoms; but Sir William Ellis hoped to induce a final crisis, and he was considering the way and means to this end when M. Jacques Bricheteau arrived.

As soon as Sallenauve found himself alone with the organist, he questioned him as to the motives that had prompted him to follow him, and it was not without indignation that he heard of the intrigue which Maxime and the Beauvisages seemed to be plotting against him. His old suspicions revived—

"Are you quite certain," he asked, "that the man I but just saw was in fact the Marquis de Sallenauve?"

"Mother Marie des Anges and Achille Pigoult," replied Bricheteau, "who warned me of this plot, have no more doubt of the marquis' identity than I have. And in all the gossip which they are trying to work up into a scandal, one thing alone seems to me at all serious, and that is, that by your absence you leave the field free to your enemies."

"But the Chamber will not condemn me unheard," replied the member. "I wrote the president to ask leave of absence; and in the event of its being refused, which is most improbable, I have asked l'Estorade, who knows my reasons for being here, to answer for me."

"You also wrote to madame his wife?"

"I wrote only to his wife," replied Sallenauve. "I announced to her the misfortune that has overtaken our friend, and at the same time begged her to explain to her husband the good offices I requested of him."

"If that is the case," said Jacques Bricheteau, "do not depend for anything on the l'Estorades. A rumor of the blow about to be dealt you had no doubt already reached them."

And after telling him of the reception he had met with, as well as the unkind speeches made by Madame de l'Estorade, Jacques Bricheteau drew the conclusion that in the impending struggle no help could be hoped for from that quarter.

"I have some right to be surprised at such a state of things," said Sallenauve, "after Madame de l'Estorade's pressing assurances of unfailing good-will; however," he added with a shrug, "nothing is impossible, and calumny has ere now undermined closer friendships."

"So now, as you must understand," said the organist, "we must set out for Paris without delay; all things considered, your presence here is really far less necessary."

"On the contrary," replied Sallenauve, "only this morning the doctor was congratulating himself on my having decided on coming, saying that at the right moment my intervention might be invaluable. In fact, I have not yet been allowed to see Marie-Gaston, reserving my appearance as a surprise at need."

"The usefulness of your presence," replied Jacques Bricheteau, "is nevertheless problematical; while, by remaining here for an indefinite period, you are most certainly imperiling your political future, your social position, everything of which the most ardent friendship has no right to demand the sacrifice."

"We will go and talk it over with the doctor," said Sallenauve at length, for he could not fail to see that Jacques Bricheteau's importunity was justified.

On being asked whether Marie-Gaston's stay in the asylum was liable to be prolonged—

"Yes, I think so," said the doctor; "I have just seen our patient, and the cerebral irritation, which must give way to the material action of medicines before we can attempt to bring any moral influence to bear, seems to me most unfortunately on the high way to a fresh outbreak."

"Still," said Sallenauve anxiously, "you have not lost all hope of a cure?"

"Far from it; I believe firmly in a favorable termination. But these dreadful disorders often present frequent alternations of aggravation and improvement; and I am beginning to foresee that the case will be a longer one than I had at first hoped."

"I have just been elected a deputy to the Lower Chamber," said Sallenauve, "and the opening of the session demands my return to Paris. It is no less required by urgent private matters which Monsieur Bricheteau came expressly to discuss. So unless I thought that my presence here would be immediately needed——"

"Go," said the doctor, "it may be a very long business. If the patient's condition had not shown a relapse, I had intended to arrange some startling scene with your help and that of Monsieur Bricheteau's music, aided too by a young lady, a relation of my wife's, who on various occasions has seconded me very intelligently—a little dramatic shock from which I hoped for good results. But, in the first place, my young relation is absent, and for the moment nothing can be done but by medical agents. So, for the moment, go!"

Sallenauve gratefully pressed the doctor's hand, seeing his eager wish to reassure him. He then took leave of Mrs. Ellis, who promised no less warmly than her husband the devoted care of a mother's watchfulness. As to Lord Lewin, Sallenauve's character had won his most friendly esteem, and his conduct in the past was a guarantee of all that might be expected of him now and in the future. So Bricheteau had no difficulty about getting off without any further delay.

They reached London at about five in the afternoon, and would have gone on to Paris the same evening but for a surprise which awaited them. Their eyes fell immediately on enormous posters, on a scale which only English "puff" can achieve, announcing at the corner of every street the appearance that same evening of SIGNORA LUIGIA at Her Majesty's theatre. The name alone was enough to arrest the travelers' attention; but the papers to which they had recourse for information supplied them, in the English fashion, with so many circumstantial facts as to the debutante's career, that Sallenauve could not doubt the transformation of his late housekeeper into one of the brightest stars that had risen for a long time above the horizon of England. If he had listened to Jacques Bricheteau, he would have been content to hail from afar the triumph of the handsome Italian, and have gone on his way. But having calculated that one evening spent in London would make no serious delay in his arrival, Sallenauve was bent on judging for himself, by his own eyes and ears, what the enthusiasm was worth which was expressed on all sides for the new prima donna.

Sallenauve went off at once to the box office, which he found closed, but he was enabled to perceive that the singer's success was immense. Every seat had been sold by two in the afternoon, and he thought himself lucky to secure two stalls at a private ticket office for the sum of five pounds.

The London opera-house had never perhaps held a more brilliant assembly; and it is impossible not to be struck by the capricious vicissitudes of human life, when we reflect that all this concourse of the English aristocracy was brought about originally by the ambition of a man who had been a felon on the hulks to rise, as a member of the police, to a rather better rank in its hierarchy.

By a no less singular coincidence the piece announced was Paesiello's "Nina, o la Pazza per Amore" (mad for love), from which Luigia had sung an air after the dinner given by Madame de Saint-Estève.

When the curtain rose, Sallenauve, having spent nearly a week at Hanwell in the midst of mad people, could all the better appreciate the prodigious gifts as an actress displayed by his former housekeeper in the part of Nina; and in the face of her heart-rending imitation, he went through a renewal of all the distress of mind he had just gone through while watching the dreadful reality of Marie-Gaston's insanity.

Bricheteau, in spite of his annoyance at first at Sallenauve's dawdling, as he called it, finally fell under the spell of the singer's power; and at last, seeing the whole house frantic with enthusiasm, and the stage strewn with bouquets, he said—

"On my word, I can wish you nothing better than a success in any degree like this on another stage!" and then he rashly added: "But there are no such triumphs in politics! Art alone is great——"

"And la Luigia is its prophet!" replied Sallenauve, smiling through the tears that admiration had brought to his eyes.

On coming out of the theatre, Bricheteau looked at his watch; it was a quarter to eleven, and by making great haste there was still time to get on board the packet starting at eleven. But when the organist looked round to urge this on Sallenauve, who was to follow him through the crowd, he no longer saw his man; the deputy had vanished.

A quarter of an hour later Luigia's dresser came into a room where her mistress was receiving the compliments of the greatest names in England, introduced to her by Sir Francis Drake. She gave the signora a card. The prima donna as she read it changed color, and whispered a few words to the maid. And she then showed such obvious anxiety to be rid of her throng of admirers, that some budding adorers could not help betraying their surprise.

As soon as she was alone, she hastily resumed her ordinary dress; the manager's carriage had soon conveyed her to the hotel where she had been living since her arrival; and, on entering her sitting-room, she found Sallenauve, who had arrived there before her.

"You here, monsieur!" said she. "It is a dream!"

"Especially to me," replied Sallenauve, "since I find you in London after having sought you in vain in Paris."

"You took so much trouble—but why?"

"You left us in so strange a manner, your moods are so hasty, you knew so little of Paris, and so many dangers might await your inexperience, that I feared everything for you."

"What harm could come to me?" said she. "And I was neither your wife, nor your sister, nor your mistress; I was only your——"

"I had believed," Sallenauve eagerly put in, "that you were my friend."

"I was your debtor," said Luigia. "I saw that I was a trouble to you in your new position. Could I do otherwise than relieve you of my presence?"

"Pray, who had impressed you with that intolerable conviction? Had I said or hinted anything to that effect? Was it impossible to discuss a plan of life for you without so far offending your susceptibilities?"

"I feel what I feel," said the Italian. "I myself was conscious that you wished me anywhere rather than in your house. You had afforded me the means of having no fears for the future; indeed, as you see, it promises to be anything rather than alarming."

"On the contrary, it promises to be so brilliant that but for the fear of seeming too presuming, I should make so bold as to ask from whose hand, happier than mine, you have obtained such prompt and efficient help."

"A great Swedish nobleman," replied Luigia without hesitation, "who spends part of an immense fortune in the encouragement of art, procured me this engagement at Her Majesty's; the kind indulgence of the public did the rest."

"Your talent, you should say. I heard you this evening."

"And were you pleased with your humble servant?" said the singer, with a coquettish curtsey.

"Your musical achievements did not surprise me; I knew your gifts already, and an infallible judge had answered for them; but your flights of dramatic passion, your acting, at once so strong and so sure of itself—that indeed amazed me."

"I have suffered much," said the Italian, "and grief is a great master."

"Suffered!" said Sallenauve; "in Italy, yes. But since you came to France I like to flatter myself——"

"Everywhere," said Luigia in a broken voice. "I was not born under a happy star."

"That 'Everywhere' has to me a touch of reproach. It is late, indeed, to be telling me of any wrong I may have done you."

"You have not done me the smallest wrong. The mischief was there!" said Luigia, laying her hand on her heart. "I alone was in fault."

"From some fancy, I dare say, as foolish as your notion that it was a point of honor that you should quit my house?"

"Oh, I was not dreaming then," said the Italian. "How well I knew what lay at the bottom of your mind! If it were only in return for all you had done for me, I ought to long

2

for your esteem, and yet I was forbidden even to aspire so high."

"But, my dear Luigia, there is no word for such ideas. Did I ever fail in consideration and respect? And beside, has not your conduct always been exemplary?"

"Yes, I have tried never to do anything that could make you think ill of me. But I was Benedetto's widow, all the same."

"What! Do you fancy that that disaster, the outcome of just revenge——"

"Nay. It was not the man's death that could lower me in your eyes; quite the contrary. But I had been the wife of a buffoon, of a police spy, of a wretch always ready to sell me to any buyer——"

"While you were in that position, I felt that you were to be pitied, but scorned? Never!"

"Well," said the Italian, "we had lived together, alone, under the same roof, for nearly two years."

"Certainly; and to me it had become a delightful habit."

"Did you think me ugly?"

"You know I did not, since I took you for the model of my best statue."

"A fool?"

"A woman cannot be a fool who puts so much soul into a part."

"Well then; it is evident that you despised me!"

Sallenauve was utterly amazed at this prompt logic; he thought himself clever to reply—

"It seems to me that if I had behaved differently, I should have given greater proof of contempt."

But he had to deal with a woman who in all things—in her friendships and aversions, in act as well as in word—went straight to the mark.

She went on as if she were afraid that he had not understood her.

"At this day, monsieur, I can say everything, for I am talking of the past, and the future is no longer in my hands. Since the day when you were kind to me, and when by your generous protection I was rescued from an outrageous insult, my heart has been wholly yours."

Sallenauve, who had never suspected the existence of this feeling, and who, above all, could not conceive of its avowal, made with such artless crudity, did not know what to say.

"I was well aware," the strange creature went on, "that I should have much to do to raise myself from the base condition in which you had seen me at our first meeting. If even at the moment when you consented to take me with you I had seen any signs of gallantry in your behavior, any hint that you might take advantage of the dangerous position in which I had placed myself by my own act, my heart would have shrunk into itself, you would have been but an ordinary man, and to rehabilitate me after Benedetto it was not enough——"

"And so," said Sallenauve, "to love you would have been an insult, and not to love was cruelty. What a woman! How is it possible to avoid offending you?"

"I did not want you to love me when you did not know me," said the singer, "when I had scarcely shaken off the mire, for then it would have been only the love of the eye and of the taste, which it is never wise to trust. But when, after living in your house for two years, you could know by my conduct that I was worthy of your esteem; when, without ever craving a single pleasure, and devoted to the care of your house, with no relaxation but the study which was to raise me to the dignity of an artist like yourself, I could, merely for the happiness of seeing you create a masterpiece, sacrifice the womanly modesty which on another occasion you had seen me defend with vehemence—then you were cruel not to understand; and your imagination can never, never picture what I have suffered, or how many tears I have shed!"

"But, my dear Luigia, you were my guest; even if I could

have suspected what you now reveal to me, my duty as a man of honor required me to see nothing, understand nothing, but on the plainest evidence."

"And was not my perpetual melancholy proof enough? If my heart had been free, should I not have been less reserved and more familiar? No—the case is plain enough: you could see nothing; your fancy was fixed elsewhere."

"Well, and if it were?"

"It ought not to have been," said the Italian stringently. "That woman was not free; she had a husband and children; and, though you chose to make a saint of her, even if I had no advantage over her excepting in youth—though that is, of course, quite absurd—it seems to me that she was not to compare with me."

Sallenauve could not help smiling. However, he replied quite gravely:

"You are altogether mistaken as to your rival. Madame de l'Estorade has never been anything to me but a head to study, and even so, of no interest whatever but for her likeness to another woman. That woman I knew at Rome before I ever saw you. She had beauty, youth, and a great talent for Art. At this day she is captive in a convent; so, like you, she has paid tribute to sorrow; as you see, all your perfections——"

"What! Three love stories, and all ending in air!" said Luigia. "You were born under a strange star, indeed! Of course when I was so misunderstood, it was only because I was under its maleficent influence, and in that case you must be forgiven."

"Then, since you admit me to mercy, pray allow me to return to my former question. The future, you tell me, is no longer in your hands; the astounding frankness of your avowal leads me to infer that, to give you such boldness, a very solid barrier must have been raised between you and me. Then what is the power by which, at one leap, you have sprung so high? Have you, then, made a bargain with the devil?"

"Perhaps so," said Luigia, laughing.

"Do not laugh," said Sallenauve. "You chose to face the hell of Paris alone; it would not at all surprise me to hear that you met with some dangerous acquaintance at starting. I know the difficulties that the greatest artists have to surmount before they can get a hearing. Do you know whom the foreign gentleman is who has leveled every road before you?"

"I know that he has put down a fabulous sum to secure my engagement; that I am to be paid fifty thousand francs; and that he did not even accompany me to London."

"Then all this devotion is free, gratis?"

"Not at all. My patron has reached the age at which a man no longer loves, but has a great deal of conceit. So his protection is to be widely proclaimed, and I have pledged myself to do nothing, say nothing, that may give the lie to his fictitious happiness. To you alone did I owe the truth; but I know you to be trustworthy, and I entreat you to keep it absolutely secret."

"And it does not seem improbable to you that this state of things should last? But how and where did you make acquaintance with this man whom you think you can for ever feed on air?"

"Through a *Dame de Charité* who came to see me while you were away. She had been struck by my voice at Saint-Sulpice during the services of the month of Mary, and she wanted to bribe me away to sing at her parish church, Notre-Dame de Lorette."

"What was the lady's name?"

"Madame de Saint-Estève."

Though he did not know all the depths of Jacqueline Collin's existence, Sallenauve had heard of Madame de Saint-Estève as a money-lender and go-between; he had heard Bixiou speak of her.

"That woman," said he, "has a notoriously bad reputation in Paris. She is an agent of the lowest intrigues."

"So I suspected," said Luigia, "but what does that matter to me?"

"If the man she has introduced to you——"

"Were such another as herself?" interrupted the singer. "But that is not likely. The hundred thousand crowns he has placed in the manager's hands have floated the theatre again."

"He may be rich and yet be scheming against you. The two are not incompatible."

"He may have schemes against me," said Luigia, "but they will not be carried out. Between them and me—*I* stand."

"But your reputation?"

"That I lost when I left your house. I was generally supposed to be your mistress; you had to give your own explanation to your constituency; and you contradicted the report, but do you imagine that you killed it?"

"And my esteem, on which you set such value?"

"I no longer need it. You did not love me when I wanted it; you will not love me when I no longer care."

"Who can tell?" said Sallenauve.

"There are two reasons against it," replied the Italian. "In the first place, it is too late; and in the second, we no longer tread the same road."

"What do you mean?"

"I am an artist, you have ceased to be one. I am rising, you are going down."

"You call it going down to rise perhaps to the highest dignities of State?"

"Whether you rise or not," cried Luigia ecstatically, "you will be beneath your past self and the splendid future that lay before you. Indeed, I believe I have deceived you; I believe if you had still been a sculptor, I should yet for some time have endured your coldness and disdain; at any rate, I should have waited till after my first trials in my art, hoping that the halo which lends glory to a woman on the stage might at last, perhaps, have made you aware of my existence—there—at your side. But from the day of your apostasy, I could no longer persist in my humiliating sacrifice. There is no future in common for us."

"What!" said Sallenauve, holding out his hand, which Luigia did not take, "are we not even to remain friends?"

"A friend—a man friend—you have already. No, it is all over and done with. We shall hear of each other; and from afar as we cross in life we shall wave each other a greeting, but nothing more."

"And this is how all is to end between you and me!" said Sallenauve sadly.

The singer looked at him for a moment, and tears sparkled in her eyes.

"Listen," said she, in a sincere and resolute tone, "this much is possible. I have loved you, and after you no man will find a place in the heart you scorned. You will be told that I have lovers: the old man whom I am pledged to own to, and others after him perhaps; but you will not believe it, remembering the woman that I am. And, who knows? By and by your life may be swept clear of the other affections which barred the way for mine, and the freedom, the eccentricity of the avowal I have just made will perhaps remain stamped on your memory—then it is not altogether impossible that after such long wandering you may at last want me. If that should happen—if, as the result of bitter disappointments, you should be brought back to the belief in Art—well, then, if time has not made love a too ridiculous dream for us, remember this night.

"Now we must part, for it is late for a *tête-à-tête*, and it is the semblance of fidelity to my elderly protector that I am pledged to preserve."

So speaking, she took up a candle and vanished into the adjoining room, leaving Sallenauve in a state of mind that may be imagined after the surprises of every kind that this interview had brought him.

On returning to the hotel whither he had taken his things on arriving from Hanwell, he found Bricheteau waiting for him at the door.

"Where the devil have you been?" cried the organist, frantic with impatience. "We might have got off by to-night's boat."

"Well, well," said Sallenauve carelessly, "I shall have a few more hours for playing truant."

"And meanwhile the enemy is pushing forward the mine!"

"What do I care? In that cave called political life must we not be prepared for whatever happens?"

"I suspected as much," said Bricheteau. "You have been to see la Luigia; her success has turned your head, and the statuary is breaking out through the deputy."

"You yourself an hour since said Art alone is great."

"But the orator, too, is an artist," said Bricheteau, "and the greatest of all; for other artists appeal to the intellect and the feelings, he alone addresses the conscience and the will. Beside, this is not the time to look back; you have a duel to fight with your opponents. Are you a man of honor or a rogue who has stolen a name? That is the question which is perhaps being discussed and answered in your absence in the full light of the Chamber."

"I am sadly afraid that you have misled me; I had a jewel in my hands, and have flung it at my feet——"

"That," retorted the organist, "is happily a vapor that will vanish with the night. To-morrow you will remember your promises to your father and the splendid future that lies before you."

The Chambers were opened; Sallenauve had not been

present at the royal sitting, and his absence had not failed to cause some sensation in the democratic party. At the office of the "National" especially there had been quite a commotion. It seemed only natural to expect that, as part owner of the paper and often to be seen at the office before the elections, having indeed contributed to its pages, he should, after being returned, have appeared there to get news when Parliament opened.

"Now he is elected," said some of the editors, commenting on the new deputy's total disappearance, "does my gentleman think he is going to play the snob? It is rather a common trick with our lords and masters in Parliament to pay us very obsequious court as long as they want supporters, and let us severely alone, like their old coats, as soon as they have climbed the tree. But we cannot allow this gentleman to play that game; there are more ways than one of turning the tables on a man."

The chief editor, less easily disturbed, had tried to soothe this first ebullition; but Sallenauve's non-appearance at the opening of the session had, nevertheless, struck him as strange.

On the following day, when the government officials were to be appointed—the presidents and secretaries—a business which is not unimportant, because it affords a means of estimating the majority, Sallenauve's absence was of more real consequence. In the office to which fate had attached him, the election of the head was carried by the Ministerialists by only one vote; thus the presence of the Deputy for Arcis would have turned the scale in favor of the Opposition. Hence the expression of strong disapproval in the organs of that party, explaining its defeat by this unforeseen defection, of which they spoke with some acrimonious surprise. They applied no epithets to the absentee's conduct, but they spoke of it as quite "inexplicable."

Maxime on his part kept a sharp lookout; he was only

waiting till the official ranks of the Chamber should be filled to lay before the House, in the name of the Romilly peasant-woman, a petition to prosecute. This document had been drawn up by Massol, and under his practiced pen, the facts he had undertaken to set forth had assumed the air of probability which attorneys contrive to give to their statements and depositions even when furthest from the truth. And now, when Sallenauve's absence was so prolonged as to seem scandalous, he went once more to call on Rastignac; and availing himself of the ingenious plan of attack suggested by Desroches, he asked the minister if he did not think that the moment had come when he, Rastignac, should abandon the attitude of passive observation which he had hitherto chosen to maintain.

Rastignac was, in fact, far more explicit. Sallenauve in a foreign land figured in his mind as a man conscience-stricken, who had lost his balance. He therefore advised Monsieur de Trailles to bring forward the preliminaries of the action that very day, and no longer hesitated to promise his support for the success of a scheme which now looked so hopeful, and from which a very pretty scandal might reasonably be looked for.

The effects of his underground influence were obvious on the very next day. The order of the day in the Lower Chamber was the verification of the returns. The deputy whose duty it was to report on the election at Arcis-sur-Aube happened to be a trusty Ministerialist, and, acting on the private instructions that had reached him, he took this view of the case:

The constituents of Arcis had elected their member according to law. Monsieur de Sallenauve had, in due course, submitted to the examining committee all the documents needed to prove his eligibility, and there was no apparent difficulty in the way of his taking his seat. But reports of a strange character had arisen, even at the time of the election, as to the new deputy's identification, and in further support of those rumors a petition had now been presented to the House to authorize a criminal prosecution. This petition set forth a very serious accusation: Monsieur de Sallenauve was said to have assumed the name he bore without any right, and this assumption being certified on an official document, was indictable as a forgery committed for the purpose of false personation. "A circumstance much to be regretted," the speaker went on, "was Monsieur de Sallenauve's absence; instead of appearing to contradict the extraordinary accusation lodged against him, he had remained absent from the sittings of the Chamber ever since the opening of the session, and nobody had seen him. Under these circumstances could his election be officially ratified? The committee had thought not, and proposed that a delay should be granted."

Daniel d'Arthez, a member of the Legitimist Opposition, whom, as we saw at Arcis, was in favor of Sallenauve's return, at once rose to address the Chamber, and begged to point out how completely out of order such a decision would be.

"The legality of the election was beyond dispute. No irregularity had been proved. Hence, the Chamber had no alternative; they must put the question to the vote, and recognize the election as regular and valid, since there was nothing to invalidate it. To confuse with that issue the question as to a petition to prosecute would be an abuse of power, because, by hindering any preliminary discussion of that question, and relieving the indictment of the usual formalities before its acceptance or rejection, it would assume a singular and exceptional character—that, namely, of a suspension of the mandate granted to their member by the sovereign power of the electors. And who," added the orator, "can fail to perceive that by giving effect to this petition for authority to prosecute, in any form whatever, we prejudge its justification and importance; whereas the presumption of innocence, which is the prerogative of every accused person, ought to be es-

P

pecially extended to a man whose honesty has never been open to doubt, and who has so lately been honored by the suffrages of his fellow-citizens."

A prolonged discussion followed, the Ministerial speakers naturally taking the opposite view; then a difficulty arose. The president for the time being, in right of seniority—for the Chamber had not yet elected its chief—was a weary old man, who, in the complicated functions so suddenly conferred on him by his register of birth, was not always prompt and competent. Sallenauve's application for leave of absence had reached him the day before; and if it had occurred to him to announce it to the Chamber at the beginning of the sitting—as he ought to have done—the discussion would probably have been nipped in the bud. But there is luck and ill-luck in parliamentary business; and when the Chamber learned from this letter, at last communicated, that Charles de Sallenauve was abroad, and had no ground to offer for this application for unlimited leave but the vague commonplace of "urgent private affairs," the effect was disastrous.

"It is self-evident," said all the Ministerialists, like Rastignac, "he is in England, where every form of failure takes refuge. He is afraid of the inquiry; he knows he will be unmasked."

This opinion, apart from all the political feeling, was shared by some of the sterner spirits, who could not conceive that a man should not appear to defend himself against so gross an accusation. In short, after a very strong and skillful speech from Vinet the public prosecutor, who had found courage in the absence of the accused, the confirmation of the election was postponed, though by a very small majority; at the same time, a week's leave of absence was voted to the accused member.

On the day after these proceedings, Maxime wrote as follows to Madame Beauvisage:

"MADAME:—The enemy met with a terrible reverse yesterday; and in the opinion of my friend Rastignac, a very experienced and intelligent judge of parliamentary feeling, Dorlange, whatever happens, cannot recover from the blow thus dealt him. If we should fail to procure any positive proof in support of our worthy countrywoman's charge, it is possible that the scoundrel, by sheer audacity, may finally be accepted by the Chamber, if, indeed, he dares show his face in France. But even then, after dragging on a sordid existence utterly unrecognized, he will inevitably ere long be driven to resign; then M. Beauvisage will be elected beyond doubt, for the constituency, ashamed of having been taken in by an adventurer, will be only too happy to reinstate themselves by a choice that will do them honor, beside having been their first instinctive selection.

"This result, madame, will be due to your remarkable sagacity; for, but for the sort of second-sight which enabled you to divine the precious truth hidden under the peasant-woman's story, we should have overlooked that valuable instrument. I may tell you, madame, even if it should inflate your pride, that neither Rastignac nor Vinet, the public prosecutor, understood the full importance of your discovery; indeed, I myself, if I had not been so happy as to know you, so as to be able to appreciate the value attaching to any idea of yours, might very probably have shared the indifference of these two statesmen as to the useful weapon you were putting into our hands. But, as the gift came from you, I at once understood its importance; and while pointing out to Rastignac the means of utilizing it, I succeeded in making my friend the minister an eager partner in the plot, and, at the same time, a sincere admirer of the skill and perspicacity of which you had given proof.

"Thus, madame, if I should ever be so happy as to be connected with you by the bond of which we have already spoken, I shall not need to initiate you into political life; you have found the path so well unaided.

"Nothing new can happen within the next week, the length of leave granted to our man. If after that date the absentee does not appear, there is, I think, no doubt that the election will be pronounced null and void; for yesterday's vote, which you will have read in the papers, is a positive summons to him to appear in his place. You may be sure that between this and his return—if he should return—I shall not fail to devote myself to fomenting the antagonistic feeling of the Chamber both by the press and by private communications. Rastignac has also issued orders to this end, and it is safe to conclude that the foe will find public opinion strongly prejudiced against him.

"Allow me, madame, to beg you to remember me to Mademoiselle Cécile, and accept for yourself and Monsieur Beauvisage the expression of my most respectful regard."

A few words of instructions to the Ministerial press had, in fact, begun to surround the name of Sallenauve with a sort of atmosphere of disrespect and ridicule; the most insulting innuendoes ascribed to his absence the sense of a retreat from his foes. The effect of these repeated attacks was all the more inevitable because Sallenauve was but feebly defended by the politicians of his own party.

On the day when his week's leave ended, Sallenauve, not having yet returned, a second-rate Ministerial paper published, under the heading of "Lost, a Deputy!" an insolent and witty article which made a considerable sensation.

That evening Madame de l'Estorade called on Madame de Camps, and found her alone with her husband. She was greatly excited, and exclaimed as she went in—

"Have you read that infamous article?"

"No," said Madame de Camps. "But my husband has told me about it; it is really disgraceful that the Ministry should order, or at least encourage, anything so utterly vile and atrocious."

"I am half-crazed by it," said Madame de l'Estorade, "for it is all our doing."

"That is carrying conscientious scruples too far," said Madame de Camps.

"Not at all," said the ironmaster. "I agree with madame. All the venom of this attack would be dispersed by a single step on l'Estorade's part; and by refusing to take it, if he is not the originator, he is at least the abettor of the scandal."

"Then you have told him——?" asked the countess reproachfully.

"Why, my dear," replied Madame Octave, "though we have our little women's secrets, I could not but explain to my husband what had given rise to the sort of monomania that possesses Monsieur de l'Estorade. It would have been such a distrust of my second self as would have hurt him deeply; and such explanations as I felt bound to give him have not, I think, made me a faithless depository of any secret that concerns you personally."

"Ah, you are a happy couple!" said Madame de l'Estorade, with a sigh. "However, I am not sorry that Monsieur de Camps should have been admitted to our confidence; the point is, to find some way out of the difficult position in which I am struggling, and two opinions are better than one."

"Why, what has happened?" asked Madame de Camps.

"My husband's head is quite turned," replied the countess. "He seems to me to have lost every trace of moral sense. Far from perceiving that he is, as Monsieur de Camps said just now, the abettor of the odious contest now going on, without having—as those had who started it—the excuse of ignorance, he seems to exult in it. He brought me that detestable paper with an air of triumph, and I found him quite ready to take offense because I did not agree with him in thinking it most amusing and witty."

"That letter," said Madame Octave, "was a terrible blow to him; it hit him body and soul at once."

"That I grant," cried the ironmaster. "But deuce take it ! If you are a man, you take a lunatic's words for what they are worth."

"Still, it is very strange," said his wife, "that Monsieur de Sallenauve does not come back ; for, after all, that Jacques Bricheteau to whom you gave his address must have written him."

"What is to be done !" exclaimed the countess. "There has been a fatality over the whole business. To-morrow the question is to be discussed in the Chamber as to whether or not Monsieur de Sallenauve's election is to be ratified ; and if he should not then be in his place, the Ministry hopes to be able to annul it."

"But it really is atrocious !" said Monsieur de Camps ; "and though my position hardly justifies me in taking such a step, a very little would make me go straight to the president of the Chamber and tell him a few home truths——"

"I would have begged you to do so, I think, even at the risk of my husband's detecting my intervention, but for one consideration—it would distress Monsieur de Sallenauve so greatly that his friend's unhappy state should be made public."

"Certainly," said Madame Octave. "Such a line of defense would evidently be contrary to his intentions ; and, after all, he may yet arrive in time. Beside, the decision of the Chamber still remains problematical, while, Monsieur Marie-Gaston's madness once known, he can never get over the blow."

"And then," added Madame de l'Estorade, "all the odious part that my husband has taken so far in this dreadful business is as nothing in comparison with a really diabolical idea which he communicated to me just now before dinner."

"What can that be?" asked Madame de Camps anxiously.

"His idea is that to-morrow I am to go with him to the gallery reserved for the peers to hear the question discussed."

"Really he is losing his wits!" said Monsieur de Camps. "It is quite like Diafoirus the younger, who offers his bride-elect the diversion of seeing a dissection——"

Madame de Camps shook her head meaningly at her husband, as much as to say: "Do not pour oil on the flames." She merely asked the countess if she had not shown Monsieur de l'Estorade how monstrous such a singular proceeding would appear.

"At the very first word I spoke to that effect, he flew into a rage," said Madame de l'Estorade, "telling me that I was apparently only too glad to perpetuate a belief in our intimacy with *this man*, since, on an opportunity when I could so naturally proclaim our rupture to the public, I so resolutely declined it."

"Well, then, my dear, you must go," said Madame Octave. "Domestic peace before all things. Beside, after all, your presence at the sitting may equally well be regarded as a proof of kindly interest."

"For fifteen years," said the ironmaster, "you have reigned and ruled at home, and this is a revolution which seriously shifts the focus of power."

"But, monsieur, I beg you to believe that I should never have made such use of the sovereignty, which indeed I have always tried to conceal."

"Do I not know it?" replied Monsieur de Camps warmly, as he took Madame de l'Estorade's hands in his own. "But I agree with my wife—this cup must be drained."

"I shall die of shame as I listen to the infamous charges the Ministerial party will bring! I shall feel as if they were murdering a man under my own eyes, whom I could save by merely putting my hand out—and I cannot do it——"

"Yes, it is so," said Monsieur de Camps. "And a man, too, who has done you signal service; but would you rather bring hell into your house, and aggravate your husband's unhealthy state?"

"Listen, my dear," said Madame de Camps. "Tell Monsieur de l'Estorade that I also wish to go to this sitting; that it will give less cause for comment if you are seen there with a person who is uninterested and merely curious; and on that point do not give way. Then, at any rate, I shall be there to keep your head straight on your shoulders and preserve you from yourself."

"I should not have dared to ask it of you," replied Madame de l'Estorade, "for one does not like to ask any one to assist in evil-doing; but since you are so generous as to offer it, I feel I am a degree less wretched. Now, good-night, for my husband must not find me out when he comes in. He was to dine with Monsieur de Rastignac, and no doubt they have plotted great things for to-morrow."

"Go then; and in an hour or so I will send you a note, as though I had not seen you, to ask if you have any power to admit me to the Chamber to-morrow, as the meeting promises to be interesting."

"Oh! To be brought so low as to plot and contrive——" said Madame de l'Estorade, embracing her friend.

"My dear child," replied Madame de Camps, "it is said that the life of the Christian is a warfare; but that of a woman married to a certain type of man is a pitched battle. Be patient and take courage."

And so the friends parted.

At about two o'clock on the following day Madame de l'Estorade, with her husband and Madame de Camps, took her seat in the peers' gallery; she looked ill, and returned the bows that greeted her from various parts of the Chamber with cool indifference. Madame de Camps, who had never before found herself in the parliamentary Chamber, made two observations: In the first place, she exclaimed at the slovenly appearance of so many of the honorable members; and then she was struck by the number of bald heads which, as she looked down on them from the gallery that gave her a bird's-eye view of the assembly, surprised her greatly.

She then listened while Monsieur de l'Estorade named the notabilities present; first of all the bigwigs, who need not be mentioned here, since their names dwell in everybody's memory; then Canalis the poet, who had, she thought, an Olympian air; d'Arthez, whose modest demeanor greatly attracted her; Vinet, who, as she said, was like a viper in spectacles; Victorin Hulot, one of the orators of the Left Centre.

It was written by the finger of fate that Madame de l'Estorade should be spared no form of annoyance. Just as the sitting was about to open, the Marquise d'Espard, escorted by Monsieur de Ronquerolles, came into the gallery, and took a seat close to her. Though they met in society, the two women could not endure each other. Madame de l'Estorade scorned the spirit of intrigue, the total want of principle, and the spiteful, bitter temper which the marquise concealed under the most elegant manners; while Madame d'Espard had even deeper contempt for what she called the "pot-boiling" virtues of the countess. It must be added that Madame de l'Estorade was two-and-thirty, and of a type of beauty that time had spared; while Madame d'Espard was forty-four, and, in spite of the arts of the toilet, her looks were altogether *passé*.

"Do you often come here?" she said to the countess, after a few indispensable civilities as to the pleasure of meeting her.

"Never," said Madame de l'Estorade.

"I am a constant visitor," said Madame d'Espard.

Then, with the air of making a discovery—

"To be sure," she added, "you have a special interest in the meeting to-day. Some one you know, I believe, is on his trial."

"Yes, Monsieur de Sallenauve has visited at my house."

"It is most distressing," said the marquise, "to see a man who, as Monsieur de Ronquerolles assures me, was quite a hero in his way thus called to account by the police."

"His chief crime, so far, is his absence," said the countess drily.

"And he is consumed by ambition, it would seem," Madame d'Espard went on. "Before this attempt to get into Parliament he had matrimonial projects, as you no doubt know, and had tried to marry into the Lanty family—a scheme which, so far as the handsome heiress was concerned, ended in her retirement to a convent."

Madame de l'Estorade was not astonished to find that this story, which Sallenauve had believed to be a perfect secret, was known to the marquise; she was one of the best-informed women in Paris. An old Academician had called her drawing-room, in mythological parlance, "The Temple of Fame."

"They are about to begin, I think," said the countess, who, always expecting to feel Madame d'Espard's claws, was not sorry to close the conversation.

The president had in fact rung his bell, the members were settling into their places, the curtain was about to rise.

To give the reader a faithful account of the sitting, we think it will be at once more exact and more convenient to copy the report as printed in one of the papers of the day.

## CHAMBER OF DEPUTIES.

MONSIEUR COINTET (Vice-President) in the Chair.

*May 23d.*

The President took the chair at two o'clock.

On the Ministers' bench were the Keeper of the Seals, the Minister of the Interior, and the Minister of Public Works.

The report of the last meeting was read and passed.

The order of the day was to discuss the validity of the election of the member returned by the borough of Arcis-sur-Aube.

*The President*—The representative of the Commission of Inquiry will read his report.

*The Reporter*—Gentlemen, the strange and unsatisfactory position in which Monsieur de Sallenauve has thought proper to place himself has not ended as we had reason to hope. Monsieur de Sallenauve's leave of absence expired yesterday, and he still remains away from the sittings of the Chamber; nor has any letter from him applying for further extension reached the President's hands. This indifference as to the functions which Monsieur de Sallenauve had sought, it would seem, with unusual eagerness (murmurs from the Left), would under any circumstances be a serious defection; but when it is coupled with the prosecution now threatened, does it not assume a character highly damaging to his reputation? (Murmurs from the Left. Applause from the Centre.) Your Commissioners, compelled to seek the solution of a question which may be said to be unexampled in parliamentary annals, when considering the steps to be taken, were divided by two opposite opinions. The minority, of which I am the sole representative—the Commissioners being but three—thought that a plan should be laid before you which I may call radical in its character, and which aims at settling the difficulty by submitting it to its natural judges. Annul M. de Sallenauve's election *hic et nunc*, and send him back to the constituency which returned him, and of which he is so faithless a representative: this is the first alternative I have to offer you. (Excitement on the Left.) The majority, on the contrary, pronounced that the electors' vote must be absolutely respected, and the shortcomings of a man honored by their confidence must be overlooked to the utmost limits of patience and indulgence. Consequently, the Commission requires me to propose that you should officially extend M. de Sallenauve's leave of absence to a fortnight from this date—(murmurs from the Centre. "Hear, hear," from the Left)—with the full understanding that if by the end of that time M. de Sallenauve has given no sign of life, he is to be regarded as simply having resigned his seat without entangling this House in any irritating and useless discussion of the matter. (Excitement on all sides.)

M. le Colonel Franchessini, who, during the reading of the report, had been engaged in earnest conversation with the Minister of Public Works on the Ministers' bench, anxiously begged to be heard.

*The President*—M. de Canalis wishes to speak.

*M. de Canalis*—Gentlemen, M. de Sallenauve is one of those bold men who, like me, believe that politics are not a forbidden fruit to any intelligent mind; but that the stuff of which a statesman is made may be found in a poet or an artist quite as much as in a lawyer, an official, a doctor, or a landowner. In virtue, then, of our common origin, M. de Sallenauve has my fullest sympathy, and no one will be surprised to see me mount this tribune to support the recommendation of the Commission. Still, I cannot agree to their final decision; for the idea of our colleague being regarded, by the mere fact of his prolonged absence beyond the limit of leave, as having resigned his seat, is repugnant both to my conscience and my reason. You have heard it remarked that M. de Sallenauve's carelessness as to his duties is all the less excusable because he lies under a serious charge; but supposing, gentlemen, that this charge were the actuating cause of his absence. (Laughter from the Centre.) Allow me—I am not so guileless as the laughers seem to fancy. It is my good fortune, by nature, that base suggestions do not occur to me; and that M. de Sallenauve, with the high position he had achieved as an artist, should plot to take his seat in this Chamber by means of a crime, is a theory I refuse to admit. Two foul spiders are ever ready to spin their web about a man with such a stain on his birth—Chicanery and Intrigue. But I, far from admitting that he would have fled before the charge brought against him, I say, suppose that at this moment, abroad, he were collecting the evidence for his defense? ("Hear, hear; well said!" from the Left.) In this belief,

—a very plausible one, as it seems to me—far from being justified in requiring a strict account of his absence, ought we not rather to regard it as a proof of respect for this House, as feeling himself unworthy to take his place in it till he was in a position to defy his accusers?

*A Voice*—Ten years' leave of absence, like Telemachus, to look for his father. (General laughter.)

*M. de Canalis*—I did not expect so romantic an interruption! But since we are referred to the Odyssey, I may remind you that Ulysses, after suffering every outrage, at last drew his bow, very much to the discomfiture of the suitors. (Loud murmurs from the Centre.) I vote for a fortnight's further leave, and a reopening of the question at the end of that time.

*M. le Colonel Franchessini*—I do not know whether the last speaker intended to intimidate the Chamber; for my part, such arguments affect me very little, and I am always prepared to return them to those who utter them. ("Order, order," from the Left.)

*M. le Président*—No personalities, colonel.

*M. le Colonel Franchessini*—At the same time, I am so far of the same opinion as the last speaker that I do not believe that the delinquent has fled from the charge brought against him. Neither that accusation, nor the effect it may have on your minds or on others, nor even the annulling of his election, has any interest for him at present. Do you wish to know what M. de Sallenauve is doing in England? Then read the English papers. They have for some days been full of the praises of a prima donna who has just come out at Her Majesty's theatre. (Groans and interruptions.)

*A Voice*—Such gossip is unworthy of this Chamber.

*M. le Colonel Franchessini*—Gentlemen, I am more accustomed to the blunt speech of camps than to the proprieties of the Chamber; I am perhaps rash in thinking aloud. The honorable gentleman who spoke last said that he believed that

M. de Sallenauve had gone in search of evidence for his defense. I say—not I believe, but I know, that a wealthy foreigner has extended his protection to a handsome Italian who was formerly honored by that of our college Phidias. (Fresh interruptions. "Order, order; this is not to be allowed!")

*A Voice*—Monsieur le Président, will you not silence this speaker?

Colonel Franchessini, folding his arms, waited till silence should be restored.

*M. le Président*—I must request the speaker to adhere to the question.

*M. le Colonel Franchessini*—I have never deviated from it; however, as the Chamber refuses to hear me, I can but say that I vote with the minority. It seems to me a very natural course to send Monsieur de Sallenauve back to his constituency, and so ascertain whether they meant to elect a deputy or a lover. ("Order, order!" A great commotion; excitement at the highest pitch.)

M. de Canalis hastily tried to mount the tribune. *

*M. le Président*—The Minister of Public Works wishes to speak, and as one of the King's Ministry, he has always a right to be heard.

*M. de Rastignac*—It is no fault of mine, gentlemen, that you have not been saved from this scandal in the Chamber. I tried, out of regard for my old friendship with Colonel Franchessini, to persuade him not to speak on so delicate a matter, since his inexperience of parliamentary rule, aggravated by his ready wit and fluency, might betray him into some regrettable extravagance. It was to this effect that I advised him in the course of the short conversation we held at my seat before he addressed the House; and I myself asked to be heard after him expressly to correct any idea of my collusion

---

* It must be remembered that the speaking member of the French Chambers does not address his audience from his seat, but mounts the provided rostrum after being recognized by the president.—Pub.

in the indiscretion he has committed—in my opinion—by descending to the confidential details with which he has thought proper to trouble you. However, against my intention, and so to say, against my will, I have mounted the tribune, though no ministerial interest detains me here, may I be allowed to make a few brief remarks? ("Speak, speak!" from the Centre.)

The Minister of Public Works proceeded to show that the absent deputy's conduct was characterized by marked contempt for the Chamber. He had treated it with cavalier indifference. He had indeed asked leave of absence; but how? By writing from abroad. That is to say, he first took leave, and then asked for it. Had he, as was customary, assigned any reason for the request? Not at all. He simply announced that he was compelled to be absent on urgent private business, a trumpery pretext which might at any time reduce the assembly by half its members. But supposing that M. de Sallenauve's business were really urgent, and that it were of a nature which he thought it undesirable to explain in a letter to be made public; why could he not have laid it in confidence before the President, or even have requested one of his friends of such standing as would secure credit for his mere word, to answer for the necessity for his absence without any detailed explanation.

At this moment the Minister was interrupted by a bustle in the passage to the right; several of the deputies left their places; others standing on the seats and craning their necks were looking at something. The Minister, after turning to the President, to whom he seemed to appeal for an explanation, went down from the tribune and returned to his seat, when he was immediately surrounded by a number of deputies from the Centre, among whom M. Vinet was conspicuous by his gesticulations. Other groups formed in the arena; in fact, the sitting was practically suspended.

In a few minutes the President rang his bell.

*The ushers*—Take your seats, gentlemen.

The members hastily returned to their places.

*M. le Président*—M. de Sallenauve will now speak.

M. de Sallenauve, who had been talking to M. d'Arthez and M. de Canalis since his arrival had suspended business, went up to the tribune. His manner was modest, but quite free from embarrassment. Everybody was struck by his resemblance to one of the most fiery of the revolutionary orators.

*A Voice*—Danton minus the smallpox.

*M. de Sallenauve* (deep silence)—Gentlemen, I am under no illusion as to my personal importance, and do not imagine that I myself am the object of a form of persecution, which would rather seem to be directed against the opinions I have the honor to represent. However that may be, my election seems to have assumed some importance in the eyes of the Ministry. To contest it, a special agent and special press writers were sent to Arcis; and a humble servant of the Government, whose salary, after twenty years of honorable service, had reached the figure of fifteen hundred francs a year, was suddenly dismissed from his post for being guilty of contributing to my success. (Loud murmurs from the Centre.) I can only thank the gentlemen who are interrupting me, for I suppose their noisy disapprobation is meant for this singular dismissal, and not to convey a doubt of the fact, which is beyond all question. (Laughter from the Left.) So far as I am concerned, as I could not be turned out, I have been attacked with another weapon; judicial calumny combined with my opportune absence——

*The Minister of Public Works*—It was the Ministry evidently that procured your extradition to England?

*M. de Sallenauve*—No, Monsieur le Ministre, I do not ascribe my absence either to your influence or to your suggestions; it was an act of imperative duty, and the result of no one's bidding; but as regards your share in the public accusations brought against me, I shall proceed to lay the facts before this assembly,

and leave the matter to their judgment. (A stir of interest.)
The law which, in order to protect the independence of a
member of this Chamber, lays down the rule that a criminal
prosecution cannot be instituted against any member without
the preliminary authority of the Chamber, has been turned
against me, I must say with consummate skill. The indictment, if presented to the Attorney-General in Court, would
have been at once dismissed, for it stands alone without the
support of any kind of proof; and, so far as I know, the
Ministry of this nation is not in the habit of prosecuting anybody on the strength of the allegation of the first comer. I
cannot, therefore, but admire the remarkable acumen which
discerned that, by appealing to this Chamber, the charge
would have all the advantages of a political attack, though
it had not the elements of the simplest criminal case.
(Murmurs.) And then, gentlemen, who is the skilful parliamentary campaigner to be credited with this masterly device?
As you know, it is a woman, a peasant, claiming only the
humble rank of a hand-worker; whence we must infer that the
countrywomen of Champagne can boast of an intellectual
superiority of which hitherto you can surely have had no conception. (Laughter.) It must, however, be added that
before setting out for Paris to state her grievance, my accuser
would seem to have had an interview, which may have thrown
some light on her mind, with the Mayor of Arcis, my ministerial opponent for election; and it is furthermore to be supposed that this magistrate had some interest in the prosecution
to be instituted, since he thought it his duty to pay the
traveling expenses both of the plaintiff and of the village
lawyer who accompanied her. ("Ha-ha!" from the Left.)
This remarkably clever woman having come to Paris, on whom
does she first call? Well, on that very gentleman who had
been sent to Arcis by the Government as a special agent to
insure the success of the ministerial candidate. And who
then made it his business to apply for authority to prosecute?

*The ushers*—Take your seats, gentlemen.

The members hastily returned to their places.

*M. le Président*—M. de Sallenauve will now speak.

M. de Sallenauve, who had been talking to M. d'Arthez and M. de Canalis since his arrival had suspended business, went up to the tribune. His manner was modest, but quite free from embarrassment. Everybody was struck by his resemblance to one of the most fiery of the revolutionary orators.

*A Voice*—Danton minus the smallpox.

*M. de Sallenauve* (deep silence)—Gentlemen, I am under no illusion as to my personal importance, and do not imagine that I myself am the object of a form of persecution, which would rather seem to be directed against the opinions I have the honor to represent. However that may be, my election seems to have assumed some importance in the eyes of the Ministry. To contest it, a special agent and special press writers were sent to Arcis; and a humble servant of the Government, whose salary, after twenty years of honorable service, had reached the figure of fifteen hundred francs a year, was suddenly dismissed from his post for being guilty of contributing to my success. (Loud murmurs from the Centre.) I can only thank the gentlemen who are interrupting me, for I suppose their noisy disapprobation is meant for this singular dismissal, and not to convey a doubt of the fact, which is beyond all question. (Laughter from the Left.) So far as I am concerned, as I could not be turned out, I have been attacked with another weapon; judicial calumny combined with my opportune absence——

*The Minister of Public Works*—It was the Ministry evidently that procured your extradition to England?

*M. de Sallenauve*—No, Monsieur le Ministre, I do not ascribe my absence either to your influence or to your suggestions; it was an act of imperative duty, and the result of no one's bidding; but as regards your share in the public accusations brought against me, I shall proceed to lay the facts before this assembly,

and leave the matter to their judgment. (A stir of interest.)
The law which, in order to protect the independence of a
member of this Chamber, lays down the rule that a criminal
prosecution cannot be instituted against any member without
the preliminary authority of the Chamber, has been turned
against me, I must say with consummate skill. The indictment, if presented to the Attorney-General in Court, would
have been at once dismissed, for it stands alone without the
support of any kind of proof; and, so far as I know, the
Ministry of this nation is not in the habit of prosecuting anybody on the strength of the allegation of the first comer. I
cannot, therefore, but admire the remarkable acumen which
discerned that, by appealing to this Chamber, the charge
would have all the advantages of a political attack, though
it had not the elements of the simplest criminal case.
(Murmurs.) And then, gentlemen, who is the skilful parliamentary campaigner to be credited with this masterly device?
As you know, it is a woman, a peasant, claiming only the
humble rank of a hand-worker; whence we must infer that the
countrywomen of Champagne can boast of an intellectual
superiority of which hitherto you can surely have had no conception. (Laughter.) It must, however, be added that
before setting out for Paris to state her grievance, my accuser
would seem to have had an interview, which may have thrown
some light on her mind, with the Mayor of Arcis, my ministerial opponent for election; and it is furthermore to be supposed that this magistrate had some interest in the prosecution
to be instituted, since he thought it his duty to pay the
traveling expenses both of the plaintiff and of the village
lawyer who accompanied her. ("Ha-ha!" from the Left.)
This remarkably clever woman having come to Paris, on whom
does she first call? Well, on that very gentleman who had
been sent to Arcis by the Government as a special agent to
insure the success of the ministerial candidate. And who
then made it his business to apply for authority to prosecute?

nauve, I regret the interruptions; be so good as to go on with your speech.

*M. de Sallenauve*—To resume briefly: The application for authority to prosecute, of which you have heard, has now, no doubt, lost much of its importance in the eyes of my colleagues, even of the more hostile. I have here a letter in which the peasant-woman, my relation, withdraws her charge and confirms the statements I have had the honor of laying before you. I might read the letter, but I think it better simply to place it in the President's hands. ("Quite right, quite right!") As regards the illegality of my absence, I returned to Paris this morning; and by being in my place at the opening of this sitting, I could have been in my seat in Parliament within the strict limits of the time so generously granted me by this Chamber. But, as M. de Canalis suggested to you, I was determined not to appear here till the cloud that hung over my character could be cleared off. This task filled up the morning. Now, gentlemen, it is for you to decide whether one of your colleagues is to be sent back to his constituents, for a few hours' delay in coming to claim his seat in this Chamber. After all, whether I am to be regarded as a forger, a desperate lover, or merely as a careless representative, I am not uneasy as to what their verdict will be; and after the lapse of a few weeks, the probable result, as I believe, will be that I shall come back again.

On all sides cries of "Divide."

On descending from the tribune, M. de Sallenauve was warmly congratulated.

*The President*—I put it to the vote: Whether or not, the election of M. de Sallenauve, returned as Deputy for Arcis, is or is not valid?

Almost every deputy present rose to vote in favor of the admission of the new member; a few deputies of the Centre abstained from voting on either side.

M. de Sallenauve was admitted and took the oaths.

*M. le Président*—The order of the day includes the first reading of the Address, but the Chairman of the Committee informs me that the draft will not be ready to be laid before this Chamber till to-morrow. Business being done, I pronounce the sitting closed.

The Chamber rose at half-past four.

NOTE:—This Scene of Political Life remained unfinished by the Author.—PUBLISHER.

# THE MIDDLE CLASSES.

Translated by Jno. Rudd, B.A.

*To Constance-Victoire.*

*Here, madame, is one of those works, we know not whence, which falls into an author's mind and affords him pleasure before he can estimate how it will be welcomed by the public, the supreme judge of our generation. Feeling assured of your compliance at my infatuation, to you I dedicate this book: is it not right that it should be yours as in other days tithes belonged to the church, in memory of God who makes all things grow, all ripen, both in the fields and in our intellects?*

*Some lumps of clay, left by Molière at the base of the colossal statue of Tartuffe, have been moulded by a hand more audacious than able; but, at whatever distance I may be 'neath the greatest of humorists, I shall be satisfied to have utilized these little pieces from before the curtain of his stage to show up the modern hypocrite at work. The reason that most encouraged me in this difficult undertaking was finding it incompatible with any religious question, since for you, so pious, I must necessarily avoid them, in spite of what a great writer calls* the general indifference to religious matters.

*May the double meaning of your names be a prophecy of the book! Be pleased to regard this as a respectful recognition by one who ventures to call himself the most devoted of your servants.*

De Balzac.

## PART I.

THE turnstile Saint-Jean, of which a description seemed unnecessary at the time of the commencement of the study entitled "A Second Home;" this primitive relic of old Paris has no longer an existence but in that story. The erection of the Hôtel de Ville, as it stands to-day, has cleared out the whole quarter.

In 1830 passers-by could still see the turnstile painted on the sign of a wine-dealer, but that house, its last sanctuary, has since been torn down. Alas! old Paris is vanishing with frightful rapidity. Here and there, in these works, there will remain some typical house of the Middle Ages, like that described at the opening of the "Cat and Racket," one or two such specimens still exist; for instance, the house occupied by Judge Popinot, Rue du Fowarre, is an example of old bourgeoisie dwellings. Here, the remains of the Fulbert house; there, the old basin of the Seine during the reign of Charles IX. Why does not the historian of French society, like a new "Old Mortality," search out these singular records of the past like the old man of Walter Scott's restored the tombstones? Certainly, for nearly ten years, the protests of literature were not superfluous; art is beginning to disguise with its flowers the hideous fronts of the trading marts in Paris, and which one of our writers has merrily compared to *commodes*.

It may be remarked that the creation of a municipal commission *del ornamento* which supervises, in Milan, the architecture of the street-fronts, and which compels every proprietor to submit his plans thereto, dates from the twelfth century. Now who can have failed to note in that pretty capital the effects of patriotism for their town alike in the middle-class and the nobles, and to admire to the full the character and originality of the buildings?

The startling and hideous speculations which, year after year, squeeze a suite of rooms into the space of a salon, waging war to the death against the gardens, must inevitably influence the manners of Parisians. Before long we shall be compelled to live out of our houses more than in them. The sanctity of private life, the liberty of the home, where can it be found? It means an income of fifty thousand francs. Again, few millionaires even permit themselves the luxury of a little mansion, protected by a courtyard from the street, and sheltered from the prying eyes of the public by the leafy shade of a garden.

By leveling all fortunes, the Code which regulates the successions, or legacies, has produced these phalansteries in which to lodge thirty families, bringing in one hundred thousand francs a year. Thus, in fifty years we shall be able to count the houses resembling that occupied, at the time we begin this story, by the Thuillier family; really a curious house and well deserving of a detailed description, if only done for the purpose of comparing the middle-class lives of other days with those of our own time.

The situation and appearance of the house, the frame to this picture of manners, has the imprint, the aroma, of the lower middle-class, which may attract or repulse the attention according to each one's inclination.

To commence, the Maison Thuillier did not belong to either M. or Mme., but to Mademoiselle Thuillier, the eldest sister of M. Thuillier.

This house, purchased in the first six months following the revolution of 1830 by Mlle. Jeanne-Brigitte Thuillier, senior, is situated near the middle of the Rue Saint-Dominique-d'Enfer, to the right on entering by the Rue d'Enfer. Thus the house occupied by M. Thuillier has a southern exposure.

The progressive movement of the Parisian populace toward the higher ground on the right bank of the river Seine, deserting the left bank, had for a long time prevented the sale of properties in the Latin quarter, so-called, who, for various reasons, which will be deduced from the character and habits of M. Thuillier, determined his sister to purchase a freehold; this one she was able to buy for the merely nominal price of forty-six thousand francs; the fixtures and so forth amounted to six thousand additional, or fifty-two thousand francs in all. A detailed description by the proprietor, in the style of an advertisement, and the changes made by M. Thuillier will fully show the way in which some fortunes were made in July, 1830, while others lost their all.

On the street the front was of stucco masonry, weather-beaten and rain-furrowed, and grooved by the plasterer's tool in imitation of blocks of stone. This kind of house-front is so common in Paris, and so ugly, that the town ought to give prizes to owners who are willing to build their new facades of carved stone. This drab wall, pierced by seven windows, was raised three stories, and terminated in a mansard roof covered with tiles. The carriage gate, wide and strong, showed in make and style that that part of the building toward the street had been erected during the Empire, one part of the courtyard utilized having formerly formed part of a very large, older habitation, surviving from the time when the Enfer quarter enjoyed more favor.

On one side was found the janitor's lodge; on the other the stairs went up the front. Two wings, adjoining the neighboring houses, had formerly served as the stables, coach-house, kitchens, and servants' quarters; but, since 1830, these had been converted into warehouses.

The right side was rented by a wholesale stationer, called M. Métivier nephew; the left side by a bookseller named Barbet. The offices of each tradesman were over the warerooms, the bookseller being on the second and the stationer on the third floor of the house on the street. Métivier nephew, more a commission agent for paper than a merchant; Barbet, more a bill-broker than a bookseller, had one of these extensive premises in use for storing job lots of paper bought from necessitous manufacturers; the other of editions of works given as pledges for loans.

This shark of the booksellers and this pike of the paper trade lived on good terms with each other, and their transactions, having none of the bustle or energies of retail trade, brought so few carriages into that habitually quiet courtyard that the janitor was compelled to weed-out the grass now and again from between the paving-stones. MM. Barbet and Métivier, who fill but a minor part in this story, made but few visits to their landlord, and their exactitude in paying their rent caused them to be classed as good tenants; they were regarded as very honest people in the eyes of the Thuillier circle.

On the third floor on the street side were two suites of rooms, one occupied by M. Dutocq, clerk to a justice of the peace, an old, retired government employé, a frequenter of the Thuilliers' salon; the other by the hero of this Scene. We must be content for the present, though, to know what rent he paid—seven hundred francs—and the position he had taken in the heart of the place, three years previous to the curtain rising on this domestic drama.

The clerk, a bachelor of fifty, occupied, out of the two suites of the three, the larger one; he had a cook and paid a rent of one thousand francs. Two years after her acquisition, Mademoiselle Thuillier was getting seven thousand francs in rent for one house; the former owner had furnished it with outside shutters, had restored the interior, ornamenting it with mirrors, without succeeding in either letting or selling it; and the Thuilliers, very handsomely lodged, as will be seen, had the enjoyment of one of the most beautiful gardens in the quarter, whose trees shaded the deserted little street, the Rue Neuve-Sainte-Catherine.

Situated between the courtyard and the garden, that part of the house which they occupied seemed to have been the caprice of some wealthy citizen, in the days of Louis XIV., or that of a president of the Parlement, or some quiet, peace-loving student. This lodge had five windows and was of two stories above the first floor, being prettily capped with a four-gabled roof, ending in a weathercock, pierced by handsome, large chimneys and oval windows. Perhaps this structure was built from the remains of some great mansion; but, after studying the plans of old Paris, I have been unable to find anything to substantiate this theory; and, for that matter, the title deeds of Mlle. Thuillier mention as proprietor, under Louis XIV., one Petitot, the famous painter of camels, he having it from President Lecamus. It is probable that the president lived here during the erection of his celebrated mansion on the Rue de Thorigny.

Thus the Robe and Art had alike left their traces. But, then, what a liberal idea of necessity and pleasure had ruled in the arrangements of the interior of this lodge! To the right, on entering the hall, is a spacious vestibule whence ascends a stairway of stone, with two windows overlooking the garden; under the stairs is the doorway to the cellar. From the vestibule, which communicates with the dining-room, with windows to the courtyard. This dining-room has a side-door to the kitchens adjoining Barbet's warehouse. At the back of the stairs on the garden side was a fine, large study, with two windows. The first and second stories each formed a separate set of two suites of rooms; and the servants' quarters were indicated, under the four-gabled roof, by the oval windows. A handsome, large stove ornamented the great vestibule; its two glass doors, facing each other, gave ample light. This hall was paved in black and white marble, and had a decorated coffered ceiling, the joists of which had at one time been painted and gilded, but had, since the Empire, undoubtedly been whitewashed. Facing the stove was a red marble basin. The three doors of the study, of the salon and the dining-room were surmounted with oval panels containing pictures which cried aloud for much-needed restoration, though the decorations were not without merit.

The salon, wainscoted in wood, recalled the century of magnificence by its Languedoc marble mantel, in its ceiling with ornamented corners, and by the shape of its windows, in which were preserved the little diamond panes. The dining-room, level with the salon and having double doors between, was floored with marble; the ceiling of chestnut-wood was unpainted; but the atrocious modern paper-hangings had replaced the tapestry of the olden time. The study, modernized by Thuillier, was now utterly discordant.

The gold and white panels of the salon were so faded that nothing but red lines could be perceived where the gold had formerly been, and the white was yellow, streaky, and falling off. The Latin words, *Otium cum dignitate*, had never, to the eyes of a poet, had so excellent a commentary as in this noble dwelling. The iron-work of the balustrade to the stairs was worthy the magistrate and the artist; but, to discern their traces to-day in the remains of a dignified antiquity, the observing eyes of the artist are necessary.

The Thuilliers and their predecessors had much dishonored this gem of the higher bourgeoisie by their middle-class habits and lack of taste. Can you imagine walnut-wood chairs with horsehair seats; a mahogany table with an oilcloth cover; a crumb-cloth under the table; lamps of black metal; a cheap paper with a red border; execrable black and white engravings on the walls; and cotton curtains with red borders in this dining-room in which Petitot and his friends had feasted?

Can you conceive of the effect of this in the salon where the portraits of M. of Mme. of Mlle. Thuillier, by Pierre Grassou, the painter of the middle-classes; of card-tables that had done twenty years' service; of consoles of the time of the Empire; a tea-table supported on a huge lyre; a coarse mahogany suite upholstered in printed velvet on a chocolate ground; of the mantel, with its clock which

represented la Bellone of the Empire; of candelabra with
fluted columns; of curtains of worsted damask and of embroidered lawn, looped back with stamped brass chains? A
second-hand carpet covered the floor. The handsome vestibule was furnished with benches covered with plush, the
carved panels being hidden behind wardrobes of divers dates,
which had been removed from the various apartments formerly
occupied by the Thuilliers. A shelf covered the marble
basin and bore a smoky lamp dating from 1815. As a finish-
ing touch, fear, that hideous bugbear, had provided double
doors both on the garden and the courtyard sides of the
house, strongly sheathed in iron, which stood back against the
wall by day and at night were securely closed.

It is an easy matter to explain the deplorable desecration
of this monument of private life of the seventeenth century
by the same life of the nineteenth century. At the commencement of the Consulate, perhaps, some master-builder,
having acquired this little mansion, conceived the idea of
making some use of the ground facing the street; he had
most likely pulled down a beautiful coach-way gate flanked by
little lodges which added importance to this pretty *séjour*, to
use an old French word, and the shrewdness of a Parisian
builder implanted its blight on the front of this elegance; as
the newspapers and their printing-presses, the factories and
their warerooms, trade and its counting-rooms, have ousted
the aristocracy, the old bourgeoisie, finance and the law,
wherever they once displayed their splendor. A curious study
is that of the title-deeds in Paris! A mad-house, on the Rue
des Batailles, occupies the site where once stood the dwelling
of the Chevalier Pierre Bayard du Terrail; the third estate
has built a whole street where once stood the Hôtel Necker.
Old Paris is going—following the kings who are gone. For
one *chef d'œuvre* of architecture saved by a Polish princess,*

* The Hôtel Lambert, Ile Saint-Louis, occupied by the Princess Czar-
toriska. [Note in original edition.]

how many smaller palaces have fallen, like Petitot's dwelling, into the hands of Thuilliers. Here are the reasons which led Mademoiselle Thuillier to become the owner of this house:

At the fall of the Villèle ministry M. Louis-Jérôme Thuillier, who had then been for twenty-six years a clerk in the Bureau of Finance, became second clerk; but he had barely had his fill of the joys of authority in that subaltern position, once the smallest of his hopes, when the events of July, 1830, compelled him to resign. He very ingeniously calculated that his pension would be honorably and munificently dealt with by the new men, who would be only too well pleased to have the disposal of another place at their command; and this was well reasoned, for it was at once granted at seventeen hundred francs.

When the prudent sub-chief first spoke of retiring from the administration, his sister, far more the partner of his life than was his wife, trembled for the employé's future.

"What would become of Thuillier?" was the question Madame and Mademoiselle Thuillier addressed to each other with equal fears; they were then living in a small flat on the third floor, Rue d'Argenteuil.

"Getting his pension into proper shape will occupy him for some time," said Mlle. Thuillier; "but I think I will so place my savings as to keep him pretty well occupied. Yes, by giving him an estate to manage it will be almost equal to his being in the service."

"Oh! my dear sister, you will save his life!" cried Mme. Thuillier.

"Well, I have always foreseen this crisis in Jérôme's life!" replied the old maid, with an air of patronage.

Mlle. Thuillier had too frequently heard her brother remark: "Such-a-one is dead; he only lasted two years after he retired!" She well remembered hearing Colleville, Thuillier's intimate friend, employed in the same office, jesting about the climacteric of bureaucracy, and saying: "We shall some time come to it the same as the rest!" not to realize the danger threatening her brother. The transition from activity to idleness is, in fact, the critical time for the employé. Those who cannot enter upon some substituted occupation for the one they have left change remarkably: some die; a great number take to fishing, a distraction very akin to their former labors (*sic*) in the office; some others, malicious men, become stock-brokers, lose their savings in the concern, and are glad to finish by taking a situation in the business, after the first bankruptcy and liquidation, which becomes successful in the hands of more capable ones on the lookout for just such chances; then the ex-clerk can rub his, now empty, hands and say: "I always knew there was a great future for this business." But most of them keep up a constant struggle against their old habits.

"Some of them," said Colleville, "are devoured by a spleen"* (he pronounced it "splane") "peculiar to government clerks; they die of suppressed *circula(r)tion;* afflicted with red-tape worm. The little Poiret could not see a blue-bordered cardboard box without his face changing color; he turned from yellow to green."

Mlle. Thuillier was looked upon as the good genius of her brother's household; that she had plenty of force and decision her personal story will demonstrate. This relative superiority enabled her to gauge her brother, though she adored him. After seeing the wreck of her hopes founded on her idol, she experienced a feeling of maternity which caused her to overestimate the social qualities of the sub-chief.

Thuillier and his sister were the children of the head porter to the Minister of Finance. Jérôme had escaped, thanks to his being short-sighted, from every possible form of requisition and conscription. His father's ambition was to make him an employé. At the opening of this century there were

*Blue devils.

so many places to fill in the army that it caused many vacancies in the offices, thus the removal of inferior clerks gave the burly old Thuillier a chance so see his son take his first decrees in the hierarchy of bureaucracy.

The porter died in 1814, at the time when Jérôme was to succeed the old sub-chief, but all the fortune he was able to leave him was this hope. Old Thuillier and his wife, who died in 1810, had retired in 1806, with a retiring pension their sole fortune, having expended their earnings in giving Jérôme his education and in supporting him and his sister.

We know the effect of the Restoration on the bureaux. The suppression of forty-one departments caused the dismissal of a horde of clerks, honest men quite prepared to accept offices inferior in grade to those formerly occupied by them. The rights of these men were further impinged upon by the pretensions of exiled families ruined by the Revolution. Squeezed between these two sources, Jérôme thought himself more than lucky not to be dismissed on some frivolous pretext. Till the day when by chance he became second-clerk he had quaked about his retiring pension.

This short review explains the limited conceptions and lack of general knowledge of M. Thuillier. He had acquired Latin, mathematics, history, and geography, as boys are taught at school; but he had not risen higher than is known as the second class, his father having profited by the chance of getting him into office, boasting of his son's "splendid hand." So, though little Thuillier wrote the first inscriptions in the ledger, he was not up in rhetoric or philosophy.

A cogwheel in the ministerial machine, he but little cultivated letters and still less troubled art; he acquired a superficial knowledge of his own line; and when, on the occasion of his rise, under the Empire, he mixed with the higher class of employés, he caught the superficial manner which concealed the porter's son, but he utterly failed to catch a ready wit. His ignorance caused his silence, and his silence well served him. He was accustomed to render, under the Imperial regime, that passive obedience which is so appreciated by superiors; and it was to this quality that he afterward owed his promotion to the grade of sub-chief. This routine life gave him a great experience; his silent manner covered his lack of education.

Mlle. Thuillier, knowing how her brother abhorred reading and his inability to replace the tasks of the office by any business, had wisely resolved to give him the care of her property, the culture of the garden, the little trivialities of middle-class life found in the intrigues of the neighborhood.

The transplanting of the Thuillier household from the Rue d'Argenteuil to the Rue Saint-Dominique-d'Enfer, the attention necessary to the purchase, the selection of a janitor, the search for good tenants, kept Thuillier fully occupied through 1831 and 1832. When this phenomenal transplantation was effected, when the sister saw that Jérôme had survived his uprooting, she found him still other employment, as we shall learn, for she recognized a similar disposition to her own in Thuillier, which it may not be useless to here describe.

Although only the son of a minister's porter, Thuillier was what is known as a fine man; above the medium height, slight, of agreeable physiognomy when he wore his spectacles, but ugly, like most persons afflicted with myopia, when he doffed them; for the habit of looking through glasses had cast a species of mist over his eyeballs.

Between the age of eighteen and thirty, young Thuillier was a favorite with women in that social sphere that exists in the lower middle-class and ends below the chiefs of the departments; but, as all are aware, under the Empire the wars left Parisian society somewhat bereft by absorbing every man of energy into the fields of battle; and perhaps, as suggested by a celebrated physician, this is the cause of the decadence of the generation that lived during the middle of the nineteenth century.

Thuillier, compelled to shine by accomplishments other than intellectual, learned to waltz and dance so well as to become noted for it in the city; he was called "Handsome Thuillier;" he was an expert billiard player; he was clever at cutting out figures; his friend Colleville had so well instructed him that he could troll out some fancy ballads in great style. All this resulted in gaining him that spurious success which deceives the young and deludes them as to the future. From 1806 to 1814 Mlle. Thuillier believed in her brother as Mlle. d'Orleans believed in Louis-Philippe; she was proud of Jérôme, she saw him arrive at the highest post in the office; thanks to the popularity which at that time gave him the entrance to some salons where he most decidedly would not have been seen only for the circumstances which, under the Empire, made society a perfect medley.

He acquired a habit of looking at himself in the glass, posing with his hands on his hips to set off his figure, and assuming the deportment of a dancing-master, all of which helped to prolong the lease of his nickname "Handsome Thuillier."

But the truth in 1806 became mockery in 1826. He still retained some vestiges of the dandy's dress of the Empire, nor were they unbecoming to the dignity of an old second-clerk. He still wore the white cravat with numerous pleats in which his chin was buried, the two ends of which menaced passers-by as they projected to the right and left of a neatly tied knot, in former days fastened by the hands of dainty beauties. He followed the fashions at a respectful distance, but he adapted them to his own style; he wore his hat far back; low shoes in summer with fine stockings; his overcoat was reminiscent of the *levites* of the Empire; he would not abandon his pleated shirt-frills and white vests; he was all the time making play with his thin cane, the style of 1810, and held himself upright. None who saw Thuillier promenading the boulevards would have taken him for the son of a

man who served the employés' breakfasts in the Bureau of
Finance, and who wore the livery of Louis XVI.; he more
resembled an imperial diplomat or a sub-prefect.

Another household transplanted into the same neighborhood
was that of which M. Colleville, Thuillier's most intimate
friend, was the head. But before painting Pylades it is first
indispensable to have done with Orestes, as it is necessary to
explain why Thuillier, Handsome Thuillier, found himself
without a family, for a family cannot be without children;
and here must be revealed one of those deep mysteries which
lie entombed in the arcana of private life, and whose symptoms arise at times to the surface when the anguish of a hidden
sorrow becomes too great to be silently borne, as instance
that of Mme. and Mlle. Thuillier, for, up to the present, we
have only seen, so to speak, the public life of Jérôme Thuillier.

Marie-Jeanne-Brigitte Thuillier, four years older than her
brother, had been immolated on her brother's altar; it was
easier to give him a profession than to give the other a mar-
riage-portion. Ill-fortune, to certain natures, is a lighthouse
illuminating the dark and squalid in social life. Superior to
her brother, alike in energy and commonsense, Brigitte possessed a nature which the sledge-hammer of persecution had
made dense, compact, and of great resistance, not to mention
inflexible. Jealous of her independence, she made up her
mind, by some means, to leave behind her the life at the
porter's lodge and become the sole arbiter of her fate.

At fourteen years of age she took up her abode in a garret,
some few steps from the Treasury, then in the Rue Vivienne,
not far from the Rue de la Vrillière, where to-day the Bank
stands. She bravely started out in an unfamiliar business,
privileged, thanks to her father's patrons; and which consisted of manufacturing cash-bags for the Bank, the Treasury,
and other great banking houses. She had, at the end of three
years, two workwomen employed. Placing her savings in the
Funds, by 1814 she owned an income of three thousand six

hundred francs a year, which had been made in fifteen years. She spent but little, dining every day with her father as long as he lived; now, as all know, the Funds during the last convulsions of the Empire went down to forty-odd francs—so this result, apparently exaggerated, is easily explained.

On the death of the old porter, Brigitte and Jérôme, one aged twenty-seven, the other twenty-three, united their destinies. The brother and sister had the fullest affection for each other. So when Jérôme, then in the time of his success, needed any money, his sister, dressed in coarse woolen cloth, her fingers showing the wear of the thread with which she sewed, always had a few louis to offer him. In Brigitte's eyes Jérôme was the most handsome man and more charming than any other in the whole French Empire.

To keep house for this adored brother, to be initiated into the secrets of Lindoro and Don Juan, to be his servant, his faithful spaniel, was Brigitte's ideal dream; she immolated herself with ardor to an idol whose egoism she could aggrandize by her sacrifice. She sold her business to her forelady for fifteen thousand francs, then went and established herself in the Rue d'Argenteuil with Thuillier, making herself the mother, protector, slave, of that "darling of the ladies."

Brigitte, with the natural prudence of a maid who owed her all to her own discretion and toil, hid the extent of her fortune from her brother; she no doubt was afraid of the prodigalities of such a man of the world, bringing to the common stock but six hundred francs; this, though, with the eighteen hundred of Jérôme's, enabled her to make both ends meet each year.

From the first day of their partnership, Thuillier listened to his sister as to an oracle; he consulted her in the smallest affairs, concealed no secrets from her, and thus gave her a taste of the fruits of domination which became the besetting sin of her nature. But, really, the sister had been altogether sacrificed to her brother, she had staked her all on his heart, she lived but in him. Brigitte's ascendency over Jérôme was singularly confirmed by the marriage she procured for him about 1814.

Seeing the violent nip of the new-comers, which came with the Restoration, in all the government offices, particularly by the return of the old society which trampled under foot the middle-classes, Brigitte understood, and indeed her brother explained to her, the social crisis that bade fair to extinguish all their hopes. Further success was out of the question for Handsome Thuillier among the nobility who had succeeded in routing the plebeians of the Empire.

Under these conditions a woman, as zealous as Brigitte was, wished and determined to have her brother marry, quite as much for her own sake as for his, for only she herself could achieve his happiness, Madame Thuillier being merely the indispensable accessory for the production of one or two children. Though Brigitte's intellect did not compare with her will, for all that she had the instinct of despotism; for though she had received no education, she went straight ahead with the persistency of a nature accustomed to succeed. She had a natural genius for household management, the sense of thrift, and a love of work. She divined that she would never be successful in marrying Jérôme in a higher sphere than their own, where the family would make inquiry as to their style of life, possibly to be alarmed at finding a mistress already established in the dwelling; she searched, therefore, in a grade below their own for the people she might dazzle, and she came across the very party.

The senior messenger of the Bank, named Lemprun, had an only daughter called Céleste. Mlle. Céleste Lemprun would inherit her mother's fortune, the only daughter of a truck-farmer. This property consisted of some acres of land in the environs of Paris which the old man still worked; then the fortune of old Lemprun, a man who, after being employed in the banks of Thélusson and Keller, had entered the service of the Bank at its foundation, would also be hers. Lemprun, then the head messenger, enjoyed the respect and esteem of the government and the inspectors.

The Board of Directors, hearing that the marriage of Céleste, to an honorable employé in the Bureau of Finance, was arranged, promised a present of six thousand francs; this gift added to the twelve thousand francs given by old Lemprun, and twelve thousand francs given by Sieur Galard, the truck-farmer at Auteuil, made a *dot* of thirty thousand francs. Old Galard and M. and Mme. Lemprun were enchanted with this alliance; the chief messenger knew Brigitte for one of the most worthy and respectable young women in Paris. Brigitte gave lustre by her descriptions of investments in the Funds and informing the Lempruns that she would never marry, and neither the chief messenger nor his wife, people of the Golden Age, allowed themselves to criticise Brigitte. They were especially struck by the high position of Handsome Thuillier, and the marriage had been settled, to use the accustomed formula, to the general satisfaction of all.

The governor and secretary of the Bank acted as witnesses for the bride, the same as M. de la Billardière, chief of his department, and M. Rabourdin, chief of the bureau, did for Thuillier.

Six years after this marriage old Lemprun was the victim of a most audacious robbery, spoken of in the journals of that time, but quite forgotten in the events of 1815. The thieves had completely eluded every search. Lemprun wished to pay for the loss, and, although the Bank charged the amount to profit and loss, the poor old man died of vexation caused by the disaster. He regarded it as a blow at his probity of seventy years' standing.

Mme. Lemprun abandoned all her inheritance to her daughter, Mme. Thuillier, going to live with her father at Auteuil, where the old man died of an accident in 1817. Afraid of either managing or letting her father's fields, Mme. Lemprun begged Brigitte, at whose capabilities and honesty she was astonished, to realize the estate of old Galard and so arrange things that her daughter should take everything, allowing her fifteen hundred francs a year and leaving her the house at Auteuil. The fields of the old truck-farmer, sold in lots, brought thirty thousand francs, and the two fortunes, added to the *dot*, amounted in 1818 to ninety thousand francs.

At the beginning of that year, with the results of operations on 'Change, Thuillier's salary and the dividend on Bank shares, the annual sum passing through Brigitte's uncontrolled hands, amounted to eleven thousand francs. It is necessary to have this financial question understood, not only to dissipate objections, but to leave a clear course for the drama.

From the very first Brigitte broke in the unfortunate Mme. Thuillier by a free use of the spurs and making her feel the curb. This luxury of tyranny was quite useless; the victim promptly yielded. Céleste had been reckoned up by Brigitte, who found her devoid of pluck and education, accustomed to a sedentary life, a tranquil atmosphere, and of excessively mild nature; she was pious as the word; she had expiated by hardest penace each involuntary fault that could cause pain to another. She was quite ignorant of life; accustomed to be waited upon by her mother, who did her own housework; compelled to keep in a state of rest by a lymphatic constitution, becoming fatigued at the least exertion. She was just a daughter of the people of Paris, where the children, rarely pretty, are the production of poverty, overwork, of airless homes, without freedom of action, and the lack of every convenience of life.

At the time of her wedding Céleste was a little woman, a faded blonde, nauseatingly so; fat, slow, and of most stupid appearance. Her too-large forehead, prominent, and suggesting water on the brain; and under that dome of a waxy hue a face evidently too small and ending in a point like the snout of a mouse, gave fear to arise that at some time she would lose her mind. Her pale blue eyes and lips, set in a petrified smile, did not disabuse one of this idea. She had, on the solemn day of her wedding, the attitude, air, and manner of one condemned to death, and who hopes it will soon be over.

"She's a bit soft!" said Colleville to Thuillier.

Brigitte was the good knife that should stab this nature, which presented so violent a contrast to her own. She possessed a sort of beauty in her correct, regular features, but it had been massacred by toil which, from infancy, had bound her hard down to uncongenial, rough work, and by the secret privations she had voluntarily undergone to increase her competency. Her dappled skin had the hue of steel. Her brown eyes were surrounded with black, or, rather, bruised circles; her upper lip was ornamented with dark down, looking somewhat as it had been smoked; she had thin lips, and her imperious forehead had once been crowned with hair that was black, but which was now changing to chinchilla. She was as erect as any handsome woman, and everything about her betrayed a life of toil, suppressed fires, and, as is said of the huzzars, "at the cost of her achievements."

To Brigitte Céleste was but a fortune to pick up, a mother to mate, one subject more in her empire. She very soon reproached her for being "flabby"—a constant word of hers— and this jealous old maid, who would have despaired if she had found a managing sister-in-law, took a savage delight in stinging this feeble creature into activity. Céleste, ashamed of seeing her sister-in-law displaying such vim and energy in her household duties, made an effort to assist her; she fell ill; at once Brigitte gave her whole care to Mme. Thuillier, she nursed her like a sister, saying before Jérôme:

"You are not strong enough; eh, well, do nothing, my pet!" she made the most of the incapacity of Céleste with that display of pity by which the strong, pretending much compassion for the weak, manage to chant their own eulogy.

When Mme. Thuillier's health was reëstablished, Brigitte

would say, in such manner that none could help hearing: "Dish-rag, good-for-nothing," and the like. Céleste would weep in her own room, and, when Thuillier surprised her in tears, he excused his sister, saying:

"She's all right, but she's hot-tempered; she loves you in her way; she is just the same with me."

Céleste, remembering the maternal care she had received, pardoned her sister-in-law. Brigitte looked upon her brother as king of the house; she lauded him to Céleste and treated him as an autocrat, a Ladislas, an infallible pope. Mme. Thuillier, bereft of her father and grandfather, and all but abandoned by her mother, who came on Thursdays to see her, while they visited her on Sundays in the summer, had no one but her husband to love; first, because he was her husband, and also because he remained to her Handsome Thuillier. And sometimes he really treated her as though she were his wife; all these reasons combined caused her to worship him. Now Thuillier dined at home, but went to bed very late; he went to balls in his own circle alone and precisely the same as though he was a bachelor. Thus the two women were always together.

Céleste assumed a passive attitude, and, agreeable to Brigitte's desire, became a regular slave. The Queen Elizabeth of the household passed from despotism to a sort of pity for this perpetually sacrificed victim. Finally she laid aside her high and mighty airs, her stinging words, her tone of contempt, when she was assured that she had broken her sister into passive slavery.

The poor creature might have become something in the household that lived upon her money—though she was unaware of the fact—all of which she obtained being the crumbs that fell from the table; she had one chance by which her spirit might have been roused to defend herself, to be something, but, alas! that chance did not materialize.

Six years had gone, but Céleste had not borne a child.

This infecundity, which, month after month, caused her torrents of tears, for a long time did but add fuel to Brigitte's flame; she reproached her for being no good at all, not even to bear children. This old maid, who had promised herself the pleasure of loving her brother's child, was slow in becoming used to the idea that this sterility was irremediable.

At the time when this story commences, in 1840, at the age of forty-six, Céleste had stopped crying, for she was mournfully certain that the power of becoming a mother had departed. Time, ample means, the incessant little frictions of daily life, had rubbed off the corners, and that, together with Céleste's lamblike resignation and sweetness, led to a serene, mild fall. Brigitte became as fond of Céleste as she was of her. And the two women were further united by the sole sentiment they had ever known—their adoration for the happy and selfish Thuillier.

This spurious motherhood, quite as absorbing as the real, needs an explanation which brings us to the heart of the drama and is the reason why Mlle. Thuillier found plenty of occupation for her brother.

Thuillier had entered as a supernumerary in the bureau at the same time as Colleville, who has already been spoken of as his intimate friend. Compared to the dull and rigid household of Thuillier's, social nature had formed Colleville's as a perfect contrast, and though it was impossible that this peculiar contrast is far from moral, it needs to be added that before jumping to a conclusion of the drama, unfortunately only too true, it were as well to read the story to the end, otherwise the author cannot be held responsible.

This Colleville was the only son of a talented musician, formerly the first violin at the opera during Francœur's and Rebel's time. Colleville and Thuillier were inseparable friends, having no secrets from each other; their friendship, commenced when they were but fifteen, remained cloudless in the year 1839.

Colleville, beside being an employé, was what was known as a "Cumulator" in the bureau; he was first clarionet at the Opera-Comique—thanks to his father's name—now, when a bachelor, he was better off than Thuillier, and often shared with his friend. But, contrary to Thuillier, Colleville married to please himself Mlle. Flavie, natural daughter of a celebrated dancer who pretended that she was a de Bourgnier, one of the richest contractors of his day, but who had been ruined in 1800, and who more completely forgot his child, as he cherished doubts as to the faithfulness of this famous comediénne.

By her appearance and birth Flavie was destined to a grievous fate at the time when Colleville, who had frequent occasion to visit her mother, who had lived luxuriously, fell in love with Flavie and married her. Prince Galathionne, her protector, in September, 1815, when the illustrious dancer was bringing her brilliant career to a close, gave twenty thousand francs as a wedding-present, and her mother added a most elaborate trousseau. The frequenters of her house and her comrades at the opera made her presents of jewelry and plate, so that the Colleville household was much richer in superfluities than cash. Flavie, raised in luxury, at first had a charming suite of rooms which had been furnished by her mother's decorator, and where this young wife held court, airing her taste for the arts, artists, and for a certain elegance.

Mme. Colleville was at once pretty and piquante, bright, gay, gracious, and an expounder of that name—a jolly good fellow. The dancer, now aged forty-three, retired from the stage and went to live in the country, which deprived her daughter of the benefit to be derived from her mother's luxury and extravagance. Mme. Colleville's house was very pleasant, but tremendously expensive. Between 1816 to 1826 she had five children. A musician in the evening, from seven to nine in the morning Colleville kept the books of a merchant. By ten o'clock he was at the bureau. Thus by blowing into a wooden pipe in the evening, and writing out accounts in double entry in the morning, he made seven to eight thousand francs per annum.

Mme. Colleville played the lady of high society; she received on Wednesdays; she gave a musicale each month, and a dinner every fortnight. She only saw Colleville at dinner in the evening; when he returned toward midnight, she very often had not yet come in. She was at the play, for she often had a box given her, or she would leave word for Colleville to call for her at some house where she was at a dance or a supper. Excellent fare was provided by Mme. Colleville, and the society, somewhat mixed, was excessively amusing; she received famous actresses, painters, men of letters, and some wealthy men. Mme. Colleville's elegance was on a par with that of Tullia, the operatic premier danseuse, of whom she saw a great deal; but, though the Collevilles dipped into their capital, often finding it difficult to make both ends meet, at the month's end Flavie was never in debt.

Colleville was very happy; he still loved his wife and was always her good friend. Ever welcomed with an affectionate smile and infectious, pretty manner, he yielded to her irresistible graces and fascination. The ferocious activity he employed in his three several callings were well suited to his character and temperament. He was a big, burly, good-natured fellow, florid, jovial, lavish, and full of whims. In ten years there had not been a single quarrel in his household. He passed at the bureau as a scatterbrain, the character given all artists, but they were superficial thinkers who mistake the constant haste of a busy man for the bustle of a muddler.

Thanks to the relations of Mme. Colleville, the theatre and the department bowed to the exigencies of the cumulatist, who, in addition to his other duties, was training a young man earnestly recommended by his wife, a great musician of the future, who often took his place in the orchestra, being promised his succession.

As a matter of fact, in 1827, this young man became the first clarionet, on Colleville's retirement.

All the criticism that Flavie aroused was in the words: "She is a *little bit* of a flirt, this Madame Colleville!"

The eldest of the Colleville children, born in 1816, was the living image of the jolly Colleville. In 1818 Mme. Colleville thought the cavalry was everything, even ranking the arts; she smiled upon a sub-lieutenant of the Saint-Chamans dragoons, the young and wealthy Charles Gondreville, who afterward died in the Spanish campaign; her second son was already destined for a military career. In 1820 she looked upon the bank as the foster-mother of industry, the backbone of the State, and the great Keller, the famous orator, was her idol; then she had another son, François, who was to go into mercantile pursuits and would never lack the protection of François Keller.

Toward the end of 1820, Thuillier, the intimate friend of M. and Mme. Colleville, and Flavie's admirer, felt the necessity of confiding his sorrows to the bosom of that excellent woman, to whom he recounted his conjugal miseries; for six years he had tried for children, but God had not blessed his efforts; for poor Mme. Thuillier had vainly said *novenas;* she had even gone to Notre-Dame de Liesse! He depicted Céleste in every phase, and the words "Poor Thuillier" fell from Mme. Colleville's lips, who, on her part, was much depressed; just now she had no predominant opinion. She poured her vexation into Thuillier's heart. The great Keller, the hero of the Left, was awfully mean; she had seen the wrong side of glory, the follies of the bank, the shallowness of the Tribune. The orator never spoke, save in the Chamber, and he had treated her very badly.

Thuillier was indignant.

"It's not only brutes that know how to love," said he; "take me!"

And Handsome Thuillier was said to be making up to Mme.

Colleville, paying her "attentions," in the words of the Empire.

"Ah! you are mashed on my wife!" said Colleville, laughing. "But lookout or she'll shake you like all the others."

A shrewd speech, allowing Colleville to preserve his marital dignity in the bureau. In 1820–21 Thuillier, under his authority as a friend of the family, was able to assist Colleville, who had so frequently of old helped him; during eighteen months he had loaned the Collevilles ten thousand francs, never intending to afterward speak of it. In the spring of 1821 Madame Colleville was confined with a handsome little girl, to whom M. and Mme. Thuillier acted as godfather and godmother; she was named Céleste-Louise-Caroline-Brigitte. Mlle. Thuillier wished that one of her names should be given to this little angel. The name of Caroline was a compliment to Colleville.

Old Mamma Lemprun took upon herself the putting out to nurse of the pretty creature, which was kept under her own eyes at Auteuil, where Céleste and her sister-in-law went to see her twice each week. As soon as Mme. Colleville was about again, she said to Thuillier, very frankly and in a serious tone:

"My dear friend, if we wish to remain good friends, you cannot be more than my friend; Colleville loves you: well, then, one in the family is quite enough."

"Explain to me," said Handsome Thuillier to Tullia, the dancer, who had made a call on Mme. Colleville, "why women are so little attached to me. I am not the Apollo Belvidere, but on the other hand neither am I a Vulcan; I am passable, I am intelligent, I am faithful——"

"Would you have the truth?" asked Tullia.

"Yes," said Handsome Thuillier.

"Well, then, although sometimes we may love an idiot, we can never love a fool."

These words killed Thuillier; he couldn't get over it; he

had a spell of melancholy and accused women of being fantastical.

"Didn't I give you the tip?" said Colleville; "I am not Napoleon, dear boy; I might be sorry if I were; but I have my Joséphine—a pearl!"

The minister's secretary, des Lupeaulx, who was supposed by Mme. Colleville to have more influence than he really had, of whom she used afterward to say: "He was one of my mistakes," was during a long time the great man of the Colleville salon; but as he had not the power necessary to have Colleville named for the division of Bois-Levant, Flavie had the good sense to resent his attentions to Mme. Rabourdin, wife of the chief of the bureau, a minx, as she said, to whose home she had never been invited, and whom on two different occasions had had the impertinence to stay away from her musicales.

Mme. Colleville acutely felt the shock of young Gondreville's death; she was quite inconsolable; she saw in it, she said, the hand of God. In 1824 she mended her ways, talked economy, gave up her receptions, occupied herself with her children, and became a good mother of her family; and her friends had no knowledge of an attendant favorite; but she went to church, she reformed her dress, she wore sober colors, she talked of Catholicism and the proprieties, and all this mysticism resulted in the production of a bouncing boy, in 1825, whom she named Théodore, that is to say, "the gift of God."

So, in 1826, the good times of the Congregation, Colleville was appointed sub-chief in Clergeot's division, becoming, in 1828, a revenue collector in a Paris arrondissement. He also obtained the cross of the Legion of Honor, which in the end entitled him to the education of his daughter at Saint-Denis. In 1832, by the advice of Mlle. Thuillier, he settled near them, where he obtained a clerkship in the mayor's office, paying one thousand crowns.

Charles Colleville had just entered the Naval School. The colleges to which the other young Collevilles went were in the same quarter. The seminary of Saint-Sulpice, where the youngest was to be entered some day, was close by the Luxembourg. Finally, Thuillier and Colleville should properly end their days together.

In 1833 the Colleville family, after leading a life first of show and dissipation, then of tranquil retirement, was become reduced to middle-class obscurity, on a total income of five thousand four hundred francs.

Céleste was now twelve; she promised to be pretty; she needed masters; that would cut down their income by two thousand francs. Her mother felt the need of placing her under the eyes of her godfather and godmother. So she had adopted the proposition, so wisely thought out, of Mlle. Thuillier, who, without committing herself, gave Mme. Colleville to understand pretty plainly that her brother's, her sister-in-law's, and her own fortune were destined for Céleste.

The little frolic had seen more of Mlle. and Mme. Thuillier than of her mother until she went home, after Mme. Lemprun's death, in 1829. In 1833 she fell more than ever under Flavie's management, who tried to do her whole duty by her, and, without being severe, she was very strict with her; overdoing it, as women do who are tortured by remorse. Flavie, without being a bad mother, was rigid enough with her daughter; she had her properly instructed, and, remembering her own early training, vowed secretly that she would make an honest woman of Céleste and not a light one. She took her to mass, and she had her prepared for her first communion under the direction of a Paris curé, who has since become a bishop. Céleste was the more pious because Mme. Thuillier, her godmother, was a perfect saint, and the child adored her godmother; she felt that she was more genuinely loved by this poor, lonely woman than by her mother.

Thuillier had not been able to withstand the action of the

rolling-mill of administrative routine, where the brains are worn thin in proportion as they are flattened out. Used up by fastidious work, beside counting his successes as a lady's man, the ex-sub-chief had lost all his best faculties by the time he had moved to the Rue Saint-Dominique, but his drawn features, which wore a rather arrogant expression, with a mixture of self-satisfaction, which may have been the fatuity of the superior employé, deeply impressed Céleste. She alone adored that sallow face. She knew that she was the joy of the Thuillier household.

The Collevilles and their children, together with an ex-clerk of La Billardière's division, Monsieur Phellion, formed the nucleus of Mlle. Thuillier's society. Phellion was one of the most respected men in the arrondissement; he had become, too, a major in the National Guard. He had one daughter, formerly an under-teacher in the Lagrave school, now married to a professor in the Rue Saint-Hyacinthe, M. Barniol.

Phellion's eldest son was a professor of mathematics in a royal college and gave lessons, coached pupils, and devoted himself, as his father expressed it, to pure mathematics. The second son was at the College of Engineers. Phellion had a pension of nine hundred francs, some little interest on his savings during thirty years of thrift, and owned a little house with a garden attached, in which he lived on the Impasse des Feuillantines. (In thirty years he had not once used the old term *cul-de-sac*.\*)

Dutocq, clerk to a justice of the peace, had formerly been employed in the ministry of finance; he had been sacrificed on one of those necessities of a government which is representative; he had permitted himself to be made the scapegoat in a scandal occurring in the office of the committee on appropriations, for which he received a fairly round sum; this had enabled him to purchase his clerkship. This man, of little

\* Blind alley or court.

honor, the spy of the bureau, was not received in the manner he thought his due by the Thuilliers; but his landlord's coldness only made him more persistent in his visits.

He remained a bachelor, and indulged his vices; his life was carefully hidden, and he was an adept at flattering his superiors. The justice of the peace had a great esteem for Dutocq. That infamous person made himself tolerated by the Thuilliers by base and gross adulation which never fails in its effects. He knew the bottom of Thuillier's life, his relations with Colleville, and more so with madame; they feared his formidable tongue, and the Thuilliers, without admitting him to their friendship, permitted his visits on sufferance.

The family that became the flower of the Thuilliers' salon was that of a poor, petty clerk, who had been the object of compassion in the bureau, and who, driven by penury, had left the bureau in 1827 to throw himself into trade with an idea.

Minard foresaw a fortune in one of those perverse conceptions which are a disgrace to French commerce, but which, in 1827, had not yet been blown on by publicity. Minard bought some tea and mixed it with dried tea-leaves; then he practiced changing the constituents of chocolate, altering it so that he could sell it as a bargain. This trade in colonial produce, begun in the Saint-Marcel quarter, set Minard up in trade; he had a factory, and, through his connections, was now able to obtain the raw materials from their source; thus on an honorable and large scale he carried out the business he had started in such a shady manner. He became a distiller, enormous quantities of raw imports were handled by him, till he came to pass, in 1835, as the richest trader in the Place Maubert quarter. He bought one of the most beautiful houses on the Rue des Maçons-Sorbonne;* he had been deputy and, in 1839, was named for mayor of his arrondissement and

* Now the Rue Champollion.

judge of the Chamber of Commerce. He kept a carriage, had a country place near Lagny; his wife wore diamonds at the Court balls, and he flaunted the rosette of officer of the Legion of Honor in his button-hole.

Minard and his wife were always excessively beneficent. Perhaps they wished to restore retail to the poor what they exacted wholesale from the public. Phellion, Colleville, and Thuillier encountered Minard during the elections, which resulted in an acquaintance, soon to become intimate, between the Minards, Collevilles, and Thuilliers, because Madame Zélie Minard appeared enchanted to introduce her "young miss" to Céleste Colleville. The Minards gave a fine ball for Céleste's *début* into society, she being then sixteen-and-a-half; her dress befitted her name and seemed prophetic of good for her life.

Minard's eldest son was a barrister; he had the hope of succeeding some of those advocates who, since 1830, by their political opinions had become estranged from the Court; he was the genius of the family, and his mother, not less than his father, aspired to see him well married.

Zélie Minard, formerly an artificial flower-maker, had an ardent passion for moving in the higher social circles, which she thought to penetrate into by the marriage of her son and daughter, while Minard, wiser than she, and, being imbued with the power of the middle-class resulting from the Revolution of July, had his every fibre infiltrated with a desire for wealth.

He haunted the Thuilliers' salon to learn Céleste's prospects as an heiress. He knew, like Dutocq and Phellion, the scandal occasioned by Thuillier's intimacy with Flavie, and with half an eye he was able to see the idolatry of the Thuilliers for their goddaughter. Dutocq, eager for admission to the Minards, fawned on them prodigiously. When Minard, the Rothschild of the arrondissement, first appeared at the Thuilliers, he compared him, almost wittily, to Napoleon, as he now saw him burly, fat, and flourishing, whereas, when he last knew him at the bureau, he was lean, pale, and sickly.

"When you were in La Billardière's division," said he, "you were like Napoleon before the 18th Brumaire, and I see you now the Napoleon of the Empire."

Nevertheless Minard treated him coldly and extended no invitation for a visit to his house; so he made a mortal enemy of the venomous clerk.

The Phellions had designs on Céleste, it struck them that she was the very thing for their son the professor. So they lined up a phalanx of seven, all fairly faithful to each other; the Colleville family was equally numerous, so that on occasional Sundays there would be as many as thirty persons in the Thuillier salon. Thuillier renewed his acquaintance with the Saillards, the Baudoyers, the Falleixs,* all people of importance in the Place-Royale quarter, and frequently invited to dinner.

Mme. Colleville, among the women, was the most distinguished personage of this circle, like as also Minard's son and Professor Phellion were its superior men; for all the others, without education and ideas, and risen from the lower ranks, were types of the absurd in the lower middle-classes. Although a fortune made in the past seems to possess merit, Minard was but an inflated balloon. He floundered in long-drawn phrases, took obsequiousness for politeness and the form for the spirit, and uttered his commonplaces in such style and mouthings that they were accepted as eloquence. These phrases which say nothing and answer every purpose—progress, steam, asphalt, National Guard, order, democratic spirit, power of coöperation, legality, motion and resistance, intimidation—seemed at each political crisis to have been invented for Minard, who then paraphrased the ideas of his newspaper. Julien Minard, the young barrister, suffered under his father what his father suffered under his wife. In fact, with her for-

* See "Les Employés."

tune, Zélie had assumed pretensions, though she could never learn to speak decent French; she had become fat, and in her handsome attire looked like a cook who had married her master.

Phellion, that model of a lower bourgeois, was equally blessed with virtues and absurdities. A subordinate during his bureaucratic life, he highly respected social superiority. In the presence of Minard he was silent. He had admirably resisted, by his own efforts, the critical times of superannuation, and this is how: never had the worthy and excellent man had a chance of indulging his tastes. He loved the city of Paris; he took intense interest in the improvements and embellishments; he was the man who would be arrested, for two hours running, by the demolition of a house.

He could stand surprised, bravely planted on his two feet, nose in air, watching for the fall of a stone which the mason was dislodging with a crowbar from the top of a wall, and did not even quit his place when the stone fell; when all was over off he would go as happy as an Academician at the damning of a melodrama. Veritable components of the great social comedy, Phellion, Laudigeois, and the like, represent the functions of the antique chorus. They weep when others weep, laugh when expected to laugh, singing in chorus over public catastrophes and popular rejoicings, triumphant in their own corner over the triumphs of Algiers, Constantine, Lisbon, and Saint-Jean-d'Ulloa; equally deploring the death of Napoleon and the fatal disasters of Saint-Merri and the Rue Transnonnain; regretting the famous men who are the most unknown of them.

Still Phellion showed two faces; if any street fighting occurred he stoutly declared himself in the sight of his neighbors; he would be in his place on the parade ground of his regiment, the Place Saint-Michel; he pitied the government, but he did his duty; he would help suppress a riot, supported the reigning dynasty, and when the political trials followed made excuses for the culprits. These "weather-cockish" opinions were harmless and permeated his political views:

Answerable for all was the Colossus of the North. As for England, she was like the old "Constitutionnel," a double-dealing gossip; by turns Machiavellian Albion and a model country—Machiavellian when she jostled the interests of France or bruised Napoleon; a model country when the faults of his government were in question.

This honorable old man was always dignified; dignity was the keynote of his life. He raised his children with dignity; in their eyes he was always the father; he insisted on respect being paid him at home, as he honored power and his superiors. He never had a debt. A juryman, his conscience made him sweat blood and water as he followed the pleadings of a trial; he never laughed, not even should the court laugh, or the judge or public authorities. Always at the service of all, he gave his care, his time, all except his money. Félix Phellion, his son, the professor, was his idol; he thought him capable of gaining the Academy of Science. Thuillier, between the audacious stupidity of Minard and the candid simplicity of Phellion, was like a neutral element, but there was in him that of each in his melancholy experience. He hid his addled brain by his banalities, like as he covered the yellow skin of his skull under the thin wisps of his gray hair, artfully combed back by the barber.

"In all other walks of life," said he, speaking of the bureau, "I could surely have had better luck."

He had seen the good, that which is possible in theory and improbable in practice; the results contradicted the premises; he would relate the intrigues, the injustice of the Rabourdin affair.

"After that, how much is one to believe?" said he. "Ah! a queer thing is the administration, and I am very happy in not having a son, so that I cannot see him hustling for a post."

Colleville, always gay, rotund, good-fellow, joker, and quibbler, inventing his anagrams, always hustling, represented the bourgeois meddler and mocker, the ability without the success, persistent hard work without result, but also the resigned jollity, narrow intelligence, art wasted (he was an excellent musician), for he only played now to amuse his daughter.

The women of the Thuillier salon were all for the jesuits; the men defended the University; but the women generally listened. A man of intelligence, if he could have endured the tedium of these soirées, would have laughed as much as at a comedy by Molière, to hear, after a long discussion, such a speech as this:

"The Revolution of 1789 could have been averted, eh? Louis XIV.'s borrowing opened the way. Louis XV., an egoist, a man with the spirit of ceremony" (he had said: "If I were Chief of Police I would abolish cabriolets") "a dissolute king—you know all about his *dear* park!*—contributed largely to open the gulf of revolution. M. de Necker, a malevolent Genevese, agitated it. Foreigners have always had it in for France. The Maximum did much harm to the Revolution. By right, Louis XVI. ought not to have been condemned; a jury would have acquitted him. Why was Charles X. overthrown? Napoleon was a great man and the details which attest his genius are found in anecdotes of him. He took five pinches of snuff a minute, keeping it loose in his vest pocket lined with leather. He checked off all the contractors' accounts, and went to the Rue Saint-Denis to learn the cost of things. Talma was his friend; Talma taught him all his gestures, and yet he always refused to decorate Talma. The Emperor mounted guard one time for a sentry who had fallen asleep and thus saved him from being shot. For these things the soldiers worshiped him. Louis XVIII., although a smart man, showed a lack of justice in

* *Parc aux cerfs.*

regard to him when he spoke of him as Monsieur de Bonaparte. The fault of the present government is that it allows itself to be led, instead of leading. It places itself too low. It fears men of energy; it should have torn up the treaties of 1815 and demanded the Rhine of Europe. The ministry plays too much with the same men."

"There, you have displayed enough intelligence now," said Mlle. Thuillier, after one of these luminous reflections; "the altar is dressed, come and play your little game."

The old maid ended all these discussions, such a bore to the women, by this suggestion.

If all these anterior facts, all these generalizations had not been given, as the gist of the argument, to provide a fitting set for this Scene, giving a due idea of the spirit of this society, perhaps the drama would be the sufferer. This sketch is faithfully and historically truthful, and shows up a social stratum of some importance in this chronicle of manners, more especially when the political system of the younger branch took it as its fulcrum.

The winter of the year 1839 was, in some sort, the time when the Thuillier salon attained its greatest splendor. The Minards were seen there nearly every Sunday; they commenced by passing an hour there when they were obliged to attend other soirées, and oftener than not Minard would leave his wife there, taking with him his daughter and his eldest son, the barrister. This assiduity of the Minards was caused by a meeting between Messrs. Métivier, Barbet, and Minard, on one evening when these two important tenants had remained later than usual to chat with Mlle. Thuillier. Minard was apprised by Barbet that the old demoiselle took of him in the neighborhood of thirty thousand francs in notes each six months; and that she took a like amount from Métivier, so that she must have in her hands at least one hundred and eighty thousand francs.

"I loan on books at twelve per cent., taking only the best

names. Nothing suits me better," said Barbet, in conclusion. "I say that she must have one hundred and eighty thousand francs, for she cannot give notes for more than ninety days at the Bank."

"She has, then, an account at the Bank?" said Minard.

"So I believe," answered Barbet.

Friendly with a governor of the Bank, Minard learned that Mlle. Thuillier had in fact an account there amounting to about two hundred thousand francs, guaranteed by a deposit of forty shares of stock. This security was, he said, unnecessary; the Bank had the highest regard for a person so well known as the responsible manager of Céleste Lemprun's affairs, the daughter of an employé who had seen as many years of service as the Bank had been in existence. Mlle. Thuillier had not once overdrawn her account in twenty years. She always placed in sixty thousand francs in notes at three months, which came to about one hundred and sixty thousand. The deposited shares represented one hundred and twenty thousand francs, so there was no risk, for the notes were of the full value of sixty thousand francs. "Indeed," said the comptroller, "if she sent us, in the third month, one hundred thousand francs in notes we should not reject a single one. She has a house of her own which is not mortgaged and is worth more than one hundred thousand francs. Beside, all the notes come through Barbet and Métivier, and are thus endorsed with four signatures, including her own."

"Why does Mademoiselle Thuillier work so hard?" asked Minard of Métivier. "Why, this is the very one for you," he added.

"Oh! as to me," replied Métivier, "I can do better by marrying one of my cousins; my Uncle Métivier has promised me his business; he has a hundred thousand francs in the Funds and only two daughters."

However secret Mlle. Thuillier might be, saying nothing of her affairs to any person, not even her brother; and although she amassed in one lump sum her own investments and those of Mme. Thuillier's beside her own, it was almost an impossibility that no ray of light should at length pierce through the wooden bushel measure in which she secured her treasure.

"Céleste will have two hundred thousand francs from us in cold cash," said the old maid, in confidence to Barbet; "and Madame Thuillier on the signing of her contract will settle her property upon her. As for myself, my will is made. My brother is given a life interest in all, and Céleste will have the reversion. Monsieur Cardot, my notary, is my executor."

Cardot, the notary, presented a suitor in the person of Maître Godeschal, attorney-at-law, successor to Derville, a man of thirty-six, very capable, who had paid one hundred thousand francs on his connection, which two hundred thousand francs of a dot would clear off. Minard soon cleared him off the deck by informing Mlle. Thuillier that Céleste would have for a sister-in-law the famous Mariette, an opera-dancer.

"She was one of that sort," said Colleville, alluding to his wife, "and she doesn't intend returning."

"Monsieur Godeschal is altogether too old for Céleste," said Brigitte.

"And then," added Mme. Thuillier, timidly, "would it not be better for her to marry some one of her choice and be happy?"

The poor woman had perceived in Félix Phellion a true love for Céleste, a love such as a woman, crushed by Brigitte and chilled by Thuillier's indifference, who cared no more for the society of his wife than for that of a servant-girl, might well dream of, bold at heart, shy on the surface, at the same time strong and timid, concentrated before all, and expanding to the heavens. At twenty-three, Félix Phellion was a gentle young man, who had been well brought up by his father; one who loved learning for its own sake. He was of medium height, with light, chestnut hair, gray eyes, a much freckled skin, of easy manners, very little given to gesticulations, thoughtful, never talking nonsense, never contradicting any one, incapable of a sordid thought or an egoistical calculation.

"That's the kind of husband I should have liked mine to have been!" Mme. Thuillier often told herself.

About the beginning of 1840, in the month of February, the personages whose silhouettes have here been made, were assembled in the Thuilliers' salon. It was near the end of the month. Barbet and Métivier waited, as they each wanted to borrow thirty thousand francs from Mlle. Brigitte. Céleste and Prudence Minard were sitting together. Young Phellion listening to Mme. Thuillier could gaze at Céleste.

On the other side of the fireplace, enthroned on an easy-chair, was the Queen Elizabeth of the family, dressed as plainly as when she was thirty years old, for prosperity was unable to cause a change in her habits. Her chinchilla hair was surmounted by a gauze bonnet ornamented with Charles X.-Geranium flowers; her Cornith-plum colored stuff gown might have cost as much as fifteen francs; her embroidered collarette, worth about six francs, hardly hid the deep hollow produced by the two muscles which attach the head to the spine. Monvel, when he played Augustus in his latter days, had no sterner profile than this autocratic knitter of stockings for her brother. In front of the fireplace posed Thuillier, prepared to receive any arrivals; by his side stood a young man whose entree had produced a great effect, when the janitor, who on Sunday donned his best clothes to act the footman, had announced "Monsieur Olivier Vinet."

He was here as the result of a confidential hint given by Cardot to this young magistrate's father, a famous public prosecutor. Cardot had estimated the present value of the money to be left to Céleste at seven hundred thousand francs at least. Vinet's son had appeared delighted at being given the privilege of going on Sunday as a guest of the Thuilliers. Large marriage-portions in these days lead to the grossest follies without the least pudency.

Ten minutes after, another young man, who was chatting with Thuillier before the arrival of Vinet, raised his voice in the heat of a political discussion, making the young lawyer do the same by the force of the debate. The question was the vote by which the Chamber of Deputies overthrew the ministry of May 12th, in refusing the grant demanded for the Duc de Nemurs.

"Most decidedly," said the young man, "I am very far from belonging to the dynastic party, and I am quite as far from approving the elevation of the bourgeoisie into power. The middle-class has no more right now than the aristocracy had then to preëminence in the State. But the French middle-classes set up a new dynasty for themselves, a royalty of their own, and how did they treat it! When the people allowed Napoleon to raise himself, he created on his side a splendid monumental edifice; he was proud of his grandeur, he nobly gave his blood and his sweat for the purpose of consolidating the Empire. Between the magnificence of the aristocratic enthronement and the Imperial purple, between the great and the populace, the bourgeoisie are mean and niggardly; they drag down the powers that be to their own ignoble level, instead of trying to raise themselves. The economies of the candle-ends of the back-shops they practice on their princes; but what is a virtue in their storehouses is a fault and a crime in high places. I wish for many things that would be good for the people, but I would retrench by cutting off ten millions from the new civil list. Now almost all-powerful in France, the bourgeoisie ought to insure the happiness of the people, of splendor without extravagance and grandeur without privilege."

Olivier Vinet's father was not quite in harmony with the present government—he had not yet obtained the robes of keeper of the seals, his great ambition; so the young judge hardly knew how to answer.

"You are quite right, monsieur," said Olivier Vinet. "But before beginning the parade, the middle-class owes a duty to France. The luxury of which you speak comes after duty. That which you seem to think as worthy of reproach was a necessity of the moment. The Chamber is far from having a full part in affairs; the ministers work far less for France than for the crown, and the Parliament wishes to see a ministry, like that in England, which has a strength of its own, not a reflected, borrowed power. The day that the ministry acts for itself and represents the power of the executive in the Chamber, the same as the Chamber represents the country, so soon will the Parliament be liberal to the crown. That's the milk in the cocoanut; I merely give it without saying aught of my personal opinion, since the duties of my office require, in politics, a species of fealty to the crown."

"Leaving the political question," replied the young man, whose accent indicated a son of Provence, "it cannot be the less true that the bourgeoisie have failed to understand their mission; we see public prosecutors, first presidents, peers of France riding in 'busses, judges who have to live on their salaries, prefects without private means, ministers in debt; while the middle-class, who have now possession of all these places, ought to do honor to them as before the aristocracy did honor; instead of holding them with the intention of making a fortune, as has been demonstrated in numerous scandalous trials, they should be occupied with a due expenditure——"

"Who is this young man?" said Olivier Vinet, hearing him with wonder. "Is he a relative? Cardot should have accompanied me the first time."

"Who is the little monsieur?" asked Minard of Barbet. "I have seen him here several times."

"He is a tenant," replied Métivier, dealing the cards.

"A barrister," said Barbet in a low voice; "he has a small suite on the third-floor front. Oh! he's no great shakes, and owns nothing."

"What's his name?" asked Olivier Vinet of M. Thuillier.

"Théodose de la Peyrade; he is a barrister," whispered Thuillier.

All turned around to look at the young man, and Mme. Minard could not refrain saying to Colleville:

"He's a good-looking young fellow."

"I have made an anagram of his name," said Céleste's father; "the letters of Charles-Marie-Théodose de la Peyrade spell out this prophecy: *Eh! Monsieur payerer, de la dot, des oies et le cher*—Be careful, my dear Madame Minard, to keep from giving him your daughter."

"They find him nicer looking than my son," said Mme. Phellion to Mme. Colleville; "what do you think?"

"Oh! as for looks," replied Mme. Colleville, "it would be a toss-up for choice."

Vinet looked around at the roomful of middle-class people and thought it might be amiss to exalt them; he made out that it was monstrous to try and save out of the emoluments of an appointment, everything had so increased in cost, and so on.

"My father," said he, in conclusion, "allows me a thousand crowns a year, and, including my salary, I can hardly make both ends meet."

When the young lawyer ventured on this treacherous ground, the Provençal, who had led up to it, winked at Dutocq, just as he was about taking his place at *bouillotte*.

"I have not yet had the pleasure of hearing you in court," said Vinet to M. de la Peyrade.

"I am the lawyer of the poor; I only plead before justices of the peace," replied the Provençal.

When Mlle. Thuillier heard the young barrister's remarks as to the necessity of spending one's whole income, she took on a most prim and ceremonious look, of which the Provençal and Dutocq both well knew the significance. Vinet shortly after took his leave, taking with him Minard and Julien.

"The higher bourgeoisie," said Dutocq to Thuillier, "will conduct themselves just as the aristocracy were formerly wont to do. The nobles wanted girls with money to improve their lands; our parvenus of to-day want handsome portions to feather their nests."

"That is what Monsieur Thuillier was saying this morning," replied the Provençal, with careless mendacity.

"His father," replied Dutocq, "married a demoiselle de Chargebœuf, and he has assumed the ideas of the nobility; he must have a fortune at whatever cost; his wife keeps it up in royal fashion."

"Oh!" said Thuillier, stirred up by the envy of the middle-class against each other, "turn such people out of their places, and down they go to the mud they sprang from!"

Mlle. Thuillier was so rapidly knitting that it might be said to have been a machine that was driven by steam.

"Now you can come in the game, Monsieur Dutocq," said Mme. Minard, as she rose. "My feet are cold," she added, going to the fire, which made the gold on her turban scintillate like fireworks in the light of the candles in the hanging "Aurore," which vainly strove to illuminate the spacious salon.

"He is but a Saint-John,* this suckling-barrister!" said Mme. Minard, glancing at Mlle. Thuillier.

"A Saint-John, say you?" said the Provençal, "that is exceedingly witty, madame——"

"But madame is witty at all times," said Handsome Thuillier.

Mme. Colleville was studying the Provençal at this time, so it affords a good opportunity to describe this singular person

* Correggio's "St. John," at the breast.

who played a great rôle among the Thuilliers, and who merits the appellation of a great actor.

There exists in Provence, particularly at the port of Avignon, a race of men with blonde or chestnut hair, of delicate skin and almost weak eyes, whose pupils are rather soft, calm, or languishing, than fiery, ardent, or deep, as those of Southerners mostly are. It may be observed, by the way, that, among Corsicans, a people subject to sudden fits of fury and dangerous angers, one often encounters blondes of apparently passive natures. These fair complexioned men, apt to be stout, dull eyes, green or blue, are the worst species in Provence, and Charles-Marie-Théodose de la Peyrade afforded a splendid type of this race, whose constitution would amply repay examination on the part of medical science and philosophical physiology. There is in their make-up a species of bile, of bitter humor, which mounts to their head, rendering them capable of ferocious deeds, done apparently in cold blood.

Born in the neighborhood of Avignon, the young Provençal was of medium height, well proportioned, rather stout, clear but dull complexion, not livid, not pale, not florid, but gelatinous, for that face can only be thus described. His eyes, coldly blue, generally wore a deceptive air of melancholy, which no doubt had for women a great charm. His high forehead did not lack nobleness, his light chestnut hair, thin, with a natural curl at the ends, agreeably finished it. His nose was exactly that of a hunting dog—broad, cleft at the tip, inquisitive, intelligent, prying, always alert; it lacked good-nature, but showed irony and sarcasm; but this double-faced nature was only to be detected when he was off his guard—a thing which rarely happened; it was only when he was in a fury that he vented the sarcastic wit and satire which poisoned his infernal jesting.

His mouth was prettily shaped, his lips were red and like a pomegranate, seeming to be the marvelous instrument of a voice of which the medium tones were sweet, Théodose usually spoke in that register, and the higher notes of which vibrated like the sounds of a gong. The falsetto being the voice of his nerves and his rage. His face, denuded of expression by his command, was oval. His manner, which accorded with the calm, priest-like demeanor of his face, was full of reserve and propriety.

Charm, when it has its source in the heart, leaves a deep impression; when it is produced artificially, like spurious eloquence, it may enjoy a passing triumph; it will strive for effect at whatever cost.

Among all maniacs the heart resembles those boxes with compartments in which sugar-plums are arranged in assorted colors; *suum cuique tribuere* is their device, they measure each duty by the dose. Now this youth of seven and twenty was a philanthropist, but only among the very poor, the paupers of the Saint-Jacques and Saint-Marceau quarters; the decent poor of the middle-class, capable men of genius on their uppers, he would not grant admittance into charity's fold. There are philanthropists who have only pity for the sins of condemned criminals. Certainly vanity is at the root of all philanthropy, but in our Provençal it was calculation, a part to be played, a hypocrisy liberal and democratic, played with such perfection that no actor could have achieved. He acknowledged himself as having been at one time a fervent disciple of Saint-Simon, but this was an error only to be ascribed to the faults of extreme youth. An ardent Catholic, like all the people of his district, he attended early mass and concealed his piety. He was like all philanthropists in that he was sordidly parsimonious, he gave nothing to the poor but his time, his counsel, his eloquence, and such money as he could pluck from the wealthy.

To finish this portrait of the Advocate of the Poor, it may not be amiss to relate his *début* into the Thuillier family.

Théodose had come toward the end of the year 1837; he

had been admitted as an attorney five years previously, and he then went through his term in Paris to become a barrister; but some unknown circumstances, as to which he retained silence, had prevented him from being duly registered as a barrister in Paris, and so he still remained an attorney.

He furnished his third floor as befitted his profession, and became an advocate in the Assize Court. The whole of the year 1838 was given up to this change in his situation; he led a perfectly regular life; he studied in the morning till time for dinner, sometimes going to the courts to listen to important cases. Having, with difficulty, said Dutocq, made friends with Dutocq, he helped some unfortunates in the faubourg Saint-Jacques, whom he had recommended, by arguing their cases before the tribunal; out of charity he obtained them the interest of pleaders, who, by the statutes, take each their turn in defending the causes of the impecunious; and by taking none but absolutely sure cases he gained each one. He thus made a connection with some lawyers, these praiseworthy efforts made him known, and he soon became a registered member of the Paris bar. He became the advocate of the poor before the justices of the peace, and was always the protector of the common people. These services of Théodose's caused his clients to express their gratitude and admiration in the lodges of the janitors, and, in spite of the young advocate's injunctions, a good many of these traits were retailed before their masters. Delighted to have so excellent and charitable a man as a tenant, the Thuilliers were wishing to attract him as a frequenter of their salon; they questioned Dutocq about him. The clerk spoke like an envious man; while doing the young man justice, he said that his avarice was something remarkable, though that might be caused by his poverty.

"I have inquired about him. He belongs to the family of la Peyrades, an old family of the county of Avignon; he came here at the end of 1829 to look up an uncle who possessed, or was so supposed, a considerable fortune; he finally discovered this relative's residence three days after the death of the old man, and the sale of the effects of the deceased only just sufficed to pay his debts. A friend of this useless uncle pressed one hundred louis upon him, and told him to seek his fortune by engaging in the study of the law, and to try for the higher walks of his profession; this hundred louis defrayed all his expenses for more than three years in Paris, where he fared like an anchorite; but, as he was unable to find his unknown benefactor, the poor student suffered from the greatest distress in 1833.

"He then, like all licentiates, turned to politics and literature, barely able to support himself; for his father, the youngest brother of the uncle, who had died in the Rue des Moineaux, has eleven children living with him on a little domain called Canquoëlles. At length he got on the staff of a ministerial paper edited by the famous Cérizet. The government, after this man left his own party to support them, did not prevent his being ruined by the Republicans. This will account for his being at the present time a mere copying clerk under me.

"Well, when Cérizet was flourishing—and who is a right good sort of a fellow, but a little too fond of the women, good cheer and dissipation—he befriended Théodose and was very useful to him. In 1834 and 1835, he was again pretty hard up, notwithstanding his talent, for his work on a ministerial newspaper told against him. 'Only for my religious principles,' he said to me at that time, 'I should throw myself into the Seine.' But at last it seems that his uncle's friend heard of his straitened circumstances and again came to his relief; money enough was sent to enable him to receive his diploma, but he never learned the name of his mysterious protector. But he will get on! He will secure a brilliant position; he has tenacity, probity, and courage! He studies—he perseveres."

Gradually Maître le Peyrade attended the Thuilliers more frequently than at first; he was invited to all their dinners, and if at any time he called to see Thuillier about four o'clock he would join their meal, taking "pot-luck." Mlle. Thuillier saying:

"We are sure then that he has dined well, the poor young man!"

A social phenomenon, which must certainly have been observed, but which has not hitherto been formulated, or published, if you will, although it deserves being established, is that of a return to the habits, jests, and manners of their primitive condition of certain people, who from youth to old age have raised themselves above it. So Thuillier had, morally speaking, relapsed into the porter's son; he would use some of his father's little jokes, and at length permitted to appear on the surface of his life, in his declining years, a little of the mud of his early days.

About five or six times a month, when the soup was good and thick, he would say, like it was something quite new:

"This shin soup is better to get than a kick on the shins!"

Hearing this joke for the first time, Théodose, who did not know it, lost his gravity and laughed with such heartiness that Thuillier, Handsome Thuillier, felt his vanity immensely tickled, such as it had never been before. This explains why on the same morning of the soirée:

"You are more witty than you think!"

Had received this answer:

"In any other career, my dear Théodose, I should have traveled far on the good road, but the Emperor's fall broke my neck."

"There is yet time for you," said the young advocate. "Whence comes it that that mountebank Colleville has the cross?"

There, Maître de la Peyrade touched the raw place that Thuillier had hidden from all eyes, even those of his sister, who knew nothing of it; but this young man, interested in studying all the bourgeois' traits, had guessed the secret envy eating up the heart of the ex-sub-chief.

"If you will so honor me, you with all your experience, by being guided by my counsel," the philanthropist went on, "and more than all will never speak of our compact with any person, not even your excellent sister, at least without my consent, I will undertake to have you decorated with the acclamations of the whole quarter."

"Oh! if we could but accomplish this," Thuillier had exclaimed, "you don't know what I would do for you!"

This will explain why Thuillier had so visibly puffed himself out, when Théodose had been so audacious as to proffer him his opinions.

In the arts, and perhaps Molière ranked hypocrisy in the arts by always classing Tartuffe with the comedians, there exists a pitch of perfection above talent to which only genius can attain. There is so little difference between the work of genius and the work of talent that the man of genius only can appraise the distance which separates Raphael from Correggio, Titian from Rubens. Plenty of peasant-women carry their children the same way as the celebrated Madonna of Dresden carries hers. Eh, well, the acme of art, in a man of such strength as Théodose, is to have said of him later: "All the world would have been taken in!"

In Colleville Théodose saw the clear, critical insight of an unsuccessful artist. He knew that Colleville did not like him; Colleville had begun to believe in his anagrams; none of them had failed as prophecies. As an employé he had been mocked at for having rendered Minard's anagram—*J'amassai une si grande fortune,** or I amassed such a large fortune. Minard was then very poor, but after ten years events had justified it. Now Théodose's anagram was unlucky. His wife's, too, made him tremble; he had never told it to any

* *Vide* "Les Employés."

one, for Flavie Minard Colleville gave : *La vieille C \* \* \*, nom flétri, vole* (Old Madame C., a blighted name, steals).

After the game was ended, Colleville drew Thuillier aside and said :

"You allowed him to step a bit too far, this young advocate. He was quite too forward in this evening's conversation."

"Thanks, my friend, a man warned is twice armed!" answered Thuillier, mocking in his sleeve at Colleville.

"Madame," said he in the ear of the pious Mme. Colleville, for he could judge that Colleville was speaking of him to Thuillier, " believe me, that if any one here can appreciate you it is myself. One can only say on seeing you, here is a pearl fallen in the mire, for a woman is only as old as she seems; many a woman of thirty, not at all to be compared with you, would only be too happy to have your tall, sublime figure and lovely face on which love has set its stamp without ever having filled the void in your heart. You have given yourself to God, I know. I am too religious to wish to be more than your friend ; but you have given yourself to Him for the reason that you have never found a man worthy of you. Certainly you have been loved, but you have never been worshiped. But here comes your husband, who has never been able to provide a position for you in harmony with your deserts ; he hates me because he imagines that I should dare to love you, and thinks to hinder my speaking to you as he suspects that I may be about telling you that I think I have found a sphere for you in which is your high destiny. No, madame," said he, in a louder voice, " it is not the Abbé Gondrin who this year is the Lenten preacher in our humble church of Saint-Jacques du Haut-Pas ; it is Monsieur d'Estival, one of my compatriots, who devotes himself to preaching in the benefit of the poorer classes, and you will hear one of the most unctuous preachers that I know, a priest of little attractiveness outwardly, but what a soul !"

"Then my desires will be accomplished," said poor Mme. Thuillier; "I never could at all understand our famous preachers."

A faint smile was noticed on the lips of Mlle. Thuillier and on those of several others.

"They occupy too much of their discourse in theological demonstrations; this has been my opinion for some time," said Théodose. "But I never talk religion, and only that Madame *de* Colleville——"

"There are, then, demonstrations in theology?" queried, innocently, the professor of mathematics.

"I cannot think, monsieur," replied Théodose, looking at Félix Phellion, "that you ask that question seriously."

"Félix," said old Phellion, coming ponderously to the help of his son, as he noted an expression of pain on Mme. Thuillier's face; "Félix divides religion into two categories; he regards it from the human standpoint and from the divine; tradition and reason."

"What heresy, monsieur!" said Théodose. "Religion is one; it places faith before all."

Old Phellion, nailed with this speech, looked at his wife:

"It is time, my good friend——"

And he looked at the clock.

"Oh! Monsieur Félix," said Céleste, in a whisper to the candid mathematician, "cannot you, like Pascal and Bossuet, be at the same time wise and pious?"

The Phellions leaving, the Collevilles soon followed, and none remained but Dutocq, Théodose, and the Thuilliers.

The flatteries addressed by Théodose to Flavie were of the commonest character, but it should be remarked in the interest of this story that the advocate studied these vulgar spirits; he sailed on their waters, he spoke their language. His painter was Pierre Grassou, not Joseph Bridau; his novel was "Paul and Virginie." The greatest living poet for him was Casimir Delavigne; in his eyes the mission of art was its utility. Parmentier, *the author of the potato*, was to him worth twenty Raphaels; the man in the blue blouse appeared to him as "A Sister of Charity." These expressions of Thuillier's he would at times repeat.

After further eulogizing religion and saying that "Science had pensioned off God," and a few "Bless me's!" Théodose went away, after bidding good-night to the three Thuilliers, accompanied by Dutocq.

"That young man is full of strength?" said the sententious Thuillier.

"Yes, on my faith," replied Brigitte, putting out the lamps.

"He is religious," said Mme. Thuillier, being the first to go.

"Môsieur," said Phellion to Colleville, when they reached the School of Mines, and after he had looked around to see that no one could overhear him; "I surrender to the superior knowledge of others, yet I cannot but see that this young advocate plays the master just a bit too much at the Thuilliers."

"It's my private opinion," said Colleville, who was walking with Phellion behind his wife, Céleste, and Mme. Phellion, "that he is a jesuit, and I've no use for such—the best of them are no good. To me, a jesuit is craftiness; he cheats with intent; it is a pleasure for him to deceive, and, as the saying goes, to keep his hand in. That's my opinion, and there are no flies on it."

"I understand you, môsieur," replied Phellion, who had given his arm to Colleville.

"No, Monsieur Phellion," remarked Flavie, in a high, head voice, "you don't understand Colleville; but I well know his meaning, and it would be best for him to say no more."

"You are quite right, my wife," said Colleville.

As they bade each other good-night, at the corner of the Rue Deux-Églises, Félix said to Colleville:

"Monsieur, your son François could, by being pushed, enter the École Polytechnique; I offer to assist him in passing the examination this year."

"That is too good to refuse! thank you, my friend," said Colleville; "we will attend to it."

"Good!" said Phellion to his son.

"There is nothing slow about that!" exclaimed his mother.

"Why, what is there in it?" asked Félix.

"That is a clever method of paying court to the parents of Céleste."

"May I never solve my problems if I ever gave it such a thought," exclaimed the young professor. "I found, by talking to the young Colleville, that François had a vocation for mathematics, so I thought it only my duty to so inform his father——"

"Good, my son!" repeated Phellion. "I would not have you otherwise. My wishes are granted; in my son I find probity, honor, and every public and private virtue I can desire."

After Mme. Colleville had gone to bed, she said to her husband:

"Colleville, don't be so ready to crudely pronounce judgment on people unless you know them thoroughly. When you speak of jesuits I know you are thinking of priests, and to oblige me I must beg you to be more careful in expressing your opinions on religion in the presence of your daughter. We are our own masters in respect to sacrificing our own souls, but not those of our children. Do you wish to see your daughter a creature without religion? Beside, my ducky, we are at the mercy of the world, we have four children for whom to provide, can you say that at some time or other you may not need the help of this one or that one? Do not make enemies; you have none; you are a good fellow, and thanks to that quality, which is so charming in you, we have got along in life pretty smoothly thus far——"

"There, that will do!" said Colleville, who had thrown his coat over a chair and was now removing his cravat; "I was wrong, you were right, my beautiful Flavie."

"At the first chance, my burly lamb," said the cunning prattler, patting her husband's cheeks, "do the civil to that little advocate; he is pretty fly; we need him on our side. He is playing a part, eh? Well, play the comedy with him; be his apparent dupe, and, if he is smart, if he has a future, make him your friend. Think you that I want to see you forever the mayor of an arrondissement?"

"Come, here, wife Colleville," said the smiling ex-clarionet of the Opéra-Comique, tapping on his knees as a sign for his wife to perch thereon, "let us toast our tootseys and chat. When I look at you I am more than ever convinced of this truth, that the youth of women is in their figure——"

"And in their hearts——"

"In both," answered Colleville; "a light figure and a heavy heart——"

"No, big silly—deep."

"What is so nice about you is that you have preserved your fresh complexion without growing fat! But, there—you have small bones. I tell you what, Flavie, if I had to begin life over again I should not wish for any other wife than thee."

"And you know very well that I always liked you better than *the others*. How unfortunate that monseigneur is dead! Do you know what I should like?"

"No."

"A job under the city, a place at about twelve thousand francs, something like a cashier's, either in this municipality or at Poissy, or as agent."

"Either would suit me."

"Well, then, if that monster of an advocate could do something; he can intrigue, you bet. I'll sound him—just leave him to me—and more than all else, don't buck against his game at the Thuilliers."

Théodose had touched the sore spot in Flavie Colleville's heart, and this deserves an explanation which may, perhaps, give a synthetic touch on the lives of women.

At forty years of age, a woman, particularly if she has tasted the poisoned apple of passion, becomes aware of a solemn dread; she perceives that two deaths are hers; the death of the body and the death of the heart. Dividing women into two great categories which answer to the common idea of them, the so-called virtuous and the culpables, it is permissible to say, that all alike, after that terrible time of life, resent the anguish of that acute pain. If virtuous and defrauded in their nature's cravings, be it borne with courage or resignation, whether they have buried their revolt in their hearts or at the foot of the altar, they cannot say, without some feeling of horror, that: "all is over for me." This thought has such strange and infernal depths that we very often find in it the cause of those apostasies which now and again surprise and astonish the world.

The culpables—they are in one of those dizzy positions which frequently, alas, end in death or terminate in passions as tremendous as the situation. Either she has been happy in an atmosphere of incense, moving only in the flowery air of flatteries which is one long caress, so how can she renounce it? Or, a phenomenon more fantastic than rare, she is spurred to her play like a gambler making a double or quit throw, for, to her, the last days of her beauty are the last things that she risks on the cards of despair.

"You have been loved, but never worshiped!"

These word of Théodose, accompanied by a look which read, not in her heart, but in her life, was the missing word of an enigma, and Flavie felt herself divined.

A young officer, two dudes, a banker, a clumsy little young man, and the poor Colleville, this was a grievous outfit,

Once in her life Madame Colleville had dreamed of happiness, but she had never felt it; then death had hatefully broken off the only passion in which Flavie had found any real charm. For two years she had listened to the voice of religion, which had told her that neither the church nor society speaks of happiness, of love, but of duty and resignation; that, in the eyes of these two great powers, happiness lies in the satisfaction arising from painful or costly duties, and that the reward is not of this world. But she heard a more clamorous voice, so, as her religion was but a necessary mask, not a conversion, and as she dared not remove it, for she looked upon it as a resource for the future, she hung on to the church, the same as a man at the cross-roads in a forest, seated on a bank, reading the guide-posts of the road, but trusting to chance as to what might happen when the night came.

She knew that Théodose had surreptitiously watched her; she had dressed at him, wearing at times her dress of gray moire, her black lace, and her headdress of flowers twisted in her mechlin, making the most of herself, and he had known it—every man does when a woman dresses for him.

Flavie had been expecting, Sunday after Sunday, that Théodose would make a declaration. She said to herself:

"He knows I am ruined and he has not a sou! Perhaps, though, he is really pious!"

Théodose had no desire to hurry matters, and, like a competent musician, he had marked the place in the symphony where he meant to give the thump on the big drum. As he went to bed he reflected:

"The wife is on my side; the husband cannot suffer me; just now they are quarreling, and I shall come out on top, for she can do as she wills with her husband."

The Provençal was mistaken, as there had not been the least dispute, and Colleville slept beside his dear Flavie while she said to herself:

"Théodose is a superior man."

The following Sunday he was almost certain to find Madame Colleville at church; in fact, they came out at the same time, meeting on the Rue des Deux-Églises. Théodose offered Flavie his arm, which she accepted, telling her daughter to walk on in front with her brother Anatole.

"Have you done me the honor and favor of thinking over what I so clumsily said the other day?" asked the wheedling advocate of the pretty *dévotée* as he pressed her arm to his heart with a movement at once gentle and firm, for he pretended to dissemble his feelings and appear respectful against his impulse. "Do not mistake my intentions," he continued, receiving a look from Madame Colleville—one of those glances with which women who have tasted and practiced passion can express either severe reproof or a secret community of sentiment.

Then he told her how Christian charity embraces the strong equally with the weak, that its treasures are for all. That it was sad to see so refined, elegant, and graceful a woman in such dire surroundings, adding:

"Oh, if only I were wealthy. Ah, if I had but power, your husband, who is certainly a good devil, should become a receiver-general, and you could make him a deputy.

"But I am poor and ambitious, my first duty is to crush my ambition. I find myself at the bottom of the bag like the last number in a lottery; I can only offer my arm where I fain would give my heart. All my hopes rest on a good marriage, and, believe me, I should make my wife's lot a happy one; not only that, but I should raise her to be one of the first in the State if only she finds me the means for my advancement. It is a lovely day, come for a stroll in the Luxembourg?"

The listless arm held in his own indicated a tacit consent, and, as she deserved the honor of a species of violence, he dragged her more rapidly along, adding:

"Come along, we shall never have such an excellent opportunity. Oh!" he cried, "your husband sees us; he is at the window; walk more slowly."

"There is nothing to fear from Monsieur Colleville," said Flavie, smiling. "He leaves me the absolute mistress of my actions."

"Oh! here is the woman of whom I have dreamed!" exclaimed the Provençal, with that ecstasy and accent emanating only from the souls and spoken by the lips of Southerners.

"Pardon me, madame," said he, checking himself and returning from that lofty sphere to the exiled angel whom he piously regarded. "Excuse me! to return to what I was saying—— Ah! how can I be otherwise than sensible of the sorrows I myself experience when I see the lot of a being to whom life should only bring joy and happiness? Your sufferings are mine; I am no more in my right place than you are in yours. Ah! dear Flavie, the first time it was granted me to see you was on the last Sunday in the month of September, 1838. You were lovely; I shall often recall you in that little dress of *mousseline de laine*, colored like the tartan of some Scottish clan. On that day I said to myself: 'Why is this woman at the home of the Thuilliers, and why, above all, should she ever have had relations with a Thuillier?'"

"Monsieur!" said Flavie, startled at the rapid flow which the Provençal gave to the conversation.

"Oh! I know all," cried he, with an expressive shrug of the shoulder, "and can explain everything to myself; I do not esteem you the less. There! these are not the faults of an ugly or humpbacked woman. You have to gather the fruit of your error, and I will help you. Céleste will be very rich —and there is where your future prospects must be found; you cannot have more than one son-in-law, so choose him with care. An ambitious man may become a minister, but you become humiliated; he would annoy you, and make your

"EH, WELL, YES, I LOVE YOU." A, O HE

daughter unhappy; and, if he loses her fortune, he will certainly never re-make it. Eh, well, yes, I love you," said he; "and I love you with an affection without bounds; you are above a crowd of petty considerations that bind simpletons. We understand each other——"

Flavie was simply astounded; nevertheless, she was sensible of the excessive frankness of speech; she said to herself: "There is no mystery in such talk as this." But she was fain to acknowledge that never before had she been so deeply moved and agitated as by this young man.

"Monsieur, I don't know by whom you have been misled in regard to my past life, and by what right you——"

"Ah! pardon me, madame," interrupted the Provençal, with a frigidity bordering on scorn; "I have been dreaming! I said to myself: 'She is all that;' but I was deceived. I now know why you will always remain aloft on the fourth floor in the Rue d'Enfer."

A gesture of the arm toward the window at which Colleville stood emphasized this retort.

"I have been frank, I expected reciprocity. Many a day I have gone without bread, madame; I managed to live, studied, obtained the grade of licentiate in Paris, my whole capital being two thousand francs; and I came through the barrière d'Italie with five hundred francs in my pocket, vowing, like one of my compatriots, that some day I would become the leading man in my country. And the man who has often rifled his breakfast out the restaurateurs' baskets into which his leavings were thrown, and which are emptied outdoors at six o'clock in the morning, when the second-hand eating-houses can find nothing more fit to take—that man will not shrink from any available chance. Eh, now! do you believe me the friend of the people?" said he, smiling; "fame needs a loud voice; she cannot be heard speaking with half-closed lips; and without renown, what is the use of talent? Say, now, have I not opened all before you? Open your heart to me. Say to me: 'We are friends,' and we shall all some day be happy."

"My God! why did I come here with you? Why did I take your arm?" cried Flavie.

"Because it is your destiny!" replied he. "Eh, my dear and best-loved Flavie," added he, pressing her arm to his heart; "you did not expect commonplaces from me, did you? We are brother and sister—that is all."

And they turned toward the Rue d'Enfer.

Flavie experienced a great fear beneath the satisfaction that a woman finds in violent emotions, she wrongly imagined this dread for a new passion beginning; but she was under a spell and walked along in deep silence.

"Of what are you thinking?" he asked, when half-way along the path.

"Of all that you brought me here to say," she replied.

"But," he answered, "at our age, we skip the preliminaries; we are not children, and we both live in a sphere in which we should understand each other. In short, believe me," he added, as they turned into the Rue d'Enfer, "I am wholly yours," and he made a profound salutation.

"The irons are in the fire!" said he to himself, as his eye followed his giddy prey.

On returning to his home, Théodose found on his landing a person who in this story figures somewhat as a sub-marine, or otherwise like unto a buried church upon which has been erected the front of a palace.

The sight of this man, who had vainly pulled his door-bell, startled the Provençal, but he did not betray his hidden emotion. This man was Cérizet, Dutocq's copying-clerk.

Cérizet, only eight and thirty, looked like a man of fifty, who has become old by all that ages a man. His bald head offered to view a yellow skull barely covered by a rusty, discolored wig; his face, pale, flaccid, irregularly chiseled and harsh, seeming all the more ugly by a much-disfigured nose, but not so badly so as to necessitate his wearing a false one; from the bridge at the forehead to the nostrils it existed as nature had made it, but disease had destroyed its wings toward the end, leaving two holes of fantastic appearance, thickening his pronunciation and impeding his speech. His eyes, formerly fine, but now weakened by every manner of vice and wear, by nights formerly given to work; they had become trimmed with red and gave a damaged appearance; his look, when stirred by an expression of malice, had frightened both judges and criminals, even those who are afraid of nothing.

His denuded mouth, apparently only containing a few blackened stumps of teeth, was sinister; it was frothy with a white saliva which did not, however, moisten his thin, pallid lips.

Cérizet, a little man, less lean than shrunken, endeavored to correct the misfortunes to his person by his apparel, and, if his dress was not magnificent, it was at least scrupulously clean, which, perhaps, only intensified its wretchedness. Everything about him seemed doubtful—his age, his nose, his looks. It was impossible to say whether he was eight and thirty or sixty; whether his faded blue trousers, neatly strapped, would presently be in fashion or dated from the year 1835. His limp boots, carefully blacked, resoled for the third time, had most likely trodden the carpets of ministers' offices. His overcoat, trimmed with heavy braid, drenched by the rains, with oval buttons that indiscreetly displayed their moulds, showed by its cut that it had once been elegant. His collar and satin tie happily hid his lack of linen, but at the back the teeth of the buckle had frayed it, and the satin shone with the friction and grease of his wig. In the days of its youth his vest had not been wanting in smartness, but it was one of those vests which are to be purchased for four francs out of the depths of a ready-made tailor-shop. Each article had been carefully brushed, including the bruised and shining stovepipe hat. Everything harmonized and matched the black gloves which hid the hands of this Mephistopheles.

He was an artist in evil. Becoming the owner of a printing business by acting treacherously to his master, he afterward figured as the publisher of a liberal newspaper; there he became the pet victim of the Royalist ministers after the Restoration, being known as the "unfortunate" Cérizet. In 1830 his patriotic renown gained him a sub-prefecture, whence he was ousted after six months; he raised such a hullabaloo about it, saying he had been condemned unheard, that Casimir Perier's ministry made him the editor of an anti-Republican paper in the pay of the government. Afterward he went into business and was mixed up in one of the most disastrous joint-stock companies that ever called for criminal prosecution; quite serenely he accepted his severe sentence, blaming the Republicans for it. His term of imprisonment was passed in a lunatic asylum. The government cast him off; they were ashamed of a man with such a disgraceful swindling record, done in combination with a retired banker named Claparon, and which brought him down to a well-deserved reprobation. In the depths of his misery this man dreamed of revenge, and, as he had nothing to lose, he was ready for anything that might encompass it. Dutocq and himself were as one in their habitual depravity. Cérizet was to Dutocq what the greyhound is to the courser.

Cérizet, who knew all that misfortune can bring, lent money in trifling loans on short time at ruinous interest; he had commenced as Dutocq's partner, and this old gutter-snipe had become the street-hawker's banker; this push-cart huckster's bill-discounter was the gnawing worm of two faubourgs.

When the advocate of the poor arrived, he let into his apartments Cérizet and Dutocq. All three crossed a small room paved in red encaustic tiles, which by their waxed surface reflected the daylight entering through two cotton curtains. From it they went into a little sitting-room furnished with red curtains, a mahogany suite, covered with red Utrecht velvet; on a wall was a bookcase filled with law books. The mantel was ornamented with vulgar gewgaws, a clock with four mahogany columns, and candlesticks under glass-shades. The study, where, in front of a coal-fire, the three friends seated themselves, was that of a sucking-calf of the law; it was furnished with an office desk, an armchair, little, green silk curtains at the windows, a green carpet, a set of pigeon-holes, and a couch, over which hung an ivory crucifix mounted in velvet. The bedroom, kitchen, and the rest of the rooms overlooked the courtyard.

"Well," said Cérizet, "how goes it? Is everything on the go?"

"Yes," replied Théodose.

"Confess that I had a bright idea, eh?" cried Dutocq, "when I thought up a scheme to get round that imbecile of a Thuillier——"

"Yes, but I'm not behindhand," exclaimed Cérizet. "I have come this morning to give you the cord for tying the thumbs of the old maid so as to make her spin like a teetotum. Don't make any mistake! Mademoiselle Thuillier is everything in this matter; only get over her and you have captured the town. Talk little, but talk well, like people who know their business. My old associate, Claparon, you know, is an idiot; he will always remain what he has always been—a mere stalking-horse. Just now his name is being used by a notary of Paris in association with some builders, who, builders and notary, are all going to the dogs! Claparon is the scapegoat, he has not yet been a bankrupt, but every one must have a beginning, and, at this very moment, he is hiding in my den at the Rue des Poules, where he will never be discovered. My Claparon is furious, he hasn't got a sou; and among the five or six houses which have to be sold, one is a perfect gem of a house, built of squared stone and right near the Madeleine— it has a front patterned like a melon and ravishing sculpture—

but, not being finished, it might be given for at most one hundred thousand francs; by spending twenty-five thousand francs on it, the buyer in two years could make ten thousand francs per annum. In helping Mademoiselle Thuillier to secure this, you can gain her esteem, for you can give her to understand that such can be picked up through you every year. Vanity can be worked by flattering its self-conceit; money-grubbers either by an attack on or replenishing their purses. And as, after all, working for Thuillier is working for ourselves, it is only fair to let her profit by this lucky stroke."

"And the notary," said Dutocq, "why does he let it slip?"

"The notary, my poor boy? It is he who saves us. Being compelled to see his connection in fact ruined, he is reserving this part of the crumbs of his cake. Believing in the honesty of that imbecile Claparon, he has instructed him to find a nominal purchaser; for he looks equally for prudence and confidence. We just allow him to think that Mademoiselle Thuillier is an honest maiden lady, who gives the use of her name to poor Claparon, and then both Claparon and the notary will be caught. I owe this little turn to my good friend Claparon for letting me in to bear the brunt of the matter in his stock concern, which was smashed by Couture, in whose skin you would hate to find yourselves!" said he, with a flash of infernal hatred in his dull, fishy eyes. "I have said, monseigneurs!" added he in a rough voice, which passed loud through his nose-holes, and assuming a dramatic pose, for once, at a time of extreme poverty, he had been an actor.

As he finished the door-bell rang, and la Peyrade went to open the door.

"Are you altogether sure of him?" said Cérizet to Dutocq. "I detect a manner about him—in short, I have known traitors."

"He is completely in our hands," said Dutocq; "so I

haven't given myself the trouble of watching him; but, between ourselves, I did not think him so smart as he is. We had an idea that we had placed a sorrel horse between the legs of a man who didn't know how to ride, and the lubber is an old jockey! And there you are!"

"He had better lookout!" said Cérizet, in an undertone. "I can puff him over like a castle of cards. As to you, Daddy Dutocq, you can watch him at work and see him at every moment; just keep him under surveillance. I'll feel his pulse, too; I'll get Claparon to employ him to get rid of us; then we can judge where we stand."

"That's a good scheme," said Dutocq; "your eyes are as good as most folks."

"We are all in the same boat; that's all there is to it!" replied Cérizet.

When the advocate reappeared Cérizet was examining all in the study.

"It is Thuillier," said Théodose. "I expected him calling. He is in the salon. It won't do for him to see Cérizet's overcoat," added he, smiling; "the frogs on it would startle him."

"Bah! you rescue the unfortunate, that is your part in the play. Do you need some money?" asked Cérizet, and brought out one hundred francs from his trousers' pocket. "There, see, that looks well;" and he placed the pile on the mantel-shelf.

"We shall be able to get out through the bedroom," said Dutocq.

"Well, then, adieu," said the Provençal, as he opened the door for them leading from the office to the bedroom. "Come in, my dear Monsieur Thuillier," he called out to the dude of the Empire.

When he saw that he had reached the door of his office, and could no longer see on to the landing, he went to let out his two associates by the other way.

"In six months you should by rights be the husband of Céleste, and doing well. You're a lucky dog; you haven't found yourself in the police dock twice, as I have—the first time in 1825 under a constructive process, or treason, following a series of articles that I never wrote; and the second time for appropriating the profits of a concern that didn't pan out! Now set the pot a-boiling; by a paper-sack! Dutocq and myself need that twenty-five thousand francs, each of us, as soon as may be; be of good courage, my friend," added he, proffering his hand to Théodose, and proving him by his grip.

The Provençal gave his right hand and wrung his with much unction.

"My dear boy, you may be well assured that in every position I attain I shall not forget that from which you rescued me by placing me on horseback here. I am your bait, but you give me the greater portion, and I should be worse than a convict who has become a police-spy if I did not play a square game."

Cérizet, as soon as the door was closed upon him, peered through the key-hole to try and catch the expression on the other's face, but the lawyer had turned his back and went to join Thuillier, so his suspicious ally could not detect aught.

Théodose, though, saw a multiplying chance of success; he flattered himself that he could get rid of his sordid friends, although all he had he owed to them.

"Well, my dear Théodose," said Thuillier, "we have been hoping to see you each day since Sunday, but each evening has seen our hopes delayed. As this Sunday is our dinner-day, my sister and wife charged me to bid you come——"

"I have had so much business," said Théodose, "that I have not had two minutes to give to a soul, not even you, whom I count in the number of my friends, and with whom I have particularly wished to speak."

"How! You seriously think of that you told me?" exclaimed Thuillier, interrupting Théodose.

"If you hadn't called to clinch the business, I should not esteem you as I do," said Théodose, smiling. "You have been a sub-chief; therefore you must have more or less ambition, and in you it is legitimate, or the deuce is in it. See, now! between you and me, when we see a Minard, a gilded blockhead, complimented by the King and doing the swagger-act in the Tuileries; a Popinot in the track of becoming a minister—and you, a man inured into the work of the administration, a man who has had thirty years' experience, who has seen six governments, left to transplant his balsam seedlings! What then? I am frank, my dear Thuillier, I want to give you a push, because you will pull me after you.

"Well, then, here is my plan. We have to name a member of the Municipal Council for this arrondissement, and that man must be you!—and," said he, emphasizing the word—"must be *you!* Some day you will most assuredly be the deputy from the arrondissement, when we reëlect the Chamber—it's not far off. The voices which nominate you for the Municipal Council will be there when the time for electing a deputy comes; you leave it to me."

"But what means have you?" exclaimed Thuillier, fascinated.

"You shall know; but leave me alone to manage this long and difficult business; if you commit any indiscretion on what we have said as to our plans or the arrangements between us, I leave you to yourself, and remain yours truly!"

"Oh! you may count on the absolute dumbness of an old sub-chief; I have had secrets——"

"Good! but you must keep these secrets from your wife, your sister, and Monsieur and Madame Colleville, when we are with them."

"I won't let a muscle play in my face," said Thuillier, putting it in repose.

"Good!" replied la Peyrade; "and I will test you. To be eligible, it is necessary to pay your full taxes, and you don't do this."

"Your pardon! for a seat in the Municipal Council I am all right; I pay two francs and eighty-six centimes."

"Yes, but for the Chamber the amount is five hundred francs, and there is no time to be lost, for possession is necessary for a year."

"The devil!" said Thuillier. "Here in a year's time I have to be assessed at five hundred francs."

"By the end of July, if not earlier, you may be paying it; my devotion to you leads me to confide to you the secret of an affair by which you may gain thirty or forty thousand francs a year with a capital of one hundred and fifty thousand at the most. But, in your household, it is your sister who for a long time has had the direction of your affairs; with that I have no fault to find; she has, as I said before, the best judgment in the world; therefore it will be requisite, as a start, that I conquer her esteem; the affection of Mademoiselle Brigitte may be accomplished by proposing this investment to her, and here is why: If Mademoiselle Thuillier has not faith in my relics, we should get into trouble; then how are we to suggest to your sister that she should purchase the property in your name? It were better that the idea should come from me. You shall, in the meantime, both be enabled to judge of this business. As to the means I have to push you into the Municipal Council of the Seine, here they are:

"Phellion has the disposition of one-fourth of the votes in the quarter; he and Laudigeois have lived there thirty years; they are looked upon as oracles. I have a friend who controls another fourth, and the curé of Saint-Jacques, who is not without a certain influence due to his virtues, may secure some votes. Dutocq, by his intimacy with his justice of the peace, will do his utmost for me, especially if it is not done for my personal benefit; finally Colleville, as secretary to the mayor, represents one-fourth of the votes."

"Why, you are right; I am elected!" cried Thuillier.

"You think so?" said la Peyrade, and his voice had an alarming irony; "well, then, only go to your friend Colleville asking him to assist you; you will see what he says. Every success in election matters is not made by the candidate himself, but by his friends. He must ask for nothing for himself, he must leave himself in the hands of his friends; you must wait to be begged to accept it, seeming to be without the ambition."

"La Peyrade!" exclaimed Thuillier, rising and taking the hand of the young advocate; "you are an awfully smart man."

"Not up to you, but I have my little merits," replied the Provençal, smiling.

"And if we succeed, how can I recompense you?" asked Thuillier, innocently.

"Ah! that's it! You will think me impertinent; but bear in mind that there is within me a feeling which must be my excuse; for it has given me the pluck to try every resource. I am in love, I give you my confidence——"

"But with whom?" said Thuillier.

"Your darling little Céleste," replied la Peyrade; "and my love is surety for my devotion to you; what would I not do for a *father-in-law!* It is but selfishness, I do but work for myself——"

"Chut!" cried Thuillier.

"Eh, my friend," said la Peyrade, taking Thuillier by the hips, "if I had not had Flavie for me, and if I had not known all, should I speak of it to you? Only mind this, don't mention a word on this subject to her. Listen to me, I am of the stuff that ministers are made, I do not want to wear Céleste until I have won her. To become a deputy for Paris you must first annul Minard; wipe him out, you must still hold your influence over him; to this end let them still hope to win Céleste, and we'll trick them all. I don't want her for her fortune, I want her for herself. You see that I have no underhand scheme, while you six months after entering the Council will have the Cross, and as soon as you are elected deputy will be made an officer of the Legion of Honor. Well, then, trust to me; do not think of making me a member of your family until you have the ribbon in your button-hole, on the day following that on which you enter the Chamber; nevertheless, I can do still more: I can get you forty thousand francs a year."

"For only one of these three things you could have our Céleste."

"What a gem!" said la Peyrade, raising his eyes to heaven. "I am foolish enough to pray God for her every day. She is charming—she is very like you, very. Well, well, you need not fear my discretion. My God, it was Dutocq who told me all. Till this evening. By-the-by, don't forget that you never intended Céleste for me. Above all, say nothing to Flavie."

As Thuillier went out he said to himself:

"That's a very superior man! We shall get along together famously, and, my faith, it would be hard to beat him as a match for Céleste;" and so forth.

The house toward which Théodose soon afterward went his way had been the *hoc erat in votis* of Phellion during twenty years past; it was as much the house of Phellion as the braiding, the brandebourgs, were an integral portion of Cérizet's overcoat and its indispensable ornament.

This building, planked up against a great house, of the depth of one room only, some twenty feet, had a species of little wing or lean-to on either side, each having one window. It had for chief charm a garden some thirty fathoms wide, but longer than the frontage by the width of a court from the street, and a row of lime-trees.

This edifice of rough stone, stuccoed over, three stories high, was yellow-washed, with Venetian blinds above and plain, broad shutters below, painted green. The kitchen occupied the first floor of the wings at the end, by the courtyard; a stout, strong girl, protected by two great dogs, was the cook and janitor. The front had five windows, beside the two wings which projected about six feet, and was in the "Style Phellion." Above the door he had inserted a marble tablet, on which was inscribed in letters of gold: *Aurea mediocritas.* Over a sun-dial he had a tablet on which was traced this sage maxim: *Umbra mea vita sic!*

He had lately restored the window-sills with Languedoc red marble which he had picked up in a stonemason's yard. At the end of the garden was a colored statue which passers-by thought looked like a nurse suckling a baby. This small freehold, which had been long coveted by the Phellions, had cost eighteen thousand francs in 1831.

Such was the retreat of this great but unknown citizen, who now enjoyed the sweets of repose, after having paid his debt to his country by working in the Bureau of Finance from which he had retired as first-clerk after thirty-six years' service.

In 1832 he had led his battalion of the National Guard in the attack at Saint-Merri, but his neighbors saw tears in his eyes at the thought of being compelled to fire on the misled Frenchmen. His virtuous hesitancy gained him the esteem of his quarter, but it lost him the decoration of the Legion of Honor. The worthy man only wished this to fill his cup of happiness. He had thought of asking Minard to help him in his secret ambition, but had not as yet been able to screw himself up to this point.

When la Peyrade presented himself the family was complete, each one being present in their Sunday best and sitting before the fire in the salon—a room wainscoted in wood, painted in two tints of gray—they all started when the cook announced the very man whom they had all been discussing in reference to Céleste, Félix's love carrying him so far as to cause him to go to mass in order to see her.

"Alas! the Thuilliers appear to me to be set upon a really dangerous man," said Mme. Phellion; "he took Madame Colleville on his arm this morning and they went off together to the Luxembourg."

"He has something peculiarly sinister about him," cried Félix, "has that advocate; if told that he had committed some crime, I should not be at all astonished."

"You are going too far," said his father; "he is cousin-german to Tartuffe, that immortal figure cast in bronze by our honest Molière, for Molière, my children, had honesty and patriotism for the basis of his genius."

Thus speaking he perceived Geneviève enter, who said:

"Here is Monsieur de la Peyrade, who wishes to speak to monsieur."

"To me!" cried M. Phellion. "Bid him enter!" added he with that solemnity in little things that gave him a ridiculous air, but not so to his family upon whom it always imposed, and all of whom accepted him as their king.

"To what do we owe the honor of your visit, monsieur?" said Phellion severely.

"To your importance in the quarter, my dear Monsieur Phellion, and to public affairs," replied Théodose.

"Then we will pass through to my study," said Phellion.

"No, no, my friend," said Mme. Phellion, a little woman, as flat as a flounder, and who still retained on her face the grim severity which is habitual to the professor of music in young ladies' seminaries; "we will leave you here."

An upright Erard piano placed between the two windows and fronting the fireplace proclaimed her pretensions to still rank as a virtuoso.

"Am I so unhappy as to cause you to take flight?" said Théodose, pleasantly smiling at the mother and daughter.

"You have a delightful retreat here," continued he, "and you only need the presence of a pretty daughter-in-law to enable you to pass the remainder of your days in that *aurea mediocritas*, the vow of the Latin poet, in the midst of family joys. Your antecedents merit this recompense, after all that you have done, my dear Monsieur Phellion; you are at once a good citizen and a patriarch——"

"Môsieur," said Phellion, quite embarrassed; "môsieur, I have done my *jooty* (duty) and that is *orl* (all)."

At the word "daughter-in-law," spoken by Théodose, Mme. Barniol, who was as like her mother, Mme. Phellion, as two drops of water resemble each other, looked at Mme. Phellion and Félix in a manner which seemed to say: "Can we be mistaken?"

The desire to talk about this incident occasioned the four to go out into the garden, for, in March, 1840, the weather was quite fine, at least in Paris.

"Commandant," said Théodose when alone with the honest burgher, who was flattered at being thus addressed, "I came to speak with you on election matters."

"Ah! yes, we have to nominate a municipal councilor," said Phellion, interrupting him.

"And it is in reference to a candidate that I have ventured to trouble your Sunday enjoyment; but, perhaps, we may not, after all, go beyond the family circle."

It was impossible that Phellion could be more Phellion at this moment than Théodose was Phellion.

"I will not allow you to say another word," replied the commandant, profiting by a pause made by Théodose to cut in: "My choice is made."

"We have, then, the same idea," cried Théodose, "people of good intent meet on a common ground the same as men of genius."

"I don't know about that being so this time, it would be phenomenal," answered Phellion. "This arrondissement has had as a representative on the Municipal Council the most virtuous of men, who was also a great judge, you know, the late Monsieur Popinot, who died as councilor of State. When it was necessary to replace him, his nephew, who inherits his beneficence, was not then a resident in the quarter, but, since then, he has purchased and now occupies the house that belonged to his uncle, on the Rue de la Montagne-Sainte-Geneviève; he is doctor at the Polytechnic and also at one of the hospitals; he is an ornament to our quarter; by these titles, and to honor in the person of the nephew the memory of the uncle, some residents of the quarter and myself have resolved to carry Dr. Horace Bianchon, member of the Academy of Sciences, as you know, and one of the new glories of the illustrious school (of medicine) of Paris. A man is not great in our eyes simply because he is celebrated, but the late Councilor Popinot was, in my opinion, nearly a Saint-Vincent de Paul."

"A doctor is not an administrator," replied Théodose; "and I have come to ask your vote for a man which in your own interests demands the sacrifice of any predilection, which after all is a matter of indifference to the public."

"Ah! monsieur!" cried Phellion, rising and posing like Lafon in his "La Glorieux" attitude, "can you so belittle me as to think that my personal interests can ever influence my political conscience? On the side of public matters, I am a citizen, nothing more, nothing less."

Théodose smiled in his sleeve at the thought of the struggle about to pass between the father and the citizen.

"Don't engage your convictions too earnestly, I entreat you," said la Peyrade; "for the happiness of your dear Félix is at stake."

"What do you mean by those words?" asked Phellion, standing in the middle of the room, in the favorite pose of the famous Odilon Barrot.

"Why, I have come on behalf of our mutual friend, the

worthy and excellent Monsieur Thuillier, whose influence over the destinies of the lovely Céleste Colleville are not unknown to you. Your admirable son might make any family proud of his entry into it; now you cannot better further his marriage with the charming Céleste than by earning the eternal gratitude of the Thuilliers, which you can do by recommending him to your fellow-citizens for their suffrages. I have devoted myself, monsieur, to the service of the humble, as did the late Councilor Popinot, a sublime man, as you say; and if my destiny were not in some sense religious, and thus antagonistic to the obligations of marriage, my taste, my further vocation, would be for the service of God by His church. I am not always on the carpet like other philanthropists; I do not write, I work, for I am a man who has vowed to do all for the good of Christian charity. I have guessed at the ambition of our friend Thuillier, and I wished to contribute to the happiness of two beings, made for each other, by offering you the means of gaining access to the heart, a somewhat cold one, of Thuillier."

Phellion was dumfounded by this excellent harangue, cleverly spoken; he was dazed, startled; but he remained the same Phellion; he went toward the advocate and extended his right hand, and la Peyrade gave him his.

Both gave one of those wrings of the hand such as were given, about August, 1830, between a bourgeoisie and a man of the morrow.

"Môsieur," said the commandant, with feeling, "I judged you wrongly. What you have given me the honor of confiding here will here die," pointing to his heart. "Real worth is so rare, that in our weak nature we are apt to be distrustful of it when it appears. In me you have a friend, if you will allow me to do myself the honor of taking such title. But, môsieur, you must learn to know me; I should sink in my own estimation if I proposed Thuillier. No, my son must never know happiness at the cost of a bad act done by his father. I shall not change my vote to another candidate to there find my son's interest. That is virtue, môsieur!"

La Peyrade took out his handkerchief, rubbed it into his eye and brought forth a tear, and said, extending his hand to Phellion and turning his head:

"There, monsieur, is the sublimity of private life and political life in conflict! Not for anything would I have missed this spectacle—my visit is not wasted. What would you? in your place I should do the same. You are the noblest work of God—an honest man; a good man, a fellow-citizen of Jean-Jacques! More of such citizens, then, oh, France, my country, what might you not become! This is me, monsieur, I crave the honor of being your friend."

"What's happening?" cried Mme. Phellion, who was looking at the scene through the window. "Your father and that monster of a man are embracing each other!"

Phellion and the advocate went out to rejoin the family in the garden.

"My dear Félix," said the old man, pointing to la Peyrade, who bowed to Mme. Phellion, "be very grateful to this worthy young man; he will be more helpful than injurious to you."

For about five minutes the lawyer walked under the leafless lime-trees with Mme. Phellion, and during that time gave them a bit of counsel, which was to bear fruit that evening; the first happy result being to cause the ladies to admire his talents, candor, and other inappreciable qualities.

After he had bidden them adieu, Mme. Phellion took her husband's arm to reënter the salon, and said to him:

"And what, my friend, you, so good a father, made you by an excessive delicacy throw obstacles in the way of so good a marriage for our Félix?"

"My dear little woman," replied Phellion, "the great men of antiquity, such as Brutus and others, were never fathers when they had to be citizens. The middle-class has, even more than the aristocracy which it is called upon to replace, to exercise the hightest virtues. Monsieur de Saint-Hilaire thought not of the loss of his arm when he saw Turenne lay dead before him. Shall I betray such feelings in the bosom of the family where I have taught them? No. Weep to-day, my dear, to-morrow you will esteem me!" he added, as he perceived tears in the eyes of his little skinny wife.

These grandiloquent words were spoken on the threshold of the door over which was written: *Aurea mediocritas.*

"I should have added: *et digna!*" added Phellion, pointing upward to the tablet; "but those two words are too eulogistic."

"But, father," said Marie-Théodore Phellion, the future engineer of roads and bridges, when they were again in the salon, "it seems to me that a man does not fail in the matter of honor by changing his determination in regard to an unimportant matter when it does not concern the public."

"Unimportant, my son!" cried Phellion. "Between ourselves, and Félix partakes my convictions, Môsieur Thuillier is without any kind of capacity; he knows nothing. Horace Bianchon is a capable man; he would get a thousand things done for the arrondissement, and Thuillier not one. Beside, if man does not blame, God will. My conscience is free from blame, and I wish to leave my memory unblemished to you. Therefore nothing can change my opinion."

"Oh! my good father," cried the little Mme. Barniol, throwing herself on a cushion at the knees of Phellion, "don't mount the high horse! There are lots of imbeciles and simpletons in the Municipal Council, but France goes on just the same. He'll vote the same as others, this brave Thuillier. Remember that Céleste will have five hundred thousand francs perhaps."

"She might have millions," said Phellion, "yet I would leave them there. I will not propose Thuillier, when my duty to the memory of the great virtues of the best man who ever lived says nominate Horace Bianchon. From high in the heavens, Popinot contemplates and applauds me," cried Phellion enthusiastically.

"My father is right," said Félix, arousing from a brown study; "he deserves our respect and love, like as he has always done in the course of life, unpretending and honored. I love Céleste as much as I love my family, but I do not wish to rise at the cost of my father's honor; and," he added, "the moment the question becomes one of conscience, let no more be said."

Phellion, his eyes filled with tears, went to his eldest son, took him in his arms, and said:

"My son, my son!" in a broken voice.

"This is all rubbish," said Mme. Phellion, in a whisper to Mme. Barniol; "come and help me dress, we must put an end to this; I know your father, he is an obstinate. To carry out the scheme which that noble and pious young man gave me, Théodore, I shall need your support—therefore be ready, my son."

At this moment Geneviève came in and delivered a letter to M. Phellion.

"An invitation to dine with the Thuilliers, my wife, myself, and Félix," said he.

The magnificent and startling idea of the advocate of the poor had caused as much turmoil at the Thuilliers as upset at the Phellions; and Jérôme, without confiding anything to his sister, for he piqued himself on his honor to his Mephistopheles, had gone to her room and said:

"Good little woman" (he always caressed her heart with these words), "we shall have some top sawyers to dinner to-day; I shall invite the Minards, so let us have a good dinner; I have written the Phellions an invitation, it is a little late, but with them it won't matter. As to the Minards, I must throw dust in their eyes; I need them."

"Four Minards, three Phellions, four Collevilles, and ourselves—that is thirteen."

"La Peyrade, fourteen; it might be as well to invite Dutocq; he can give us a push; I'll go up to him."

"What are you up to?" cried his sister; "fifteen to dinner, that means at least forty francs sent dancing!"

"Don't regret that, my good little woman; above all, be as adoring as possible to our young friend la Peyrade. He is a friend—he will prove it! If you love me, care for him like the apple of your eye."

And he left Brigitte stupefied.

"Yes, yes, I will wait till he does prove it," said she to herself. "He can't catch me with pretty words, not me! He is a nice boy, but, before carrying him my heart, I must study him a little more."

Thuillier invited Dutocq; then off to Zélie, whom he bamboozled into coming; then to the Minards. Minard had bought one of those great, sumptuous dwellings which the old religious orders had erected in the vicinity of the Sorbonne. As he ascended the broad, stone stairway, with a balustrade, which showed how well the second order of arts had flourished under Louis XIII., he envied the mayor his hôtel and position.

In this handsome house, with a garden in the rear and a courtyard in front, lived a retired grocer, a successful cheat. Thuillier's name opened the doors of the salon where, among red velvet and gold, in the midst of the most magnificent Chinese stuffs, a poor woman sat, who at every popular ball crushed the hearts of the princes and princesses at the Château.

"Is she not rightly given the name of 'the Caricature?'" said a smiling pseudo-lady of the bed-chamber to a duchess who could not refrain from laughing at the appearance of Zélie tricked out in her diamonds, red as a poppy, squeezed into a spangled dress, and rolling about like one of the barrels of her old store.

"Can you pardon me, fair lady," said Thuillier, wriggling around and ending by striking an attitude, number two of his repertoire of 1807, "for having left on my desk this invitation which I really thought had been sent you? It is for to-day; perhaps I come too late——"

Zélie examined her husband's face, as he advanced to meet Thuillier, and responded:

"We had intended going to have a look at the country and dine by *chance* at a restaurant, but we can readily renounce the project, all the more willingly because it seems to me so devilish common to go out of Paris on a Sunday."

"We can have a little hop to the piano for the youngsters, if there'll be enough of us, and I presume there will be, as I sent word to Phellion, whose wife is intimate with Madame Prou, the successor——"

"The successtress," interrupted M. Minard.

"Oh, no," replied Thuillier, "it would be successoress, as we say the mayoress, of the demoiselle Lagrave, and who was a Barniol."

"Is it necessary to dress?" asked Mme. Minard.

"Oh, well, yes!" said Thuiller; "I should get in trouble with my sister. No, no, though, it is only in the family. Under the Empire, madame, we learned to know each other by dancing. In those glorious days, a good dancer was as much as a fine soldier. To-day people are too matter of fact——"

"We won't talk politics," said the mayor, smiling. "The King is a great man and very smart. I live in admiration of my times and its institutions which we have given ourselves. The King understands what he is doing when he develops our industries; it is a hand-to-hand fight with England, and this second peace is doing us more good than all the wars of the Empire."

"What a deputy Minard would make," said Zélie naïvely. "Between you and I, he tries to speak when we are alone; you would help to get him returned, would you not, really, Thuillier?"

"No talking politics," replied Thuillier. "Come at five o'clock."

"That little Vinet, is he to be there?" asked Minard. "Without doubt he has an eye on Céleste."

"Then he may order his crepe," answered Thuillier. "Brigitte would not lend ear to him."

Zélie and Minard exchanged smiles of satisfaction.

After inviting the Laudigeois when he left the Minards, he then called on the Collevilles to be sure that Céleste wore a pretty toilette. He found Flavie somewhat pensive, and Thuillier had to overcome her indecision.

"My old and my ever-young love," said he, putting his arm about her waist, for she was alone in her room, "I cannot have any secrets from you. I have a most important affair on hand. I cannot say more, but I can ask you to be particularly gracious to a young man——."

"Who?"

"Young la Peyrade."

"And why, Charles?"

"He holds my future in his hands; then, too, he is a man of genius. Oh! I know. Between us it is give and take."

"How! You want me to play the coquette with him?"

"Not too much, my angel," replied Thuillier, with a fatuous air.

And off he went without noticing a species of amazement that had befallen Flavie.

"That is a power," said she to herself, "that young man. We shall see."

At half-past four Théodose was at his post; he had assumed a simple air, part servile, and a soft voice; and first he went with Thuillier into the garden.

"My friend, I have not the least doubt of your success, but I must once more impress upon you at all times to keep absolute silence. If any one questions you about Céleste give evasive answers, such as you learned so well at the bureau."

"All right!" answered Thuillier. "But is it a certainty?"

"You will see the dessert I have prepared. Be modest, above all. Here are the Minards, leave me to lime them."

After saluting them, la Peyrade kept close by M. the Mayor, and at an opportune moment he took him aside and said to him:

"Monsieur the Mayor, a man of your political importance does not face the ennui of dining here without having some end in view; I do not for a moment ask your motives, I have no right so to do; it is not my part here below to interfere in the business of this world's powers; but pardon my boldness and deign to listen to the counsel that I can give you. If I am able to do you a service to-day, you are in a position to render me two to-morrow, so if you listen to me a moment it is in my own interest. Our friend Thuillier is in despair at being a nobody, and he is intending to become something, a personage in the arrondissement."

"Ah!" said Minard.

"Oh! nothing much; he wants the nomination as a member of the Municipal Council. I know that Phellion, divining an equal advantage from doing him a service, intends to propose our poor friend as a candidate. Well, perhaps you might find it necessary to your project to be forehanded with him. The nomination of Thuillier will not only be favorable to you—I should think it would also be agreeable; he will do well in the council; there are worse than he there. And then if he is indebted to you for his advancement he will see through your eyes; he will regard you as the shining light of the town——"

"My dear sir, I thank you," said Minard; "you have rendered me a service which I shall never forget, and that proves to me——"

"That I don't care for the Phellions," replied la Peyrade, profiting by the mayor's hesitation, fearing that he might bring forth some speech disdainful of the advocate. "I hate people who trade on their honesty and make cash of their noble sentiments."

"You thoroughly understand them," said Minard; "they are sycophants. That man, all his life, for the past ten years, is explained by that scrap of red ribbon," added the mayor, showing his own button-hole.

"Lookout, though," said the lawyer, "his son loves Céleste and is in the citadel."

"Yes, but my son has twelve thousand livres of income himself——"

"Oh!" said the advocate, with a shrug, "Mademoiselle Brigitte said the other day that she wanted at least that from suitors for Céleste. And, after all, before six months are over, you will see that Thuillier will have a freehold bringing in forty thousand francs a year."

"The deuce! I never doubted it," replied the mayor. "Well, he shall be a member of the council."

"In any case, don't mention me in the matter," said the advocate of the poor, who pressed forward to greet Mme. Phellion, who had just arrived. "Well, my fair lady, have you succeeded?"

"I waited until four o'clock, but the worthy and excellent man would not listen at all; he is too much occupied to accept such a charge, and Monsieur Phellion has a letter in which Dr. Bianchon thanks him for his good intentions, and says that, for himself, his candidate is Monsieur Thuillier. He is using his influence in his favor and prays my husband to do the same."

"And what says your excellent spouse?"

"'I have done my duty,' he replied. 'I have been no traitor to my conscience, and henceforth I am wholly for Thuillier.'"

"Well, that's all fixed then," said la Peyrade. "Forget my visit, the whole credit of the idea is your own."

9

Then turning to Mme. Colleville, with a most respectful attitude, he said:

"Madame, be so good as to introduce me to our good Papa Colleville; I propose a little surprise for Thuillier, and he must be in the secret."

As la Peyrade played his part for Thuillier's benefit, Mme. Colleville was hearing such remarks as made her ears tingle; it was a mystery to her.

"I wish I knew what Messrs. Colleville and la Peyrade are saying that they laugh so much?" said Mme. Thuillier, simply, looking out through the window.

"They are speaking just such rubbish as all men talk between themselves," answered Mlle. Thuillier, who frequently attacked the men by a kind of instinct natural in old maids.

"He is incapable of such a thing," said Phellion, gravely; "for Môsieur de la Peyrade is one of the most virtuous young people whom I have met. I put him on a par with Félix; nay, I wish that my son had a little of Môsieur Théodose's pretty piety."

"He is, in fact, a man of merit, who will get on," observed Minard. "As for me, my best wishes—I won't say my protection—are his."

"He spends more in lamp-oil than bread," said Dutocq; "that I know."

"His mother, if she still survives, must be proud of him," said Mme. Phellion, sententiously.

"You may confide to him your secrets and your fortune," said Thuillier; "in these days that is not such a small thing to say of the best of men."

"It is Colleville who is making him laugh," cried Dutocq.

Just then Colleville and la Peyrade were at the bottom of the garden, the best friends in the world.

"Gentlemen," said Brigitte, "soup and the King must not be kept waiting; hand in the ladies."

This pleasant jest, inherited from the janitor's lodge,

ushered the whole party, with the exception of the dreadful Cérizet, into the dining-room. Every principal character in this drama was seated around the board.

The characteristics of the middle-class cook in 1840 is necessary to a picture of its manners; good housekeepers may learn a lesson therefrom. A woman does not for twenty years occupy herself in making cash-bags without looking up some means of filling a few. Now Brigitte had this peculiarity, with the thrift necessary for laying the foundation of a fortune she combined that of dispensing sufficient for necessities. Her relative extravagance, when it had to do with her brother or Céleste, was the antitype of miserliness. As a fact, she often commisserated herself for not being avaricious.

The soup offered was *bouillon*, extremely pale; for, even on an occasion such as this, she had enjoined the cook to make plenty of it; then, as the beef had to serve the family on the morrow and the day after, the less of its juices it furnished to the bouillon, the more substantial it would be. The beef, underdone, was always removed at a little speech of Brigitte's, said by her as Thuillier essayed to carve :

"I guess it's rather tough; never mind, Thuillier, no one will care to eat of it, we have other things."

The bouillon was, in fact, flanked by four dishes standing on hot copper double plates off which the silver-plating was worn. At this dinner, called the *candidature*, the first course was composed of two ducks *aux olives*, having opposite a large pie *aux quenelles* and an eel with tartar sauce, with a *fricandeau* on endive. The second course had for its centrepiece a fine roast goose stuffed with chestnuts, a corn-salad ornamented with slices of red beet, opposite a dish of cupcustards, and a tureen of sweet turnips looked down upon a bowl of macaroni. This dinner, well suited to be that of a janitor's wedding festivities, would be produced, for, at the most, twenty francs; the relics would keep the house for two days, and Brigitte would say :

"*Dame;* when one receives, the cash goes! It's frightful."

The table was lighted by two hideous silver-plated candlesticks with four branches, in which twinkled that economical candle called the *Aurore*. The linen was resplendently white, and the old thread-pattern plate was a paternal heritage, the fruit of a purchase made during the Revolution by old Thuillier, and had served in the quasi restaurant he had kept in his lodge, but which was suppressed in 1816 in all the offices. Thus the fare harmonized with the dining-room, with the house, and with the Thuilliers, whose fate it was not to rise above their own style. The Minards, the Collevilles, and la Peyrade exchanged a few smiles, which communicated a satirical, but not expressed thought. They alone knew of any superior luxury, and the Minards said plainly enough that they had some afterthoughts in accepting such a dinner. La Peyrade, who sat beside Flavie, whispered her:

"You see they need some one who can teach them how to live; you are eating what is commonly called cag-mag, an old friend of mine. But these Minards; what horrible cupidity! Your daughter would be lost to you. These parvenus have the vices of the great nobles of other days, without their elegance. Their son, who has twelve thousand francs income, can well find a family in the *Potash* set without dragging their rake here on speculation. It is a pleasure to play upon such people like as if they were a bass or a clarionet."

Flavie listened with a smile; she did not remove her foot when Théodose lightly pressed it with his boot.

As the dishes of the second course were being removed, Minard, afraid that Phellion would forestall him, said to Thuillier, very gravely:

"My dear Thuillier, if I accepted your dinner it was because I had an important communication to make to you, one which honors you so much that I choose to have as witnesses all your guests."

Thuillier became pale.

"You obtained for me the Cross?" cried he, as he got a look from Théodose, and to prove that he was not without finesse.

"You will have that some day," replied the mayor; "but this is more than that. The Cross is a favor due to the good opinion of a minister, whereas this is now the question, so to say, of an election due to the sentiments of your fellow-citizens. In a word, a great number of the electors of your arrondissement have cast their eyes upon you, and wish to honor you with their confidence by charging you with their representation of this arrondissement in the Municipal Council of Paris, which, as all the world knows, is the council general of the Seine."

"Bravo!" said Dutocq.

Phellion rose.

"Monsieur the Mayor has anticipated me," said he, in a voice broken with emotion; "but it is so flattering for our friend to be the object of interest on the part of all good citizens, and to obtain the public vote from all parts of the capital, that I must not complain of being the second in line; beside I bow to the power of authority!" (And he bowed respectfully to Minard.) "Yes, Môsieur Thuillier, many electors think of giving you their votes in that portion of the arrondissement where I have my humble Penates; and you have the particular advantage of being designated by an illustrious man (Sensation), by a man whom we designed to honor for the sake of one of the most distinguished inhabitants of the arrondissement, who was, I might say, for twenty years its father. I allude to the late Monsieur Popinot. But his nephew, Doctor Bianchon, one of our glories, has, owing to his pressing duties, declined to serve us. He thanked us for the compliment paid, but indicated for our suffrages the candidate of Monsieur the Mayor, as being, in his opinion, the more capable from the position he formerly occupied."

And Phellion sat down amid an acclamative murmur.

"Thuillier, you may count on your old friend," said Colleville.

At this moment the guests were all touched by the sight presented by old Brigitte and Mme. Thuillier. Brigitte, pale as if about to faint, let the slow tears run unheeded down her cheeks, tears of deepest joy; and Mme. Thuillier sat as though struck by a thunderbolt, her eyes fixed. All at once the old maid sprang into the kitchen, crying to Joséphine the cook:

"Come into the cellar, my girl; we must get out the wine from behind the fagots."

"My friends," said Thuillier, in a choking voice, "this is the grandest day in my life, happier than that of my election, should I permit myself to ask the suffrages of my fellow-citizens" (Certainly, of course!), "for I feel myself much run down with thirty years of public service, and you may surely believe that a man of honor has need to consult his strength before he assumes the functions of an *ædile*."

"I expected nothing less of you, Monsieur Thuillier," cried Phellion. "Pardon me, this is the first time in my life that I ever interrupted any one, and one who was formerly my superior, too; but under the circumstances——"

"Accept, accept," cried Zélie. "In the name of the little man! we need such men as you for governor."

"Resign yourself, my chief," said Dutocq; "and long live our future councilor—— But we have nothing to drink——"

"Well, all is said," replied Minard, "you are our candidate, eh?"

"You think too much of me," said Thuillier.

"That's all right," cried Colleville; "a man who for thirty years has worked in the galleys of the Bureau of Finance should be a treasure to the town."

"You are much too modest," said young Minard; "your capacity is not unknown to us; it is remembered even at the bureau."

"As you all insist——"

"The King will be well pleased with our choice, I can tell you that," said Minard, interrupting Thuillier in a pompous manner.

"Gentlemen," said la Peyrade, "will you permit a recent inhabitant of the Saint-Jacques faubourg to make a little remark, which may not be unimportant?

"The influence of the mayor of an adjoining arrondissement, immense in ours, where he has left such an excellent memory—that of Monsieur Phellion, the oracle—yes, I repeat it, the oracle"—noticing a negative gesture of Phellion's— "of his battalion; the influence of Monsieur Colleville, powerful by his frank urbanity; that of Monsieur the Clerk of the Peace, no less valuable; and my own humble efforts, all are pledges of success, but they are not success itself. To obtain triumph let us here and now pledge ourselves to keep a profound silence as to our intentions. Otherwise, we should excite, not willing or desiring it, envy and the like passions, which would erect obstacles in our path necessary to be overcome. Some would see good in our efforts, others evil; it is not for me to judge between such in the presence of minds before whose superiority I bow; I content myself by pointing out the dangers our friend must encounter. The writ for election may not take effect for another month. From now until then imagine the intrigues! Do not offer, I entreat you, our friend Thuillier to the blows of his opponents; let us not deliver him over to public discussion, that modern harpy, the trumpet of calumny and envy, the pretext of inimical feelings calculated to belittle all that is great, that dishonors all that is sacred, and befouls the respectable. Rather let us do as the third party is doing in the Chamber—vote and say nothing!"

Envy had turned Minard's son green and yellow.

"Perfectly true and well said," cried Minard.

"Unanimously carried," said Colleville.

"Whoso desires the end adopts the means," said Phellion, emphatically.

At this moment appeared Mlle. Thuillier, followed by two domestics; stuck in her belt was the key of the cellar, and three bottles of champagne, two of old hermitage, and one of Malaga wine were placed upon the table; but she herself carried a little bottle with respectful care, much like a fairy Carabosse, which she placed before herself. In the midst of the hilarity caused by this abundance of choice cheer, a fruit of her gratitude, poured out by the old maid in the delirium of her joy, there arrived numerous dishes of dessert: a heaped-up dish of raisins, figs, almonds, and nuts;* pyramids of oranges; confections, candied fruits brought from the depths of her closets, and which, but for the circumstances, would have never figured on the table-cloth.

"Céleste, they will bring you a bottle of brandy that my father got in 1802; make an orange salad!" cried she to her sister-in-law. "Monsieur Phellion, open the champagne; this bottle is for you three! Monsieur Dutocq, take this one! Monsieur Colleville, you can make the corks pop!"

The two maids distributed champagne glasses, claret glasses, and liqueur glasses, for Joséphine carried in three more bottles of Bordeaux.

"The year of the comet," cried Thuillier. "Gentlemen, you have caused my sister to lose her head."

"And this evening punch and cakes," she said. "I have sent out to the drug-store to buy some tea. My God! if only I had known that this dinner had to do with an election," exclaimed she to her sister-in-law, "I would have served the turkey."

A general laugh greeted this speech.

"Oh! we have a goose," said Minard's son, smiling.

"It's an ill wind that blows no one good,"† exclaimed Mme. Thuillier, as she saw *marrons glacés* and *meringues* handed round.

---

\* *Quatre-mendiants*—"the four beggars;" a popular French dessert.
† *Les charrettes y versent*—the carts are unloading.

Mlle. Thuillier had a face of fire; she was a superb sight; never had a sister's love assumed such a frenzied expression.

"To those who know her it is quite touching," remarked Mme. Colleville.

The glasses were filled, whereupon la Peyrade said:

"Let us drink to something sublime!"

All looked up in astonishment.

"To Mademoiselle Brigitte."

All arose and with one voice cried: "*Vive Mademoiselle Thuillier.*"

After a toast by Phellion to M. Minard and his wife, Thuillier proposed:

"The King and the royal family; I add nothing, the toast says all."

"To the election of my brother," said Mlle. Thuillier.

La Peyrade was the next on his feet.

"To the ladies, that bewitching sex to whom we owe our happiness, not to mention our mothers, sisters, and wives."

After the hilarity caused by this toast, Colleville, already gay, exclaimed:

"Wretch! you have stolen my speech."

After some conversation and a few unimportant toasts, Céleste Colleville said, timidly:

"Mamma, will you allow me to give a toast?"

The poor girl had seen the puzzled face of her godmother; she, the mistress of the house, had the expression of a dog which is in doubt which master to obey; she consulted each countenance and was oblivious of herself, but the joy on a face so unaccustomed to its visits had the effect of a pale wintry sun behind a mist, which grudgingly shone through the flabby, faded features. Her ill-dressed hair and dingy attire—combined with her woeful look of joy—stimulated the affection of the young Céleste, who, alone in the world, knew the value of that woman's heart; suffering from all, yet consoling herself in God and this child alone.

"Let the dear child give her little toast," said la Peyrade to Mme. Colleville.

"Go on, my daughter," said Colleville; "we have the hermitage yet to drink, and it's hoary with age."

"To my good godmother!" said the girl, inclining her glass respectfully before Mme. Thuillier and holding it toward her.

The poor woman, quite scared, looked through a veil of tears, alternately, at her sister and her husband; but her position in the family was so well understood, and the homage paid by innocence to weakness had such a lovely side to it, that the emotion was general; every man rose and bowed to Mme. Thuillier.

"Ah! Céleste, I wish I had a kingdom to lay at your feet!" said Félix Phellion.

"Now, it's my turn," said Colleville, posing like an athlete. "Listen to me. To friendship! Empty your glasses; refill your glasses. Good. To the fine arts! the flower of social life. Empty your glasses; refill your glasses. To another such festival the day after the election!"

"What is in that little bottle?" asked Dutocq of Mlle. Thuillier.

"This," said she, "is one of my three bottles of Madame Amphoux liqueur; the second is for Céleste's wedding, and the last for the christening of her first child."

The dinner ended with a toast by Thuillier, suggested to him by Théodose, when the Malaga sparkled in the glasses like so many rubies.

"Colleville, gentlemen, drank to *friendship;* for myself, I drink, in this generous wine, *to my friends.*"

Cheers greeted this speech; but Dutocq remarked aside to Théodose:

"It is murder to pour such Malaga down such a class of throats."

"Ah! if we could only imitate this, my dear," said Minard's wife to her spouse, after tasting it; "what fortunes we could make."

"Yes," answered Minard, "but ours is made."

"Don't you think, sister, that we had better take coffee in the salon?" said Brigitte to her sister.

Mme. Thuillier obediently assumed the air of mistress of the house and arose.

"Ah! you are a great wizard," said Flavie Colleville to la Peyrade, as she took his arm.

"And yet I only care to bewitch you," replied he.

"Madame Phellion will play the piano," cried Colleville. "We must all dance to-night—the bottles, Brigitte's twenty-sous-pieces, and our little girls. I'll go and fetch my clarionet." He handed his empty coffee-cup to his wife, and smiled to see her such a good friend of la Peyrade's.

"What have you done and said to my husband?" asked Flavie of the seducer.

"Well, since you tell me all your secrets," said he, letting himself out in a spirit of gayety, always Provençal and always apparently so charming, so natural, so unaffected, "I won't conceal from you a pain that I have in my heart." He led her to a window and said, smiling:

"Colleville, poor man, has seen in me the artist crushed by all these bourgeois; silent before them because I was misunderstood, misjudged, repelled; but he felt the heat of the sacred fire which was devouring me. Yes, I am," said he in a tone of intense conviction, "an artist in words after the manner of Berryer; I could make juries weep by weeping myself, for I am as nervous as a woman. Then your husband, who looks upon the middle-classes with horror, made game of them with me; we began by laughing, but eventually became serious, and he found me as strong as himself. I told him of the scheme to make *something* of Thuillier; I showed him all the good he could do himself by becoming a political manikin, if only, said I, to be called a *de* Colleville, and to put your charming wife in the position I should like to see her, as the wife of a receiver-general, whence you could become a deputy. Good reasons disguised in a jest have the knack of penetrating deeper into some minds than if soberly stated; so Colleville and I became the best friends in the world. Don't you remember at table he said: 'Wretch, you have stolen my speech.' By the end of the evening we shall be theeing and thouing. I shall before long invite him to a jolly party, such as always allures artists who have become broken to domestic rule, and get him to kick over the traces. It will make us as solid friends as he and Thuillier are, or more so, for I have told him that Thuillier will be bursting with jealousy when he sees his rosette. Colleville will adopt me; so that I may visit at your house by his invitation. But what wouldn't you make me do? Lick lepers, swallow live toads, seduce Brigitte— yes, I would impale my heart on that picket-fence, if I needed her for a crutch to drag me to your knees!"

"You are, I must own, a most extraordinary man."

"Oh, no; my smallest as well as my greatest efforts are but the reflection of the flame which you have kindled; I intend to become your son-in-law, so that we may never part. My wife, oh, my God! she could be no more than a machine to bear children; but the supreme being, the divinity, will be you," he whispered in her ear.

"You are Satan!" said she, with a sort of terror.

"No, I am something of a poet, like all the people of my country. Come, be my Joséphine. I'll come and see you to-morrow at two o'clock; I long to see the pearl in its shell."

He slipped cleverly away after these words, not giving her a chance to reply.

Flavie, who in all her life had not been made love to in the language of romance, sat still, but happy; her heart palpitated; she told herself it was difficult to resist such influence. Théodose was admirably dressed and the only person present who had the deportment of a gentleman; in fact, he was the only one with any style or air among the now rapidly arriving guests.

Madame Prou, *née* Barniol, came with two school-girls aged seventeen, confided to her motherly care by families residing in Martinique. M. Prou, a professor of rhetoric in a school managed by priests, was of the Phellion model, but instead of expanding on the surface in phrases and demonstrations, and posing as an example, he was dry and sententious. He enjoyed much influence in that part of the quarter bounded by the boulevard of Mont-Parnasse, the Luxembourg, and the Rue de Sèvres. Phellion at once button-holed him on behalf of Thuillier.

Félix, still under the deep emotion imparted by Céleste's generous act and the cry that sprang from the girl's heart, though no one but Mme. Thuillier still bore it in mind, became inspired by one of those ingenious impulses which form the artlessness of true love; but he was not to the "manor born;" mathematics had made him rather absent-minded. He stationed himself by Mme. Thuillier, imagining that Céleste would be thither attracted. This ruse was admirably successful.

"Who but must love Céleste?" said Félix to Mme. Thuillieur.

"Poor little dear, no one in the world loves me but her," replied the poor slave, restraining her tears.

"Oh! madame, we both love you," said this candid Mathieu Laensberg, smiling.

"What are you talking about?" asked Céleste of her godmother.

"My child," replied the pious victim, drawing her godchild down to her and kissing her on the forehead, "he said you both loved me."

"Do not be angry at my presumption, mademoiselle," said the future candidate for the Academy of Sciences; "but allow me the honor of realizing it. It is my nature—injustice revolts me deeply. Yes, the Saviour of the world was right in promising the future to the meek heart, to the sacrificed lamb. But innocence is the sole consolation of the martyr. Happy the man whom you will choose."

"Dear godmother, with what eyes does Monsieur Félix see me?"

"He properly appreciates you, my little angel; I shall pray God for both of you."

Noticing her daughter glowing with happiness, exhaling rapture through every pore of her face, beautiful in the loveliness of the first roses of an indirect declaration, Flavie felt a pang of jealousy in her heart; she went to Céleste and whispered to her:

"You are not behaving at all nicely, my daughter, everybody is observing you; you will compromise yourself by talking so long with Monsieur Félix without knowing whether it has our approval."

"But, mamma, my godmother is here."

"Ah! pardon me, dear friend," said Mme. Colleville, "I did not see you."

"Like all the rest of the world."

This retort stung Mme. Colleville, who took it as a barbed arrow. She glanced haughtily at Félix, and said to Céleste: "Sit there, my daughter," seating herself beside Mme. Thuillier and pointing to a chair at her side.

Madame Thuillier sat pensively listening to the noise of a witch's Sabbath made by her sister-in-law, a real horse at hard work, lending her hand to help the two servants clear the table, take everything out of the dining-room, to make room for the dancers, vociferating like the captain of a frigate on his quarter-deck while preparing for an attack: "Have you any currant syrup? Run out and buy some orgeat!" or, "There's not enough glasses! and too little *eau rougie!* (wine and water); take those six bottles of *vin ordinaire* and make more. Keep an eye on Coffinet, the porter, that he

IT WERE USELESS TO PAINT A BALL OF THIS KIND

doesn't get at anything! Caroline, my girl, wait at the sideboard; you shall have a slice of ham if they keep it up till the morning hours. But no waste, mind you. Keep an eye on everything. Pass the broom here, and do you put more oil in the lamps; don't have any accidents. Arrange the remains of the dessert, so as to make a show on the buffet! Why doesn't my sister come and give us a lift? I can't think what she's about—a dawdle, her! My God! how slow she is! Here, take away these chairs; they need all the room they can get!"

The announcement of a dance at the Thuilliers had got noised about in the Luxembourg. As a consequence the salon was full of Barniols, Collevilles, Phellions, Laudigeois, and the like.

"And you, Brigitte, are you ready?" said Colleville, rushing into the dining-room; "it is nine o'clock. They are packed as close as herrings in the salon; the whole faubourg Saint-Antoine is rushing in. Can't we move the piano in here?"

It were useless to paint a ball of this kind. The toilettes, faces, conversations, were all in keeping with one detail which will surely suffice the least lively imagination; they were all of one character and color. They passed round, on tarnished shabby trays, common glasses filled with wine, *eau rougie*, and *eau sucrée*. At longer intervals appeared the trays bearing *orgeat* and syrups. There were five card-tables for twenty-five players and eighteen dancing couples. At one o'clock in the morning Mme. Thuillier, Mlle. Brigitte, Mme. Phellion and her husband were dragged into a vulgar country dance known as *la Boulangère*, in which Dutocq figured with a veil over his head, and looking like a Kabyl.* When this interminable round had lasted for a full hour, and Brigitte announced supper, they wished to carry her in triumph; but she perceived the necessity of hiding a dozen bottles of old Bur-

* Berber, native of Barbary.

gundy wine. Everybody was so well pleased, matrons as well as maids, that Thuillier was able to say :

"Well, this morning, we little thought we should have such fun to-night."

"One never has so much pleasure," said Cardot, "than at this sort of impromptu dance. Don't talk to me of parties at which each one is on his ceremony!"

This opinion is an axiom among the middle-classes.

"Ah, bah!" said Madame Minard, "for me I love my papa's way. I love those of my mamma."

"We did not mean that remark for you, madame ; at your home pleasure elects to reign," said Dutocq.

The *Boulangère* finished. Théodose drew Dutocq from the buffet, where he was preparing to eat a slice of tongue, and said :

"Let's be off, for to-morrow we must see Cérizet ; we need to think over that affair ; it is not quite so easily managed as Cérizet seems to think."

"And why?" asked Dutocq, eating his tongue sandwich as he went toward the salon.

"But you know the laws?"

"I know enough to be aware of the dangers of the business. If the notary wants the house and we filch it from him, he has ways and means by which to recover it ; he can put himself in the skin of a recorded creditor. By the present state of the law of mortgage, when a house is sold at the behest of creditors, and if the amount realized is not sufficient to pay all creditors, they have the right to bid it in ; and the notary, once caught, will be twice shy."

"This has been one of the greatest days in our life," said Brigitte to her brother, when, at half-past two o'clock in the morning, they were alone in the deserted salon. "What an honor to be chosen by your fellow-citizens."

"You don't tumble to one fact, though, Brigitte ; we owe all this, my child, to one man——"

"To whom?"

"Our friend la Peyrade."

It was not on the next day, Monday, but the next but one, Tuesday, that Dutocq and Théodose called on Cérizet, it having been called to the latter's attention the fact that on Sundays and Mondays he took advantage of a total lack of business, these days being devoted to dissipation by the common people. The house to which their steps were bent is a striking feature of the faubourg Saint-Jacques. It has never been known, and no commission has inquired into, why or for what reason or cause certain quarters of Paris sink into vice and vulgarity, morally as well as physically; how the old centres of the Court and the church, the Luxembourg and the Latin quarter, have become what they are to-day, in spite of the finest palaces in the world, in spite of the soaring dome of Sainte-Geneviève, that of Mansard's on the Val-de-Grâce, and the charms of the Jardin des Plantes. One asks himself why the elegance of life has shaken the dust of that quarter from off its feet—the Phellion and Thuillier houses swarm here, and boarding-houses displace the formerly so numerous noble and religious edifices; and why mud and dirty forms of trade and poverty have fastened on this hill, instead of spreading out upon the plain beyond the old and noble city. Once dead, the angel whose beneficent sway had blessed this quarter, the lowest form of usury rushed in. To the Councilor Popinot succeeded a Cérizet; and, stranger still, a good matter for study, the effects produced, socially speaking, were little different. Popinot loaned without interest, and was willing to lose; Cérizet lost nothing, and compelled the unfortunates to work hard and learn wisdom. The poor adored Popinot, but they did not hate Cérizet. Here is the lowest round of Parisian finance. At the top the firm of Nucingen, the Kellers, the du Tillets, the Mongenods; a little further down, the Palmas, the Gigonnets, the Gobsecks; still lower, the

Samanou, the Chaboisseaus, the Barbets; then, ending, after the pawnshops, that king of usurers, who spreads his nets at the corners of the streets to entangle all the various forms of misery and miss none—that sharp spider, Cérizet.

This house, blotched with nitre, the walls of which oozed a fetid humidity, was enameled all over with huge slabs of mold. Standing at the corner of the Rue des Postes and the Rue des Poules, it showed a first floor partly occupied by a vendor of the commonest kind of wine, a bright-red bottle painted as a sign; the windows decorated with red calico curtains; furnished with a leaden counter and armed with formidable bars.

Above the door of an odious court hung a frightful lantern, on which was painted "Night Lodgings Here." The outer walls displayed iron cross-clamps, apparently to show the insecurity of the building of which the wine merchant was the owner, and who occupied the entresol in addition to the store. Madame the Widow Poiret (*née* Michonneau) kept the furnished rooms, which composed the second, third, and fourth floors, arranged in chambers for the use of laborers and the poorest class of students.

Cérizet occupied one room on the first floor and one in the entresol, to which he ascended by an interior stairway; this upper room looked out upon a horrible courtyard, from which arose mephitic odors. Cérizet gave forty francs for his breakfast and dinner; he thus conciliated the hostess of this boarding-house; he made himself acceptable to the wine-dealer, too, by procuring him an enormous trade in his wines and spirits, profits realized before the sun was up. The counting-rooms of the Sieur Cadenet were opened even before those of Cérizet, who began his operations on Tuesday, by three o'clock in the morning in summer and five in winter.

The opening of the Great Market, which so many of his male and female clients attended, determined Cérizet's early hours for his frightful transactions. Cadenet, in consideration of the custom of Cérizet's clients, had rented to him the two rooms for eighty francs a year, giving him a lease for twelve years, and which Cérizet alone had the right to break, without paying indemnity, at three months' notice. Every day Cadenet brought up a bottle of excellent wine for the dinner of this precious tenant; and when Cérizet was "short," he had only to say: "Cadenet, my good fellow, let me have a hundred crowns." But he always faithfully repaid them. Cadenet was said to have proof that the Widow Poiret had put in Cérizet's hands some two thousand francs for investment; this may explain his rapid increase in business.

The "lender by the little week" was perfectly safe in his den, where he could have, if needed, strong assistance. For on certain mornings there would be not less than sixty to eighty people, men and women, either in the wine-dealer's, in the court, sitting on the stairs, or in his office, for the distrustful Cérizet would only admit six persons at once. The first comers were the first served, and, as each one was only admitted according to his number, the wine-dealer or his head-helper chalked it on the men's hats and on the backs of the women.

They would sell, like cabmen in a line, one number high up for one lower down, with something to boot. On certain days when business was pressing in the Market, a head number would fetch as much as a glass of brandy and a sou. The numbers as they went out of Cérizet's office bawled out the succeeding numbers, and, if any dispute arose, it was soon quieted by Cadenet saying:

"When you succeed in getting the police here, will you get your advances? *He* would shut up shop."

Cérizet's name was *He*. When, in the course of the day, an unfortunate, despairing woman, without an atom of bread in the house, seeing her children pale with hunger, would come to borrow ten or twenty sous:

"Is *He* here?" she would anxiously ask the wine-dealer or his head-helper.

Cadenet, who seemed like an angel to these poor mothers, would reply:

"He told me you were an honest woman and that I might give you forty sous. You know what you must do." And, a strange thing, *He* was blessed, even as had been Popinot before him.

But they cursed Cérizet on Sunday morning, when accounts were straightened up; they cursed him still more on Saturday, when it became necessary to work in order to pay the sum borrowed, with interest. Still he was Providence, he was God, from Tuesday to Friday, every week.

His office was formerly the kitchen of the next story; the floor was bare, smoke still discolored the once whitewashed walls and ceiling, and the stone floor retained and exhaled moisture. The window was furnished with inside shutters of iron and enormously thick, and fastened with an iron-bar. The door commanded respect by a similar armor.

At the end of the room, in an angle, was a spiral stair brought from some demolished store and bought by Cadenet on the Rue Chapon, who had fitted it into the entresol. To prevent all communication with the second floor, Cérizet had stipulated that the door opening on to the landing should be walled up. The place had thus became a fortress. He shaved himself before a glass on the mantel. He owned two pairs of muslin sheets and six cotton shirts; the rest of his attire being of equal elegance. Once or twice Cadenet had seen Cérizet dressed as a fashionable dandy; so it must be that he kept hidden away in the bottom drawer of his bureau a complete disguise in which he could go to the opera, or see society and yet not be recognized, for, only for his voice, Cadenet would have asked him: "What can I do for you?"

Cérizet, Cadenet and his two helpers lived in the bosom of frightful misery, but preserved the calmness of undertakers in the midst of the heirs of the deceased, of old sergeants of the

Guard among heaps of the dead; they no more shuddered when they heard the cries of the famishing or of despair than do surgeons groan when they hear their patients in the hospitals; they said, as the soldiers and the nurses said: "Have patience, a little courge! Be brave! No use to kill yourself! One can get used to anything; have a little reason!"

Although Cérizet took the precaution of hiding the money necessary for his morning's operations in the double seat of the chair on which he sat, never taking out more than one hundred francs at a time, and always between the exit of one batch of clients and the entry of another—keeping his door locked and not opening it until the cash was in his pocket— as a matter of fact, he need have feared nothing from the numerous despairs which found their way to this rendezvous of money. Undoubtedly there are many different ways of being honest and virtuous, and the "Monograph of Virtue"* has no other basis than this social axiom. Cérizet depended on the honor of his clients; he never made a mistake, nor did his poor borrowers; it was the reciprocity of capital and desires. Many times Cérizet, who was born one of the people, had corrected one week the unseen error of a previous week, to the benefit of some poor devil who had not discovered it. He went by the name of dog, but he was an honest dog; his word in the midst of that city of sorrows was sacred. A woman died who owed thirty francs.

"There are my profits," said he to the assemblage, "and you howl at me! Nevertheless I shall not trouble the kids; in fact, Cadenet has taken them bread and piquette" (wine-lees or paltry wine).

Since that, a smart business stroke, it was said of him in the faubourgs:

"He's not such a bad sort."

* The *Monographie de la vertu;* a work in the same vein as the *Physiologie du marriage*, on which the author has been working since 1833, when it was first announced.—AUTHOR'S NOTE.

The "loan by the little week," as heard from Cérizet's customers, is not, taking all things into account, so cruel a system as the pawnbroker's. Cérizet gave ten francs on Tuesday on condition that he received twelve on Sunday morning. In five weeks he doubled his capital, but he had frequent compositions. His kindness consisted in accepting, from time to time, eleven francs and fifty centimes, and the rest stood over. When he loaned fifty francs for sixty to a little huckster, or a hundred francs for one hundred and twenty to a vendor of peat, he ran some risk.

When they arrived at the Rue des Poules by way of the Rue des Postes, Théodose and Dutocq saw a great crowd of men and women, and, by the light from the lamps in the wine-dealer's windows, they were horrified at seeing that mass of red faces, seamed, grimy, and haggard; dejected by suffering, withered, distorted, bloated with wine, emaciated with spirits; some resigned, some threatening, some jeering, some sarcastic, and others stupefied, all clad in the miserable rags which no caricaturist can surpass in his most extravagant phantasies.

"I shall be recognized," said Théodose. "We were foolish to come here in the midst of his business."

"Then let us all meet at the Cheval Rouge, on the Tournelle quay," replied Dutocq. "It won't matter about them seeing me."

Dutocq went alone into the midst of that congress of beggars, and he heard his own name from mouth to mouth, for it was almost impossible that some jail-bird should be met who was not familiar with his justice-court, just as sure as Théodose would have encountered some client.

In these quarters the justice of the peace is the supreme tribunal; all legal authority is centred in his court, especially since legislation has made his decisions final in all cases involving not more than one hundred and forty francs. A passage was made for the clerk, who was not feared less than the Judge himself. He saw women on the stairs, a horrible display like flowers ranged on stages, amongst them were some young, pale, and suffering. The diversity of colors in fichus, bonnets, dresses, and aprons rendered the comparison more exact, perhaps, than it should be. Dutocq was nearly asphyxiated when he opened the door of the room in which already sixty persons had left their odors.

"Your number! the number!" shouted a host of voices.

"Hold your jaw!" cried a hoarse voice from the street, "that's the judge's pen!"

"It can't be done like that, Daddy Lantimèche," Cérizet was saying to a tall, old man, who appeared to be about seventy, standing in front of him, a red woolen cap in his hand, showing a bald head, and a breast covered with white hairs visible through his shabby blouse. "Tell me what you want a hundred francs for? even to get back one hundred and twenty it can't be let loose like a dog in a church."

The five other customers present, among whom were two women nursing infants, one suckling her baby, the other one knitting, burst out laughing.

When he saw Dutocq, Cérizet rose respectfully and went hastily to meet him.

"You can have time to think about it; for, see you, I'm not satisfied—a hundred francs demanded by a blacksmith's helper."

"But it's to start an invention," cried the old workman.

"An invention and a hundred francs, you don't know the laws; it takes two thousand francs," said Dutocq. "You must get a patent, you need backers."

"That's the truth," said Cérizet, who reckoned on such chances; "go now, daddy, and come again to-morrow morning at six o'clock; we can't talk invention before others."

Cérizet listened to Dutocq, whose first words were:

"If all goes right, half profits."

"Why did you get up as early as this to say that to me?"

asked the distrustful Cérizet, much annoyed at the mention of half profits. " You could have seen me at the office."

And he looked askance at Dutocq, who, while telling him how matters stood, speaking of Claparon and the necessity of pushing Théodose's affair as rapidly as possible, seemed confused.

"You could have seen me at the office," replied Cérizet, as he conducted Dutocq to the door.

"There's one," said he, resuming his seat, "who seems to me to have blown out the lantern so that I may not see clearly. Well, I'll give up that job as copyist. Ah! your turn, my little mother!" he exclaimed. "You invent children! That's amusing, too. It's a good enough game, and they all do it."

It is useless to recount the conversation which took place between the three associates, the more so as they alluded to the arrangements to be the basis of certain confidences between Théodose and Mlle. Thuillier; but it is essential to say that la Peyrade's craftiness seemed to dismay Cérizet and Dutocq. Now, the banker of the poor, finding his antagonists such strong players, resolved to make sure of his own stake at the first chance. To win the game by cheating expert gamblers is an inspiration to the votaries of the green-cloth. From this came the terrible blow that la Peyrade was destined to receive.

He had his hands filled in following the twinings of Dutocq and Cérizet; they were both experts in humbug. An immobile face like Talleyrand's would have made them break at once with the Provençal, it was necessary to make a show of confidence and of playing above-board, which is certainly the acme of art. To delude the pit is an every-day triumph, but to take in Mlle. Mars, Frédérick Lemaître, Potier, Talma, and Monrose is the height of acting.

The day after this conference la Peyrade dined with the

Thuilliers, and on the pretext of paying a visit carried off his wife, leaving Théodose with Brigitte. Neither Théodose, nor Thuillier, nor his sister were duped by this comedy; but the old buck of the Empire gave it the name of diplomacy.

" Young man, do not take advantage of my sister's innocence, respect it," said Thuillier as he departed.

To get the upper hand of Brigitte would be in this long struggle like carrying the great redoubt of the Moskowa. But it was necessary to possess that old maid as the devil was said to possess man in the Middle Ages, and to prevent any possible awakening by her. He had studied and measured the ground for the past three days. Flattery, that almost infallible means in adroit hands, would not be listened to by a woman who for a very long time had known that she was without beauty. But to a man of powerful will nothing is impregnable; the Lamarques could never have failed to carry Caprea.

"You have shown your affection for us," said Brigitte, when they were alone.

"Your brother has told you?"

"No; he merely said you wished to speak with me."

"Yes, mademoiselle, for you are the man of the family; but in reflecting over this matter I find a number of dangers, such as a man risks only for those who are near and dear to him. A whole fortune is involved, thirty to forty thousand francs a year, and not in the least speculative—a freehold. The need of giving a fortune to Thuillier fascinated me from the first. I told him frankly that in working for his interests I advanced my own, as I will later also explain to you. If he wishes to be a deputy, two things are absolutely necessary: to comply with the law as to assessment, then to win some kind of celebrity for his name. If I push my devotion to the extent of assisting him in writing a book on some political question—no matter what—so as to get him that celebrity, I must needs think of his property also; it would be absurd of you to give him this house."

"What! for my brother? Why, I'd put it in his name to-morrow," exclaimed Brigitte; "you don't know me."

"I do not entirely know you," said la Peyrade, "but I know enough to cause me to regret that I did not acquaint you with the whole business since its origin."

"But this business," said Brigitte, "of what nature are the obstacles?"

"Mademoiselle, the difficulty is existent in my conscience—I certainly could not help you in this matter without first consulting my confessor. To the world, oh, the affair is perfectly legal, and I am—you understand me—an authorized barrister, a member of the bar controlled by most rigid rules; I am incapable of suggesting an enterprise which might give rise to blame. My excuse, first, is that I don't accept a single liard out of it."

Brigitte was on a gridiron, her face was aflame; she broke her wool, knotted it together again, and did not know how to contain herself.

"One can't do that," said she; "in this day a rental of forty thousand francs means a property costing one million eight hundred thousand francs."

"Well, you shall see the property and estimate its probable revenue, of which I can make Thuillier the owner for fifty thousand francs."

"Well, then, you only get us that!" exclaimed Brigitte, wound up to the highest pitch by the key of her avarice. "Go on, my dear Monsieur Théodose——"

She stopped short.

"Well, mademoiselle."

"You will perhaps have labored to your own advantage."

"Ah! if Thuillier has told you my secret, I leave your house."

Brigitte looked up.

"Has he told you that I love Céleste?"

"No; as I'm an honest woman!" exclaimed Brigitte; "but I myself was just about to speak of her."

"And to offer her to me? Oh! no, may God forgive us; I want her only of her free choice. No, no, all I ask of you is your good-will and favor. Promise me that, treat me as a son; should you do this I will abide by your decision in this matter; I will not consult my confessor. You can help me in so many ways, you could attend to the details of our fortune, so that I need not neglect anything that would tend to my political career. I admired you on Sunday evening. How you made things fly; I guess the dining-room was cleared out in ten minutes. Without leaving your home, all was at hand for the refreshments and supper. 'There,' said I to myself, 'is a mistress-woman.'"

Brigitte's nostrils dilated, she breathed in the words of the young lawyer. He looked askance at her to enjoy his triumph; he had twanged the chord responsive.

"Now here is where we stand, my dear aunt, for you are an aunt in some sort——"

"Hush you, naughty fellow!" said Brigitte, "and go on."

"Well, the matter crudely is this: remark that I compromise myself by telling you these secrets, for they are confided to me as an attorney. We are both, therefore, as it were, committing a crime—*lèse-cabinet* or legal high treason. A notary of Paris (although the law does not permit speculation by notaries) was in copartnership with an architect; they bought land and built upon it; just now they are embarrassed—the bottom dropped out of things. Among these houses is an excellent one not quite finished; this must consequently be sold at a great loss, so that the price asked is only one hundred thousand francs, although the land and building cost at the least four hundred thousand. The interior to complete will run up to fifty thousand more. Now, by its location, this house, when completed, will bring in at least forty thousand francs, exclusive of taxes."

T

"Well, and of what does the difficulty consist?"

"Just this: the notary wants to save this piece of cake from the wreck he must abandon; under the name of a friend he is the creditor who petitions for the sale of the property by the assignee of the bankruptcy. It has not gone into court, the costs would count up so rapidly; the sale is by voluntary agreement. This notary's friend is a client of mine; my client is a poor devil who says to me: 'There's a fortune to be made out of that house by tricking the notary.'"

"That's fair in trade," said Brigitte quickly.

"If this were the only obstacle," answered Théodose, "it would be as a friend of mine said to a pupil of his who complained of the difficulties encountered in producing a masterpiece of painting: 'My dear boy, were it not so footmen would paint.' But, mademoiselle, if we get the better of this notary —for he deserves it, he has compromised many private fortunes—it might be hard to do it at a second turn. When one purchases real estate, that is at a low price at forced sale, the mortagees have the right, until the expiration of a certain fixed time, to buy it in; that is to offer a larger sum and keep the property. If this trickster can't be tricked as to the sale being a genuine one and hindered from raising the price until the time limit expires, well, then, some other scheme must be worked. But is this business legal? Shall a man undertake such for the benefit of a family he seeks to enter? That is a question my mind has been revolving for the past three days."

It must be admitted that this made Brigitte pause; Théodose put forth the last resource:

"Take to-night for reflection; to-morrow we will talk it over."

"Listen, my boy," said Brigitte, looking almost lovingly at the lawyer; "the first thing is to see the house. Where is it?"

"Near the Madeleine. In ten years that will be the heart of Paris. And, you know, land has been in request there since 1819; du Tillet the banker made his fortune there. Birotteau, the perfumer, Roguin, the notary, were ruined by speculating there too wildly."

"Can we go there to-morrow?"

"Dear aunt, I am at your command."

"Mercy me! don't call me that before folk. As to this business," she went on, "one must see the house before deciding."

"It has six stories; nine windows in front, a fine courtyard, four stores and stands on a corner. Oh! that notary is smart. But events may occur that will depreciate the Funds, one hundred and twenty-two, it is a fabulous price; I should hurry to sell your own and Madame Thuillier's and purchase this fine piece of property for Thuillier; and you could recover the fortune of that poor, pious creature by the savings from the rental."

Brigitte licked her lips; she saw how she might keep her own fortune intact, and enrich her brother by making this use of Mme. Thuillier's fortune.

"My brother is right," said she to Théodose, "you are a remarkable man, you will go far——"

"And he will march before me," replied Théodose, with an artlessness that captivated the old maid.

"Till to-morrow, then, toward noon, when we will view the house," said Brigitte, holding out her hand for Théodose to shake; but he pressed upon it a kiss, respectful and tender.

"Adieu, my boy," said she, as she reached the door; "it is God himself who has placed him in our house," she added to herself.

Five days later, in the month of April, the ordinance was issued for the nomination of a member of the Municipal Council; it was inserted in the "Moniteur" and placarded all about Paris. Brigitte was in a charming humor; she had verified the statements of Théodose; the property had been inspected by old Chaffaroux, a wealthy ex-contractor, an uncle of the Comtesse du Bruel, formerly Tullia the dancer, at one time a crony of Flavie Colleville's, who had been privately requested to do this office for Brigitte. Poor Grindot, the architect who was interested with the notary in this speculation, thought he was being employed in the interests of the contractor; the old fellow thought he was acting in the interest of his niece, Flavie, and he passed it as in his opinion only thirty thousand francs would be necessary to thoroughly finish the property. Thus in one week la Peyrade became Brigitte's god; she proved to him that fortune should be seized when it presented itself.

"Beside, if there is any sin in the affair," said she, as they stood in the middle of the garden, "you can confess it."

"There, my friend," said Thuillier, "what, the devil! a man owes himself to his relations."

"I have decided to do it," said la Peyrade. "Only, my good friend, and you too, my little aunt, keep absolute secrecy regarding me in this matter; and do not pay heed to the calumnies which the men I nip will serve out against me. I shall become, see you, a vagabond, ambitious, a swindler, a jesuit—can you hear such unmoved?"

"Be easy," said Brigitte.

From that day forward Thuillier was "my good friend." Good friend was the name given him by Théodose, with a variety of inflections of voice fitted to the occasion. My "little aunt," a name which vastly flattered Brigitte, was only used by him in the privacy of the family circle. The activity of the Thuillier workers was extreme. Great and small put their hands to the plough. On April 30th, Thuillier was elected by an immense majority and was proclaimed member of the Council-general of the department of the Seine. On May 1st he went to the Tuileries with the municipal body to congratulate the King on his fête day. He returned radiant. He had trod the path of Minard.

Ten days later a yellow placard announced the sale of the house after due publication; the price of upset being seventy-five thousand francs; the final adjudication to be made on July 1st. On this matter Claparon and Cérizet had an argument by which the latter pledged fifteen thousand francs to Claparon, if he kept the notary deceived until the expiration of the time needed to withdraw the property. This money was to go through la Peyrade's hands, being furnished by Mlle. Thuillier. The young notary, one of those who run after fortune instead of leisurely following it, saw another future ahead; he was trying to so manage his present affairs as to be at liberty to lay hands thereon. He had an interview with Claparon at midnight at which he offered him ten thousand francs to secure him, this amount only to be paid on receipt of a counter-deed from the nominal purchaser of the property. He felt sure of his man, for he knew that Claparon needed this amount to extricate himself from his liabilities.

Then Cérizet offered twelve thousand francs to Claparon and at once demanded fifteen thousand from la Peyrade, intending to put the balance in his own pocket. All these scenes between the four men were seasoned with pretty words about sentiment and honesty, on the honor that men owed to each other in business transactions. Meanwhile Théodose was assisting the new councilor in writing his masterly work; he became absolutely necessary to him; he was each day more convinced that Théodose's marriage to Céleste was a necessity. Now Théodose made an admirable "friend of the family;" he disarmed jealousy by his manner of effacing himself; he was more like a new piece of furniture than anything else; this allayed all the suspicion of the Mindards and Phellions, who fondly thought he had been found too light in the balance by both Brigitte and Thuillier.

"He thinks that perhaps my sister may put him in her will," said Thuillier to Minard, one day; "he doesn't know her, though."

This speech, prompted by Théodose, calmed Minard's distrust. It gave him what he wanted more than all, the contempt of his antagonists. For four months in succession his face maintained the torpid expression of a snake which has swallowed and is digesting its prey.

"And you," said he to Flavie, the evening before the purchase of the house, "don't you pity me? A man like me, creeping like a cat, having to choke down every retort, chewing my gall, submitting to your rebuffs."

"My friend, my child," said Flavie, who still remained undecided about him.

All this time Félix Phellion was instructing young Colleville. Flavie was for ever making for him either a purse, a pair of slippers, a cigar case, and so on for the happy young man. Old Phellion rubbed his hands as he realized how things were; he already saw Céleste wedded to his fine, his noble Félix.

As stated, the final sale was fixed for the end of July. Théodose, therefore, advised Mlle. Thuillier to be prepared with the necessary cash; accordingly, she sold out her own and sister-in-law's Funds. The catastrophe of the treaty of the four powers, an insult to France, but now a matter of history, is necessary to be retold that the reader may thus understand that Funds declined from July to the end of August; this was caused by the prospect of war, a fear which M. Thiers did too much to promote; they fell twenty francs and Three-per-cents went down to sixty. This also had an evil influence on real estate in Paris, which rapidly declined. All this caused Théodose to be regarded as a prophet. Thus, when the purchase was completed, Thuillier's importance was magnified tenfold. Meanwhile, Théodose, assured of his supremacy, put on a rather less servile manner. Brigitte and Thuillier said to him once:

"Nothing can take from you our esteem; in this house you are in your own home; the opinion of Minard and Phellion, which you seem to fear, is not of more value to us than a line by Victor Hugo. Let them talk; hold your head up!"

She saw her brother secure of his forty thousand francs per annum, exclusive of his pension; she had reinvested Mme. Thuillier's fortune in Three-per-cents at sixty, which brought her in twelve thousand francs. Her own balance was also thus invested and was of the annual value of ten thousand francs; for the future she would only invest in the Funds; she had now, herself, a total income of eighteen thousand francs, beside the house in which they lived and which she valued at eight thousand.

"We are worth quite as much as the Minards," she said.

"Don't be too ready to sing victory," said Théodose; "the right of exemption does not expire for a week yet. I have attended to your affairs, but my own are in an awful mess."

"My dear boy, you have friends!" cried Brigitte; "and if you ever need twenty-five louis, you can find them here."

Théodose at this speech exchanged a smile of meaning with Thuillier, who hastened to take him off, saying to him:

"Excuse my poor sister; she sees the world through the mouth of a bottle. But if you want twenty-five thousand francs, I will lend them to you—out of my first rents," he added.

"Thuillier, I have a rope around my neck," cried Théodose. "Ever since I have been a lawyer I have had to give acceptances. But mum, not a word," added Théodose, frightened himself at having let the cat out of the bag. "I'm in the clutches of scoundrels, but I hope to best them."

In telling this secret Théodose had a double purpose: first, to test Thuillier, next to avert a terrible blow, liable at any day to be dealt him in the secret, sinister struggle in which he was engaged. This was it:

In the midst of the deep poverty through which he had passed, none but Cérizet had gone to see him in the garret where, in cold weather, he had lain in bed for lack of clothes. He had but one shirt left. For three days he lived on one loaf of bread, carefully cut into measured pieces, and asking himself: "What next?" Just then his former protector appeared, just pardoned out of prison. Of the projects which these two men then formed before the fire of kindling-wood, one wrapped in his landlady's bed-quilt, the other in his infamy, it is needless to recapitulate. The following day, Cérizet, who had talked with Dutocq, returned, bringing with him a pair of trousers, a vest, coat, hat, and boots, all purchased in the Temple; then carried him off to dinner. The Provençal ate at Pinson's, Rue de l'Ancienne Comédie, half of a dinner costing forty-seven francs. At dessert, between two glasses of wine, Cérizet said to his friend:

"Will you sign acceptances for me for fifty thousand francs, giving yourself the title of barrister?"

"You couldn't raise five thousand francs on them," replied Théodose.

"That doesn't concern you; you'll pay all right; this is our business, or monsieur's who has just regaled us. It is an affair in which you risk nothing, but by which you will obtain the title of barrister, a good clientage, and the hand of a girl in marriage of the age of an old dog, and who is worth not less than twenty to thirty thousand francs a year. Neither Dutocq nor myself can marry her; we must rig you up, give you the air of an honorable man, feed and lodge you, and fix you up generally. Therefore, we shall need our guarantee. I don't say this for myself, but for monsieur, who will have the use of my name. We equip you as a pirate that does the white slave trade, eh! If we don't capture that *dot*, well, we'll try some other little scheme. Between ourselves we needn't handle things with tongs—that's sure. We'll give you instructions later. Here's the stamps."

"Waiter, a pen and the ink!" cried Théodose.

"That's your sort of man," said Dutocq.

"Sign 'Théodose de la Peyrade,' and add 'Barrister, Rue Saint-Dominique-d'Enfer,' under the words: 'Accepted for ten thousand francs.' We'll date the notes and sue you, of course secretly, so as to be able to capture and imprison your body. The privateer-owner must have some security when the captain and brig are at sea."

On the morrow the clerk of the judge served la Peyrade for Cérizet, secretly. The Tribunal of Commerce has hundreds of such cases every term. The strict rules of the Association of Barristers would cause the disbarring of a member liable to be committed to Clichy. Thus Cérizet and Dutocq had their measures taken to secure twenty-five thousand francs each out of Céleste's *dot*. Now, when Théodose signed the notes he only saw his living assured, but when he saw the horizon growing clearer, as he rose step by step to a higher position on the social ladder, then he wished to be rid of his two associates. Now, in asking twenty-five thousand francs of Thuillier he hoped to settle his notes to Cérizet on a fifty per cent. basis.

Up to the present neither of the three men had kicked or groaned. Each knew his own strength and recognized his danger. Equals in distrust, in watchfulness, and in apparent confidence; equals also in stolid silence and gloomy looks when mutual suspicion arose to the surface, betrayed by the play of their features or words. For two months past Théodose had gradually acquired the strength of a detached fortress. But Dutocq and Cérizet had under their skiff a mass of powder, the torch already alight; but the wind might blow out the match or the devil flood the mine.

A reaction of envy was gathering like an avalanche in Cérizet. Dutocq saw himself at the mercy of his copyist, who had become enriched. Théodose would have liked to burn his partners, if only he could be assured that their papers would be consumed with them. Théodose lived three lives in hell as he thought of how the cards might turn, then of his own game, and then of the future. His speech to Thuillier was the cry of despair; he had thrown his sounding-lead into the waters of the old bourgeois and had found there no more than twenty-five thousand francs.

"And," said he to himself, "perhaps nothing, one month hence."

He now hated the Thuilliers with a profound hatred. But he held Thuillier by the harpoon stuck into the man's vanity —that of the projected work, "Taxation and Redemption;" he intended rearranging the ideas of "The Globe" in its Saint-Simonism, and coloring them with his fervid Southern diction.

The evening before the right of redemption of equity expired Claparon and Cérizet proceeded thus: Cérizet, to whom the other had given the password and the address of the notary's retreat, went out to him, and said:

"One of my friends, Claparon, whom you know, has asked me to call upon you; he expects you to-morrow evening, you know where; he has the paper you expect from him; he will exchange it with you for the ten thousand francs, but I must be present, for of that amount five thousand belongs to me; I give you notice, monsieur, that a blank remains for the name."

"I shall be there," said the notary.

The poor devil waited the whole night with what agony one may imagine, for his safety or inevitable ruin were in the balance. But at sunrise, instead of Claparon, he saw an officer of the Tribunal of Commerce, who produced a judgment against him in due form, requiring him to accompany him to Clichy.

Cérizet had bargained with a creditor to deliver the unlucky notary up for one-half the amount of the debt. Out of the ten thousand he had reserved for Claparon he was compelled to disgorge six thousand to obtain his liberty.

Cérizet then went to the notary and said:

"Claparon is a scoundrel, monsieur; he received five thousand francs from the alleged purchaser of your house, which makes him the owner. Threaten him with disclosing his retreat to his creditors and to have him adjudged a fraudulent bankrupt, then he'll turn over half of it to you."

In his rage the notary wrote Claparon an abusive letter; he, in despair, feared arrest, and Cérizet promised to obtain a passport for him.

"You have played me many a trick, Claparon," said Cérizet; "but listen to me, then you can judge me. All I possess is one thousand crowns—I'll give you that. Go to America, and trade and make your fortune there, the same as I am trying to make mine here."

That very evening Claparon, cleverly disguised by Cérizet, left by the diligence for Havre. Thus Cérizet remained master of the fifteen thousand francs demanded by Claparon, and awaited Théodose with tranquillity. He had another string to his bow.

"The limit of the equity is passed," said Théodose, going himself to find Dutocq to get him to bring Cérizet to his office.

"You won't be able to settle this transaction anywhere but in Cérizet's place, since Claparon is in it," replied Dutocq.

Théodose went between seven and eight o'clock to this banker of the poor, whom the clerk had notified. They promenaded the miserable kitchen like two beasts in a cage, playing the scene thus:

"Have you brought the fifteen thousand francs?"

"No, but I have them home."

"Why, then, have not you them in your pocket?"

"I'll explain why," replied the advocate, who, between the Rue Saint-Dominique and the Estrapade, had laid out his course of action.

The Provençal, writhing on the gridiron to which his partners had bound him, had a bright idea which flashed up from the bosom of the hot coals. Peril at times has gleams of light.

"Good!" said Cérizet, "now the farce begins."

This was a sinister word and seemed to be forced through the nose with horrible accent.

"You have placed me in a most splendid position, and I shall never forget it, my friend," said Théodose, with emotion.

"Ah! that's it, eh!" said Cérizet.

"Listen to me; you don't know my intentions."

"So? truly!" replied the loaner by the little week.

"No."

"You don't intend to put up those fifteen thousand francs."

Théodose looked fixedly at Cérizet and shrugged his shoulders. These two things caused the latter to keep silence.

"Would you, in my position, knowing yourself within range of a cannon loaded with grape-shot, live thus without making an effort to end it? Listen to me. You are in a dangerous trade; some time you will be glad of good, solid protection in the courts of Paris. I, if I continue in my present course, shall become deputy attorney-general, maybe attorney-general, in three years' time. To-day I offer you a devoted friendship which will be of service to you. Here are my conditions."

"Conditions?" cried Cérizet.

"In ten minutes I will bring you twenty-five thousand francs for all the claims you hold against me."

"And Dutocq? And Claparon?" exclaimed Cérizet.

"Leave them in the lurch," said Théodose, in his friend's ear.

"How sweet!" replied Cérizet. "And you play this little three-card-monte, finding that you hold fifteen thousand francs that don't belong to you."

"But I add ten thousand to them. See here, you and I know each other."

"If you have power enough to get ten thousand francs out

of your bourgeois," said Cérizet, eagerly, "you can quite as easily ask fifteen. For thirty, I'm your man. Frankness for frankness."

"You ask the impossible," exclaimed Théodose. "At this moment, if you had Claparon to deal with, your fifteen thousand francs would be lost, for the house is Thuillier's now."

"I'll see what Claparon has to say," replied Cérizet, pretending to go and consult Claparon, mounting upstairs to the chamber whence he had just gone, bag and baggage, in a hack.

The five minutes during which Théodose heard what he believed to be the murmur of two voices was positive torture to him, for his whole life was the stake. Cérizet came down, a smile upon his lips, his eyes brilliant with an infernal malice, dancing with glee, he was a Lucifer in his gayety.

"I know nothing," said he, shrugging his shoulders; "but Claparon, he knows it all. He used to work hand in glove with some top-notch bankers. When I told him what you wanted he laughed and said: 'I don't doubt it.' To-morrow you will have to bring me those twenty-five thousand francs you offered me; and no less beside to redeem your acceptances, my boy."

"And why?" asked Théodose, who felt as if his backbone were liquefying; as though melted by the discharge of some interior electric shock.

"The house is ours."

"And how?"

"Claparon has formally bid it in under the name of a dealer, the first one to take proceedings against him, a little toad named Sauvaignou. Desroches, the attorney, has the matter in hand, and to-morrow morning you'll receive due notification. This business will compel me, Claparon, and Dutocq to raise the wind. What would become of me without Claparon? So I must forgive him. I forgive him; you may not believe it, my dear friend, but we actually embraced each other. Change your terms."

The last words were appalling, especially in the comment offered by the face of Cérizet, who was amusing himself by playing a scene from "Légataire," in the midst of which he studied attentively the Provençal's character.

"Oh! Cérizet, and I wished you so well!"

"See you, my dear," replied Cérizet, "between us this is needed," and he struck his heart, "of which you haven't the least bit. When you imagined you had us—then came the squeeze. I saved you from vermin and the horrors of starvation. You'll die like an idiot. We put you on the way to fortune, we put you inside a pretty society-skin, by which you could have grasped a fortune—and after all that! Well, now I know you; we tramp under arms."

"Then it is war," said Théodose.

"You fired first," said Cérizet.

"But if you demolish me—then farewell to all your hopes; and if you are not able to down me, you have an enemy in me."

"Exactly what I said to Dutocq yesterday," answered Cérizet, coolly. "But how can it be helped. We chose between the two—circumstances govern cases. I'm a pretty good fellow," he went on after a pause, "to-morrow bring me your twenty-five thousand francs and Thuillier shall retain the house. We'll help you at both ends, but you must pay—— Now after what has passed that's not so much amiss, eh?"

"Say to-morrow at noon," said the Provençal, "for there are a number of irons to heat."

"I'll endeavor my best with Claparon, but he's a pretty tough fellow when he's in a hurry."

"Oh, well! to-morrow then," said Théodose, in the tone of a man decided on his course.

"Good-morning, friend," said Cérizet in such a horrible nasal tone that degraded the most beautiful word in the language. "There goes a sucker," said he to himself, looking after Théodose passing down the street like a man in a daze.

As he left the idea came to him to go to Flavie and tell her everything. Southern natures are thus—strong up to a certain point of passion, then a collapse. He entered. Flavie was alone in her chamber; she saw Théodose and thought he had come to violate or kill her.

"What is the matter?" she cried.

"I—I— Do you love me, Flavie?" said he.

"Oh! can you doubt it?"

"But absolutely love me—even if I were a criminal?"

"Has he then killed somebody?" said she to herself; answering him with a nod of assent.

Théodose, happy at even grasping this branch of willow, burst into a passion of sobs, torrents of tears ran down his cheeks. Flavie went out and said to her maid: "I am not at home to any one;" then she closed all doors and returned to Théodose.

"I have but you in the world," cried he, seizing Flavie's hands and kissing them with a sort of fury. "If you only remain true to me—as the body is to the soul—then," he added, recovering himself with infinite grace, "I should have the courage."

He rose and paced the room.

"Yes, I can struggle; I will recover my strength, like Antæus, from a fall; with my own hands will I strangle the serpents that entwine me, that give me serpent-kisses, that slaver my cheeks, that suck my blood, my honor. Oh! that poverty! Far better have died than lived for this. A coffin is a softer bed in comparison than my present life. For eighteen months I have been *fed on bourgeois;* and after that horrid feast, when all is propitious of attaining an honest, fortunate life and a great future, when I was about seating myself at the banquet of society, the executioner taps me on the shoulder: 'Pay thy tithes to the devil, or die!' And I, shall I not trample them underfoot! and I, shall I not ram my arm down their throats to their very entrails! Ah! yes, I will, I will. See you, Flavie, my eyes are dry. And presently I shall laugh; I feel my power. Oh! say to me that you love me—say it once again. At this moment it sounds like the word 'Pardon' to the condemned?"

"You are terrible, my friend," said Flavie. "Oh! you bruise me."

She knew nothing of the meaning of this, but she fell on the couch half-dead, so agitated was she by this scene; and then Théodose flung himself on his knees before her.

"Pardon me! forgive me," he said.

"But what does it all mean!" she asked.

"They wish to ruin me. Oh! promise me Céleste; you shall see in what a glorious life I will make you a sharer. If you hesitate—well, that will mean you shall be mine; I will have you!"

He started up with such vehemence that Flavie, terrified, rose and walked away.

"Oh! my angel! at your feet, there—what a miracle. For certainly God is for me. Thanks, my good angel; great Théodosius! you have saved me."

Flavie admired that chameleon being; he was a fervent Catholic; he reverently crossed himself; it was as fine as the communion of Saint-Jérôme.

"Adieu," he said, in a melancholy voice; then rushed away; but in the street he turned and saw her at the window, he made a sign of triumph.

"What a man!" said she.

"My good friend," said Théodose, in a gentle, calm voice, almost coaxing, to Thuillier, after reaching home, "we have fallen into the hands of atrocious scoundrels; but I intend giving them a little lesson."

"What is wrong?" said Brigitte.

"Well, they want twenty-five thousand francs, and so, to get the better of us, have arranged to bid in the property. Put five thousand francs in your pocket and come with me; I'll assure you that house. I am making implacable enemies for myself," he exclaimed; "they seek to destroy me morally. Should you despise their calumnies and feel no change toward me, I shall be content. And what is this, after all? If I succeed, you have paid for the house one hundred and twenty-five thousand francs instead of paying one hundred and twenty."

"Will it happen again?" demanded Brigitte, uneasily, whose eyes dilated with a horrible suspicion.

"None but preferred creditors have the right of redemption, and as in this case there is but one that has used this right, we can take it quietly. His debt is but two thousand francs; but of course there are the costs of the lawyers in affairs like this which must be paid, and it wouldn't be amiss to give a perquisite of a thousand francs to the creditor."

"Go, Thuillier," said Brigitte; "take your hat and gloves, and get the cash—you know where."

"As I let that fifteen thousand francs go without result, I don't wish any more money to pass through my hands. Thuillier can pay it himself," said Théodose, when he found himself alone with Brigitte. "You have made twenty thousand francs by the bargain I made with Grindot; he thought he was assisting the notary, and you own a property which in five years will be worth nearly a million. It is at a corner of the boulevard."

Brigitte was uneasy, and listened exactly like a cat that smells mice under the floor. She looked very earnestly, and half doubtfully, at Théodose.

"What is it, little aunt?"

"Oh! I shall be in deadly fear until we are the real owners," she replied.

"Where are we going?" asked Thuillier.

"To Maître Godeschal, whom we must employ as our attorney."

"But we refused Céleste to him," exclaimed the old maid.

"The more reason for employing him," said Théodose.

Godeschal was Derville's successor, whose head-clerk he had been for more than ten years. There was the utmost intimacy between them, and ties like these in Paris form a true fraternity. They give and take, in all possible concessions, on the strength of the old proverbs: "Pass me the rhubarb, I'll pass the senna," or, "One good turn deserves another;" which is put in practice, in every profession, between ministers, officers, lawyers, merchants, everywhere, in fact, where enmity has not raised too strong barriers between the parties.

Now la Peyrade, a smart man, had not trailed his robe about the Palace so long without being aware how best these judicial amenities would serve his ends. It was eleven o'clock at night, but la Peyrade was not wrong in thinking that a newly fledged attorney would be found in his office, even late as it was.

"To what do I owe this visit, Monsieur l'Avocat?" said Godeschal, meeting la Peyrade.

Foreigners, provincials, men of the world, perhaps, are not aware that barristers (*avocats*) are to attorneys what generals are to marshals; a strict line of demarkation divides them. However venerable may be the attorney, however competent, he must go the barrister. The attorney is the one who lays out the campaign, who collects the munitions of war, and sets everything on the move; the barrister gives battle. It is not explained why the law gives the client two men instead of one, any more than it is known why the author needs both a printer and publisher. The Association of Barristers forbids its members to perform any act pertaining to that of the attorney. It very rarely happens that a barrister sets foot in an attorney's office, they meet in the Palace of Justice; but, in society, these barriers are thrown down, and sometimes barristers, in a position similar to that of la Peyrade, demean themselves by calling upon an attorney; but such occurrences are rare, and special urgency is urged as an excuse.

"Eh, *mon Dieu*," said la Peyrade, "it is a grave affair, and between us we must settle a very delicate piece of business. Thuillier is below in a carriage, and I come, not in my capacity as a barrister, but as a friend of Thuillier's. You are in a position in which you can be of immense service to him, and I told him that you were of too noble a soul (for you are a worthy successor of the great Derville) not to place at his direction your utmost capacity. This is the business."

After explaining wholly to his own advantage the trick which must, he said, be balked by ability, and lawyers meet more clients that lie than those who speak the truth, the barrister developed his plan of campaign.

"You ought, my dear maître, to go this very night to see Desroches, explain the whole plot, persuade him to send for this client of his to-morrow, this Sauvaignou; we between us three will properly confess him; if he wants a perquisite of say a thousand francs we'll stand that, in addition to five hundred each for yourself and Desroches, only provided that Thuillier obtains from Sauvaignou a letter renouncing his bid before ten o'clock to-morrow. This Sauvaignou, what does he want? His money! Well, then, such a peddler as that wouldn't resist the appeal of a thousand-franc bill, so especially if he is but the agent of a cupidity backing him. The fight between him and the others is no matter of concern to us. Come, do your best to get the Thuillier family out of this."

"I'll go at once and see Desroches," said Godeschal.

"No; not before Thuillier gives you a power of attorney and five thousand francs. Money talks in such a case as this."

La Peyrade's whole future and fortune lay in the outcome; for he had arranged to meet Godeschal at Desroches' office on the morrow at seven o'clock. It is not astonishing, therefore, that he disregarded the traditions of the bar and went thither to study Sauvaignou and to take part in the struggle.

As he entered and made his salutations he examined Sauvaignou. He was, as his name indicated, from Marseilles, and was foreman to a master-carpenter, or rather a kind of clerk of the works, standing between the master-carpenter and the workmen. The profit of the work consisted in what he could make out of the price paid him by the boss-carpenter and the labor he employed; he received no profit out of the materials used. The master-carpenter had failed. Sauvaignou at once appealed to the Tribunal of Commerce and had a lien placed on the property. He was a little, squat man, who wore a gray linen blouse, cap on head, and sat in an armchair in the office. Three bills of a thousand francs each laying before him, on Desroches' desk, showed la Peyrade that the engagement was over, and the attorneys worsted. Godeschal's eyes told the rest, and the glance which Desroches, the most feared of every attorney in Paris, cast on the "poor man's advocate" was like the blow of a pick in a grave. Stimulated by danger the Provençal was magnificent; he laid his hand on the three bills of one thousand each, and folded them as if about to put them into his pocket.

"Thuillier won't make the deal," said he to Desroches.

"Well, then, we are all agreed," replied the terrible attorney.

"Yes; your client must now hand over to us fifty thousand francs expended by us in furnishing the property, under the contract between Thuillier and Grindot. I did not inform you of that yesterday," said he, turning to Godeschal.

"You hear that?" said Desroches to Sauvaignou. "I shall not touch this case without being guaranteed."

"But, gentlemen," said the tradesman, "I cannot deal with this matter until I have seen the worthy man who gave me five hundred francs on account for having signed a power of attorney to him."

"Are you from Marseilles?" said la Peyrade to him, in Sauvaignou's own *patois*.

"Yes, monsieur."

"Well, poor devil, you, don't you see they wish to ruin you? Don't you know what to do? Pocket those three thousand francs, and, when the other fellow turns up, take out your rule and give him a pounding; tell him that he is a scoundrel, that he wants you to do his dirty work, that instead of doing this you revoke your power of attorney, and that, further, you will return him the five hundred francs the first week in which there are three Thursdays. Then be off to Marseilles with that three thousand five hundred francs and your savings. If anything goes wrong, let me know through these gentlemen; I'll get you out of the scrape, for not only am I a good Provençal, but also one of the leading barristers in Paris and the friend of the poor."

When the workman found a compatriot supporting his own wishes, also learning that he was really a barrister and able to do as promised, he signed the relinquishment, but stipulated for three thousand five hundred francs; this with the cross receipts settled the whole matter.

"You must at once acquaint your man with what is done and let him know that the proxy is revoked," said Desroches to Sauvaignou, as he sent the latter out through his back office.

"There is something behind all this," said Desroches to Godeschal after Théodose had gone.

"The Thuilliers get a magnificent freehold for next to nothing, that's all," Godeschal replied.

"La Peyrade and Cérizet seem to me like two divers fighting under the sea. What am I to tell Cérizet, who placed the affair in my hands?" asked Desroches as the barrister returned.

"Say that Sauvaignou forced your hand," said la Peyrade.

"And you fear nothing!" said Desroches pointedly.

"What, me? I have only given Cérizet a lesson."

"To-morrow I shall learn the whole," said Desroches to Godeschal; "no one blabs like a beaten man."

At eleven o'clock la Peyrade was in the court of the justice of the peace; he saw Cérizet come in, pale with rage, his eyes full of venom; he said in his ear, in a calm, firm voice:

"My friend, I also am a pretty good sort of fellow myself; I still hold these twenty-five thousand francs in bank-bills at your disposal; they are yours in exchange for my acceptances."

Cérizet gazed at the advocate of the poor, but was quite unable to make any answer; he was green; his bile had struck in.

"I am now incontestably a property owner," cried Thuillier when he returned from his notary, Jacquinot, the son-in-law and successor of Cardot. "No human power can now dispossess me; so they say!"

"Ah!" said Brigitte, "what an awful fright our dear Théodose gave me."

"Halloo! my best friend; but what do you suppose Cardot said? he asked me who had put me in the way of this stroke, and said that I ought to give him at least ten thousand francs as a present. As a fact, I do owe all to him."

"But he is the same as our own boy," said Brigitte.

"Poor fellow, I'll do him the justice of saying that he does not ask for anything."

"Well, my good friend," said la Payrade, who returned at three o'clock from the justice of the peace, "here you are, Mister Richman."

"And through you, my dear Théodose."

"And you, little aunt, have you come to life again? Ah! you were not so much afraid as I was. I put your interests before my own. *Tenez!* I couldn't breathe freely till eleven o'clock; still I am sure now of having two mortal enemies at my heels in the persons of the two whom I tricked for you. As I came home I wondered what had possessed me by your influence to make me commit this sort of crime! Whether the honor of being one of your family and becoming your son will ever efface from my conscience the stain I have put upon it."

"Bah! you can confess it," said Thuillier, the freethinker.

"Now," said Théodose to Brigitte, "you may pay in security the price of the house, eighty thousand francs, and thirty thousand to Grindot, in all, with the costs you have paid, one hundred and twenty thousand francs; the last twenty thousand make it in all one hundred and forty thousand. If you lease the whole to one tenant, ask for the last year's rent in advance, and reserve for me and my wife all the floor above the entresol. You can then even get forty thousand francs a year for twelve years. Then, if at any time you wish to move nearer the Chamber and desire to quit this quarter, you can stay with me; there are stables and coach-house, and so forth, pertaining to it. Meanwhile, Thuillier, I am going to get you the cross of the Legion of Honor."

Hearing this last promise, Brigitte cried:

"My faith! my boy, you've done our business so well that I shall leave you that of leasing the house."

"Don't abdicate, good aunt," said Théodose; "and God preserve me from taking one step without you. You are the good genius of the family. You will have forty thousand francs in hand inside of two months. And, beside all, that won't prevent Thuillier from handling his ten thousand in rent per quarter."

After having thrown this hope at the old maid, who was jubilant, he took Thuillier into the garden and said, without beating about the bush:

"My good friend, find some means to get me ten thousand francs from your sister; but don't let her know they are for me; tell her they are needed for the formalities of getting the Cross; that you know just who will get the cash."

"That's all right," said Thuillier; "I can repay her when I get my rents."

Théodose now hurried off to Mme. Colleville, to whom he cried as he entered:

"I have conquered; we shall have secured for Céleste a property worth a million francs, a life interest in which will be given in her marriage-contract by Thuillier; but keep my secret, or your daughter will be in demand by the peers of France. Now dress yourself and let us call upon the Comtesse du Bruel, she can get Thuillier the cross. While you are getting under arms I'll do a little courting of Céleste; you and I can talk in the carriage."

Now he had noticed that Félix and Céleste were alone in the salon; for her mother had full faith in Céleste. The couple were discussing religion. Félix, like most geometricians, chemists, mathematicians, and great naturalists, had subjected religion to reason; he saw in it a problem as insoluble as the squaring of the circle. In *petto* a deist, he still professed the religion of the majority of the French, without attaching more importance to it than to the new laws of July. There must needs be a God in heaven, the same as there must be a bust of the King in the mayor's office. The young girl professed a horror for atheism, and her confessor had told her that a deist was cousin-german to an atheist.

"Have you thought, Félix, of the promise you made me," asked Céleste, when Mme. Colleville had left them.

"No, my dear Céleste," replied Félix.

"Oh! to break a promise," cried she, dolefully.

"It would have been profanation," said Félix. "I love you so much, and with a tenderness which makes me so weak against your requests, that I promised something against my conscience. Conscience, Céleste, is our treasure, our strength, our mainstay. How could you desire me to go to church and kneel before a priest in whom I can only see a man. You would despise me if I obeyed you."

"So, my dear Félix, you will not go to church?" said Céleste, casting a tearful look at the man she loved. "If I were your wife, you would leave me to go alone, eh? You do not love me as I love you—for until this moment I have had in my heart a feeling for an atheist against the command of God?"

"An atheist!" cried Félix. "Oh! no. Listen, Celeste; I know of a certainty that there is a God; I believe that, but I have a much higher opinion of Him than your priests have; I have no desire to bring Him down to my level, I try to raise myself to Him. I hearken to the voice He has planted within me, a voice which honest men call conscience, and I try to not betray that divine ray as it reaches me. I will never injure any person; I will not do aught to break the commandments of universal morality, which formed those of Confucius, Moses, Pythagoras, Socrates, as well as of Jesus Christ. I remain before God; my acts shall be my prayers; I will never lie, my word is sacred; and I will do nothing vile or evil. These are the precepts of my virtuous father, these I wish to leave to my children. What can you ask more than this?"

This profession of faith caused Céleste to sadly shake her head.

"Read attentively," said she, "'The Imitation of Christ.' Strive to be converted to the holy church, Catholic, Apostolic, and Roman, then you will learn how absurd your words are. Listen, Félix, marriage, says the church, is not the affair of a day, the satisfaction of desire; it is made for all eternity. What! shall we be united by day and night, shall we be one flesh, one spirit, and yet speak two languages, have two faiths in our hearts, two religions; a cause of perpetual dissension? Could I address myself in peace to God when He always had His right arm bared against you? Your deistic blood, your convictions, might animate my children. Oh, my God! how wretched for a wife. Do not place a gulf between us. If you loved me, you would already have read the 'Imitation of Christ.'"

The Phellions, children of the "Constitutionnel," have no love for priests. Félix had the imprudence to reply to this species of supplication from the depths of an ardent soul:

"You are repeating, Céleste, the lesson taught by your confessor, and nothing can be more fatal to happiness, I think, than the interference of priests in one's household."

"Oh!" cried Céleste, "you do not love me;" for she was pierced to the quick, being inspired of love.

She enveloped herself in noble silence; Félix went to the window and thrummed upon the panes; a music familiar to those who have indulged in poignant reflections. The Phellion conscience argued thus:

"Céleste is a rich heiress, and, by yielding, contrary to the voice of natural religion, to her ideas, it would be done for the purpose of making an advantageous marriage: an infamous act. I ought not, as a father of a family, to allow a priest to have any influence in my home; if I submit to-day I do a weak act, which will lead to many such, pernicious to the authority of a father and husband. All this is beneath the dignity of a philosopher."

Then he returned to his beloved.

"Céleste," he said, "on my knees I beg you not to confound things. Each has his own way of salvation; as to society, it is not obeying God to obey its laws. Christ said: 'Render unto Cæsar the things which are Cæsar's.' Cæsar is the body politic. Forget this little quarrel, dear."

"Little quarrel!" cried the young enthusiast. "I wish for you to have my whole heart as I would have all yours; but you would divide it into two parts. Is not that awful? You forget that marriage is a sacrament."

"Your priests have turned your brain," cried the mathematician, impatiently.

"Monsieur Phellion," said Céleste, hastily interrupting him, "that's enough of this subject."

It was at this point of the controversy that Théodose, who

had not disdained to listen outside the door, deemed it judicious to make his entry. He found Céleste pale and the young professor uneasy as a lover should be who has just vexed his mistress.

"I heard the word 'enough,' has there been too much?" asked he, looking by turns at Céleste and Félix.

"We were talking religion," replied Félix. "I was telling mademoiselle how evil the influence of clerics must be in a family."

"That was not the point at all, monsieur," said Céleste, sharply; "but that I wanted to know if husband and wife could be of one heart when one was an atheist and the other a Catholic."

"Is it possible that there are atheists?" exclaimed Théodose, showing signs of deep amazement. "Is it that a Catholic could possibly marry a protestant? But it is impossible that safety can be found for a married couple unless there is perfect agreement in their religious opinions. I am, of a truth, from the Comtat, of a family which counts a pope among its ancestors; for our arms are: *gules* with a key *argent*, our supporters, a monk holding a church and a pilgrim bearing a staff, the motto being: '*J'ouvre et je ferme*,' or, I open and I shut. I am, I may say, fiercely dogmatic on the subject. But to-day, thanks to our system of modern education, it is not in the least strange that religion should be called in question. But, as I tell myself, I would never marry a protestant even if she possessed millions; nor even if I had lost my reason for love of her. Faith is outside discussion. *Una fides, unus Dominus*—one faith, one Lord—that is my living motto."

"You hear!" cried Céleste, looking at Félix.

"I am not too devout," la Peyrade continued. "I go to mass every morning at six o'clock, that I may not be observed; I fast on Fridays; I am, in short, a son of the church; I would not commence any undertaking without prayer, after the ancient custom of my ancestors; but I do not obtrude my religion on people. In the Revolution of 1789 an incident occurred that bound us more firmly than ever to our holy mother, the church. A poor young lady of the elder branch of la Peyrades, who owned the little estate of la Peyrade (for we are the Peyrades of Canquoëlle, but both branches inter-inherit), well, this demoiselle married, six years before the Revolution, a barrister, who after the fashion of the times was a Voltairean, that is, an unbeliever, or, if you like, a deist. He took up all the revolutionary ideas, practicing the pleasing rites of which you have heard, in the worship of the goddess of Reason. He came to our part of the country soaked in the fanaticism of the Convention. His wife was very handsome; he compelled her to play the rôle of Liberty; the poor unfortunate went mad—she died insane. Ah, well, as things seem to be going, we may yet see another 1793."

This romance, forged on the spot, made such an impression on the young, fresh imagination of Céleste that she rose, curtsied low to the two young men, and retired to her chamber.

"Ah, monsieur, why did you tell her that?" exclaimed Félix, stricken to the heart by the cold look of indifference cast upon him by Céleste.

"I am ready," said Mme. Colleville, appearing in a tasteful toilet. "But what ails my poor daughter? She is crying!"

"Crying, madame!" cried Félix. "Tell her, madame, that I will at once begin to study the 'Imitation of Christ.'"

An hour later Mme. Colleville, Céleste, Colleville, and Théodose were entering the Thuilliers' home to dine with them. Théodose and Flavie took Thuillier into the garden, where Théodose said:

"My good friend, you will have the Cross within a week. Listen, this dear friend will tell you all about our visit to the Comtesse du Bruel."

Théodose left them, having caught sight of Desroches approaching, convoyed by Brigitte; a chilling, dread presentiment bade him go to meet the attorney.

"My dear maître," whispered Desroches to Théodose, "I am here to see if you can at once furnish twenty-five thousand francs, plus two thousand six hundred and eighty francs, sixty centimes, for costs."

"Are you Cérizet's attorney?"

"He has placed all the acceptances into Louchard's hands; you know what you must expect after arrest. Is Cérizet wrong in believing that you have twenty-five thousand francs in your desk? You offered them to him; he finds it only natural that they should not make their home with you."

"I am greatly obliged for the course you have taken, my dear maître," said Théodose; "I expected this attack."

"Between ourselves," replied Desroches, "you jollied him finely. The rascal will stop at nothing to be revenged upon you, for he will lose all if you are willing to cast off your robe, throw it to the sharks, and go to prison."

"Me?" exclaimed Théodose. "I shall pay him. But even then he will still retain five acceptances of mine, each of which is for five thousand francs: what does he mean to do with them?"

"Oh! after the affair of this morning, it is impossible to guess; but my client is a crafty, mangy dog, and has, without a doubt, his little schemes."

"See, now, Desroches," said Théodose, taking the hard, lean lawyer by the waist; "have you not got the notes?"

"Will you pay them?"

"Yes; in three hours."

"Good; then be at my place at nine o'clock; I'll receive the cash and give you the acceptances; but, mind, at half-past nine they pass to Louchard."

"All right, this evening at nine o'clock," said Théodose.

"At nine," said Desroches, embracing the whole company in a comprehensive glance.

At daybreak the following morning, Théodose went to the banker of the poor to see what effect his prompt payment had had upon his enemy, and to make one more effort to rid himself of his horse-fly.

He found Cérizet in colloquy with a woman; he was imperatively requested to keep at a distance and not to interrupt the interview. Théodose had a presentiment, though a vague one, that the result of this conference would in some wise affect Cérizet's arrangements as to himself, for he saw on his face the change that comes of hope.

"But, my dear Mamma Cardinal——"

"Yes, my worthy sir——"

"What do you want?"

"It must be decided——"

These beginnings and ends of sentences were the only gleams of light on the animated conversation.

Mme. Cardinal was one of Cérizet's first customers; she was a fish-hawker. As she stood in Cérizet's office she had all the value of an isolated masterpiece of her kind; she was a perfect type of her species.

She was mounted on muddy *sabots*—peasants' wooden shoes—but her feet, beside being well inclosed in gaiters, were further protected by good, thick woolen stockings. Her print dress, enriched with flounces of mud, bore the imprint of the strap which supported the huckster's basket, cutting across the back to below the waist. Her principal garment was a shawl of rabbit-skin cashmere, so-called, the two ends of which were knotted behind above her bustle—for only this fashionable word will properly describe the cabbage-like effect produced by the pressure of the basket upon her form. A coarse neckerchief served as a fichu, which revealed a red throat covered with wrinkles, like the surface of the ice on the Villette pond after skating. Her coiffure was a yellow bandanna twisted into the shape of a picturesque turban.

Short and stout, a skin rich in color, Mother Cardinal took

her morning nip of brandy. She had once been handsome. The Market had reproached her, in their vigorous figure of speech, of having earned more than one day's wages at night. Her voice, to be brought down to the pitch of ordinary conversation, had to be stifled by her as is done in a sick-room; but then it came out thick and muffled from a throat so used to shouting the names of each fish in its season in a tone to reach the deepest recess of the highest garrets. Her nose, à la Roxelane, her well-shaped mouth, her blue eyes, all that had at one time made up her beauty, was now buried in folds of vigorous fat which plainly told of an open-air life and occupation. The stomach and bust could have been recommended as being of an amplitude worthy of Rubens' pencil.

"And do you wish to see me lying on straw?" said she to Cérizet. "What do I care for the Toupilliers? Ain't I a Toupillier myself? Where do you wish me to fish for those Toupilliers?"

This savage outburst was silenced by Cérizet with a prolonged "hush!" always obeyed by every conspirator.

"Well, go and see what you can do about it and then come back to me," said Cérizet, pushing her toward the door and whispering in her ear.

"Well, my dear friend," said Théodose to Cérizet, "so you have got your money?"

"Yes," answered Cérizet; "we have measured our claws, they are equally sharp, long, and strong. What follows?"

"Am I to tell Dutocq that you have received twenty-five thousand francs?"

"Oh! my dear friend, not one word, if you love me," exclaimed Cérizet.

"Listen," said Théodose. "I must know once for all what it is you want. I have firmly made up my mind not to stay for another twenty-four hours on the gridiron to which you have bound me. You may cheat Dutocq all you like, I don't care about that, but I intend to know where I stand. It is a fortune that I have paid you, twenty-five thousand francs, for you must have made ten thousand by your traffic; it ought to give you a start as an honest man."

"Here are my conditions, take them or leave them, they are not subject to discussion. You will get for me the lease of Thuillier's house for eighteen years, then I hand you out one of the five acceptances canceled. You won't afterward find me in your way; as to Dutocq, you'll have to settle with him for the remaining four. You beat me; Dutocq is not smart enough to buck against you."

"Agreed, if you will give forty-eight thousand francs a year for the rent of the house, the last in advance, and begin the tenancy in October."

"Yes, but I shall only give forty-three thousand francs in cash, your acceptance will make the balance, the forty-eight. I have had a good look at the house, I've examined it; it's just the thing I want."

"One last condition," said Théodose, "you'll lend me a hand against Dutocq?"

"No," replied Cérizet; "you have done him brown enough now, without having me to help you baste him: you can roast him dry. But be reasonable. The poor man knows not which way to turn to pay the last fifteen thousand francs due on his position; you should remember that you can get all your acceptances back for fifteen thousand francs."

"Well, give me two weeks to get the lease."

"Not one day past Monday next. On Tuesday your acceptance for five thousand francs will be in Louchard's hands, unless you pay me on Monday or get Thuillier to grant me the lease."

"Well, Monday be it," said Théodose, as he shook hands, each saying: "So long."

For ten years Cérizet had seen a number of people getting rich by the business of sub-letting property. The principal tenant is, in Paris, to the owner of houses what farmers are to country landowners. All Paris has seen how a famous tailor built at his own cost a sumptuous structure on the site of the celebrated Frascati, paying as principal tenant fifty thousand francs as rent for the building, which in nineteen years was to become the property of the landowner. Notwithstanding the cost of construction, about seven hundred thousand francs, those nineteen years' profits in the end proved enormous.

Cérizet had seen the possibilities of the house which Thuillier had "stolen" (in his idea); he therefore arranged to sell his banking business to Cadenet and the Widow Poiret for ten thousand francs, he had amassed thirty thousand, and the two would enable him to pay the last year's rent usually demanded by Paris house-owners on a long lease, as a guarantee. He fell asleep dreaming of becoming a bourgeois, a Minard, a Thuillier. But, lo, he had a waking of which he had not dreamt. He found Fortune standing before him, pouring out riches from a gilded horn, in the person of Madame Cardinal.

Now Mme. Cardinal, widow of a porter in the Market, had an only daughter whose beauty Cérizet had often heard tell of by her mother's cronies. Olympe Cardinal was about thirteen when, in 1837, Cérizet began to "bank" in the quarter; and with a view to infamous libertinism, he had paid much attention to the mother, whom he had rescued from abject poverty, hoping to make Olympe his mistress; but in 1838 the daughter left her mother and had undoubtedly "made her own life," to use the term given by the Parisian populace to the destruction of the most precious gifts of nature and youth.

Searching for a girl in Paris is like looking for a minnow in the Seine; it is all chance if it comes to net. The chance came. Mother Cardinal, who was standing treat to a chum, visited the Bobino Theatre, where she recognized in the leading lady her own daughter, and who for three years had been under the domination of the first comedian. The mother at first was flattered to see her daughter in a lovely gauze bespangled attire, her hair dressed like that of a duchess, wearing clocked stockings, satin shoes, and applauded when she appeared; but she ended by howling from her seat:

"You shall hear from me again, murderess of your mother! I'll soon know whether measly play-actors have any right to come and debauch girls of sixteen!"

She waited at the stage-door to intercept her daughter, but she had wisely dropped down from the stage and gone out with the audience.

The next day Mme. Cardinal intended consulting Cérizet, as he was in the office of a justice of the peace, but before arriving at his den on the Rue des Poules she met a porter who lived in the same house as an old uncle of hers, one Toupillier, who told her that the old man had barely two days to call his own, being in the last extremity.

"Well, can I help that?" asked the Widow Cardinal.

"We count on you, dear Madame Cardinal; you won't forget the good advice we can give you. Here's the thing: For the last month or so your poor uncle, who has been unable to get around, trusted us to collect his rent for his house on Rue Notre-Dame de Nazareth, and the arrears of dividends due on a Treasury bond for eighteen hundred francs——"

And now the eyes of the Widow Cardinal became staring instead of wandering.

"Yes, my dear," continued the noble Perrache, a little humpbacked porter; "and being as how you are the only one who ever thinks on him, why we thought as you sometimes came to see him and brought him a bit of fish at times, why, as how he might make you his heir like."

"You might well think, you old leather-thumper," replied Mother Cardinal to the porter, who had been a shoemaker. Then she hurried off at her top-rate of speed to the wretched garret in which her uncle lived. "What?" said she, "my

Uncle Toupillier rich! The good beggar of the church of Saint-Sulpice."

"Ah!" the porter responded, "but he fed well. Every night when he went to bed he took with him his best friend—a bottle of Roussillon wine. My wife has tasted it, but he told us it was cheap stuff, six-sous wine."

"Don't you let drop one word of all this, my good fellow," said the widow. "I'll remember you if anything comes of it."

This Toupillier, an old drum-major in the Guards, had gone into the service of the church two years before 1789 by becoming the swiss (or sexton) of Saint-Sulpice. The Revolution deprived him of that post, and he fell into abject poverty. He then took up the profession of model, for he *enjoyed* a fine physique.

When worship was again allowed, he resumed his staff; but in 1816 he was dismissed, as much on account of his immorality as for his political opinions; he passed as a Bonapartist. Nevertheless, as a sort of pension, he was allowed to stand by the door and distribute the holy water. Later on an unfortunate business, which will presently be related, caused him to lose his holy sprinkler; but, still finding means to hang about the sanctuary, he was finally suffered at the door of the church as a licensed beggar. At this time, being seventy-two years old, he made himself ninety-six, going into business as a centenarian.

In the whole of Paris it was impossible to find a beard and hair such as Toupillier's. He walked bent nearly double; in one trembling hand he carried a cane—a hand that looked as if covered with the lichen that grows on granite; in the other he held out the classic hat, greasy, broad-brimmed, and battered, into which there tumbled an abundance of alms. His legs, swathed in rags and bandages, dragged along a pair of wretched overshoes of coarse-matting, hiding excellent comfortable inner soles of cork. He smeared his face with certain ingredients, which gave it an appearance of some late severe illness, and he played the senility of centenarism most admirably. He had become a hundred in 1830, although in reality but eighty years old. He was chief of the beggars, the high muck-a-muck; and all others who came to beg under the porches of the church, safe from the persecutions of the police by the protection of the sexton and holy-water sprinkler and the parish church, had to pay him a kind of tithing.

When an heir, a bridegroom, or a godfather said, as he came out of church: "Here, this is for all of you, don't bother any of my party," Toupillier, named by the sexton, his successor, to receive these alms, pocketed three-quarters and gave one-quarter only to his acolytes, and their tribute was one sou per day. Money and wine were his two last passions; but he regulated the second one, giving himself up to the first, not, however, neglecting his personal comfort. He drank only in the evening, after dinner, when the church was closed; he slept every night for twenty years in the arms of drunkenness—his last mistress. The beadle and sprinkler, with whom he most likely had an understanding, would say of him:

"He is a poor man of the church; he used to know the Curé Languet, who built Saint-Sulpice; he was sexton here for twenty years; before and after the Revolution; he is now a hundred years old."

This best of advertisements lined his hat so as none others were equal to it. He bought his house in 1826, and in 1830 invested in the Funds. From the two sources he must have made something like six thousand francs per annum, and most likely he put some out in Cérizet's manner, for the cost of his house was forty thousand francs, and he had forty-eight thousand in the Funds. His niece was as much deceived by the old man as was the public; she believed him to be a most miserable pauper, and, when she had any fish getting "high," she would carry some to the poor man.

After making an inspection of the sick man, Mother Cardinal hurried off to consult Cérizet, for she knew she was too ignorant to be able, successfully, to get the property unaided. The banker of the poor, like the other scavengers, had at last found diamonds in the slime he had been raking over, always looking to pick up such a chance. This, then, was the secret of his gentle dealing with the man whom he had promised to ruin. He was not the man to shrink from a crime should necessity arise, so especially when others might do that and reap the benefits.

"My Benjamin," said the huckster, rushing into Cérizet's office, with a face inflamed as much by cupidity as haste, "my uncle sleeps on more than one hundred thousand francs in gold; and I'm sure that the Perraches, under pretense of caring for him, have an eye on the blunt."

"Shared up among forty heirs," said Cérizet, "it won't make much of a fortune for each. Listen here, Mother Cardinal, I'll marry your daughter; give her your uncle's gold and I'll leave to you the Funds and the house for life."

"Shall we run no risk?"

"None at all."

"Done!" said Madame Widow Cardinal, clasping hands with her future son-in-law. "Six thousand francs a year—oh! the jolly life!"

"And a son-in-law like me, beside," added the amiable Cérizet.

"Now," resumed he, after they had embraced each other, "I must look over the ground. Do not leave there; tell the porter you expect a doctor. I shall be the doctor; when I come you mustn't know me."

"You're no fool, you old rogue," said la Cardinal, giving him a punch in the stomach by way of farewell.

An hour after, Cérizet, dressed in black, disguised in a rusty wig and an artistically made-up face, arrived in the Rue Honoré-Chevalier, in a coach. He asked the porter for

Toupillier's address. He was taken up the back stairs of the house, leading to the wretched garret occupied by the beggar.

The house in which Toupillier lived is one of those which have been compelled to lose one-half by being cut through in widening the street, for the Rue Honoré-Chevalier is one of the straitest in the Saint-Sulpice quarter. The owner, forbidden by law to repair it, was compelled to rent out the wretched building as it was. The coach-way to the courtyard was made in a circular form, this shape being indispensable in a street so narrow that two carriages could not pass.

Cérizet laid hands on the rope that served as a hand-rail to a kind of ladder that ascended to the room where the alleged centenarian lay dying; in this chamber was being played the odious spectacle of pretended poverty.

In Paris all that is done with an end in view is done to perfection. The would-be poor are as clever in such lines as the storekeepers in dressing their show windows, or as the sham wealthy are in obtaining credit.

The floor had never been swept; the bricks had disappeared under a litter of filth, dust, dried mud, and every kind of rubbish thrown down by Toupillier. A poor cast-iron stove, with a pipe bricked into a crumbling fire-place, was the best appearing thing in the lair. In a recess was a bed with a head-pole from which hung a curtain of green serge, eaten into lace by moths. The nearly useless window had a dense coat of greese on its panes, which dispensed with the necessity for a curtain. The whitewashed walls were fuliginously tinted with the smoke of wood and peat burned in the stove. On the mantel stood a broken water pitcher, two bottles, and a cracked plate. A miserable, worm-eaten bureau held his linen and decent clothes; the other furniture consisted of a night-table of the commonest kind, another table worth about forty sous, and two kitchen chairs, with the straw seats about gone. The very picturesque costume of the centenarian beggar hung from a nail, and below it, on the floor, the shapeless coarse hempen gaiters which served him as shoes, and, with his prodigious staff and his hat, formed a sort of panoply of poverty.

When Cérizet entered the old man did not move, even on hearing the groaning of the heavy door, armed with iron-lining and furnished with bolts to secure his domicile.

"Is he conscious?" said Cérizet, before whom Mme. Cardinal started back, for she did not recognize him until he spoke.

"Very nearly," said Mme. Cardinal.

"Come out on the stairs, for we don't want him to hear us. This is what we must do," whispered he to his future mother-in-law. "He is weak, but he isn't so very sick-looking; we shall have about eight days before us. I'll find a doctor that will suit us, do you catch on? I'll return later with six poppy-heads. In the state he is, you see, a good strong tea of poppy will send him off to sleep. I'll send you in a cot-bed, under the pretense of your sleeping here. Then we'll move him from one bed to the other; thus when we've counted the money hidden in his mattress we can easily carry it off. But we ought to know what sort of tenants there are in the barrack. The doctor will say that he has some days to live and that he should make his will."

"My son!"

"But we must learn about the occupants; for if Perrache gives the alarm—so many lodgers, so many spies."

"Bah! I know all that already," replied Mme. Cardinal. "Du Portail, the little old man who rents the second floor, has charge of a mad girl whom I heard called Lydie this morning by an old woman named Katt. The old man has only one servant, a valet, another old man named Bruno, who does everything but cook."

"Well, we must study the matter," said he, in the tone of a man whose plans are not yet decided upon. "I'll go to the mayor's office, get Olympe's register of birth, and have the banns published. Next Saturday but one, the wedding."

"How he goes it, this old rascal!" said Mother Cardinal, giving a frisky push with her shoulder to her son-in-law.

As he went downstairs Cérizet looked in the rooms used as workshops and counted the workers. Then he departed, turning over in his mind the numerous difficulties that might arise to prevent the carrying off of the gold hidden under the dying man.

"Lift it all at night, eh?" said he to himself; "why those parties are always on the watch; and in the day one would be seen by twenty people. It's hard to carry twenty-five thousand francs in gold on one's self."

Society has two forms of perfection: the first is a stage of civilization in which morality, being equally infused, does not permit of crime even in thought; the jesuits have reached this point, which was presented in the early church; the second is the state of another civilization in which the mutual supervision of its citizens renders crime an impossibility. The end which modern society has placed in view is the latter, namely, that a crime shall offer such difficulties that a man must be really without reason to attempt it. To live at ease crime must have a sanction like that granted by the Bourse, or like that given to Cérizet by his clients, who never grumbled, and who would, indeed, be troubled in mind if their flayer had not been found in his kitchen on Tuesdays.

"Well, my dear sir," said the porter's wife, as Cérizet went past the lodge; "how is that friend of God, the poor man?"

"I am not the doctor," Cérizet made answer, who now decidedly renounced the part; "I am Madame Cardinal's man of business; I have advised her to have a cot-bed brought in, so she may be here day and night, though she may have to engage a regular nurse."

"I could give her good service," said Mme. Perrache; "I nurse women in confinement."

"Well, we'll see," said Cérizet. "I'll arrange all that. Who is your second-floor tenant?"

"Monsieur du Portail. He has lodged there thirty year. He is a man with a good income, a very respectable man. You know, bondholders, who live on the Funds. For more than eleven years he has been trying to restore the reason of a daughter of one of his friends, Mademoiselle Lydie de la Peyrade. She gets the best of advice, I tell you; why, only this morning there were two celebrated physicians what had a consultation. But up to now nothing has cured her; they have to watch her pretty close, too, I tell you; for at times she gets up in the night."

"Mademoiselle Lydie de la Peyrade!" exclaimed Cérizet. "You are quite sure that is her name?"

"Madame Katt, her nurse, who does the little cooking for the household, has told me a thousand times, though, as a general thing, neither Monsieur Bruno, the valet, nor Madame Katt chatter much. We have been porters here for twenty years and haven't yet found anything out about Monsieur du Portail. Beside that he owns the house alongside. You can see the door, there. Well, you see, he can go out that way and receive his company and us know nothing about it."

"Then you didn't see the gentleman who is talking to him in the garden go by this way?"

"Not much! Certainly not!"

Now as Cérizet was coming down the rickety ladder he had seen the second-floor tenant in conversation with the Comte Martial de la Roche-Hugon, an important member of the government.

"Ah!" said Cérizet, as he got into the coach, "this is the daughter of Théodose's uncle. Du Portail may be the benefactor who one time sent two thousand five hundred francs to my rascal. I might send an anonymous letter to the little old fellow telling him of the danger that Monsieur l'Avocat is in owing to those twenty-five thousand francs' worth of acceptances."

An hour later a complete cot-bed had arrived for Mme. Cardinal, to whom the inquisitive porter's wife offered her services to bring her something to eat.

"Do you want to see the curé?" asked Mme. Cardinal of the old man; she had noticed that the arrival of the bed had roused him from his somnolence.

"I want some wine," he replied.

"How do you find yourself now, Father Toupillier?" asked Mme. Perrache, coaxingly.

"I tell you I want some wine," repeated the old fellow with a scarcely looked-for insistent energy.

"We must first know if it is good for you, Unky Bunky," said she, caressingly. "Wait till the doctor gives his idea."

"Doctor! I won't have one," cried Toupillier. "What are you doing here, anyhow? I don't want anybody."

"My good uncle, I just came to know if you could fancy a bit of something tasty; I have a nice fresh flounder: eh! a *teenty* flounder served with a dash of lemon-juice?"

"It's fine, is your fish," answered Toupillier; "it is real stinking; the last you brought me, six weeks ago, is still in the closet; you can take it away with you."

"Gracious me, how ungrateful sick people are," said la Cardinal, speaking low to Lady Perrache.

"Leave me alone, I want nobody here; I only want some wine; leave me in peace," said Toupillier, angrily.

"Don't get vexed, little uncle; we'll find you some wine."

"The wine at six—Rue des Canettes," cried the beggar.

"Yes," said Mother Cardinal; "but let me count up my coppers. I want to get the best he has in the cellar. You see, an uncle is a kind of second father; we ought to do what's right by him."

While speaking she sat down, her legs wide apart, on one

of the two dilapidated chairs, then turned out on her apron all the contents of her pockets: a knife, her snuff-box, two pawn-tickets, some crusts of bread, and a handful of coppers, from which she extracted a few silver-pieces. Then spying behind the night-table a dirty bottle which might hold about two litres:

"Wasn't it Rue des Canettes that he said?" she asked the portress.

"Corner of Rue Guisarde," was the reply. "Mister Legrelu, a big, fat man, with fine whiskers and a bald head." Then, dropping her voice, "his six-at wine is the *best* Roussillon. It will be quite sufficient to let him know that you come from his customer, the beggar of Saint-Sulpice."

"I don't need telling twice," said la Cardinal; she opened the door and made a false start, for she returned and said: "What does he burn in the stove, in case I need to heat anything for him? I must get in some food and fuel; I hope nobody will see what I bring."

"I'll lend you a rush-basket," said the ever-officious portress.

"Thanks! I'll buy a market-basket," answered the fish-hawker, who was more anxious as to what she could carry away than what she might bring. "I guess there's an Auvergnat somewhere about here who sells wood and charcoal?"

"At the corner of the Rue Férou—you'll easily find the place; a fine establishment, where the logs are painted on an awning like so many bottles; they look like faces that want to talk to you."

She had hesitated, had Mme. Cardinal, about leaving the portress alone with the sick man. She now acted a part of deep hypocrisy:

"Madame Perrache," said she, "you won't leave him, the dear man, not till I return?"

Cérizet was yet undecided on the course to adopt; when alone, he saw the difficulties of playing doctor, with a nurse, notary, and others complicating matters. It might be a long and troublesome affair to bring the old beggar to making a will; it was true that, unless a will was made, the income in the Funds and the house in Rue Notre-Dame de Nazareth would go to the heirs-at-law, Mme. Cardinal only getting her share. He therefore resolved on the simplest manœuvre—the poppy-heads. He was on his way back with this simple narcotic when he encountered Mme. Cardinal, basket on arm, who had already secured the desired panacea.

"So!" said the usurer, "this is how you guard your post?"

"I had to go out to fetch him some wine," replied la Cardinal. "He howled like one broiling on a gridiron that he wanted to be left in peace, and that he be given his booze. The man's idea is that Roussillon is the one thing needed for his cure; I'll give him a bellyful; when he's boozy, perhaps he'll be quieter."

"Quite right," said Cérizet, pompously. "It is bad policy to contradict a sick person; but this wine can be improved by medicating it with these"—lifting one of the lids of the basket, he here slipped in the poppy-heads—"it will enable the poor man to get a nap for five or six hours; this evening I'll call upon you; I don't fancy there'll be much to prevent us examining the value of the heritage."

"I twig!" said Mme. Cardinal, with a wink.

When Mme. Cardinal reached her uncle's garret she relieved Mme. Perrache, giving her adieu at the door, as she received a quantity of wood already sawed. Into an earthen pot of the right size to fit the hole in the stoves of the poor in which they put their soup-kettles—into this she threw the poppy-heads, and poured over it about two-thirds of the wine she had brought; then she lighted the fire under the pot so as to get the decoction as soon as possible.

The crackling of the wood and the warmth spreading about the room brought Toupillier out of his stupor. Seeing the stove lighted—

"A fire here!" cried he; "do you want to burn the house down?"

"Why, Unky Bunky," replied la Cardinal, "this is wood that I bought myself, to warm your wine. The doctor doesn't wish you to drink it cold."

"Where is it, that wine?" asked Toupillier, who was calmed by the thought that the fire was not burning at his expense.

"It must boil first," said his nurse; "the doctor insisted on that. Still, if you'll keep quiet I'll give you a little, just to wet your whistle; but don't say anything about it."

"I won't have a doctor come here; they are scoundrels who put men out of the world. Come, give me that wine."

When she passed it to him he grasped it with his bony, eager fingers, gulped it down at a breath, and—

"What a little drop, and watered beside," he said.

"Ah, now! don't say that Unky Bunky; I fetched it myself from old Legrelu's. But when the rest has simmered a bit you can have it all, the doctor says."

At the end of fifteen minutes she brought him a cup filled to the brim with the mixture. The avidity with which he drank it did not permit him to notice the taste of the wine, but as he swallowed the last drops the bitter, nauseating taste betrayed itself; he flung the cup on the bed and cried out that she had poisoned him.

"Get out! there is your poison," replied the huckster, pouring the few drops that remained into her own mouth, declaring that if the wine did not taste as usual it was because his mouth had a "bad taste."

Before the dispute was ended the narcotic began to take effect; in an hour he was sound asleep.

She had an idea that it would be as well to avoid the vigilance of the Perraches, if they wished to transport the treasure, so she amiably called in the portress, after throwing out the poppy-heads, and said to her:

"Take a taste of *his* wine. You would have thought when you listened to his talk that he was ready for a barrel, wouldn't you? Well, a cupful satisfied him."

"Here's to you!" said the portress, clinking glasses with la Cardinal, who was careful to fill her glass with the natural wine.

A less distinguished connoisseur than the beggar, Mme. Perrache found nothing amiss in the insidious liquid, for when she drank it had become cold; she declared that it was quite velvety and wished her husband could have had some. After a long gossip the two separated. Mme. Cardinal ate some food and then indulged in a siesta which lasted until dark.

She had barely taken a glance at Toupillier when a cautious knock was heard on the door, and Cérizet entered.

"Well?" said he, as he came in.

"Well, he's taken the dose. He's been for these four hours as dead as Jesus. He was dreaming and talking of diamonds, just now."

"These beggars pile up everything when they get miserly," said Cérizet.

"By-the-by, little father, what was your idea in telling Mme. Perrache that you are my man of business and not a doctor? It was arranged this morning that you were to come as a doctor——"

"I saw that the woman was going to propose a consultation, so I got out of it like that."

"Did they notice you come in, those porters?"

"It seemed to me that the woman was asleep in her chair," replied Cérizet.

"She should be—sound," said la Cardinal, with a significant shrug.

"What! Really?" asked Cérizet.

"*Parbleu!*" said the fish-hawker. "Enough for one is enough for two; I gave her the rest of the dose."

"As to her husband," said Cérizet, "he is there, for as he drew his thread he made me a gracious sign of recognition, which I could well have dispensed with, as I passed."

"Leave it till night has fallen; then we'll have a little game that will bother him."

In fact, a quarter of an hour after, with a nerve that astonished the usurer, she carried through a farce of seeing a "monsieur" out, who begged her to not take such trouble. Making a manner of seeing the pretended doctor as far as the gate on the street, half-way across the courtyard she pretended that the wind had blown out her light, and, under the pretext of relighting it, she extinguished Perrache's light as well. All this play, accompanied with much gesticulations and loquacious vociferations, was so cleverly done, that the porter before any judge would not have hesitated to make oath that the doctor, whom he had ushered in that evening, had come down from the beggar's room and left the house between nine and ten.

When she returned to the room she acted on Béranger's hint and hung up her old shawl at the window, as though to screen Lisette's amours. In the Luxembourg life's stir is over early. Before ten all was quiet, inside the house as well as out. If it did not take long to find the treasure la Cardinal could have the front gate left open, so that in case of having to fetch medicine she could get handily to the drug-store. Then if the porters acted as porters mostly do, when in their first slumber, pull the cord of the latch without getting out of bed, Cérizet could get out at the same time, and they could thus carry off at least a portion of the cash and place it securely away.

Toupillier, under the brawny hands of the fish-hawker, was soon transferred to the other bed, and the mattress was eagerly searched. At first they found nothing, and the fish-hawker, being pressed to explain how that morning she was sure of her uncle sleeping on one hundred thousand francs in gold, was obliged to confess that her conversation with Perrache and her brilliant imagination were the basis of her pretended certainty. Cérizet was furious. After all this time cherishing the idea and hope of a fortune, and making up his mind to embark on dangerous and compromising undertakings, in the end to find himself face to face with emptiness! The disappointment was so cruel that, only that he dreaded an encounter with so muscular a future mother-in-law, he would have been carried to extreme rage.

At the least he could vent his choler in words. Rudely assailed, la Cardinal would only keep saying that all was not yet lost, and, with the faith that removes mountains, continued to tumble the bed over from top to bottom.

So that she might have nothing to reproach herself with, la Cardinal, notwithstanding Cérizet's objections, who thought it ridiculous, insisted on removing the sacking of the bedstead bottom; certainly the vainless search had whetted her faculties, for when she lifted the wood frame she heard the sound of some small object, which had become detached, as it fell on the floor.

Ascribing to this detail a possibly undue importance, the eager explorer soon got a light and after some time found a small polished steel barrel among the filth, of which the use to her was an inexplicable mystery.

"That's a key!" exclaimed Cérizet, who at once changing from indifference let his imagination off at a gallop.

"Ah, ah! you see?" said la Cardinal, triumphantly; "but what can it open?" added she, after reflection; "a doll's trunk?"

"That's not all," answered Cérizet. "This is a modern invention and very strong locks may be opened with this little instrument."

At the same time he made a rapid survey, embracing all the furniture in the chamber, went to the bureau, drew out the drawers, looked into the stove, under the table; but not a thing could he see of a single lock which this little key would fit.

Mme. Cardinal struck a bright idea.

"Stay," said she; "I noticed that as he lay on his bed the old thief never ceased to keep his eye on the wall opposite him."

"A closet concealed in the wall? anyway that's not impossible," said Cérizet, taking up the candle.

After he had carefully examined the door in the alcove which faced the head of the bed, he found nothing but heavy hangings of cobwebs and dust. He then tried the sense of touch. which is occasionally keener, and sounded and felt the wall all over. At the spot where Toupillier had ever kept his eyes he found a circumscribed space which was certainly hollow; and it was wood. He rolled his handkerchief into a ball and rubbed the spot hard, and under the layer of dirt thus cleaned he found a little oak board closely adjusted in the wall; on one end of this board was a little round hole, this was the keyhole that the key fitted.

While Cérizet unlocked the door, which he did without difficulty, la Cardinal, who held up the candle, became pale and gasping; but, cruel disappointment, the closet was opened and nothing was to be seen but an empty space. Leaving the fury to fulminate her despairing exclamations and to salute her uncle's soul with every conceivable abusive epithet of which she could think, Cérizet kept calm and quiet.

After putting his arm in the opening and around the bottom of it, he cried:

"Here is an iron box!"

Then he snatched the candle out of the bottle in which it was stuck and moved it around the iron cover he had found.

"It has no keyhole," said he; "it must have a secret lock."

After feeling about it for some time he said:

"Ah! I have it." Under the pressure of his fingers the

lid sprang open. During this time Mme. Cardinal's life seemed to be suspended. The iron side had arisen, and, among a mass of gold thrown loosely into a deep recess, lay a red morocco case, which from its size and general appearance promised magnificent booty.

"I take the diamonds for the *dot*," said Cérizet, when he saw the splendid jewels it contained. "You, my mother, would not know how to dispose of them; I'll leave the gold for your share. As to the Funds and the house, they are not worth the trouble of getting the worthy man to make another will."

"Just a minute, my boy!" replied la Cardinal, who found this division rather too summary; "we will first count the cash."

"Hush!" said Cérizet, stopping in a listening attitude.

"Why?" asked la Cardinal.

Cérizet made her a sign to remain silent, and listened with more attention.

"I hear the sound of steps on the stairs," said he soon after; then he hastily restored the jewel-case in the closet and vainly tried to lower the panel.

"Indeed, yes, somebody is coming. Ah, bah! it is only the mad girl, I suppose; she does walk in the night."

If it was the insane girl she had a key to the room, for it was inserted in the lock; la Cardinal was too late in trying to bolt the door, so blew out the light to give less chances of discovery by the darkness. Useless precaution! the spoilsport carried a candle in his hand.

When she saw that the intruder in their business was a little old man of puny appearance, Mme. Cardinal, her eyes flaming, sprang before him, like a lioness seeking to protect her cubs from the hunter.

"Calm yourself, my good lady," said the old man, banteringly, "the police are sent for, they will be here in a moment."

The word "police" broke, as the common saying is, Mme. Cardinal's legs.

"But, monsieur, the police!" said she; "we are not robbers."

"Just the same, were I in your place, I shouldn't wait for them," said the little old man; "they make unfortunate mistakes at times."

"Can I *get*, then?" said the fish-hawker, incredulously.

"Yes, when you return to me anything that may by *accident* have gotten into your pockets."

"Oh! my good sir, I have nothing in my hands, nothing in my pockets; I wouldn't harm anybody in the world; I am only here to look after this poor cherub, my uncle; search me if you want to."

"That will do; now get out," said the old man.

The fish-hawker needed no second telling, but rapidly scuttled down the stair. Cérizet seemed about to take the same way.

"You, monsieur, that is another matter," said the old man; "you and I can have a little chat together; but if you prove tractable, things may be satisfactorily arranged."

It may be that the effects of the narcotic had ceased, for Toupillier now opened his eyes and looked about him with the manner of a man who wonders where he is; then, seeing his closet open, he cried out: "Thieves! thieves!"

"No, Toupillier," said the little old man; "you have not been robbed; I arrived in time; nothing has been touched."

"And you, why don't you arrest that villain?" said the beggar, pointing to Cérizet.

"Monsieur is not a thief," replied the old man; "on the contrary, he came up with me to give me his help." Then, turning to Cérizet, he said: "I think, my friend, that we had better postpone our interview until the morrow. At ten o'clock come to the next house and inquire for Monsieur du Portail."

Cérizet, finding that he was not to be treated more rigorously than Mme. Cardinal, gave his promise and slipped away; more especially as the little monsieur had recognized him as the "brave Cérizet."

The next day Cérizet did not fail to appear at the rendezvous, as directed. He was ushered into the study of Du Portail, whom he found writing. Without rising, he made a sign that his guest be seated and went on with his letter. When it was finished he rang for Bruno, his valet, and, giving him the letter, he said:

"For Monsieur the Justice of the Peace of the arrondissement."

Then he carefullly wiped the steel pen that he had used, symmetrically replaced all the articles that he had moved on his desk, and it was only when these little matters had been duly attended to that he turned to Cérizet and said:

"You know that we have lost poor Monsieur Toupillier in the night?"

"Truly, no," said Cérizet, putting on the best look of sympathy he could assume. "This is my first tidings of it."

"You at least might have expected it; when one gives a dying man a big bowl of hot wine, narcotized beside, for, after drinking but a little glass, Perrache's wife lay in a lethargy the whole night through, it becomes quite evident that this catastrophe had been arranged for and hastened."

"I am ignorant, monsieur," said Cérizet with dignity, "of what Madame Cardinal may have given her uncle. Doubtless I committed an indiscretion in helping that woman to preserve her inheritance to which she gave me assurances that she had a legal right; but I am incapable of attempting the life of that old man; such a thought never entered my mind."

"Was it you that wrote me this letter?" said du Portail, brusquely, offering a paper to Cérizet.

"A letter?" replied he, with the hesitation of a man who wonders whether to lie or speak the truth.

"I have a mania for autographs; I am positive this is yours, for I have one of them when the Opposition elevated you to the glorious state of martyr. The letter you hold in your hand tells me of the monetary straits of young la Peyrade."

"Well," said the man of the Rue des Poules, "as I knew that you had in your care a demoiselle de la Peyrade, I guessed that you were Théodose's unknown protector. Now, having a sincere affection for that poor boy, it was in his interests that I made so bold——"

"You were right," interrupted du Portail. "I am pleased to encounter a friend of his. It was this that saved you last night. But what about those twenty-five thousand francs' worth of acceptances? Is he leading a dissipated life?"

"On the contrary," replied Cérizet, "he's a puritan. He is just on the point of making a wealthy marriage."

"Ah! he is to be married; to whom, pray?"

Then Cérizet proceeded to inform him of the circumstances of Céleste Thuillier. When he had concluded du Portail said:

"But you wrote me that those acceptances were in favor of Monsieur Dutocq. Is it a kind of matrimonial brokerage?"

"Something of the sort," said Cérizet. "You know, monsieur, that such transactions are common enough in Paris; the clergy doesn't disdain putting their finger in them."

"Well, even if the marriage is a settled thing, I must get you, my dear sir, to put an end to it; I have other views for Théodose—another match to propose to him."

"Excuse me," replied Cérizet; "should this marriage be broken off, it would be impossible for him to meet those acceptances."

"Monsieur Dutocq's debt," replied du Portail, "you shall yourself pay off. Should not Théodose prove amenable to my projects, those acceptances in our hands might compel him to do so; you could sue him in your name; I will pay the notes and your costs in suing Théodose."

"That's fair, I must say, monsieur," said Cérizet. "Perhaps you may afford me some light on why you do me the honor of confiding this matter to my hands."

"You mentioned a minute ago the cousin of la Peyrade, Mademoiselle Lydie de la Peyrade. That young lady, no longer in her first youth, for she is nearly thirty, is the natural daughter of la Beaumesnil, of the Theatre-Français, and de la Peyrade, commissary-general of police under the Empire, the uncle of your friend. At his death, which occurred suddenly, I, his best friend, took upon myself the care of his daughter whom he passionately loved."

"You have faithfully performed that duty," said Cérizet, anxious to let the other know that he was acquainted with some details of his inner life.

"Yes," answered du Portail, "the poor child was so cruelly tried by the death of her father that her mind became somewhat affected. But fortunately a change has occurred for the better; yesterday Doctor Bianchon and two other eminent physicians in consultation declared that marriage and a first child would infallibly restore her. You can well see that the remedy is too easy and too pleasant not to be given a trial."

"Then," said Cérizet, "it is to his cousin that you propose to marry Théodose."

"You have said it," replied du Portail. "You must not suppose, though, that by accepting this marriage he is displaying a gratuitous devotion. Lydie is agreeable in her person, is talented, has a charming nature, and can bring high favor to bear in her husband's behalf. She has also a pretty fortune, and my property will be wholly secured to her in the contract; and, added to this, she has inherited an important accession the past night."

"How!" said Cérizet; "has that old Toupillier——?"

"By a holograph will, which I have here, the beggar constitutes her his universal legatee; you see it was our property you and Madame Cardinal were trying to pillage. Beside, the will only makes a restitution."

"A restitution!" exclaimed Cérizet.

"A restitution," repeated du Portail, "and nothing is easier to establish. You remember the theft of diamonds from one of our dramatic celebrities some ten years ago?"

"Yes, certainly; the actress who lost them was the famous Mademoiselle Beaumesnil."

"Precisely, the mother of Lydie de la Peyrade."

"So that the wretched Toupillier—— But no, I remember, the thief was convicted. He was known as Charles Crochard. He was said to be, under the rose, the natural son of a great personage, the Comte de Granville."

"Well," said du Portail, "it happened thus: The robbery, you remember, was committed in a mansion on the Rue du Tournon, occupied by Mademoiselle Beaumesnil. Charles Crochard, a handsome fellow, had the run of her house."

"Yes, yes," said Cérizet, "I recall her embarrassment when she gave her testimony; and also how she lost her voice when asked her age."

"The robbery," continued du Portail, "was audaciously committed in the daytime; no sooner had Crochard got the casket than he went to the church of St. Sulpice, where he had arranged to meet an accomplice. He was to receive the diamonds from his hands, and, having a passport already provided, he was to at once start for foreign parts. It chanced that the expected one was detained for some time and was late in arriving at the church. Charles Crochard found himself face to face with a celebrated detective who knew him perfectly well, as the young rogue had had several encounters with the police already. The absence of his friend, the rencounter with the detective, and a rapid movement made by the latter troubled his mind; he thought he was being

14

watched. He lost his head under this idea, and wished himself well rid of his prize. At this moment he caught sight of Toupillier, then the holy-water distributer. 'My dear fellow,' said he, assuring himself that no one could hear him, 'will you oblige me by taking care of this little parcel? It is a box of lace. I am about calling on a countess to collect a bill; if she saw this she would want it on credit; that I don't want to do. But,' added he, 'on no account touch the paper wrapper, for there is nothing so difficult as to rewrap it in the old creases.'"

"The dummy!" exclaimed Cérizet, naïvely; "why, it was a recommendation for the man to open it."

"You are a practiced moralist," said du Portail. "One hour after, Crochard, finding nothing happened to him, presented himself at the church to recover his deposit. Toupillier was no longer in the place. You can figure to yourself how, on the next day, at first mass, Charles Crochard approached the holy-water distributer, who had returned to the performance of his duty; but night, as they say, brings counsel; the dear man, with bold effrontery, declared that nothing had been left with him, and he did not know what he was talking about."

"And not the least good to argue about it," said Cérizet, who was not far from sympathizing in so bold a play, "for that would have meant exposure."

"No doubt the robbery was already noised around," du Portail went on, "and Toupillier, a smart fellow, had rightly calculated that the thief by accusing him would discover himself. In the trial Charles Crochard never spoke one word of his misadventure, and, condemned to ten years, six of which he passed on the hulks, during his incarceration he did not open his lips about the treachery. In that interval Madame Beaumesnil died, leaving her daughter some small remains of a great fortune; she mentioned the diamonds, and expressly stated that they became hers, 'if they were ever recovered.'"

"Ah!" said Cérizet, "that made it bad for Toupillier, for having a man of your mettle to deal with——"

"All thoughts of Charles Crochard were first turned to vengeance on his release; he denounced Toupillier as the receiver of the casket. Taken under hand by Justice, he defended himself most good-humoredly, singularly so, and proved that no suspicion attached to him, and the case was dismissed. But this affair cost Toupillier his position; he obtained, not without difficulty, the right of begging in the porch of St. Sulpice. As for myself, I was satisfied of his guilt, and, without being suspected, I had the closest watch kept upon him; in order to unmask him, I did one of the smartest tricks in my life. I became the tenant of the room adjoining his on the Rue Cœur-Volant; I drilled a hole through the party-wall, and one evening saw him take out the casket from a cleverly contrived hiding-place, open it, and gaze upon the contents and fondle them. The man loved them for themselves alone; he had no thought of converting them into money."

"I understand," said Cérizet, "a mania of the same kind as Monsieur Cardillac, the jeweler, which has just been dramatized."

"The same," returned du Portail; "the wretch was in love with them, so that when I entered his room and told him I knew all, he asked me not to dispossess him of them while he lived, and at his death his whole hoard of gold, his cash in the Funds, and his house should become the heritage of Mademoiselle de la Peyrade.

"Well, my dear sir, I was not mistaken in trusting him. I exacted that he should occupy a room in the same house as myself; I assisted in building that hiding-place of his, the secret of which you so ingeniously discovered; but, in your ignorance, you did not discover that when you touched the secret spring you also rang a bell in my chamber which warned me of any attempt to steal our hoard."

"Poor Madame Cardinal," cried Cérizet, with pleasantry, "she counted her chickens too soon."

"Now, on account of the interest I feel in the nephew of my late friend, this marriage seems to me most desirable," said du Portail. "Théodose may object, owing to his cousin's mental state. You have turned up on my way; you are smart and crafty, so I put this matrimonial negotiation in your charge. You may speak to him of a pretty girl with a good fortune, with one slight drawback, but mention no names."

"Your confidence honors me," replied Cérizet; "I will justify it to the best of my ability."

"Get those acceptances from Dutocq; we shall not haggle over a few thousand francs, but when the affair is arranged Dutocq must give us his assistance. After what you have told me of the other marriage, you can scarcely waste any time," concluded du Portail.

"Two days hence I have an appointment with Théodose," said Cérizet.

"So be it," said du Portail; "that is not delaying much. Now, remember, monsieur, if you succeed you have a man who may assist you, instead of bringing you to account."

Then the pair separated.

The same as the Tourniquet Saint-Jean, the Rocher de Cancale, whence this scene is changed to, is to-day but a memory. A wine-dealer who uses a pewter-topped counter has replaced that *Temple of Taste*, that sanctuary of European fame, which had seen the passing of gastronomy under the Empire and the Restoration.

The evening of the day arranged upon for a meeting la Peyrade had received this simple word from Cérizet :

"To-morrow, lease or no lease, at the Rocher, at six thirty." Dutocq received his invitation by word of mouth ; but his time was "quarter past six, sharp." It was evident that Cérizet wanted that fifteen minutes with him before the arrival of la Peyrade. That fifteen minutes the usurer intended to employ in jockeying Dutocq in the purchase of the acceptances; he thought a sudden proposition to purchase would be accepted more readily than if time were given for thinking. Moreover, let it be said that Cérizet was bound to try and scrape something out of his dear friend; it was an instinct, his nature. He had the same horror of a straight line as the amateurs in English gardens have of a straight path.

At a quarter after six Dutocq punctually made his appearance, for a dinner at the Rocher de Cancale was something of an event.

"It is funny," said he, "that we again meet; the three emperors, except that our present tryst is preferable to our former one."

"My faith!" replied Cérizet, "I don't quite know that the results justify the change, for, frankly, where are the profits of our triumvirate?"

"Well, but it was a bargain," said Dutocq, "with a long term attached. It can't be claimed that la Peyrade has lost much time, pardon the pun, in becoming installed at the *T(h)uileries*. The rascal has gone ahead pretty fast."

"Not so fast but that his marriage is anything but a settled matter," said Cérizet.

"Not settled; why?"

"Yes, I am charged to propose to him another wife. I am not so sure that he will be allowed to choose."

"But what, the devil! my dear, lending your hand to help on another marriage when you know we have the first hypothecated!"

"My friend, one cannot always control circumstances. I saw that the other was gone overhead; I look now to guide our feet to pastures new."

"They can't fool me: la Peyrade signed the acceptances and he must pay them."

"The question is, will he pay them? You are not a merchant, neither is Théodose; suppose he disputes the acceptances; he might deny their validity. The tribunal might annul them as having been given without consideration received. Now you, as clerk to a justice, might find that the chancellor could have a little case with you; as for myself, I've seen to my interests. I choose to save myself by a sacrifice."

"What kind of a sacrifice?"

"*Parbleu*, I have sold my share," said Cérizet.

"Who was the buyer?"

"Who, think you, would step into my shoes but those urging on this other marriage?"

"Doubtless, then, my share would be of use also?"

"Well, you see, I could not offer them until I had seen you."

"On what terms?"

"I let them have my acceptances for fifteen thousand francs."

"Oh! then your game is to make a commission out of mine to make up your loss—if you've had one—beside, it may be but a scheme between you and la Peyrade," said Dutocq.

"At least, my dear, you don't mince your words; you have an infamous thought and state it with charming abandon."

"Well, I withdraw the insinuation, as you say that you are going to make the offer to Théodose in my presence."

"See here, my poor friend, how I reasoned; I said to myself: 'This good Dutocq is being pressed for the last payment on his office; he will find enough to pay it off at one stroke; events have shown that uncertainties exist about the compromising of la Peyrade; here's cash down, on the nail;' the bargain ain't so bad, either."

"All the same, it's a loss of two-fifths."

"You just spoke of commissions; you only help me over

this other matter and I don't fear but what I can obtain you a round twenty thousand francs."

"Then you think this new proposal may not be acceptable to la Peyrade? Why should he object? Is it then some heiress from whom the rascal has already had something!"

"All that I can say is that trouble is expected in concluding it."

At this moment the door opened and the other guest arrived. "You may serve dinner," said Cérizet to the attendant; "we expect no one else."

They could see that Théodose had begun to take his flight toward higher social spheres; elegance had become his constant ambition. He had made an evening toilet, dress suit and patent-leather shoes, while the other two received him in loose coats and muddy boots.

"Gentlemen," said he, "I think I am somewhat late, but that devil of a Thuillier, with the pamphlet I am concocting for him, is one of the most intolerable of human beings. I was so unfortunate as to arrange to revise the proofs with him; at each paragraph we had a fight: 'What I don't understand,' he kept saying, 'the public can't understand, either. I'm not a man of letters, but I am a practical man;' and it was the same battle over every sentence. I thought this seance would never come to an end."

"What would you, my dear?" said Dutocq; "when a man wants to get there he must have some courage; once the marriage is made you can hold up your head."

"Oh! yes," said la Peyrade, "I'll raise it; for since you have given me this bread of bitterness, I've become heartily tired of it."

"Cérizet," said Dutocq, "has to-day some more succulent food to place before you."

For the time being nothing more was said, they had to do justice to the goodly cheer ordered for them by Cérizet in honor of the first tenant. It was not until dessert was served that Cérizet decided to ask la Peyrade what resolution had been come to in reference to the lease.

"Nothing, my dear," replied la Peyrade.

"How, nothing? I left you time enough to decide in."

"And, in fact, something is decided; there will be no first tenant, Mademoiselle Brigitte will herself sub-let the house."

"That's a different story," said Cérizet, with a lordly air. "After your promise to me, I avow that I did not expect such a result as this."

"What could I do, my dear? I made my promise subject to contingencies; I wasn't able to give another turn to the business. In her quality as master-woman and sample of perpetual motion, Mademoiselle Thuillier has reflected that she might as well undertake the task of managing the property and pocketing the profits herself that you intended making. I put in all I could about the annoyances, inconveniences, and so forth, but 'Bah! rubbish!' she replied; 'it will stir my blood and be good for my health.'"

"But this is pitiable," said Cérizet; "the poor old maid doesn't know what it means to get tenants from top to bottom."

"I used all those arguments," replied la Peyrade, "but only to strengthen her resolution. There you are, my dear democrats, you fomented the revolution of '89; you thought it an excellent speculation to dethrone the nobles by the bourgeoisie; it ends in yourselves being elbowed out. It seems like a paradox, but you've found out now that the country-jay can't be forced down and kept under like the noble. The aristocracy had a care for its dignity; it prohibited itself a host of petty details, even of learning to write; it found itself dependent on a host of plebeian servitors to whom it confided three-fourths of the actions of their lives. But to-day utilitarian theories rule: 'We are never so well served as by ourselves.' 'It's not disgraceful to know one's own business;' and a thousand other middle-class proverbs, which have done away with the need of intermediaries. Why should not Brigitte Thuillier have the pretensions to manage her house, when dukes and peers of France go personally to the Bourse, when the same persons sign their own leases, and read them first, and discuss every point with the notary at his own place, one whom they formerly accounted as a scrivener?"

"What you are preaching," said Cérizet, carelessly, "is mighty clever; but it seems to prove, also, that you are not on such a footing of intimacy with Mlle. Thuillier as you would have us believe. I begin to think that the marriage is far from being so settled a matter as Dutocq and myself fancied."

"Without doubt," replied la Peyrade, "there are yet some careful touches to be given to our sketch before it is finished, but I think it nears completion."

"For my part I am of the contrary opinion, you have lost ground, and the reason is simple; you have done an immense service to these people, and they will never forgive you for it."

"Well, wait and see," said la Peyrade; "I hold them by more than one string."

"No, you are wrong. If I were you I shouldn't feel quite so sure of treading on solid ground; if something else turned up that presented a good chance——"

"What! because I couldn't get you the lease to eat, must I throw the handle after the axe?"

"I repeat to you," said Cérizet, "that I'm not looking at it from the side of my own interests; but as you have doubtless and truly tried your level best to promote them, I think that the way in which you have been pushed aside is a disquieting symptom."

"*Ah! ça!*" said la Peyrade, "what are you getting at? Is it that you have something to propose to me? What's it to cost?"

"My dear fellow," replied Cérizet, ignoring this impertinence, "yourself shall judge of the value of finding a young woman, well brought up, adorned with beauty and talent, a *dot* equivalent to or no less than Céleste's, in her own right, *plus* one hundred thousand francs in diamonds (as Mlle. Georges says on her posters in the provinces), beside political influence for her husband's benefit."

"And this treasure you have in your hand?" asked la Peyrade, with an incredulous air.

"Better than that, I am authorized to make you the offer; I may even say that I am charged so to do."

"My friend, either you are mocking me, unless, as I suppose, this phœnix has some prohibitory defect."

"I acknowledge," said Cérizet, "that there exists one slight defect, but not on the score of family, for she has none."

"Ah!" said la Peyrade, "of course, a natural child—what beside?"

"Beside? Well, she is not so young as to wear the hood of St. Catherine; she is, say, about twenty-nine; but an elderly girl can be imagined into a young widow—nothing easier."

"And is that all the venom?"

"Yes, all that is irreparable."

"What do you mean by that? A case of rhinoplasty?"

This so pertinent a word, as addressed to Cérizet, was given with an aggressive air; this manner, indeed, had been noticeable throughout the dinner, even in the conversation of the barrister. But it was not to the purpose of the negotiator to resent it.

"No," he responded; "we have as good a nose as feet and waist; but we might perhaps have a touch of hysteria."

"Very good!" said la Peyrade, "and as from hysteria to insanity there is but a step——"

"Well, yes," eagerly interrupted Cérizet; "sorrows have left our brain slightly deranged, but the doctors, after a care-

ful diagnosis, say that after bearing a first child not the least
trace of this trouble will remain."

"I willingly admit that Messieurs the Doctors are absolutely
infallible," replied the barrister; "but, in spite of your discouragements, you must excuse me if I still continue to address Mademoiselle Colleville. It is perhaps ridiculous to
avow this, but the fact is that I am gradually falling in love
with that little girl. It is not that she is very beautiful, or
that the glamour of her *dot* has enamored me, but in that child
is an innocent mind joined to sound sense; and, what to my
mind is of more consequence, she possesses a sincere and solid
piety."

"Yes," said Cérizet, who, having been on the stage, may
well have remembered Molière's: "Your hymen shall be
soaked in sweetness and joy."

This allusion to Tartuffe was keenly felt by la Peyrade, who
hotly retorted:

"The contact of innocence will disinfect me of the vile
company I have kept for so long a time."

"And you will pay your acceptances, which I urge you to
do without delay," said Cérizet. "Dutocq here was just saying that he would like to see the color of your money."

"Me? oh, not at all," said Dutocq; "I think, on the
contrary, our friend is perfectly right in his delay."

"Well, for myself," said la Peyrade, "I am quite of
Cérizet's opinion; I hold that the less the debt is due, and
therefore the more insecure, the sooner should one free himself by paying it."

"But, my dear la Peyrade," said Dutocq, "you speak so
bitterly."

Drawing from his pocket a portfolio, la Peyrade said:

"Have you the acceptances with you, Dutocq?"

"Faith, no, dear fellow," said the clerk; "I don't carry
them around, beside they are in Cérizet's hands."

"Well," said the barrister, as he arose, "whenever you

V

bring them to my office, the cash is ready. Cérizet can prove that."

"What! are you leaving us without waiting for coffee?" said the usurer, much amazed.

"Yes; at eight o'clock I have an arbitration case. Beside, all has been said; you haven't got the lease, but you have gotten your twenty-five thousand francs, and Dutocq can have his whenever he likes to present his acceptances at my office; I don't see anything that should prevent me going about my own affairs, therefore I give you a cordial good-day."

"Dear me!" said Cérizet, as la Peyrade went out, "this means a rupture."

"And carefully prepared at that," remarked Dutocq. "With what an air he produced his portfolio!"

"But where the devil did he get his money?" asked the usurer.

"No doubt," replied the clerk, ironically, "whence he got that with which he paid off in full your acceptances on which you made such a sacrifice."

"Well, I was instructed to buy up your acceptances; you will recollect that I had risen to twenty thousand when he came in."

"All right, when we leave here we'll go to your house for those notes; I mean to give him the chance to pay me while his humor is hot."

"Quite correct; for I can tell you right here that there will very soon be an upset in his life."

"Then you were really serious about that crazy marrying him. I must say that I should have adopted the same course; Ninas and Ophelias are very interesting on the stage, but in our households——"

"In the households, when they bring a *dot*, we become their guardian," replied the sententious Cérizet. "Really we get a fortune and not a wife."

"Let's have our coffee elsewhere," said Cérizet; "I want

to get out of this room, I can't breathe in it." He rang for the garçon; "the bill?" said he.

"But, m'sieur, it is paid."

"Paid! and by whom?"

"By the gentleman who just left. Shall I bring in the coffee—it is paid for, before he left?"

"An excellent reason for refusing it," answered Cérizet angrily. "It is really inconceivable that in a house like this such a blunder should be allowed. What do you think of such impertinence?" he bitterly added, when the waiter had gone.

"Pshaw! it's only a schoolboy's move to show that he has money in his pocket; it is something new to him."

"No, no, that's not it at all," said Cérizet; "it was his way of emphasizing the rupture. 'I will not even owe a dinner to you' is what he says."

Dutocq was the guide to a low café in the Passage du Saumon, where Cérizet soon recovered his good humor; like a fish who had been out of water returned to his native element, so Cérizet had become so degraded that he felt ill at ease in good society resorts. In this vulgar place a game of pool was being played. Now Cérizet enjoyed the reputation of being a skillful player in the establishment, and he was entreated to take a cue. In the parlance of the place he "bought a ball;" that is, one of the players sold him his turn and score.

Soon after, in his shirt-sleeves, a pipe between his teeth, he made a masterly stroke which evoked tumults of applause. He looked triumphantly around, graciously receiving the admiration of the gods, when his eyes alighted on a terrible killjoy. Standing amongst the spectators, looking over his hand resting on his cane, du Portail was watching him. Cérizet reddened, lost his presence of mind, made a few bad strokes, and was soon out of the game. As he was gloomily donning his coat du Portail brushed by him:

"Rue Montmartre, at the end of the court," said he in a low voice.

When they met Cérizet was so dumb as to try and explain why he was found in such disreputable company.

"But," said du Portail, "to see you there I had also to be there myself."

"That is true," replied the usurer; "I was astonished to find a quiet inhabitant of the St. Sulpice quarter there."

"That proves to you," retorted the other, in a tone which effectually cut off curious questioning, "that I am in the habit of going everywhere, and my lucky star usually leads me to those whom I wish to meet. Well, what have you done?"

Cérizet explained all that had occurred, and that there was no chance of Dutocq's acceptances being secured.

"Then does he regard his marriage with the demoiselle Colleville as a settled thing?"

"Not only that, but he pretended that it is a love-match. He tried to persuade me of that by a long, tiresome tirade."

"Well, now cease your charge; you have failed in this, but I have other uses for you."

As he spoke he hailed a passing hack, nodded to Cérizet, got in and told the man to drive to the Rue Honoré-Chevalier.

As he walked down the Rue Montmartre, to regain the Estrapade quarter, Cérizet puzzled his brain in guessing what that little old man, with curt speech, imperious manners, and a tone that seemed to cast a spell as strong as a grappling-iron over a person, could be; why, too, should a man like him come such a distance to spend his evening, especially in such a place where he must assuredly be out of his element? He had just reached the Market when he was rudely aroused from his meditation by a rough shake and a punch in his back. He turned hastily around, and found himself face to face with Mme. Cardinal. For the past two days she had been taking "drops of consolation" over her defeat in the numerous liquor-dealers' taverns of the quarter. With thickened speech and face aflame:

"Well, papa," said she to Cérizet, "how did you come on with the little old man?"

"I gave him my word," replied the usurer, "that so far as I was concerned it was all a mistake. You, my poor Madame Cardinal, behaved in this affair with much heedlessness; why should you ask me to assist you in getting your uncle's inheritance when it has for a long time been manifest that he had a natural daughter to whom he had left all. That little old man is her guardian."

"Ah! talk to me of guardian," said la Cardinal, "a nobby guardian. To talk as he did to a woman of my age, only because she wanted to find out if her uncle had anything to leave. And then to talk to me, me! of the police! It's horrible, it's *degustating!*"

"Come!" said Cérizet, "you got off very well, Mammy Cardinal."

"Well, and you, you who broke the locks and said you would accept the diamonds under pretense of marrying my daughter. As if she wanted you, my daughter, my legitimate daughter, like she is. 'Never, my mother,' said she to me; 'I will never give my heart to a man with half a nose, like his.'"

"So you've found her, then?"

"Only last evening; she has left her drunken actor, and is now, I flatter myself, in a splendid position; she can eat money, has a coach hired by the month, and is much esteemed by a barrister who would marry her off the reel, but he has to wait for the death of his parents; for his father happens to be mayor, and the government would be against it."

"My worthy woman," said Cérizet, "what the devil are you gabbling about? 'It happens that his father is his mother*——'"

---

* *Parce que le père se trouve être maire: mère*—mother; *maire*—mayor.

"What stuff! Mayor of his arrondissement, the eleventh, Monsieur Minard, a retired cocoa-dealer, enormously rich."

"Oh! very good, I know him. And you say that Olympe is living with his son?"

"Well, that is to say, not living together, for that makes talk, that he visits her with a good motive; he lives at home with his father, but he has bought their furniture and him and my daughter has took a lodgings, where it and my daughter is housed, on the Chaussée-d'Antin: stylish quarter, ain't it?"

"It seems nicely arranged," said Cérizet.

"Yes; and there's something I want to consult you about."

"What is it?"

"It's this: my daughter's in luck, I ought not to go on crying fish up and down the streets; and then I find myself disinherited by my uncle; it seems to me, therefore, that I've a right to a *elementary* allowance."

"You dream, my poor woman. Your daughter is a minor; it's you should be feeding her; she ought not to provide the alimentaries."

"Then," said Mme. Cardinal, vexed and disagreeable, "that means that us who have nothing must give to those who have plenty. That's a proper sort of a law; it's as bad as your guardians who prate about sending for the police. Well, yes, I'd like to see 'em send the police! Let them guillotine me! It won't stop me saying that the rich are all swindlers; it's about time the people made another revolution for their *rightful rights*, my boy. You, my daughter, the barrister Minard, and that little old guardian, see you, you would all be done away with."

Seeing that his ex-mother-in-law had worked herself up to a becoming degree of exaltation that was far from assuring, Cérizet abruptly left her, but even then she sent her epithets after him for a hundred feet or more; but he promised himself the pleasure of getting even with her the next time she came to the bank in the Rue des Poules to ask for an "easy let down."

As he neared his house, Cérizet, who was anything but brave, felt an emotion of fear; he noticed a figure ambushed by his door; as he approached nearer it detatched itself to come and meet him; happily it was none other than Dutocq. He had come for his acceptances. Cérizet returned them, with some ill-humor; he complained of the distrust implied by a visit for such a purpose at that hour. Dutocq paid no attention to his touchy susceptibilities, but the next morning presented them to la Peyrade, who paid him as he had promised. Dutocq made a few sentimental remarks when he had gotten the cash, but he was answered by a marked coolness.

As he conducted his creditor to the door he found himself face to face with a woman dressed as a servant, who was just about to ring the bell. She seemed to be known to Dutocq, for he said:

"Ah! little mother; so you feel the necessity of consulting a barrister? You are right; at the family council some serious charges were brought against you."

"Thank God! I have no fear of any one; I can walk with my head erect," answered the woman.

"Well, be careful, my dear lady, for I tell you that when you get before the judge who is to inquire into the matter, you'll be finely pulled to pieces. The relatives are furious against you; they can't get the idea out of their heads that you have become very rich."

Here Théodose requested his client to enter.

This is what had taken place the day before.

It will be remembered that la Peyrade was in the habit of attending the first mass in his parish church. For some time he had found himself the object of particular attention on the part of the woman who had just entered his house, and who, as the saying goes, like Dorine in "Tartuffe," had taken care to attend regularly at "his exact hour;" these singular proceedings had embarrassed him considerably.

An affair of the heart? This explanation scarcely comported with the saintly maturity of a person who, wearing the plain cap, known in the quarter as a *janséniste*, the nun-like covering for the hair that distinguished the female votaries of that sect. On the morning of the day of the dinner, la Peyrade went to the woman and asked if there was anything he could do for her.

"Monsieur," she replied in a mystical voice, "is I believe the celebrated Monsieur de la Peyrade, the advocate of the poor?"

"I am la Peyrade; and I have at times been able to be of service to the poor of this quarter."

"If you would listen to and grant me a consultation, monsieur."

"This is not a fitting place," replied la Peyrade, "for a conference. I live near here, Rue Saint-Dominique d'Enfer; if you will take the trouble to come to my office—"

"It will not trouble monsieur?"

"Not the least in the world; my business is to attend my clients."

"At what hour, for I would not disturb monsieur?"

"Whenever you please; I shall be home all the morning?"

"Then I will hear another mass and take the communion; I am too agitated just now. I will be at monsieur's house at eight o'clock, if that hour won't be inconvenient."

At the hour named, not one minute before or past, the pious woman rang the bell, but the barrister had some difficulty in getting her to be seated and to state her case. Then that delaying little cough, so often used in like cases, seized her; but at last she touched the object of her visit.

"This is it," said she, "whether monsieur would be so kind as to let me know if it was true that a very charitable man had given a fund as a reward to servants who have faithfully served their masters?"

"There is this to say," replied la Peyrade, "that Monsieur de Montyon founded a prize of virtue which, in fact, has often been awarded to zealous and exemplary servants; but good conduct only is not enough, there must be some act of high devotion and a truly Christian abnegation."

"Religion," replied the pious woman, "enjoins humility, and so I cannot praise myself; but for twenty years I have been in the service of an old man, dull in the extreme, a *savant*, who has eaten up all his substance by inventing things, and whom I have been obliged to feed and clothe; so some people think I am not unworthy of obtaining the prize."

"That is, in fact, the conditions under which the Academy chooses its candidates," replied la Peyrade. "What is your master's name?"

"Father Picot; they all call him that in our quarter. He takes no care for his dignity; he is occupied with his own ideas; I wear myself out getting him tasty food, but if one asks him what he had for dinner he cannot remember."

"Is your master a mathematician?"

"Yes, monsieur; they have been his bane."

"Well," said la Peyrade, "let me have the testimony proving your devotion to this old man, and I will prepare a petition to the Academy and have it presented."

"Monsieur is very good," said the pious woman; "if he would allow me to speak of a little difficulty——"

"What is that?"

"They tell me, monsieur, that the prize can only be won by a very poor person."

"Not exactly so; still, the Academy does in effect try to choose people in straitened circumstances and who have made sacrifices beyond their means."

"Sacrifices! I flatter myself that I have made them; all

my little heritage from my parents has gone in keeping him, and, beside, for fifteen years I have not had a sou of wages, which, at three hundred francs a year and compound interest, would make a right pretty sum, as monsieur will allow."

At the words compound interest, which was evidence of a certain degree of cultured financial experience, la Peyrade looked upon this Antigone with attention.

"In short," said he, "this difficulty of yours——"

"Monsieur," the pious one replied, "will not deem it strange that a very rich uncle of mine has died in England and left me twenty-five thousand francs; one, too, that had done nothing for his family before?"

"Assuredly there is nothing in that but what is right and properly legal," said the barrister.

"But, monsieur, having this might lose me the prize; beside, it is in the greatest danger from my master."

"How is that?" asked la Peyrade, curiously.

"Eh! monsieur, if he only got wind of that money, it would go at one mouthful; his invention of perpetual motion and the like have already ruined both him and me."

"Then you would have the knowledge withheld from the Academy and master, both?"

"How clever monsieur is; he fully understands at once," said the religious woman, smiling.

"And what do you want to do with the money?" asked the barrister. "You want to get it out of your hands?"

"For fear that the master might swoop down upon it, certainly. How well monsieur understands; now, if it was at interest, I could get him a few delicacies now and again; that's why I should like it to bear interest."

"And as high as possible, eh?" said the barrister.

"*Dame*, yes, five or six per cent."

"Then it was about both these things that you wished to consult me?"

"Monsieur is so kind, so charitable, so encouraging."

"After a few inquiries the petition can easily be drawn; but to invest with security and secrecy, both, is rather more difficult."

"Ah! if I only dared," said she.

"What?" said la Peyrade.

"Monsieur understands me."

"Me? not the least idea in the world."

"I have prayed well this hour past that monsieur might take charge of this money; I should be sure of its safety and of nothing being said about it."

La Peyrade received at this moment the fruit of his farce of devotion to the necessitous class. The chorus of porters in the quarter had carried his praises to this domestic. He thought of Dutocq, and firmly believed that this woman had been wafted to him by Providence. He resolved to play a deep game.

"My dear lady," said he to his pious client, "I am in no need of money; and I am not rich enough to pay you interest on twenty-five thousand francs without investing it. All I could do would be to put it in the hands of the notary Dupuis in my name, a pious man whom you may see every Sunday on the wardens' bench in our parish church. Notaries, you know, give no receipt, therefore I cannot give you one. I can but leave a note among my papers, which will be found at my death, showing the transaction. You see, it is a confidential business; it is only done to oblige a pious and devoted person who possesses charitable sentiments."

"If monsieur can find no other way——"

"That is the only one that seems possible," said la Peyrade. "However, I don't know but what I can get you six per cent., and I will see that it is paid promptly. But on the least indiscretion on your part the money will be at once returned to you."

"Oh! monsieur, think you that I am a woman who would talk about what she should keep silent?"

"My blessing! my dear lady, we must provide against everything in such a business. Take time to think it over. Come again in a day or two, I may evolve another plan; I confess this does not please me over-well; I may think of other difficulties that have escaped my notice."

This adroit menace thrown in clinched the business.

"I have reflected," said piety; "with a man so religious as yourself, monsieur, I cannot see any risk."

And, taking from under her chemisette a little pocket-book, she drew out twenty-five bank-bills. Her manner of counting them, the dexterity she showed, was to la Peyrade a revelation. The woman was well accustomed to handling cash, and a singular idea struck him:

"Suppose that I am receiving stolen—— No," said he; "in order to draw up your petition I must make a few inquiries, so in the ordinary course of things I will wait on you presently. At what hour are you alone?"

"On the stroke of four, monsieur goes for a promenade to the Luxembourg."

"And where do you live?"

"No. 9 Rue du Val-du-Grâce."

"Well, then, four o'clock; if, as I believe is likely, I find all is right, then I can take your money."

"Oh! monsieur is prudent," said she, thinking the matter settled. "This money, thank God, I have not stolen, and monsieur can so inform himself about me in the quarter."

"That is just what I shall be compelled to do," said la Peyrade, who did not quite like, under the exterior of simplicity, that lively intelligence which penetrated his every thought.

"As monsieur pleases," said the pious one; "you are doing me too great a service to complain of your precautions."

And, after an unctuous salutation, she went out, carrying her money with her.

"The devil!" thought la Peyrade, "that woman is as

strong as myself; she swallows an affront with a gratified air and without the shadow of a grimace."

The information he gathered in the quarter was contradictory; some gave his client the name of saint, others presented her as a very cunning, artful woman; but, summing all up, there was nothing that inculpated her morality or such as would deter la Peyrade from accepting the good fortune that she offered him.

At four o'clock he found her of the same mind. The cash in his pocket, he went to the Rocher de Cancale, and perhaps it was the day's excitement that had caused him to assume the petulant manner he had with his two associates. In fact, the money had rather turned his brain; he had rid himself of Cérizet without even consulting Brigitte. Thus through the whole day la Peyrade had not shown himself the man so completely infallible as we had credited him with being. It is perhaps more difficult to keep one's head level in good than in evil fortune.

The Farnèsse Hercules, calm in repose, shows more fully the plenitude of muscular force than the other Hercules in violent agitation and represented in the excitement of their labors.

## PART II.

Between the two parts of this story an important event had taken place in the life of Phellion.

There is no one but has heard of the Odeon's ill-luck, that fatal theatre which had for years spelt the ruin of its directors. Rightly or wrongly the quarter in which stands this dramatic impossibility is absolutely convinced that its prosperity in a high degree depends upon it; more than once the mayor and notables of the arrondissement have tried every desperate effort to galvanize the corpse, with a courage equal to their honor.

Now to have a finger in the pie theatrical is one of the eternal, ever-living ambitions of the middle-class. Thus the successive saviours of the Odeon feel themselves amply rewarded when they are given a share, be it ever so small, in the administration of the concern. It was at such a combination of circumstances that Minard, in his quality as mayor of the eleventh arrondissement, had been called to preside over the committee on reading plays, with power to select as assessors a certain number of notables of the Latin quarter—the choice being left to him.

Now as both the Minards and Phellions had seen the advance made by la Peyrade in the securing of Céleste's *dot*, they each felt a loss of that prejudice which had formerly animated them; there is nothing binds and soothes men so much as a feeling of checkmate felt in common. Thus when the mayor had to bring to head the question of the composition of his dramatic customs-house, he gave immediate thought to Phellion.

One can well understand that so high and sacred a mission

was not lightly undertaken by a man of Phellion's solemnity; to himself he said that he was called upon to exercise magistracy, priesthood.

"To judge men," he had replied to Minard, who was astonished at his hesitation, "is an alarming task; but to judge of intellects—who can believe himself equal to such a mission?"

Phellion, to use his own term, had become a member of the Areopagus presided over by Minard, and he had just come home from the exercise of his functions both "delicate and interesting," quoting himself again, when the conversation we are about to repeat took place.

The session of the committee had been particularly stormy. On discussing a tragedy, having for title "The Death of Hercules," those classically imbued and the others tinctured with romance, carefully balanced by the mayor in forming the committee, had nearly come to the hair-pulling stage. Twice had Phellion asked to put in a word, and every one was astounded at the flood of metaphors with which the speech of a major of the National Guard could flow when his literary convictions were assailed. The result of the vote was a victory for the opinions of which Phellion was the eloquent mouthpiece.

As they descended the stairs together Phellion remarked to Minard: "'The Death of Hercules' reminded me of Luce de Lancival's 'Death of Hector;' it is full of sublimity."

"Yes," said Minard, "it is in good taste. It is far better literature than Colleville's anagrams."

"Oh!" said Phellion, "they are mere witticisms; they have nothing in common with the severe accents of Melpomene."

"And yet," replied Minard, "I can affirm that he attaches much importance to that stuff. But it seems to me that not only Colleville, but his wife, daughter, the Thuilliers, and the rest of the whole coterie have assumed airs of importance, hardly justified by their having moved into the Madeleine quarter."

"What would you?" said Phellion; "it requires a strong head to stand the fumes of opulence. Our friends have grown very rich by the purchase of that house; we must excuse a little intoxication; yesterday they gave us a good housewarming dinner, well spread and succulent."

"I also," said Minard, "have, I flatter myself, given a few remarkable dinners at which men high in the government have not disdained to attend, but I am not unduly puffed up."

"You, Monsieur le Maire, you have for a long time enjoyed a handsome mode of life in your high commercial capacity; our friends have but just made their fortunes; they have hardly got their sea-legs yet."

"Are you going through the Luxembourg?" asked Minard.

"I shall go that way, but not to stay. I have to meet Madame Phellion at the end of the broad walk; she will await me there with the Barniol children."

"Well," said Minard, "I shall have the pleasure of saluting Madame Phellion."

Minard quite realized that Phellion had not voluntarily followed him in his caustic remarks on the Thuilliers, so he did not offer to renew the subject, but he felt sure that Mme. Phellion would reëcho his animadversions.

"Well, fair lady," said he, "and what did you think of the dinner yesterday?"

"It was well put up," replied Mme. Phellion, "and the *potage à la bisque*,\* I could tell, showed the hand of a master, like Chevet, who must have replaced their own cook. But there seemed a lack of gayety; there was none of the cordiality that marks our little reunions in the Latin quarter. Beside, one could hardly fail to see that Madame and Mlle. Thuillier did not seem at home. I felt like I was dining with

---

\* A rich soup.

Madame —— what's her name? I cannot keep myself in mind of it."

"Torna, Comtesse de Godollo," said Phellion, interrupting. "Still the name is most euphonistic."

"Euphonistic as you wish, my friend; but for me, I can't think it's a name at all."

"It is a Magyar, or, vulgarly speaking, a Hungarian name. Our name, for instance, may be said to be borrowed from the Greek."

"That is possible, but we have the advantage of being well-known, not only in our own quarter, but in the whole world of education, where our parvenus have conquered an honorable position; not like that Hungarian countess who makes rain and sunshine in the Thuilliers' house. Whence came she? How comes it that having all the manners of a great lady, with such a distinguished air, she should fall into the arms of Brigitte, who, between us, tastes of the sod, and is so the porter's daughter as to nauseate one?"

"Dear me," said Minard, "don't you know how the intimacy began between the Comtesse de Godollo and the Thuilliers?"

"That she is a tenant of theirs, she occupies the entresol."

"True, but there's more than that in it. Zélie, my wife, had it from Joséphine, who was quitting their service for ours, but did not, as our own Françoise, change her mind about getting married. You must know, fair lady, that it was Madame de Godollo who caused the migration of the Thuilliers; she was, one might say, their upholsterer."

"How, their upholsterer!" cried Phellion, "that stylish woman of whom one might truly say: *Incessa patuit dea,* which, in French, is so imperfectly expressed by saying: 'the bearing of a queen.'"

"Permit me," said Minard; "I don't mean she was actually their upholsterer, but when Mademoiselle Thuillier decided by la Peyrade's advice to manage the house herself, he could not persuade her to move into that sumptuous apartment where they received us yesterday."

"Five-franc pieces form her jingling music; so when la Peyrade and Thuillier urged her removal she only thought of the cost it would entail."

"There you have the universal link," exclaimed Phellion; "you see, from the summit of society, luxury sooner or later infiltrates itself through the lower classes and involves empires in ruin."

"That is a knotty point in political economy," said Minard. "But to go on: Madame de Godollo told her that a friend of hers, a Russian princess, had a fine suite of furniture, most of it entirely new. She had been recalled to Russia by the Czar, a gentleman whom it is no joke to cross; so the poor woman had no recourse but to sell at the best obtainable price. This idea of doing a good stroke of business and a chance of refurnishing decided the matter. In that old maid, you see, there is always more or less of Madame la Ressource, in 'The Miser.'"

"I think, Monsieur the Mayor, that you are in error," said Phellion; "la Ressource is a character in 'Turcaret,' a very immoral play by the late Le Sage."

"Well, be that as it may, this caused the foreign countess to get on a good footing with Brigitte. You may have observed also the signs of a coming struggle between the two influences, the personal and the real estate?"

"Why, yes," said Mme. Phellion, with a beaming expression, evincing her interest. "It did appear that the grand lady allowed herself to contradict the barrister, and with an amount of asperity, too."

"Well, his interest is waning in the house," said Minard. "He cannot get a freehold every day for his 'good friend,' as he calls him, for a crumb of bread."

"How did they get it so cheap?" asked Mme. Phellion.

"Oh! by a dirty intrigue. Desroches, the attorney, told

me all about it. Now our Thuillier finds a tit-bit in the Chamber. Eating gives appetite, but he cannot dupe us this time like he did before. That is why they turn to the Comtesse de Godollo, whom it seems has high connections in political circles. There is this further: Instead of being a parasite, like the Provençal, this foreigner has a fortune of her own which she uses beneficently. She it was who gave the two dresses of Brigitte's and Madame Thuillier's; she came herself to arrange the toilettes of our *amphitryonesses*, which accounts for them not being found in their usual dowdy fashion."

"I do not accept for my friends," said Phellion, "the derogatory remarks you make about them. There may be a lack of experience, and the noble lady may have given of her knowledge to them; but——"

"Well, but, my dear commander, what about the idea of giving Céleste to la Peyrade; is not that something beyond a mere want of experience? It is at the same time stupidity and immorality; for, really, the scandalous flirtation of that barrister with Madame Colleville——"

"Monsieur le Maire," interrupted Phellion, with redoubled solemnity, "the law-giver, Solon, decreed no punishment for parricide, declaring it an impossible crime. I think the same may be said of the gross misconduct to which you allude. That Madame Colleville granting favors to Monsieur la Peyrade and the while intending to give him her daughter is— no, monsieur, no! it is beyond imagination. Questioned on this subject before the Tribunal, Madame Colleville, like Marie-Antoinette, might respond: 'I appeal to all mothers.'"

"Nevertheless, my friend, allow me to remind you that Madame Colleville is abominably profligate and has given very sure proof of it."

"That's enough, my dear," said Phellion. "The dinner hour calls us; I fancy we have allowed our conversation to drift toward the miry banks of slander."

And each party, after mutual salutations, went their way.

It was impossible that la Peyrade should not be aware that a change was taking place in the Thuillier household. His influence was fast waning before that of the stranger; but the countess did not limit herself to a simple struggle for influence; she made no pretense of being otherwise than utterly opposed to his suit for Céleste's hand; more, she gave her approval to the love of Félix Phellion.

La Peyrade was perhaps more distressed at this because he had brought this undermining force into the heart of the citadel.

His first mistake was the sterile satisfaction of refusing the lease to Cérizet. If it had not been that Brigitte had taken the matter into her own hands, by his advice, it was unlikely that she would have become known to Madame de Godollo.

Another blunder was in persuading the Thuilliers to leave the Latin quarter. Just then Théodose looked upon his marriage as a settled thing; he therefore supported the views of the Hungarian in the sale of the furniture and in having her installed as a tenant; he felt that he thus sent the Thuilliers before him to make ready his bed in the splendid suite he intended sharing with them.

The Collevilles had followed their friends into the house in the Madeleine, where the rear entresol had been conceded to them at a price conformable to their means. But Colleville found that it lacked light and air, and, obliged to go daily from the Madeleine boulevard to the St. Jacques' faubourg, where his office was situated, he railed against the arrangement of which he was the victim, and at times rated la Peyrade as a tyrant. On the other hand, Mme. Colleville, under the pretense of being a resident in such an aristocratic quarter, had rushed into a frightful orgy of new bonnets, mantles, and dresses, which necessitated the presentation of a pile of bills and caused frequent stormy scenes in the household.

But all this was as nothing when weighed with another

cause for his diminished influence. He had promised Thuillier that the Cross should be his, after a little delay and the expenditure of ten thousand francs. Two months had elapsed since then, and yet no sign was there of that glorious bauble. To be sure, la Peyrade had mentioned an unforeseen and unaccountable obstacle which had paralyzed every effort of the Comtesse du Bruel; but Thuillier was sick of being paid in explanations, and on some days when his disappointment was particularly acute, he would often, like Chicaneau in "Les Plaideurs," be within an ace of saying: "Then give me back my cash!"

La Peyrade felt that he had reached a point at which he must strike a blow in order to restore his rapidly evaporating influence. It was just that nagging, haggling, proof-revising that afforded the barrister a chance to use a scheme both bold and deep.

One day, when they were at work on the last pages of the pamphlet, a discussion arose over the word "nepotism," which Thuillier would have eliminated from one of the sentences written by la Peyrade, declaring that he had never met with it, and that, properly, it was "neologism," which, in the literary ideas of the bourgeoisie, is about equivalent to the notion of '93 and the Reign of Terror.

Generally, la Peyrade took the ridiculous notions of his "dear friend" in good part; but this day he became highly excited; he signified that Thuillier might finish the work himself, as he was able to criticise so intelligently, and for some days he was not seen again.

Thuillier at first laid it to a mere passing effect of ill-humor, but la Peyrade's prolonged absence made him feel the necessity of seeking him and making reconciliation. He therefore visited the Provençal's room, and, with an off-hand manner, said:

"Well, my dear fellow, I find we were both right; *nepotism* means the authority that the nephews of popes take in affairs political. I have searched the dictionary, and I find no other explanation; but, from what Phellion says, it appears that in the vocabulary of politics the word has been extended to cover the influence which corrupt ministers allow certain persons to illegally exercise; I think, therefore, that we can let the term stand; at the same time, it is not so used by Napoleon Landais."

La Peyrade, who, while receiving his visitor, had pretended to be exceedingly busy in arranging his papers, contented himself with shrugging his shoulders, but made no answer.

"Well," went on Thuillier, "have you looked over the proofs of the last two sheets? For we ought to be getting along."

"If you have sent nothing to the printers," replied la Peyrade, "we are not very like to have proofs; for my own part, I have not touched the manuscript."

"But, my dear Théodose," said Thuillier, "it cannot be possible that you are vexed about such a trifle. I don't pretend to be a writer; all the same, as I sign the thing, it seems I might have my opinion about a word."

"But *Môsieu* Phellion," replied the barrister, "is a writer; and, as you have consulted him, I don't see why you shouldn't engage him to finish the work; as for myself, I promise you I won't coöperate any more."

"*Dieu!* what a temper!" exclaimed Brigitte's brother; "here you are mad as a hornet just because I doubt an expression and took another opinion. Shall I give you an idea of the confidence I have in you? The Comtesse de Godollo, to whom last evening I read a few pages, told me that the pamphlet was apt to cause me trouble with the public prosecutor; can you for a moment think anything like that would stop me?"

"Well," said la Peyrade, ironically, "I think that the oracle of your house sees the thing clearly; I have no desire to bring your head to the scaffold."

"That's all bosh. Do you or do you not intend to leave me in the lurch?"

"Literary questions," replied the barrister, "breed quarrels among the best of friends; I wish to put an end to such discussions between us."

"Théodose," said Thuillier, "you have something on your mind that you don't tell me; it is unnatural that for a simple tiff about a word you should wish to lose a friend as influential as myself."

"Well, yes," said la Peyrade, with an air of decision, "I don't like ingratitude."

"Nor I any more than you; I don't like it," said Thuillier with some heat, "and if you think of accusing me of aught so base and vile, I summon you to explain; we come out of equivocations: Of what do you complain? What reproach can you have against one whom only the other day you called your friend?"

"Nothing and everything," said la Peyrade; "your sister and yourself are too clever to openly make a rupture with a man, who, at the risk of his reputation, has put a million in your hands; but, all the same, I am not so simple but that I can detect a change. There are people about who set themselves to undermine me; and Brigitte has but one thought, and that is how to find a reasonable pretext of not keeping her promises."

"Come, come," said Thuillier, seeing a tear in the barrister's eye, by the glitter of which he was completely duped, "I don't know what Brigitte may have done, but one thing is quite certain, that I have never ceased to be your most devoted friend."

"Well, you always see Madame Godollo alongside Brigitte; she seems now that she cannot live without her."

"Oh, ho! it is perhaps a little jealousy on our mind!" said Thuillier slyly.

"Jealousy!" answered la Peyrade. "I don't know
16

whether that's the proper word; but anyhow your sister, who is not at all above the ordinary, and whom I am astonished that a man of your intellectual superiority should allow to assume a supremacy which she uses and abuses——"

"How can I help it, dear fellow?" interrupted Thuillier, sucking in the compliment; "she is so entirely devoted to me."

"I acknowledge the weakness," replied la Peyrade; "but, I repeat it, your sister cannot step in your track. What I say is that when a man of the value which you claim to recognize in me does her the honor of advising her, and who devotes himself to her as I have done, it cannot be agreeable to see himself supplanted by a woman come from who knows where, and all on account of some trumpery curtains and a few old chairs she has helped her to purchase."

"With women, as you well know, household affairs come before all else," replied Thuillier.

"Another thing I can tell you, Brigitte, who has a finger in everything, has an equal pretension to use a high hand in our love affairs; you, being so remarkably clear-sighted, must have seen that to Brigitte nothing is less certain than my marriage with Mademoiselle Colleville; now, my love has been solemnly authorized by you."

"By the rood!" said Thuillier, "I should like to see any one dare to interfere with my arrangements."

"There is some one else though outside of Brigitte, Céleste herself; in spite of the bickerings about religion, her mind is not the less filled with that little Phellion."

"But why not have Flavie put a stop to it?"

"Flavie, my dear! no one knows as much of her as you. She is a woman rather than a mother; I have found it necessary to do a little courting in that quarter myself; and you understand that, though she may will the marriage, she would not urge it very much."

"Well," said Thuillier, "leave that matter to me; I'll

speak to Céleste; I won't have a chit of a girl laying down the law for me."

"That's just what I don't wish you to do," exclaimed la Peyrade; "don't interfere in this at all. Outside of your relations with your sister you have an iron will; it shall never be said that I took advantage of your authority over Céleste to have her placed in my arms; on the contrary, I wish her to have full control in the disposition of her heart; only I think that she should be required to definitely decide between myself and Monsieur Félix, for I don't want to remain in this equivocal position. Beside all, although we agreed that this marriage should not take place until you were a deputy, yet I feel that makes too much of a bargain and sale of this business, and, more, I cannot allow my life's greatest event to be at the mercy of doubtful circumstances. Dutocq may have informed you that an heiress has been offered me who has a larger fortune than Mademoiselle Colleville. I refused that because I foolishly let my heart be won, and because an alliance with a family as honorable as your own seemed the more to be desired; but, after all, it might be as well to let Brigitte understand that, in case Céleste should refuse me, I shall not be pushed into the street."

"I can easily believe that," said Thuillier; "but as for putting all the decision of this affair at the mercy of that girl's head, and if, as you say, she has a fancy for that Félix——"

"That may be," said the barrister; "but I cannot remain any longer in my present position. You talk about your pamphlet, I am in no fit condition to finish it; you are a ladies' man and can understand the domination that those creatures fatally exercise over our minds."

"Pshaw!" said Thuillier, conceitedly, "they took to me, but I didn't often care for them; I just took them and left them."

"Yes, but I, with my Southern nature, am passionate; and then Céleste has other attractions beside fortune. Brought up by yourself, under your own eyes, you have made her an adorable child; only it was a great weakness to allow that boy, who is not in any degree suited to her, to install himself in her fancy."

"You are right ten times over; but it was first a childish fancy. Félix and she played together; you came much later, and it proves our high regard for you that when you presented yourself we renounced our former projects."

"You, yes," said la Peyrade. "With a head filled with literary manias, which are marked with bright wit and full of intelligence, you have a heart of gold; but Brigitte is another matter; your friendship is a surety, and you know what you mean."

"Well, I think that Brigitte has always wanted you and would like you for a son-in-law, if I may so speak. But in any case I intend to be obeyed."

"I think I will finish your pamphlet, for, before all else, I think of you."

"Certainly," said Thuillier, "we ought not to sink in port."

"It seems to me that a girl should be able to make up her mind in fifteen days."

"Without a doubt," replied Thuillier; "but I have the greatest repugnance in allowing Céleste to decide without appeal."

"I'll take the chances; but, between you and I, it is not shooting at a venture; it is not in fifteen days that a son of Phellion, who is, one may say, obstinacy incarnate in silliness, will make an end of his philosophical hesitations, and certainly Céleste will never accept him for her husband until he gives her proof of his conversion."

"That is probable. But if Céleste dawdles over the matter, suppose she won't accept the alternative?"

"You will have to look after that," said the Provençal. "I don't know how you manage families in Paris, but in our country of Avignon it would be without parallel that a young woman should be given such liberty. If all of you cannot prevail on a girl to exercise her own free choice between two suitors—well, the sooner you write over the door of the house that Céleste is queen and sovereign the better."

"We've not come to that yet," said Thuillier, with a firm manner. "I'll open it frankly with Brigitte, and *I will* not have any objections."

"Ah! my poor fellow," said la Peyrade, clapping him on the shoulder, "since Chrysale, in 'Femmes Savantes,' who has not continually seen many brave warriors who have struck their flags before the powerful will of women used to domineer."

"We'll see about that," said Thuillier, making a theatrical exit.

When he returned home Thuillier at once put the question before Brigitte. She, with her native wit, good sense, and egotism, pointed out that by thus hurrying on the previous arrangements for the marriage they were disarming themselves; they could not say when the election would be held, nor that when it occurred whether the barrister would be as energetic for success. "It might be," said the old maid, "the same as the Cross."

"There's a difference," replied Thuillier; "the Cross did not depend directly on la Peyrade, but his influence in the arrondissement he employs as he wills."

"And if he wills," retorted Brigitte, "after we have feathered his nest, to work on his own account? he's very ambitious."

This danger did not fail to strike the future candidate, who nevertheless thought he might depend upon the honor of la Peyrade.

"It is not a particularly delicate honor," replied Brigitte, "when a man tries to get out of a bargain he made, and his idea of dangling a lump of sugar before us about getting 'your' pamphlet finished doesn't please me at all. Couldn't Phellion help you? Or, I think, Madame de Godollo, who is well known in political circles, could hire you a journalist; there are plenty of such on their uppers; you could get the whole thing done for a twenty-crown piece."

"No, I must have Théodose, otherwise the secret might get into the papers. Beside, after all, we promised him Céleste, it is only fulfilling the promise a little earlier; the King, of course, may dissolve the Chamber at any moment."

"But if Céleste won't have him?" objected Brigitte.

"Céleste! Céleste!" ejaculated Thuillier; "she can't have whom she wills, but whom we choose."

"So you really believe," said the skeptical Mlle. Thuillier, "that should Céleste decide in favor of Félix, you can still count on la Peyrade's devotion?"

"What else can I do? Those are his conditions. Beside, he has made calculations of the whole business, he knows that Félix will not so soon decide to bring Céleste a certificate of confession, and if he does not do this that little witch will not accept him for her husband. La Peyrade plays a clever game."

"Too clever," said Brigitte; "I won't interfere; settle it as you please; all this scheming is not to my taste."

Thuillier saw Mme. Colleville, and intimated to her that Céleste must be informed of the projects about her.

When informed that she must choose between Félix and la Peyrade, the naïve child was only struck by the advantage of one side of the attractions offered; she thought she did herself a favor by consenting to an arrangement which made herself the mistress of disposing of her person and to bestow her heart as she wished. But la Peyrade had not miscalculated when he reckoned that the religious intolerance on one part and on the other side the philosophical inflexibility of Phellion would create an invincible obstacle to their coming together.

The evening of the same day when Flavie had been instructed to communicate to Céleste the sovereign will of the Thuilliers, the Phellions came to pass their evening with Brigitte, and a sharp engagement took place between the young people. Céleste did not need telling by her mother, for she had too much delicacy of feeling, that she must not allow herself to mention to Félix the conditional approval of his suit. Theological arguments occupied the time they were together, and Phellion junior was in the encounter more than usually unlucky and blundering. He would concede nothing; he took on an air of airy and ironical importance and ended by fairly putting Céleste beside herself; she made a definite rupture with him and forbade him appearing in her presence for the future.

It was just a case for lovers of experience, which the young savant was not, to turn up the very next day, for hearts never approach so near to an understanding as when they have declared the necessity for an eternal separation. But this law is not logarithms, and Félix Phellion, incapable of guessing it, believed himself seriously and very positively proscribed; to that extent indeed that during the fifteen days given to the young girl for her decision, and although he was expected by Céleste day by day and minute by minute, who thought no more of la Peyrade than if he was entirely out of the question, this deplorable boy had not the most distant thought of breaking the ban.

Luckily for this benighted lover a beneficent fairy was watching over him, and the day before the one on which Céleste must declare her choice, this came to pass. It was Sunday, the day on which the Thuilliers still affected their periodical receptions.

Convinced that the leakage, vulgarly known as the "basket dance," was the ruin of the fortunes of the best establishments, Mme. Phellion was in the habit of going in person to purchase from her tradespeople. From time immemorial in the Phellion household, Sunday was the day of the *pot-au-feu*,\* and the wife of that great citizen, in an intentionally dowdy costume, such as good housewives bundle themselves up in when they go marketing, was returning from the butcher's, followed by her cook, who carried in her basket a fine cut of rump of beef. Twice had she rung her door-bell, and threatening was the storm brewing for the servant-boy, who was placing his mistress in a position less tolerable than that of Louis XIV., who only "nearly" waited, by not opening her door. Just as she gave the bell a third feverish, excited pull, you can judge of her confusion when she perceived a coupé draw up, and descending therefrom a lady whom she recognized, at this untimely hour, as the elegant Comtesse Torna de Godollo, the Hungarian.

Becoming a scarlet-purple, the unhappy bourgeoise completely lost her head, she floundered in excuses, each more awkward than the last, when Phellion, attired in a dressing-gown and Greek cap, came out of his study to learn what the matter was. After a speech, the pomposity of which made ample amends for the *négligé* of his costume, the great citizen, with that serenity which never deserted him, gallantly offered his hand to the stranger, and after having installed her in the salon:

"Perhaps, without indiscretion, I might ask Madame la Comtesse," said he, "to what I am indebted for the advantages, so unhoped for, of this visit?"

"I desired," replied the Hungarian, "to have a talk with Madame Phellion on a subject of vital interest to her; I have taken the liberty of calling upon her, although so little known to madame."

Before Phellion could reply Mme. Phellion appeared; a cap with ribbons had replaced the market-hat and a large shawl concealed the other things lacking in the matutinal toilet. On

---

\* A popular French dish of stewed beef: the same name is given to the stock-pot.

the entrance of his wife the great citizen made as though he would retire.

"Monsieur Phellion," said the countess, "you are not out of place in our conference; on the contrary, your excellent judgment may be of the utmost benefit in clearing up a question not less interesting to your wife than to your dignified self; I allude to the marriage of monsieur, your son."

"The marriage of my son!" said Mme. Phellion, with an air of astonishment; "but I am not aware that anything of the kind is on the tapis at present."

"The marriage of Monsieur Félix with Céleste is, I think, your desire," replied the countess; "one of your projects?"

"We have never, madame," said Phellion, "taken any special steps toward that object."

"I know that full well," replied the Hungarian; "on the contrary, each one of your family seems to study how to nullify my efforts; but one thing is clear, that is, the young people love each other, and in spite of your reserve, and to prevent the unhappiness they will experience if they do not marry, it is to prevent that catastrophe that I came here this morning."

"We cannot, madame," said Phellion, "fail to be profoundly touched by your interest in——"

"But the explanation is very simple," interrupted the countess, with animation. "Céleste is a dear, innocent child, and I detect a moral value in her that makes me regret to see her sacrificed."

"It is true," said Mme. Phellion, "that Céleste is an angel of sweetness."

"While, as for Monsieur Félix, I dare to interest myself in him because, first, he is the worthy son of the most virtuous of fathers——"

"Madame, I beg——" said Phellion with a graceful obeisance.

"And further by the awkwardness of his true love, which

is apparent in his every act and word. We more mature women can find an inexpressible charm in watching the passion under a form which does not menace us with deceptions and misunderstandings."

"In fact, my son, is not brilliant," said Mme. Phellion, with a suspicion of tartness in her tone; "he is not a young man of fashion."

"But he has the more essential qualities," replied the countess; "a merit which ignores itself, which in every intellectual superiority——"

"In truth, madame," said Phellion, "you compel us to hear things——"

"That are not beyond the truth," interrupted the countess. "I have another reason: I am not particularly desirous that la Peyrade should be made happy, he is false and avaricious. On the ruin of their hopes this man counts on building his swindling schemes."

"It is certain," said Phellion, "that Monsieur de la Peyrade has dark depths which the light has never penetrated. You have told us of where we are remiss, it appears to me that you should plainly indicate what you would have us do for the future."

"Well, it is fifteen days of absence from the Thuilliers of the whole of your family; do you imagine that nothing of importance could occur in that time?" said the Hungarian.

"Of a truth, those three glorious days were enough, in 1830, to throw down a perjured dynasty and lay the foundation of the order of things under which we are now governed."

"You see it yourself," said the countess. "And on that last evening did nothing occur between Céleste and monsieur, your son?"

"Truly," replied Phellion, "a disagreeable conversation on the subject of religion; it must be allowed that our good

Céleste, who in every other respect has a most lovely nature, is a little fanatical in the matter of piety."

"I agree with you," said the countess; "but she was raised by the mother whom you know; she has never been shown the face of sincere piety; she has only seen its mask; repentant Magdalens of Madame Colleville's kind always wear an air of wishing to retire into the desert in company with a death's head and cross-bones. They think that's the best market at which to get religion. After all, now, what was it that Céleste asked of Monsieur Félix? Only that he would read 'The Imitation of Christ.'"

"He has done that, madame," replied Phellion; "he finds it a well-written book, but his convictions—that's the misfortune—have not in the least changed by its perusal."

"Do you think it shows much cleverness not to let his mistress see some little change in the inflexibility of his convictions?"

"My son, madame, has never received from me the least lesson in smartness; loyalty and the right, these are the principles I have inculcated."

"Allowing all that—need he, think you, have capped his proceedings by a long sulk, which has struck the girl's heart with despair and, also, a deep feeling of irritation."

"My son is incapable of acting thus. I know nothing of what you allude to," said Phellion.

"Nothing is more true, though. Young Colleville, home for his half-holiday, has just told us that since last Sunday but one Monsieur Félix, who had always gone with the utmost punctuality to teach him, has not been near him. Unless your son is ill, this is a grievous blunder."

The Phellions, husband and wife, stared at each other as if consulting how to reply.

"My son," said Mme. Phellion, "is not exactly ill; but, as you have seen fit to reveal this to us, a thing very strange and not at all like himself, we see, since Céleste told him that all was over between her and Félix, that a most extraordinary change has passed over him; Monsieur Phellion and myself are very uneasy about it."

"And yet," said Mme. de Godollo, "nothing but what is natural happened; lovers always make the worst of everything."

"But he is terribly excited," said Phellion. "You speak to him and he seems not to hear you; he sits at table and forgets to eat; or else he takes his food so absent-mindedly as to be, so say the medical profession, most injurious to the digestive process; his duties, his regular occupations, we have to remind him of, he so extremely regular, so punctual. The other day while he was at the Conservatory, where he now passes all his evenings, only returning home in the small hours, I went into his room and looked into his papers; madame, I was absolutely alarmed on seeing a paper covered with algebraic calculations which, by their extent, seemed to me to pass far beyond the limits of the human intellect."

"Perhaps," said the countess, "he is on the eve of the discovery of a mighty problem."

"Or else on the road to lunacy," said Mme. Phellion.

"A mind equable and calm as is his need not be afraid of that," said the countess. "But a greater danger threatens his understanding. Unless we stop it this evening by a masterstroke, Céleste is lost to him forever."

"How is that?" said the Phellions, with one voice.

"Perhaps you are ignorant of the fact that Thuillier and his sister had entered into an express engagement with la Peyrade that he should marry Céleste," said the countess.

"We at least had our misgivings," said Phellion.

"It would be useless to tell you of the manœuvres la Peyrade has practiced to hasten this marriage, but it concerns you to know that, thanks to his duplicity, Céleste was forced to decide in fifteen days between him and Monsieur Félix; that time expires to-morrow, and, owing to the unfortunate turn taken through your son's attitude, there is imminent danger of her sacrificing her wounded feelings on the altar of her love and instincts."

"But what can be done to hinder this, madame?" asked Phellion.

"Fight, monsieur; come this evening in full force to the Thuilliers; induce your son to come; lecture him until he becomes rather more flexible in his philosophical opinions. 'Paris,' said Henry IV., 'is worth a mass;' but tell him to avoid such questions; any man who loves a woman can find enough to talk about to move a woman; so little satisfies her. I will help where I can. One thing is sure, we have to fight a big battle; if we do not each one strive our utmost, la Peyrade will gain the victory."

"My son is not here, madame," said Phellion. "I wish he had been, you might have aroused him from his torpor."

"It is unnecessary to say," added the countess, as she rose, "that we must be careful not to give any appearance of collusion; it would be better, in fact, not to be seen speaking together."

"I can assure you, madame, of my prudence," replied Phellion, "and you will please to accept the assurance——"

"Of your most distinguished sentiments," interrupted the countess, laughing.

"No, madame," gravely responded Phellion, "I reserve that formula for the conclusion of my letters; but you will please accept the most unutterable gratitude of myself."

"We will speak of that when we are beyond all danger," said Mme. de Godollo, going toward the door, "and if Madame Phellion, the tenderest of mothers, will grant me a little place in her regards, I shall be fully repaid."

Mme. Phellion launched into an endless sea of compliments. The countess in her carriage was some distance away before Phellion had ceased offering his most respectful salutations.

By degrees the salon of Brigitte became more select and

less insidious, a livelier Parisian element began to infiltrate therein. The new councilor had made a number of recruits from among his associates in the council; the Latin quarter element became less. The mayor of his arrondissement and several deputy mayors had called upon him after the removal to the Madeleine quarter. Thuillier had hastened to return the civility; he had also the same experience with a number of the superior officers of the First Legion. Among others came Rabourdin, the former head of Thuillier's bureau, who had lost his wife; Rabourdin occupied as a bachelor the third floor of their house over the entresol. He was now a director in one of the numerous railroads, ever projected but always delayed by the indecision of the Chamber or rival claims; but he had now become one of the most important personages in the world of finance. At the time of his resignation, under deplorable circumstances, of his position in the bureaux, Phellion was the only one in his office who had stood by him. Being now in a position to reward his friends, Rabourdin, meeting once more his faithful subordinate, at once made him an offer of an easy, lucrative position.

"Môsieur," replied Phellion, "your kindness both touches and honors me, but my frankness owes you a confession which I trust you will not take amiss. I have no belief in these iron roads, or 'railroads,' as the English call them."

"You have a perfect right to have your own opinion," said Rabourdin, smiling, "but in the interim, until the contrary appears, we pay our servants very satisfactorily, and I should be pleased to have you with me. I know by experience that you are fully reliable."

"Môsieur," replied the great citizen, "I did my duty and nothing more. As for the offer you have been so good as to make me, I cannot accept it. Satisfied with my humble lot, I feel neither the need nor the desire to again embark on an administrative career, and, with the Latin poet, I may say:

"'Claudite jam rivos, pueri, sat prata biberunt.'"

Thus elevated in the social scale, the Thuillier salon still needed another element of vitality, and, to speak as Madelon in the "Précieuses ridicules," this "frightful lack of amusement," signified by Mme. Phellion, required remedying. Thanks to the attention of Mme. de Godollo, the great organizer, who happily profited by the former relations of Colleville with the musical world, a few artists came to make a diversion from *bouillotte* and *boston*. Out of fashion and old, these two games had to beat a retreat before whist, the only manner, said the Hungarian countess, by which respectable people can kill time.

Like Louis XVI.,* who began by putting his hand to reforms which should subsequently engulf his throne, Brigitte at first encouraged this interior revolution. But the day on which occurred the scene we are about to relate, an apparently trivial detail had revealed to her the danger of the slope upon which she was standing. The greater number of the new guests introduced by Thuillier were unaware of the supremacy of his sister in the household; upon arrival they naturally asked Thuillier to present them to "madame;" of course it was impossible that he could inform them that his wife was but a dummy queen who groaned under the iron hand of a Richelieu, the sole authority. Therefore it was not until after this presentation that they were led up to Brigitte, but the stiffness she manifested in her displeasure did not encourage them in paying her further attentions. Quick to realize this transfer of power:

"If I don't look out," said this Queen Elizabeth to herself, with that profound instinct of despotism which was her ruling passion, "I shall soon be a nobody here."

Pondering over this idea, she saw that the audacious la Peyrade would not scotch this decline of prestige; a further intuition whispered her that Félix Phellion, absorbed in his mathematical abstractions, would be a more suitable match

---

* His want of decision led to the revolution of 1792.

than the enterprising barrister. She was the first to regret that the Phellions had come without their son. Despite Mme. de Godollo's advances, this terrible lover had taken as guide the last line of Millevoye's famous elegy: *Et son amante ne vint pas*—the beloved came not.

As for Mme. de Godollo, who possessed a remarkably fine voice, she went up to ask Mme. Phellion to accompany her on the piano, to whom she whispered in her ear, between two verses of a fashionable ballad:

"Well, and monsieur, your son?"

"He is coming," replied Mme. Phellion; "his father spoke most emphatically to him; but it seems that to-night there is a conjunction of some planets; it is a grand occasion for the gentlemen of the Observatory; he did not feel as though he could dispense——"

"This is simply inconceivable, that he could be so foolish," said the countess; "was it not enough that he brought his theology here that he should now blunderingly drag in his astronomy."

Her song was finished, as the English say, amid thunders of applause. La Peyrade, who dreaded her excessively, was among the first to congratulate her, but she received his compliments most coldly, and he turned away to find consolation with Mme. Colleville. Flavie had too many pretensions to beauty not to feel an enmity toward a woman who in a manner intercepted her due homage.

"And you also mean to say that that woman sings well?" asked Mme. Colleville of the barrister.

"At least I had to tell her so," replied la Peyrade, "because there's no security of Brigitte without her. But look at Céleste; every time a tray is brought in she turns to the door."

"Don't worry me!" said Flavie; "I know what that foolish girl has in her mind; your marriage will take place only too soon."

"But is it for my own sake?" said la Peyrade; "it is necessary for the future of the whole of us. Come, there are tears in your eyes. I shall leave you; you are unreasonable. The devil! as that old prude Phellion says, if you want the end you need the means."

And he went toward a group in the centre; Mme. Colleville followed, and under the strong feeling of jealousy she had just displayed she became a savage mother.

"Céleste," said she, "why don't you sing? A number of gentlemen wish to hear you."

"Oh, mamma!" said Céleste, "how can I, with my poor thread of a voice, sing after madame. Beside, you know that I have a cold."

"That means that you intend to be disagreeable; people sing as they can, every voice has its own merits."

"My dear love," said Colleville, who had just lost twenty francs at a card-table, and found the nerve in his vexations to oppose his wife, "to say one sings as he can is a bourgeois maxim; people sing with a voice if they have one, but not after hearing an operatic voice like that of Madame la Comtesse's; for my part, I am perfectly willing to let Céleste off warbling a sentimental ditty."

"It's a grand idea to spend so much money on expensive masters," said Flavie, as she left the group, "and then get nothing in return."

"So," said Colleville, resuming the conversation in which he had been interrupted by the invasion of Mme. Colleville, "Félix no longer inhabits the earth; he passes his time among the stars?"

"My dear old colleague," said Phellion, "I am as much annoyed as yourself with my son for neglecting the oldest friends of his family; and, though the contemplation of the great luminous bodies suspended in space by the hand of the Creator present, in my opinion, more interest to me than your overwrought brain seems to imagine, yet I think that Félix shows a lack of propriety by not coming here to-night, especially as he gave me his promise."

"Science," said la Peyrade, "is a fine thing, but, unfortunately, it has the drawback of making bears and maniacs."

"Without counting," said Céleste, "the undermining of all religion."

"In that, my child, you are mistaken," said the countess. "Pascal, himself a shining example of the falsity of your view, says, if I am not mistaken, that a little science leads us away from religion but a great deal draws us back to it."

"Bring back a savant to the practice of religion, madame," said la Peyrade, "it seems to me a difficult task; these gentlemen put their studies before everything else; tell a geometrician or geologist, for example, that the church imperatively insists on the sanctification of Sunday and a suspension of every kind of work, and they shrug their shoulders, although God himself did not disdain to rest."

"Therefore by not coming here this evening," said Céleste, innocently, "he not only commits a breach of good manners, but also sins."

"But tell me, my handsome," replied Mme. de Godollo, "do you think that our assembling here to sing ballads and eat ices and speak evil of others, as is the practice in drawing-rooms, is more pleasing to God than seeing a scientific man in his observatory engaged in studying the magnificent secrets of the creation?"

"There's a time for all things," said Céleste, "and, as Monsieur la Peyrade says, 'God did not disdain to rest.'"

"But, my dear love," said Mme. de Godollo, "God has the time so to do; He is eternal."

"That," said la Peyrade, "is one of the wittiest impieties ever issued. Those kind of arguments serve the turn of folk of the world. They interpret and explain away the commands of God, they interpret, take, choose among them as they will; the free-thinker subjects them to his sovereign revision, and free-thinking is but a short distance from free-conduct."

During this tirade Mme. de Godollo was watching the clock; it now marked eleven. The salon began to empty. Only one table was going on, the players being Minard, Thuillier, and two new acquaintances. All tended to show that the hope of seeing the tardy lover was evidently lost.

"Monsieur," said the countess to la Peyrade, "do you think the gentlemen of the Rue des Postes have the honor of being good Catholics?"

"Without a doubt," answered the barrister; "religion has no more earnest supporters."

"Well, this morning," continued the countess, "I had the honor of being received by Father Anselme. He is considered the model of every Christian virtue, yet this good father is a very learned mathematician."

"I did not say, madame, that the two qualities were incompatible."

"But you did say that a good Christian would do no manner of work on Sunday; thus Father Anselme must be a miscreant; for at the moment I gained access to his room I found him standing in front of a blackboard, a piece of chalk in his hand, busy with a difficult problem, for the board was covered with algebraic characters, and, further, he didn't seem to realize that he might create a scandal, for with him was a person whom I am not at liberty to name, but it was a young scientist of great promise, who shared his profane occupation."

Céleste and Mme. Thuillier as they looked at each other saw a gleam of hope in each other's eyes.

"Then you know a number of young savants?" asked Céleste; "this one and Monsieur Félix make two."

"As for me," said la Peyrade, ironically, "I shouldn't be in the least surprised if Father Anselme's collaborator was precisely that Félix Phellion; Voltaire always kept up close relations with the jesuits who brought him up, only he did not discuss religion with them."

"Well, my young savant he does discuss it with his venerable confrère in the sciences; he explains his doubts to him, and, in fact, this was the commencement of their scientific friendship."

"And Father Anselme," asked Céleste, "does he hope to convert this young man?"

"He is sure of so doing," replied the countess. "His young collaborator, apart from religious education, which he never received, is a man of most excellent parts and the highest principles; moreover, he well knows that his conversion would give happiness to a charming young girl whom he loves and who loves him in return. Now, my dear child, you won't get another word out of me; you can fancy what you please."

"Oh! my godmother," said Céleste, yielding to the innocence of her impressions, "if it were he!"

At this moment the servant opened the door of the salon and, singular coincidence, announced: "Monsieur Félix Phellion."

The young professor entered, bathed in perspiration, his cravat askew, and himself out of breath.

"A pretty time, this," said Phellion, with severity, "to present yourself."

"My father," said Félix, moving to where Mme. Thuillier and Céleste were seated, "I was unable to leave before the close of the phenomenon; I could find no coach and have run all the way."

"Your ears must have burned on the road," said la Peyrade, sneeringly, "for you have occupied the thoughts of these ladies up to now; you have been the subject of a great problem to them."

Félix did not answer; he went to greet Brigitte, who had just entered from the dining-room. After she had reproached

him for the rarity of his visits and receiving her pardon in a
"Better late than never," he turned to his pole and was astonished to hear Madame de Godollo say to him:

"Monsieur, you must pardon my indiscretion done in the heat of conversation about you; I have told them where I met you this morning."

"Where have I had the honor of meeting you?" said Félix; "but, madame, I did not see you."

A faint smile lighted up la Peyrade's lips.

"You saw me sufficiently well to ask my confidence as to where I found you; but at least I did not go further than to say that I had seen you with Father Anselme sometimes, and that you had some scientific relations with each other; and also that you defended your doubts against his arguments the same as you do with Céleste."

"Father Anselme!" said the stupid Phellion.

"Yes, without doubt," said la Peyrade, "a great mathematician who does not despair of converting you; Mademoiselle Céleste has shed tears of joy."

Félix looked around with an air of bewilderment. Madame de Godollo looked at him with eyes the language of which a poodle would have understood.

"I wish," said he, finally, "that I could have done a thing so agreeable to Mademoiselle Céleste, but I am afraid, madame, that you labor under an error."

"Listen to me, monsieur, it seems that I must needs be more precise; and if your timidity prompts you to continue denying a step that can only honor you, then you may contradict me; I must bear the annoyance of having divulged a secret which I had promised you faithfully to keep."

Measuring each word, she said:

"I have told these ladies, because I know how they wish your salvation, and because you were accused of audaciously defying God's commandments by working on Sunday, that I had met you this morning at Father Anselme's house, a scientist like yourself, with whom you were engaged in solving a problem; I said that this had led up to other explanations between you, and that he did not despair of refuting your arguments. In confirming my words, there can be nothing to wound your self-esteem. It was only intended as a surprise for Céleste, but I was so stupid as to divulge it."

"Come, monsieur," said la Peyrade, "there's nothing ridiculous in searching for the light; you, so honorable, such a foe to untruth, can scarcely deny what madame so resolutely affirms."

"Well," said Félix, after a slight pause, "will you, Mademoiselle Céleste, permit me to say a few words to you in private, without witnesses?"

Céleste, after an approving nod from Mme. Thuillier, rose, and Félix took her hand and led her to a window recess.

"Céleste," he said, "I beg you to wait a little longer. See," he added, pointing to the constellation of the chariot,* "beyond those visible stars, there lies a future for us. As regards what has been said about Father Anselme, I cannot admit it, for it is not true. It is a pleasing story; but patience, you shall hear things——"

Céleste left him, and he remained gazing at the stars.

"He is mad," said the young girl in accents of despair, as she resumed her seat by Mme. Thuillier.

Félix confirmed this prognostication by rushing out of the room without perceiving the emotion with which his father followed him.

Shortly after this exit, which had stupefied everybody, la Peyrade approached Mme. de Godollo and respectfully said:

"You must admit, madame, that it is very difficult to draw a man out of the water when he is intent on drowning——"

"I had no idea," replied the countess, "of such unparalleled simplicity; it is too silly for anything. I shall go over to the enemy, and with that enemy I am, when he

* Ursa Major.

pleases, ready to go into a full and frank explanation in my own rooms."

The next day Théodose felt himself possessed by two curiosities: How Céleste would behave in the option presented for her acceptance? Then this Comtesse Torna de Godollo, what did she mean by what she had said; and what did she want of him?

He sent his porter for a hack and about three o'clock drove from the Rue Saint-Dominique-d'Enfer toward the fashionable neighborhood of the Madeleine. His toilet was naturally the subject of some thought, and presented a compromise between the negligent ease of morning attire and the ceremonious style of evening dress. Necessitated by his profession to wear a white cravat, which he rarely laid aside, and not being well-disposed to dispense with a dress-coat, he felt drawn to one of the extremes he was desirous of avoiding. But by buttoning his coat and wearing tan instead of lemon-colored kids he managed to "unsolemnize" himself, and thus avoided the provincial and poor-relation aspect which a man in full dress always conveys to the mind when seen on the streets of Paris.

Arrived he rang the bell, and after some little delay was ushered into a severely luxurious dining-room, where he was requested to wait. A minute later the attendant returned and he was admitted into a most coquettish and splendid salon. The divinity of the place sat before a table covered with Venetian cloth, in which gold thread sparkled among the rich embroidery. As la Peyrade went in the countess bowed without rising.

"Will monsieur allow me to seal a letter of some importance?" said the comtesse.

The barrister made a bow of assent; the handsome foreigner then took from a tortoise-shell inlaid desk a sheet of blue-tint English paper which she placed in an envelope; after she had written the address, she rose and rang the bell. The maid appeared and lighted a small spirit lamp; over the lamp was hung a silver-gilt crucible-shaped vessel, in which was a scrap of scented sealing-wax; as soon as the flame had melted this the maid poured it on the envelope and handed her mistress an armorial seal. This she impressed with her own fair hands on the wax, and said: "Take it at once to that address."

As the woman made a movement to take the letter she inadvertently let it fall, near to la Peyrade's feet, who made a quick movement to pick it up and read thereon: "M. the Minister of Foreign Affairs," added below being: "For him only."

"Thanks, monsieur," said the countess, for he had the good sense to return it to her. "Be so good, mademoiselle, as not to lose it," she added severely to the maid.

The countess then left the table and took her seat on a lounge covered with pearl gray satin. You may say that you cannot know all a woman's perfections unless you have seen her in the prismatic atmosphere of her own drawing-room; but guard against pretending to judge and know her if you have never seen her anywhere else.

"Monsieur," said she, with a smile and a slightly foreign accent which gave an added charm to her words, "I cannot help thinking what a queer thing it is that a man of your spirit and rare penetration should have an idea that you had an enemy in me."

"But, Madame la Comtesse," replied la Peyrade, allowing her to read in his eyes the astonishment he felt, not unmingled with distrust, "you will admit that every appearance was of that nature. A rival crops up when I was already justified in considering my marriage fully settled; he becomes absolutely stupid and awkward so that I could easily have set him aside, when suddenly a most unlooked-for auxiliary rushes in and assists him on his most vulnerable point."

"What a great misfortune it would be," replied the foreigner with charming audacity, "if your marriage with mademoiselle were prevented. Do you really care so very much for that schoolgirl?"

In that last word there was not more of contempt than hatred. This did not escape an observer of la Peyrade's keenness. But he only went on to say:

"Madame, the vulgar expression 'to settle down' sums up the situation, where, after a long-drawn fight, a man reaches the end of his illusions, and when he would fain compromise with his future. Now, when this end is presented in the form of a young girl with more virtue than beauty, I won't deny, but one who brings to her husband the fortune so indispensable to the welfare of conjugal companionship, why it should excite astonishment that his heart is filled with gratitude and that he should eagerly welcome the prospect of peaceful happiness?"

"I had always imagined," replied the countess, "that a man's intelligence and power should be the measure of his ambition; one, I should think, so wise as to make himself the poor man's advocate would have less modesty and fewer pastoral aspirations."

"Ah! madame," said la Peyrade, "the iron hand of necessity makes one resign himself, it forces stranger things upon us than that; the question of daily bread is one before which everybody debases himself. Apollo, was he not compelled to 'make a living' by tending Admetus' sheep?"

"Admetus' sheep-fold," objected Mme. de Godollo, "was at least a sheep-fold of royalty; but certainly Apollo would never have submitted to become the shepherd of a—bourgeois."

The pause which preceded the last word of the handsome foreigner seemed to convey the meaning of a proper name instead of the one used.

"I believe, madame, that your distinction is not less true than subtle," answered la Peyrade; "but Apollo has no choice."

"I don't like people who charge too much," said the countess, "neither do I like those who sell their goods below the market price, I am always afraid lest they should make me the victim of some knavish trick. You well know your own value, monsieur, and your hypocritical humility annoys me immensely; it shows me that my kindly overtures have not even produced the beginning of confidence between us."

"I assure you, madame, that up to now my life has not given me any reason to think myself possessed of dazzling superiority."

"Well," said the Hungarian, "perhaps I ought to admit the modesty of the man who will accept the pitiable finale of his life which I have intended to do my best to prevent."

"So, perhaps, as I myself," replied la Peyrade, "might believe in that benevolence which in order to rescue me has treated me so roughly."

The countess threw a reproachful glance at her guest; her hands toyed with the ribbons of her dress; she cast down her eyes and allowed a sigh to escape her, so faint as to be scarcely perceptible, so slight in fact that it might have passed as her regular breathing.

"You are rancorous," said she, "and judge people by yourself. After all," she added, as if in reflection, "you may possibly be right in reminding me that I have gone a long and roundabout way in meddling in interests that are none of my concern. Go on, dear monsieur, and prosper in this so glorious marriage which offers you such a combination of inducements; only let me hope that you may never repent your course, which I will no longer try to postpone."

The Provençal had not been spoilt by women. The poverty against which he had been so long struggling never leads to affairs of gallantry, and, since he had thrown off its worst clutches, his mind had been given up to the anxious work of providing for his future; with the exception of the farce played with Mme. Colleville, he had never had an affair of the heart during his whole life. We can thus understand the perplexity of this novice. Like all overbusy men when they are goaded by the demon of lust, he was content to accept the ignoble love that any night can be bought at corner crossings, and that is easily reconciled with the exterior of devotion.

Suppose this kindness, but poorly explained as it seemed to him, of which he had so suddenly become the object was but a bait to entice him toward a snare which might be used to compromise him with the Thuilliers, what a blow at his supposed shrewdness, what a part to play; that of the dog dropping the meat to grasp the shadow.

We know that la Peyrade was something after the school of Tartuffe, and the frankness which that master declares to Elmire that unless a few of the promised favors are granted he could no longer trust her tender advances, seemed almost adapted to the occasion, though there was more softness in its form.

"Madame la Comtesse," said he, "you have made of me a man who is much to be pitied; I was marching gayly to this marriage, and you take from me all my faith; and yet, what if I break it off, what can I, with that great capacity you credit me with, do with the liberty thus acquired?"

"La Bruyère has said, if I am not mistaken, that nothing so refreshes the blood as to avoid committing a folly."

"I grant that; but that is a negative benefit; I am of an age and in such a position as to desire more serious results. The interest you show in me cannot, I imagine, end at leaving a blank page. I love mademoiselle with a love, not, it is true, with an imperative, dominating passion, but still I do love her, her hand is promised to me, and before renouncing——"

"So," said the countess, briskly, "in a given case you would not object to a rupture? And," added she, in a calmer tone, "you might be ready to break it off; that is, in case a more suitable marriage were to offer?"

"At the very least, madame, I should want to definitely foresee this."

This determination to be on the safe side appeared to annoy the countess.

"Faith, monsieur," said she, "is only a virtue when it accepts without seeing. You doubt yourself, another form of stupidity. I am not happy in my proteges."

"But, madame, it cannot be very indiscreet to ask for the least intimation of what your benevolence has designed for me?"

"Very indiscreet," replied the Hungarian, coldly, "for it shows me that you only offer me a confidence on conditions. Say no more. You have gone far with Mademoiselle Colleville; you say she suits you in many things, marry her; one more attack, you won't again find me in your way."

"But does mademoiselle really suit me?" replied la Peyrade; "that is exactly where you have raised my doubts. Don't you think you are cruel in casting me first in one direction and then in another without offering anything to support me?"

"Ah! you want my opinion; well, there is one fact: Céleste does not love you."

"I think myself," said la Peyrade, "that I am on the way to a marriage of convenience."

"And she cannot love you," continued Mme. de Godollo, with animation, "for she cannot understand you. The man who should be her husband is that blonde young man, as shy and pale-faced as herself; the contact of these two natures without life and heat will result in that lukewarm duet which in the opinion of the world in which she was born constitutes the *ne plus ultra* of conjugal felicity. Enriched bourgeois, *parvenus*, there's the roof under which you intend resting after your hard labors and long trials. And don't you know that twenty times a day they will make it manifest to you that your share in the partnership is very light against their money?

"BUT DOES MADEMOISELLE REALLY SUIT ME?"
REPLIED LA PEYRADE.

The artist, the man of imagination, who tumbles into the middle-class atmosphere, shall I tell you to what I compare him? To Daniel cast into the den of lions, less the miracle of the Scriptures."

"Ah, madame!" exclaimed la Peyrade, "how eloquently you present the thoughts that have been mine so often. But I felt lashed to the cruel necessity of gaining a position."

"Necessity, position!" interrupted the countess, again elevating the temperature of her words, "words without meaning! They have no sound to men of ability, though they bar fools as though they were formidable obstacles. Necessity, does that exist for noble natures who know how to will? A Gascon minister said these words, which should be graven over every door of all careers: 'All things come to him who knows how to wait.' Are you ignorant that marriage to men of superior stamp is either a chain which rivets them to the most vulgar of existences, or a wing that bears them to the highest summits of the social world? The wife you need, monsieur, and she would not be long lacking in your career if you had not with such incredible haste offered yourself to the first fortune which turned up. The one you should have chosen is a woman capable of understanding you, able to read you; one who would be a collaborator, an intelligent confidant, not a mere incarnation of *pot-au-feu;* who to-day is your secretary, but to-morrow may be the true wife of a deputy or an ambassador; in short, one who could offer you her heart for a mainspring, her salon for a stage, her friends for a ladder, and who in return for all you gave of ardor and strength would ask no more than to sit near your throne in the glare of the prosperity and glory that she foresaw would be your lot."

Intoxicated by her own words the Hungarian was magnificent, her eyes sparkled, her notrils dilated; the perspective her vivid eloquence had unfurled she appeared to see, to touch with her hands. For a moment la Peyrade was dazzled with this kind of sunrise which burst suddenly upon his life.

All the same, he was an eminently prudent man, who had made it a rule to never lend anything except on the soundest security; he was impelled to still weigh the situation.

"Madame la Comtesse," said he, "you just now reproached me with speaking like a bourgeois, and I, in turn, fear that you talk like a goddess. I admire you, I listen to you, but I am not convinced. These devotions, these sublime abnegations, are perhaps met with in heaven; but on our earth who may boast that he has seen them?"

"You are mistaken, monsieur," said the countess, solemnly, "such cases are rare, but neither impossible nor incredible; the fault is only in not having the skill to find and the hand to grasp them when offered to you."

So saying she majestically rose.

La Peyrade comprehended that he had ended by displeasing her; he felt that she dismissed him; he rose in his turn, bowed respectfully, and begged to be allowed to call again.

"Monsieur," replied Mme. de Godollo, "among we Hungarians, a primitive people and almost savages, when a door is open, both leaves are opened; but when it is closed, it is double-locked."

This dignified and ambiguous response was accompanied by an inclination of the head. Bewildered, confounded by this behavior, which was so new to him, which bore little resemblance to that of Flavie, Brigitte, and Mme. Minard, he went away asking himself if he had played his game aright.

On leaving Mme. de Godollo, la Peyrade felt that he must have time to think. What could he see beneath the conversation, a springe or a rich wife offered to him? Under such a doubt, to press Céleste for an immediate answer was neither wise nor prudent. Consequently, in lieu of going to the Thuilliers he went home and wrote the following note:

My Dear Thuillier:

I daresay you will not think it strange that I have not presented myself at your house to-day; partly because I dread the sentence and because I do not care to be taken for an impatient, ill-bred creditor. A few days, more or less, will matter little under the circumstances, and yet Mlle. Colleville may find them desirable as giving her entire freedom of choice. I shall not call, therefore, until you write me. I am now calmer, and I have added a few more pages to our manuscript; it needs but little more to be ready for the printer. Ever yours,

THÉODOSE DE LA PEYRADE.

Two hours later a servant dressed in what was evidently the first transition toward a livery, the "male" servant spoken of by Minard, which as yet the Thuilliers did not wish to risk, brought la Peyrade this answer:

Come this evening without fail; we will talk the whole affair over with Brigitte.
Your most affectionately devoted,

JÉRÔME THUILLIER.

"Good," said la Peyrade, "there is a hitch somewhere; I shall have time to turn myself around."

When he arrived, and after talking of the weather and so forth, as people do who have met to discuss a delicate subject about which they are not sure of coming to an understanding, the matter was brought up by Brigitte, who had sent out her brother to take his walk on the boulevards, telling him to leave her to manage the business.

"My dear boy," said Brigitte, "it was a gentlemanly thing of you not to come here to-day like a 'grab-all,' to put your pistol to our throats, for we are not, as it happens, quite ready to answer you. I really think," she added, "that Céleste needs a little more time."

"So," said la Peyrade, quickly, "she has not then decided in favor of Monsieur Félix Phellion?"

"Rogue!" replied the old maid, "you fixed that last

night; but you know, also, that she inclines a little to that side."

"Well, how does Céleste take the matter? Has she refused me?"

"It is much worse than that. She accepts you, saying that she had given her word; but it is easy to see that she looks upon herself as a victim. If I were in your place, I should not consider my success either assuring or flattering."

In any other state of mind, la Peyrade would have answered that he accepted the sacrifice and would make it his business to win her heart, which, for the moment, had been given so reluctantly; but delay better suited his end.

"What is your advice?" he asked Brigitte.

"For the first thing," said Brigitte, "I would finish the pamphlet of Thuillier's, he is going crazy for it, and leave me to work your interests," replied Brigitte.

"But if I am not in friendly hands? for, little aunt, I could not help seeing that you have changed somewhat in your feelings toward me."

"I am changed toward you! and in what do you see me changed, you dreamer?"

"Oh! in little things," said la Peyrade; "but it is sure that since the introduction here of this Countess Torna——"

"My poor boy, the Hungarian has been of much service to me, I must acknowledge that; but is that any reason why I should be false to you, you who have done us much greater services?"

"Still," said the crafty la Peyrade, "you know that she has spoken much that is bad about me?"

"That's the simplest matter, whatever she may have said; those fine ladies expect the whole world to adore them, and she knows that your head is full of Céleste; but all she has said about you runs off me like water off oilcloth."

"So, little aunt," asked la Peyrade, "I am to count on you?"

"Yes; if you don't torment me and allow me to manage matters."

"Well, tell me, then, what you intend doing," said la Peyrade, with an air of jolly good-humor.

"First, I shall forbid Félix the house."

"Is that possible?" said the barrister, "or is it the least bit civil?"

"Very possible, and I shall make Phellion himself tell him. As he makes a hobby-horse of his principles, he'll see that if his son won't do what is necessary to win the hand of Céleste, that he ought to deprive us of his presence."

"And afterward?" said la Peyrade.

"Afterward I shall signify to Céleste that as she was allowed the liberty of choosing a husband from one or the other, and, as she did not choose Félix, she must put up with you, who are such a pious fellow, such as she wants. You be easy; I'll make the best of you, especially your generosity in not pressing your attentions when you might have profited thereby. But that will take quite a week, and if Thuillier's pamphlet is not finished by then, I don't know but what we shall be obliged to send him to Charenton."

"In two days the pamphlet can be ready; but are we quite sure, little aunt, that you are playing a square game? The saying is that mountains cannot meet, but men do; and, certainly, when the time for election comes, I can do Thuillier good or bad service. The other day, do you know, I had a terrible fright. I had about me a letter in which he spoke of the pamphlet as being written by me. I thought for a moment that I had lost that letter at the Luxembourg. If I had, what a scandal there would have been in the quarter."

"Is there any one who would care to play tricks on such a sly fellow as you?" said the old maid, quite understanding the covert threat implied. "But, really," added she, "why should you find fault with us? Is it not yourself that is behindhand with your promises? That Cross which was to be

18

given within a week, that pamphlet that should have been out long ago?"

"The pamphlet and the Cross will each bring the other," replied la Peyrade, rising. "Tell Thuillier to come and see me to-morrow evening. I think by then we can correct the last sheet. But don't lend an ear to the machinations of Madame de Godollo; I have an idea that she designs to make herself the entire mistress of this house; she wants to alienate all your friends, and in the meantime to appropriate Thuillier."

"In fact," said the old maid, whom the infernal barrister had touched in a tender spot, the love of authority, "I must see into this; she is a little coquette, that little madame."

Four days later the printer, the stitcher, and the hot-presser had done their work; Thuillier, in the evening, could give himself the inexpressible honor of commencing a walk on the boulevards, which he continued through the passages of the Palais-Royal, pausing before every bookstore window to steal a glance at a yellow poster, shining in black letters, with the famous title:

## DE L'IMPOT ET DE AMORTISSEMENT.

### Par J. Thuillier,

*Membre du conseil général de la Seine.*

Having managed to persuade himself that the care he had given to the proof-reading and revising had the merit of making the work his own, his paternal heart, like that of the Maître Corbeau, could not hold itself for joy. It should be added that he had but little opinion of those booksellers who did not announce this latest new work for sale, destined, as he fondly believed, to be a European event. Without really being able to see how he could punish them for their indifference, he nevertheless made a list of these recalcitrant persons, and wished them all possible evils, as though it were a personal affront.

The next day he spent in the delightful occupation of addressing a number of presentations, wrapping up fifty sample copies to which the inscription: "From the author," communicated an inestimable prize.

But the third day of the sale brought his happiness a check. He had chosen for his publisher a young man, who, rushing his business at a break-neck pace, had lately established himself in the Passages des Panoramas, where he paid a ruinous rent. A nephew of Barbet, the publisher, whom Brigitte had for a tenant in her old house; he flinched at nothing, and when his uncle recommended him to Thuillier, he was assured that unless he was restricted in the advertising that he would sell the first edition and print another within a week.

Now Thuillier had spent about fifteen hundred francs for advertising; such as sending a profusion of copies to the journals, and, after three days had gone by, only SEVEN copies had been sold, and three of these on credit. It might be presumed that the young publisher would have lost some of his assurance with this; but, to the contrary, this Guzman of the book-trade said:

"I am delighted at what has happened. If we had sold a hundred copies I should be very uneasy as to the fifteen hundred we have printed; I call this hanging fire, whereas this paltry sale goes to prove that the edition will go off with a bang."

"Then you don't think that the sale is hopeless?" said Thuillier.

"On the contrary, I take a most favorable view of this. As soon as the 'Debats,' the Constitutionnel,' the 'Siècle,' and the 'Press' have reviewed it, especially if it gets 'hammered' by the 'Debats,' which is ministerial, it will go."

"You rattle that off right easily," replied Thuillier, "but how shall we get hold of the gentlemen of the press?"

"Leave that to me," said Barbet, "I am on the best of terms with the chief editors; they say the devil is in me and that I remind them of Ladvocat in his best days."

"Then, my dear boy, you ought to have seen to this before."

"Ah! but permit me, Papa Thuillier, there's only one way of 'seeing' a newspaper-man; as you grumbled about the fifteen hundred francs, I didn't want to suggest another expense to you."

"Expense for what?"

"When you were nominated for the Council," replied the book-seller, "where was your election planned?"

"*Parbleu!* in my home," answered Thuillier.

"At your home, without doubt, but at a dinner followed by a ball and the ball followed by a supper. Well, my dear master, there are not two ways to do this business; Boileau says:

> "'We govern our times the best with our dinners,
> It's by dining alone that we keep check on our sinners.'"

"But that costs money; journalists are all a lot of gourmands."

"Pshaw! twenty francs per head, without the wine. Given, say, ten of them, with a hundred crowns you could do it fine."

"How you talk, young man," said Thuillier.

"*Dame*, everybody knows that it costs to get a nomination, and you will thus prepare for it."

"But how shall I invite these gentlemen? Must I go and invite them myself?"

"Not at all; you have sent them your pamphlet, now you beg them to meet you at Philippe's or Véfour's; they'll catch on all right."

"Ten guests," said Thuillier, entering into the idea, "I did not know there were so many important journalists?"

"Quite true," replied the publisher, "but we must have the curs, for they bark the loudest. The breakfast is sure to be well talked about; they will think you have been picking and choosing, and each one left out would become your enemy."

"If I were sure that this expense would have the desired effect," said Thuillier, with indecision.

"*If I were sure* is very pretty," said Barbet, with importance; "but, my dear master, this is money placed on mortgage; with that I can guarantee you selling the fifteen hundred copies. That at forty sous, and allowing the discounts, makes three thousand francs. You see that covers your costs and extras—more than covers them."

"So! I'll talk it over with la Peyrade," said Thuillier as he went out.

"As you will, dear master, but decide quickly, for nothing gets mildewed so soon as a book; write hot, serve hot, sell it hot; that's the rule of three for authors, publishers, and the public; outside of that everything falls flat, and is no good to touch."

When la Peyrade was consulted he did not really think so much of the plan; but now he had begun to feel the bitterest animosity against Thuillier, so he was quite delighted to see this new tax levied on his self-conceit, inexperience, and pomposity.

Now Thuillier's mania for posing as a statesman decided him on following Barbet's advice. He called upon him therefore for the list of guests. Barbet gayly produced his little catalogue. Fifteen instead of the original number were down, without counting himself or la Peyrade, whom Thuillier felt he should need in encountering a crowd of men with whom he had reason to think he would be out of place. When Thuillier had cast his eyes over the paper:

"Ah, there! my dear boy," said he to the publisher, "you have given me the names of journals that I never even heard tell of. What is this 'Moralisateur,' that 'Lanterne,' the 'Diogène,' or the 'Pelican,' and that 'Echo de la Bièvre?'"

"You do well," replied Barbet, "to fall foul of 'Echo de la Bièvre,' a paper printed in the twelfth arrondissement and read by all the rich tanners in the quarter."

"Well, pass that, then; but the 'Pelican?'"

"The 'Pelican?' why that journal is on every dentist's waiting-room table; dentists make more *puffs* than all the rest of the world; how many teeth do you suppose are daily drawn in Paris?"

"Oh! bosh," said Thuillier.

Finally the list was finished at fourteen guests and the meeting appointed at Véfour's, the one most extensively patronized by the bourgeoisie and provincials. Barbet arrived even before Thuillier, wearing a cravat so enormous as to itself become a feature among those satirical guests. The publisher had taken it upon himself to change sundry of the dishes: instead of having the champagne served in the bourgeois fashion with the dessert, he ordered it placed on the table at the commencement of the repast, properly iced, together with a few dishes of shrimps, of which the amphitryon had not thought.

Thuillier, who gave a verbal approval to these changes, was followed by la Peyrade; then a long pause before any others appeared. Breakfast was ordered for eleven, but at a quarter before twelve not a guest had come. Barbet, never at a loss, made the crushing remark that breakfasts at a restaurant were like funerals, when eleven meant twelve. As a fact, just before that hour two goat-bearded gentlemen arrived, exhaling a strong odor of the smoking-room. Thuillier effusively thanked them for the "honor" they were about to do him; and then came another long period of waiting. At one, five only of the invited guests had arrived. They took their places at table; a few polite speeches reached Thuillier's ears as to the "immense" interest the publication of his pamphlet had excited, but this failed to blind him to the fact of a dismal failure. Only for the vivacity of the publisher, who had seized the reins dropped by his patron, gloomy as Hippolytus on the way to Mycenæ, nothing could have equaled the depression and the icy coldness of this meeting.

After the removal of the oysters the champagne and Chablis had begun to give a slight rise to the temperature when a youngster in a cap rushed into the banqueting-room and gave Thuillier a most unexpected and crushing blow.

"Boss," said the new-comer to Barbet—he was a clerk in the bookseller's store—"we are done for! The police have raided us; a commissary and two men have come to seize monsieur's pamphlet; they left this paper with me for you."

"See what this says, Monsieur the Barrister," said Barbet as he handed the paper to la Peyrade. At this stroke his habitual assurance paled somewhat.

"A summons to shortly appear before the Assize Court," said la Peyrade, after reading the sheriff's scrawl.

Becoming as pale as death:

"Then didn't you fill all the necessary formalities?" asked Thuillier in a choking voice.

"Oh! This is not a question of formalities," replied la Peyrade, "it is seized as illegal printed matter, which excites hatred and contempt for the government. You will find at home, my poor Thuillier, a similar compliment awaiting you."

"But this must be treason, then!" said Thuillier, who had completely lost his head.

"*Dame!* my dear boy, you must know what you put in the pamphlet; for my part, I didn't see anything bad enough to whip a cat for."

"There's a misunderstanding somewhere," said Barbet, recovering a little courage. "It will be all explained, the result will be a fine cause for complaints to be made, is not that so, gentlemen?"

"Waiter, a pen and ink," exclaimed one of the journalists thus appealed to.

"You'll have time enough to write your article," said one of his colleagues; "what has a bomb in common with this *filet sauté ?*"

This was a parody on a famous speech of Louis XII., of Sweden, whom a cannon-ball interrupted while he was dictating to his secretary.

"Gentlemen," said Thuillier, rising, "you will excuse me; if, as Monsieur Barbet thinks, it is all a mistake, it ought to be explained immediately: I shall at once, with your permission, go to the court. La Peyrade," added he, significantly, "you will not refuse, I think, to accompany me. And you, my dear publisher, had better come with us."

"My faith, no!" said Barbet; "when I breakfast I breakfast; if the police have blundered, so much the worse for them."

"But suppose the action is a serious one?" exclaimed Thuillier, greatly agitated.

"Well, all I should say, which is perfectly true, that I had not read a single line of your pamphlet. There is only one annoying feature about it—those damned juries hate beards, so if I am to appear in court I must cut mine off."

"Come, my dear amphitryon, sit down again," said the editor-in-chief of the "Echo de la Bièvre," "we'll stand by you; I have already written an article which will stir up all the peat-hawkers, and that is a power, that honorable corporation."

"No, gentlemen," said Thuillier, "no, a man like me cannot rest a single half-hour under such an accusation. Continue without us; I hope soon to return to you. La Peyrade, are you coming?"

When Thuillier left the office of the court he could no longer indulge illusions. He was under a most serious charge, and the severe manner in which he had been received made him understand that when the trial came on he would be treated without leniency. Then he turned, as is the manner with accomplices when things turn out wrongly, upon la Peyrade in the bitterest vituperations: He had paid no attention to what he was writing; he had given full rein to his stupid ideas on Saint-Simonism; *he* didn't care about the consequences; *he* wouldn't have to pay the fine or go to prison! Then, when la Peyrade said the case did not seem serious to him, and that he looked for an acquittal, Thuillier burst furiously upon him:

"Certainly! all is very simple," replied Thuillier, "monsieur sees nothing in it; all you can see is a chance for a showy defense; but I shan't put my honor and fortune in the hands of one of your ilk. I shall take some great barrister, if the case comes to trial. I've had about enough of your collaboration."

Under the injustice of these reproaches la Peyrade felt his anger rising. He did not wish to come to an open rupture, so he left him, saying that he forgave him, as he was naturally so excited. He would wait upon him in the evening, when he would probably be calmer.

Accordingly, about four o'clock, the Provençal called at the house in the Place de la Madeleine. Thuillier was quieter, but consternation, frightful despair, had taken its place. As for Brigitte, she had no mercy in her speech; her bitter, virulent abuse was quite out of proportion to the fault. La Peyrade felt that all was lost for him in the Thuillier household, they seemed to hail with joy the chance for throwing him over. On an ironical illusion by Brigitte to the manner in which he had decorated his friends, he rose and took his leave, without their making an effort to retain him.

After walking the streets for a little while his indignation calmed down to thoughts of Madame de Godollo. To have paid her another visit immediately would have been anything but skillful, but a sufficient time had now elapsed to prove that he was the master of himself. So he turned his steps back to the Boulevard de la Madeleine, and, without asking if the countess was at home, he passed the lodge as if he was returning to the Thuilliers, and rung the bell of the entresol.

As before, he was asked to wait while the maid notified her mistress; but this time it was in a little library. He waited long and wondered at the meaning of the delay; but finally the maid reappeared :

"Madame la Comtesse," said she, "is engaged on a business matter. Would monsieur be so kind as to wait? He might amuse himself with some of the books, as she would possibly be detained for some time."

He did not open any of the rosewood cases, for he saw on a claw-footed table a medley of books. But as he opened the volumes, one after another, he fancied that a Tantalus' feast was before him; one book was in English, another German, the next Russian, and one he found with crabbed Turkish characters. Was this a polyglot joke that she had arranged for him?

One volume at length arrested his attention. The binding, he noticed, unlike those of the other books, was not so rich as pretty. It lay by itself on a corner of the table. It was open, the back upward, and the edges of the leaves rested on the green tablecloth like a tent. La Peyrade took it up, when it proved to be a volume of the illustrated edition of Scribe's works. The engraving displayed was taken from a scene at the Gymnase, entitled "The Hatred of a Woman." Few but know the story and the conclusion of the drama. The principal personage is a young widow who desperately pursues a young man. One speech is: "There are some women who would spit on the dish to cause disgust and prevent others eating of it." Hatred pursues the unhappy one everywhere. Her deviltries make him to nearly lose his reputation and do prevent his making a wealthy marriage; but it ends by her giving him more than she had deprived him of, and she makes him her husband.

If it was chance that had placed this volume in its isolated position, it was opened at the precise spot which seemed pertinent to what had passed between himself and the countess —chance is at at times adroit and clever. As he thought over this enigma the sound of an opening door reached his ear, and he detected the rather drawling voice of the countess, who was accompanying some one to the door.

"I may say then," said the voice of a man, "that you promise the ambassadress that you will honor the ball with your presence this evening?"

"Yes, commander, if my somewhat mitigated headache will permit."

"Au revoir, then, my most adorable lady," said the voice of her interlocutor. Then the door closed and silence again reigned.

The title of commander somewhat reassured la Peyrade, for it is not in common used to young fops. He was curious enough to know whom this person might be that had so long occupied the time of the countess. As he did not hear any one approaching the library he went softly toward the window and carefully opened the curtain, prepared to drop it immediately if any sound was heard. An elegant coupé, standing in waiting, was drawn up to the door. A footman in dashing livery opened the door, and a little, dandified old man, with a brisk, jaunty movement, stepped into the carriage, being rapidly driven away. La Peyrade had opportunity to notice that his breast was covered with decorations. This, taken in connection with his powdered hair, gave evidence of a diplomatic personage.

La Peyrade had returned to his book so as to be discovered reading, when the maid appeared and invited him to follow her. He replaced the volume—not in the place in which he had found it—and an instant later was in the presence of the countess. Beside her on the couch lay a gilt-edged letter in that free, large writing that betrays an official communication.

X

In her hand was a crystal bottle with a gold stopper, from which she inhaled the odor of English toilet vinegar, which permeated the room.

"You are not well, madame?" asked la Peyrade, with anxiety.

"Oh! it is nothing," said the foreigner, "but a headache; I am subject to them. But you, monsieur, where have you been? I despaired of seeing you again. Have you some important news to make known to me? The date of your marriage to Mademoiselle Colleville must be sufficiently neai that you may now state it."

This opening slightly disconcerted la Peyrade.

"But, madame," he replied almost sharply, "it seems to me that you know everything that transpires in the Thuilliers' household, you must therefore well know that the event of which you speak is not even a probability."

"No, I give you my word, I know nothing. I have strictly made up my mind to take no further interest in the affair. Madame Brigitte speaks of everything but Céleste's marriage."

"Well, madame, your judgment as to my marriage was certainly correct."

"What?" said the countess, eagerly. "Has the seizure of the pamphlet happening after Thuillier's failure to obtain the Cross led to a rupture?"

"No," said la Peyrade, "my influence in the Thuillier establishment rests on a solid foundation. The services I have rendered mademoiselle and her brother quite outweigh these two checks, which happily are not irreparable."

"You think so?" interrupted the countess, incredulously.

"Certainly," replied la Peyrade. "When Madame du Bruel seriously means to get the red ribbon she can do it in spite of all the obstacles that may be placed in her way."

The countess received this assurance with a smile, and shook her head.

"You must surely forget that it is unusual to decorate a

man who is under a summons of the court. It betokens a strong feeling against Thuillier, and perhaps against yourself, too; for you are the real culprit. The law, in this case, does not appear to have acted independently."

La Peyrade looked at the countess.

"I must confess," replied he, after that rapid glance, "that I have vainly tried to find a single phrase in the whole work that would give cause for its seizure."

"But it seems to me that the King's people must have a vivid imagination to find anything seditious in the work," said the countess. "And this proves the strength of the underground power which thwarts your every intention in favor of that excellent Monsieur Thuillier."

"Is it that you know our secret enemies?" said la Peyrade.

"Perhaps," said the countess, smiling again.

"May I dare to venture a suspicion?" asked la Peyrade, considerably agitated.

"Speak," replied Mme. de Godollo; "I won't blame you if you guess aright."

"Well, madame, our enemies, Thuillier's and mine, *are* a woman."

"Even so," said the countess. "Know you how many lines of handwriting Richelieu needed before hanging a man?"

"Four," answered la Peyrade.

"You can then satisfy yourself that a pamphlet of two hundred pages can easily furnish a—well a, say, intriguing woman with ground enough for prosecution."

"I cease my struggle," said la Peyrade. Then, assuming an air of contrition:

"My God! madame," added he, "you must, indeed, hate me."

"Not to the extent that you imagine," replied the countess; "but, after all, suppose that I did?"

"Ah, madame," said la Peyrade, "I should then be the happiest of unfortunates; for this hate would be to me a thousand times more precious than your indifference. But you hate me not. Why should you show to me that blessed feminine sentiment which is described by Scribe with such intelligence and delicacy?"

Mme. de Godollo made no immediate reply; she cast down her eyes and her deep breathing gave a tremulous tone to her voice:

"The hate of a woman!" she replied, "can a man of your stoicism be able to perceive it?"

"Oh! yes, madame," answered la Peyrade, "I do perceive it, but not to rebel against it; on the contrary, I bless the harshness that deigns to injure me. My beautiful enemy now known and confessed, I shall not despair of touching her heart, for I will never again tread a path that is not hers; never will I march under any banner that she has not made her own. In everything I will be her auxiliary, her slave; if she repulses me with her darling foot, punishes me with her white hand, I will endure it with pleasure. For all this submission and obedience I will crave but one favor—that I may kiss the print of the foot that spurns me, of bathing with tears the hand that is raised to strike me."

During this long outcry of a transported and distracted heart, which the joy of triumph had wrung from the impressible nature of the Provençal, he had glided from his chair, and at the end found himself on one knee before the countess in the conventional attitude of the stage, but which is far more common in real life than most people think.

"Rise, monsieur," said the countess, "and please answer me."

Then, giving him a questioning gaze beneath the lovely, frowning eyebrows:

"Have you carefully weighed," said she, "the meaning of what you have just said? Have you gauged the pledge, and plumbed its depths? Your hand on your heart and conscience, are you the man to redeem this promise; are you not one of the falsely humble and perfidious men who only affect to embrace our knees to make us the more easily lose our balance, both of will and reason?"

"I!" exclaimed la Peyrade; "never can a reaction occur against the fascinations which enthralled me at our first interview. I have said aloud to-day what my heart has long held; I have struggled against your allurements; it has ended in giving me a firm, deliberate will, understanding itself, and refusing to be cast down by your severity."

"Severity, that is possible," said the countess, "but you ought also to think of the kindness; we foreign women do not understand the levity with which your Frenchwomen enter upon the most solemn engagement. With us yes is a sacred bond; our word is our act. We do nothing by halves. Our family arms seem pertinent to the circumstances: ALL OR NOTHING."

"That is the understanding I have of my pledge," replied the barrister; "my first step on leaving you will be to go and put an end to that ignoble past which I once placed in the balance against my present intoxicating future."

"No," said the countess, "do it calmly and with due thought. I shouldn't like to see you lose your head and going about smashing window-panes. The Thuilliers are not such bad folk at the bottom; they humiliated you without knowing it; their world is not yours. Is that their fault? Untie the knot, don't break it. Your conversion to my belief is of very recent date. What man can be sure what his heart will say to-morrow?"

"I, madame, am that man. We men of the South do not love in the French fashion."

"But I thought," said the Hungarian, with a charming smile, "that our discussion was on hatred."

"Ah! madame, that word hurts me; the rather tell me that you love me."

"My friend," replied the countess, accenting the word,

"one of our moralists says: 'There are those who say: *this is* or *this is not;* such need take no oath;' do me the honor of counting me among such people." As she spoke she held out her hand with a graceful gesture. La Peyrade, quite beside himself, rapturously kissed it, and they bade each other adieu.

On the stairs La Peyrade stopped to exhale, one might say, the happiness with which his heart was too full. When opposite the Thuillier door he cried:

"At last I have fame, fortune, happiness; more than all, I can give myself the pleasure of revenge. After Dutocq and Cérizet I will crush you, vile bourgeoise brood?" and he shook his fist at the innocent double-door.

The next day, the tempest heaving in his breast, la Peyrade went to see Thuillier in the most hostile mood. How amazed he became when, as soon as Thuillier saw him, he threw himself into his arms.

"My friend," said the ex-sub-chief, "my political fortune is made, every paper without exception speaks this morning of the pamphlet being seized; you should see how the Opposition sheets peg into the government."

"Yes, but you have an enemy who is working against you; the same hand that prevented your getting the Cross is the one that seized your pamphlet; you are being assassinated by premeditation."

"Then if this dangerous enemy is known to you, why don't you unmask him to me?" said Thuillier.

"I don't know, but I have suspicions," replied la Peyrade; "this is what you get by playing such a deep game."

"How! a deep game?" said the simple Thuillier, who well knew he had nothing of the kind with which to reproach himself.

"Certainly," replied the barrister. "You have used Céleste as a kind of decoy-duck in your salon; the whole world has not the magnanimity of Monsieur Godeschal, who so generously forgave you and managed that business of the house."

"Explain yourself," said Thuillier, "I can't yet comprehend."

"Nothing is easier. Without counting me, how many pretenders have you had to Céleste's hand? Godeschal, Minard junior, young Phellion, Olivier Vinet, all men who have been told to walk their chalks like as I have been."

"Olivier Vinet, the substitute," exclaimed Thuillier, struck with a new light; "that's the one, of course, that caused this blow. His father, they say, has a very long arm. But it cannot be said that we made him walk his chalk, to use your expression, which seems unseemly to me; for no offer was made by him or Minard or Phellion. Godeschal is the only one who took the risk of a direct refusal, and this was done before he had even dipped his beak in the water."

"Quite true," said la Peyrade, looking for a new ground of quarrel; "sly men always brag of having fooled men of their word and decisive people."

"Now what are you aiming at by those insinuations? Didn't you properly settle everything with Brigitte the other day? It's a nice time to bother me about your love affairs while the sword of justice hangs over my head."

"Oh! that's it," said la Peyrade, ironically; "I knew how it would be when your pamphlet came out—the old cry of not getting out of me all that you expected!"

"Well, I did think that our friendship was too true and devoted for you to fling sarcasms at me when I only looked for your services."

"What services?" asked la Peyrade. "Did you not say yesterday that you would not accept my assistance under any circumstances? You said when I offered to defend you that you would employ a great barrister."

"Yes, in the first shock of surprise; I was foolish, naturally, but after reflection I see that you could better defend me than

19

others, as you know thoroughly what you have written with your own pen. You should forgive that momentary irritation. You are caustic as well as cruel."

"Well, I refuse to do anything of the kind. Things have changed since yesterday. I see to-day that you had better get some big-wig of the law, because Vinet's antagonism is taking on such proportions that I should be afraid to tackle the responsibilities."

"I understand," said Thuillier, sarcastically; "monsieur has an eye on the magistracy and does not want to quarrel with one who is slated for keeper of the seals. Quite prudent, quite; still I don't think it will help on your marriage."

"That is to say," said la Peyrade, catching the ball on its rebound, "that to get you out of the clutches of the jury is the thirteenth labor of Hercules that you would impose upon me to gain the hand of Mademoiselle Colleville. I fully expected that the exigencies would multiply in proportion to my devotion. But just that same thing has worn me out; to-day I have come to put an end to this exploitation of myself. You may dispose of Céleste's hand as you are disposed; so far as I am concerned I am no longer a suitor."

This abrupt and unexpected declaration left Thuillier speechless, the more so as that moment Brigitte entered. Her animosity had declined; she greeted him with amicable familiarity:

"Ah! there you are," said she to la Peyrade, "good wheat of a barrister!"

"Mademoiselle, I salute you," gravely responded the Provençal.

"Well," she went on, not paying any attention to la Peyrade's ceremonious manner, "the government has done it by seizing your pamphlet. You should just see how the morning papers go for it. Here," she added, passing to Thuillier a small sheet printed on sugar-paper, in coarse type and scarcely legible, "this is one that you've not yet seen; this is the journal of our old quarter, the 'Echo de la Bièvre.' It's *wrote* splendid; it's queer though how careless these journalists are; most of them write your name without the *h*—you ought to complain about it."

Never before had Brigitte troubled about the papers except to see whether they might be of a proper size in which to wrap a package; but now, under the influence of sisterly affection, she pointed out to Thuillier the especially bright spots.

"Yes," said Thuillier, refolding the paper, "that's pretty warm, beside being very flattering to me. But there is another very important matter: monsieur, here present, has come to inform me that he is no longer a claimant for Céleste's hand."

"That is he means," said Brigitte, "that he won't take on the case unless he is married out of hand as soon as it is over. Well, it seems only reasonable, poor man. When he has done that there should not be any further delay; she must accept him; everything has an end."

"You hear, my dear sir," said la Peyrade, seizing upon Brigitte's commentary; "when I have pleaded, the wedding comes. Your sister is frankness itself; she is not the least diplomatic."

"Diplomatic!" exclaimed Brigitte. "I'd like to see myself grubbing under a business; I say as I think; the workman has done his work, now he should be paid in full."

"Be quiet, do," said Thuillier; "I say that la Peyrade returns us our pledges; he claims that we are asking another service off him for Céleste's hand; he thinks he has done quite enough as it is."

"He has done us some service, undoubtedly," replied Brigitte; "we are not ungrateful to him. All the same, it was he that caused you the trouble. It seems only fair that he should get you out of it."

"There might be some sense of justice in your remarks,"

answered la Peyrade, "if I were the only barrister in Paris; but, unhappily, the streets are black over with them. Now, as to the marriage, as I don't intend being made the object of any further brutal bargaining, I am here to renounce it in the most formal manner, and nothing now prevents Céleste accepting Monsieur Phellion with all his numerous advantages."

"At your pleasure, my dear monsieur," replied Brigitte, "if that is your last word. We shall be at no loss in finding a husband for Céleste. But the reason you give is not the real one. We can't dance faster than the fiddlers go, the banns have to be published; you have sense enough to know that no wedding can take place till all formalities have been complied with, and long before then Thuillier's trial will be over."

"Yes," said la Peyrade, "and if I lose the case it will be me who has sent him to prison, the same as yesterday I caused the seizure."

"Well, it does seem to me that if you hadn't *wrote* something there would be nothing to bite at by the police."

"My dear Brigitte," interposed Thuillier, who had noted la Peyrade shrug his shoulders, "it is not la Peyrade's fault if persons high in station are conspiring against us. That little Vinet who came to one of our receptions, you remember him —well, his father is furious because we didn't want him for Céleste."

"Well, what other reason than monsieur's fine eyes had we for refusing?" said Brigitte. "After all, a substitute is a very desirable catch."

"Undoubtedly," said la Peyrade, nonchalantly; "only you see he didn't bring you a million!"

"Ah!" said Brigitte, flaming up, "if you are going to talk again about the house you got us to buy, I don't mind telling you pretty plainly that if you had had the money yourself you wouldn't have told us about it. You would have tricked the notary for yourself. Beside, we've had to pay a lot more than you said it would cost."

"Come, now," said Thuillier, "don't speak of trifles."

"Trifles! trifles!" repeated Brigitte. "Did we pay more than we expected, or didn't we?"

"My dear Thuillier," said la Peyrade, "discussion is useless; my mind is made up; I shall not be Céleste's husband, but we may be good friends;" and he rose to leave.

"One moment, monsieur," said Brigitte, barring his way; "there is one matter yet unsettled, if we are not to have anything conjointly again, perhaps you will be so good as to inform me what became of that ten thousand francs given you by Thuillier to bribe those scoundrels of government officials to get the Cross we never got."

"Brigitte," cried Thuillier with anguish, "you have the tongue of hell; you learned that from me once when I was in a bad humor, you promised you would never mention it again."

"No; but," replied the implacable Brigitte, "when people part they should settle up—pay their debts. Ten thousand francs, a real Cross is dear enough at that price; but for a Cross that has wilted away, monsieur will admit the price is rather steep."

"Monsieur," said la Peyrade, ignoring Brigitte, and pale with rage, "I am not prepared to instantly return you the amount which has been so insolently demanded. But should you be pleased to grant me some little delay and accept my note, why——"

"To the devil with a note," said Thuillier, "you owe me nothing; in fact, by what Cardot said, we are indebted to you; he said we ought to have given you not less than ten thousand francs."

"Cardot! Cardot!" said Brigitte, "he is very generous with other people's money. We were giving monsieur Céleste, that's better than ten thousand francs."

La Peyrade was too fine a comedian to allow such an affair as this pass without changing it to a scenic finale. With tears in his voice, which presently rolled down his cheek:

"Mademoiselle," said he, "when I had the honor of being received by you, I was poor; you saw me accept every indignity with forbearance, for you knew what poverty must undergo. To-day when I release you of anxiety, by giving you the chance of attaining the husband you wish for Céleste—for if you were honest you would acknowledge that you had that thought—we might still remain friends. Thank heaven, I have in my heart some religious sentiment; the gospel to me is not a dead letter, so, pray understand me, *I forgive you*. It is not to Thuillier, who would refuse to accept them, that I shall offer the ten thousand francs, which you believe me to have appropriated to my own use, but to you. If at that time you feel how unjust your suspicions were and should scruple to keep the money, you can hand it over to the Bureau of Benevolence——"

"To the Bureau of Benevolence!" cried Brigitte, interrupting him; "thanks, not much. What! for them crowd of junketing do-nothings to have that distributed amongst them; folk who would eat off the head of the good God! I've been poor myself, my boy; I made bags for people to put money in before I'd any of my own; now that I've got some I mean to keep it; so, whenever you're ready to cash up, well, I'll receive that ten thousand francs and keep it, too. If you didn't know better than to try and put salt on a cock-sparrow's tail, why so much the worse for you."

La Peyrade saw that he had missed his aim and had not in the slightest degree impressed Brigitte's granite; he cast a disdainful look at her and went out majestically. Arriving at his own home the barrister completed his emancipation by writing to Mme. Colleville that, the marriage with Céleste being broken off, he thought that propriety required his abstaining from visiting her house for the future.

The next day Colleville, on the way to his office, called on la Peyrade and asked what "stupidity" he had written Flavie, whom he had left plunged in the direst despair from it. The barrister with the utmost gravity reproduced a copy for the husband; it was certainly not a love letter that had been sent to his wife.

"And so that is what you call being a friend?" said Colleville, who for a long time had familiarly *thoud* the Provençal. "You don't marry us—but is that any reason for breaking with the girl's parents? It is as though we were responsible for Thuillier's and your quarrel. Is this the regard that you profess for us? My wife, has she not always treated you kindly?"

"I have never been received but with the utmost kindness and the greatest consideration by Madame Colleville," replied la Peyrade.

"And so for this you would let her die of grief? Never since yesterday has she laid down her handkerchief; I tell you she will be really ill."

"Well, I must frankly tell you," said la Peyrade, "that my visits have excited comment; it is my plain duty to put a stop to this calumny."

"What!" exclaimed the husband, "a man of your intelligence taking notice of such puerile twaddle. Why she has been talked about for five and twenty years has my wife, and only because she happens to be better looking than a Madame Thuillier or Brigitte. I must be a greater scoundrel than you, for this tittle-tattle has not caused a quarter of an hour's uneasiness in our household."

"I admire your strength of mind, but it is rash to go against public opinion."

"What next!" said Colleville; "I trample it underfoot, this public opinion, the prostitute! It is Minard who has done this gossiping, all because his fat cook of a wife has never attracted the attention of any decent man. He had better look after his son, who is ruining himself with an elderly actress at the Bobino."

"Well, my dear friend," said la Peyrade, "try and bring back Flavie to her senses."

"To the good speech," said Colleville, vigorously shaking the hand of the barrister; "you call her Flavie as of old; I have recovered my friend."

"Certainly," replied la Peyrade, serenely, "friends are always friends."

"Yes, friends are friends," repeated Colleville; "friendship is a present from the gods, and consoles us for all the crosses of life. I understand, then, that you will call upon my wife and replace our household's sorrow with joy and serenity."

La Peyrade made a vague promise and wondered whether the husband—a type more plentiful than supposed—was an actor or genuine.

At the time when la Peyrade was about laying the freedom he had recovered at the feet of the countess, he received a perfumed note on which he recognized the famous seal: ALL OR NOTHING, which was to govern the relations between them.

"Dear Monsieur," said Mme. de Godollo, "I have heard of your determination, thanks! But now I must arrange to take my own; I cannot, you must see, continue to reside in a sphere so far from that of ours, one, too, in which we have nothing in common. To make this arrangement so as to avoid explanations for the reason why the entresol welcomes the voluntary exile from the first floor, I shall need to-day and to-morrow for myself. Therefore, do not call to see me until the following day. By that time I shall have executed Brigitte, as they say on the Bourse, and have much to tell you.

"*Tua Tota*.
"Comtesse de Godollo."

That "wholly thine" in Latin seemed charming to la Peyrade; it did not astonish him, for he knew that the Latin tongue with the Hungarians was almost a second national language.

In the interval of waiting he was agitated with an ardent passion, which was but increased by his enforced absence. He ran lightly up the stairs and put out his hand to ring the bell, but the silken cord was missing; he thought that illness might have caused this, so that all noise should be silenced; but then he noticed that the soft carpet on the landing had been removed and the portieres taken down. He had to resign himself to take the same means employed when visiting a milliner's apprentice to make known his presence—he rapped with his knuckles. The hollow sound revealed the void within; it was *intonuere caverna*. Convinced at length of a total removal, he thought it had most probably been caused by some insolence of the old maid. But what an idea to place him in the ridiculous position called by the vulgar by the picturesque appellation of "meeting the wooden face." Being determined to fully satisfy himself, before going, he made a furious assault upon the door.

"Whose that hammering at the door as if he wanted to pull down the house?" shouted the janitor up the stairway.

"Madame de Godollo—does she not still reside here?" asked la Peyrade.

"Certainly she doesn't live here now since she's left. Had monsieur told me he was seeking her, I would have spared him the trouble of battering down the door."

"I knew she was about leaving this suite," said la Peyrade, "but was ignorant that she had already done so."

"I think it must have been done in a hurry," said the janitor, "since she went off early this morning with post-horses."

"Post-horses!" repeated la Peyrade, stupefied; "then has she quit Paris?"

"Well, people don't usually go post from one quarter of Paris to another," said the porter.

"Did she say where she was going?"

"What a funny idea, monsieur; do such folk give any account of themselves to the like of us?"

"Did she leave no messages?"

"Nothing, monsieur; except that any letters which might arrive would be called for by the little commander."

La Peyrade went away with despair in his heart. After some reflection he muttered to himself:

"These female diplomats are often charged with important secret missions, where discretion is a necessity and the utmost rapidity of motion required."

Here a sudden revulsion of feeling came over him:

"But suppose she is but an adventuress, one of those employed by foreign governments as secret agents? Suppose that the story of the Russian princess, more or less likely, being obliged to sell her furniture to Brigitte is also that of this Hungarian lady? But yet," added he, as his brain made a third revolution, "her education, manners, speech, everything, proclaim her a woman of the highest position; then, beside, if she were but a bird of passage, why try to win me over?"

La Peyrade might have continued his pleading, for and against, for a much longer time, if he had not felt himself suddenly seized by the shoulders by a strong arm, while a voice he well knew cried:

"My dear barrister, lookout! a frightful danger menaces you; you are running into it headlong."

La Peyrade turned round to find himself in Phellion's arms. A house was being torn down and Phellion, with his spoken-of fondness for the like, stood, watch in hand, looking at the workmen and calculating how long a time would elapse before a great wall would topple over.

"You there, are you deaf and blind?" ran the speech

of the man employed to warn the passers-by, in a tone that may be imagined.

"Thanks, my dear monsieur," said la Peyrade, "I should have been *erased* like an idiot only for you." And he pressed Phellion's hand.

"My reward," replied he, "is in the satisfaction of knowing that you are saved from imminent danger. I may add that the gratification is increased by a certain pride, for I was not mistaken to a moment in the time I had reckoned upon for the instant when the centre of gravity of that formidable mass would be displaced. But of what were you thinking? Perhaps of the plea you would make in the Thuillier case. You have a noble cause to defend, monsieur. Between you and I," added the great citizen in a low voice, "I think it a mean action on the part of the government."

"I am of the same opinion," said la Peyrade, "but I am not charged with the defense."

"Poor man," said Phellion; "I called to see him when the blow fell. (I am on my way to see him now.) I saw only Brigitte, who was conversing with Madame de Godollo; that is a woman who possesses strong political views. It appears that she predicted that the seizure would occur."

"Did you know that the countess had left Paris?" said la Peyrade.

"Ah! she has gone," said Phellion. "Well, monsieur, I must tell you that though there was little sympathy between you and her, yet I look upon her departure as a misfortune; she leaves a serious void in the salon of our friends; I say this because I think it, I am not used to at all disguise my feelings."

"Yes," said la Peyrade, "she is a most distinguished woman; I think, in spite of her predilections against me, that we should have come eventually to some kind of an understanding of each other; but this morning she hastily left by post."

"Post!" exclaimed Phellion. "I don't know whether monsieur agrees with me, but I think traveling post is most agreeable. It is certain that Louis XI., to whom we owe this institution, had a very happy thought; although in other matters his sanguinary and despotic rule was not, to my way of thinking, quite devoid of reproach. Only once in my life have I so traveled, but I may truly say that I found it far superior, in spite of the relative increase of speed, to the mad rush of the iron roads or 'railways,' as the English call them, and where speed is acquired at the cost of safety and the taxpayer."

La Peyrade paid but small attention to Phellion's phraseology. "Whither has she gone?" This was the one question round which all his thoughts hovered. But the great citizen continued:

"It was at the time of Madame Phellion's last confinement. She was at Perche with her mother, when I learned that serious complications had ensued, together with milk-fever. A wound in the pocket is never fatal, as they say, so, overwhelmed with terror at the danger threatening my wife, I at once proceeded to the coach-office to obtain a seat in the coach; all were taken, and had been for a week in advance. My mind was at once made up. I went to the Rue Pigalle, and, by paying gold down on the spot, I obtained a chaise and two horses; but unfortunately I had neglected the formality of a passport, without which, by the decrees of the consulate of 17 Nivôse of the year XII., they are not allowed to deliver horses to a traveler——"

The last words were a flash of light to la Peyrade; without the finish of the posting Odyssey, he started off at once to the Rue Pigalle. Arrived at the establishment of the royal post, la Peyrade wondered of whom he might best inquire. He explained to the porter that he wished to send a letter to a lady of his acquaintance; that this lady had neglected to leave her address, and he thought he might possibly learn it by means of the passport which must have been presented in order to obtain horses.

"This lady traveler, had she a maid with her? This one I picked up near the Madeleine," said a postillion who sat in a corner of the room.

"Exactly," said la Peyrade, advancing eagerly to the man of providence, and slipping a crown of a hundred sous into his hand.

"She's a rum sort of a traveler," said the post-boy; "she told me to take her to the Bois du Boulogne, there she made me drive around for an hour; then we came back to the barrier de l'Étoile, where she gave me a good tip and got into a hack, telling me to take the chaise to the man she had hired it from on the Cour des Coches, Faubourg St. Honoré."

"The name of the man?" demanded la Peyrade.

"Sieur Simonin," replied the postillion.

Armed with this information, la Peyrade took his course, and in a quarter of an hour was questioning the livery-stable keeper; that individual could only say that the chaise had been hired for half a day without horses, and that it had been returned at noon by a postillion of the royal post.

"Never mind," said la Peyrade, "I am certain that she has not left Paris, and is not avoiding me; most likely she uses this pretended journey to utterly break with the Thuilliers. Fool that I am, a letter assuredly awaits me at my home to inform me of all."

Worn out with hunger and fatigue, he took a hack to his home, but there he had to wait for the porter, Coffinet, who since Brigitte's departure had been remiss in his duties. La Peyrade had rushed at once to the lodge, but the porter and his wife were both absent, she about the house, he in a wine-shop, where between two drinks he defended the right of people to own property, as against the opinion held by a republican who was speaking disrespectfully the other way.

It was over twenty minutes before this worthy janitor re-

membered that he had certain "property" confided to him
and returned to his functions. One can figure to himself the
deluge of reproaches with which la Peyrade saluted him. He
made some kind of an excuse, and handed a letter to him which
bore the Paris postmark. Rather with his heart than his eyes
the Provençal recognized the writing; the arms and the motto,
when he turned the missive over, confirmed the hope and put
an end to the cruelest emotion he had ever experienced.

To read this letter before the janitor were profanation; by
a delicacy of feeling which all lovers will understand, he did
himself the pleasure of deferring his happiness; he would not
even break the seal of that so precious missive until, safe behind his own closed door, he could revel to his heart's content in the ravishments it promised.

Flying up the stair, two steps at a time, the amorous Provençal had the childishness to turn the key in the door; then,
installed before his desk, he, with pious dexterity, broke the
seal; it seemed as if his heart would break his ribs.

"Dear monsieur," was written, "I disappear forever, for
my rôle is played out. I give you my thanks for having rendered it pleasant and easy. By embroiling you with the
Thuilliers and Collevilles, who are now fully informed as to
your sentiments about them, and having taken great care to
expatiate to extravagant lengths, in a manner most mortifying
to their bourgeois self-conceit, on the real cause of your sudden and ruthless rupture with them, I am most happy to say
that I have rendered a most signal service to you. The girl
does not love you, and you only love the beautiful eyes of her
*dot*. So I have saved the pair of you from a hell. In exchange for the one to whom you aspired, another is destined
for you; she is richer, more beautiful than Mlle. Colleville,
and, speaking for myself, in conclusion, much freer than

"Your very unworthy servant,
"*Wife* TORNA, COMTESSE DE GODOLLO.

"P. S. For further information, apply without delay to M. du Portail, gentleman, Rue Honoré-Chevalier, near the Rue Cassette, quarter of Saint-Sulpice, who is expecting you."

When he had finished this screed, the advocate of the poor put his head in his hands; he saw nothing, heard nothing, thought nothing; he was annihilated.

Several days were necessary to la Peyrade before he could recover the shock. The blow, in fact, was a terrible one; coming out of that golden dream in which he had seen a perspective of the future in such a radiant atmosphere, he found himself the victim of a hoax which wounded him most severely in his self-conceit and all his pretensions to cunning and cleverness; broken with the Thuilliers irrevocably; loaded with a debt of twenty-five thousand francs, of course not immediately due; and also engaged by his dignity to pay Brigitte another ten thousand francs; to complete all, he felt that he was not radically cured of his passionate feelings for the feminine author of this great disaster and the instrument of his ruin. We might go further and say that he never ceased to long for her. That desire to find her he dubbed curiosity, ardor for vengeance, and, as a consequence, he evolved the ingenious deductions:

"Cérizet spoke to me of a rich heiress; the countess in her letter intimates that the whole intrigue in which she entangled me was to lead to a wealthy marriage; rich marriages are not so plentifully thrown at a man's head that two such should come my way in a few weeks; therefore, the match offered me by Cérizet and that proposed by the countess must be the same crazy girl they are so strangely bent on making me marry; therefore, Cérizet, being in the plot, must know the countess; therefore, I shall get upon the Hungarian's track through him. In any case I shall get some information about this strange choice that has befallen me; evidently these people, whoever they may be, who can use such well-dressed puppets, must occupy positions of considerable importance. I'll go, therefore, and see Cérizet."

And he went to see Cérizet.

Since the dinner at the Rocher de Cancale, the two old cronies had not met. Once or twice, at the Thuilliers, la Peyrade had asked Dutocq, who now seldom went there on account of its distance, what had become of his copying-clerk.

"He never mentions you," was the answer.

It might well be supposed, therefore, that resentment reigned in the breast of the vindictive usurer, the *manet alta mente repostum*. Such a consideration as this could not detain la Peyrade. He was not about to ask for anything; he was using the pretext of renewing the affair about which Cérizet had spoken; Cérizet never had any part in things that were not of material interest to himself; the chances were then that he would be received with enthusiasm. He called upon him at the justice of the peace office; he did not pause in the waiting-room but pushed through to the office adjoining that of Dutocq. There he found Cérizet seated at a blackened wooden desk, at which another clerk, then absent, occupied the opposite place.

Seeing the entrance of the barrister, Cérizet cast a savage look at him, without moving or ceasing from his work of copying a judgment.

"Halloo!" said he, "you, Sieur la Peyrade. Well, you made a pretty mess for your friend Thuillier with your pamphlet!"

"How are you?" asked la Peyrade, in a tone at once resolute and amicable.

"I," replied Cérizet, "as you see, am still rowing my galley; and, to follow out the nautical metaphor, may I ask what wind has blown you here; perhaps it chances to be the wind of adversity?"

La Peyrade did not answer this, but took a chair which he

placed alongside his questioner, after which he gravely said:

"My dear, we must have a few words with each other."

"It appears," said the venomous Cérizet, "the Thuilliers have become furiously chilly since the pamphlet was seized."

"They are ungrateful people; I have broken with them," said la Peyrade.

"Rupture or dismissal," replied Cérizet, "their door is none the less closed against you; from what Dutocq tells me, Brigette doesn't spare you. You see, my friend, what comes of trying to run things alone; there is no one to help smooth off the angles. If you had got the lease for me, I should have been introduced to the Thuilliers; Dutocq would not have deserted you, and we should have steered you safely into port."

"And if I don't want to arrive into port?" replied la Peyrade. "I tell you I've done with the Thuilliers; it was I broke with them first; I told them to keep out of my sunshine; and if Dutocq told you anything different, you may tell him from me that he lies: is that straight enough? It seems to me that I speak plainly."

"Oh, just so, my dear, if you are so mad at all these *Thuillierieses*, why that was the reason you should have planted me among them, then you would have seen me revenge you and show 'em up."

"You have reason on your side," said la Peyrade; "I should have been glad to sicke you at their legs; but I had nothing to do with the matter of the lease."

"Doubtless," said Cérizet, "it was your conscience that caused you to tell Brigette that the twelve thousand francs were as good in her pocket as in mine."

"It seems that Dutocq," said the barrister, "still continues on his honorable course of spy, which he practiced in the Bureau of Finance. Like others who follow that dirty profession, he makes his reports more amusing than truthful."

20

"Be careful," said Cérizet, "you are speaking of my patron in his own lair."

"Some time ago you spoke to me of a girl whom I could marry—rich, matured, and suffering the least in the world with hysteria, as you euphemistically phrased it."

"So, there! I've been waiting for this," exclaimed the usurer; "but you've been full slow in getting here."

"In offering me this heiress, what had you in your mind?"

"*Parbleu!* to assist you in making a good strike; you only had to stoop to conquer. I was charged to make a formal proposal to you; and, as there wasn't any brokerage in it for me, I relied wholly on your generosity," said Cérizet.

"You are not the only one that made me that offer; a woman made the same, eh?"

"A woman?" replied Cérizet, in so natural a tone, certainly of surprise. "Not that I'm aware of."

"Yes, a foreigner, young and handsome, whom you must have met in the family of the future bride, and who seems to be entirely devoted to them."

"Never," said Cérizet, "has there been the trace of a woman in the negotiations; I have every reason to think that I alone had the charge of it."

"What," said la Peyrade, fixing Cérizet with his eye; "do you mean to tell me that you never heard of the Comtesse Torna de Godollo?"

"Never in all the days of my life; it's the first time I ever heard the name pronounced."

"Then it must have been another match," said la Peyrade; "this was a young person much richer than Mademoiselle Colleville."

"And matured? And hysterical?" asked Cérizet.

"No; the proposal was not embellished with those accessories; there is one other detail may give you the clue; Madame de Godollo desired me, if I wished more information, to see a Monsieur du Portail, gentleman."

"Rue Honoré-Chevalier?" said Cérizet, quickly.

"Exactly."

"Then it is the same marriage offered from two different sides; the only strange thing about it is that I should not have been informed of my collaborator."

At this moment the door of the office was cautiously opened; a woman's head was seen and a voice, immediately recognized by la Peyrade, said, addressing the clerk:

"Ah! your pardon; monsieur is busy. May I be allowed to say a word to you when you are alone?"

Cérizet, whose eye was as quick as his pen, noticed this: La Peyrade sat so that the visitor could not see him, but he no sooner heard the honeyed drawl than he hurriedly turned his head to hide his features. Instead, then, of dismissing her roughly, the usual treatment accorded intruders by this least pleasant of copying-clerks:

"Come in, come in, Madame Lambert," the modest visitor heard. "You would have to wait so long a time."

"Ah! Monsieur the Advocate of the Poor," cried his creditor. "How pleased I am to meet monsieur. I have been several times to your house to see if you had attended to my little matter."

"Truly," said la Peyrade, "for some time I have had many occupations that have kept me from my office; but all is in order and the petition, properly prepared, has been sent to the secretary."

"How good monsieur is," said the pious woman, clasping her hands.

"*Tiens!* you and Madame Lambert have business together!" said Cérizet; "you never told me that. Are you old Picot's counsel?"

"Unfortunately, no," said the devotee; "my master won't take advice from any one; he is such a stupid, willful man. But, my worthy sir, is it true that another family council is to meet?"

"Certainly," replied Cérizet, "and not later than to-morrow."

"But why is this, monsieur, when the judges of the court have decided that the family have no rights?"

"Well, yes," answered the copying-clerk, "the judge of the lower court, followed by that of the court of appeals, rejected the application of the relations, the same as their application for a commission in lunacy. But now they are taking it up from another point of view and wish to have a trustee for the estate appointed. It strikes me, my dear Madame Lambert, that old Picot will be leashed up. There are some very grave allegations advanced; to pinch a little is all right, but to grab the lot is a bit too much."

"Does monsieur believe?——" said the pious woman, raising her hands and lifting her shoulders.

"I! I believe nothing," said Cérizet; "I'm not the judge in the case. But the relatives say that you have made away with considerable sums of money, beside making investments into which they mean to inquire."

"My God!" said she, "they can look; I have not a bond, a share, or a note, not the least thing of value in my possession."

"Ah!" said Cérizet, with a sidelong glance at la Peyrade, "you have obliging friends who hold—— well, it has nothing to do with me; each must manage for himself; what was it that you particularly wished to see me about?"

"I wished for you to speak for us to the justice of the peace; the vicar of St. Jacques will give us a good recommendation. It is hard that the poor man," she added, weeping, "should be tormented so. They will be the death of him."

"Well, as I told you before, the judge is against you. It's my opinion that you make yourself out to be much poorer than you are; if my friend, la Peyrade, was not bound by the obligations of his profession——"

"I," interrupted la Peyrade, quickly, "I know nothing of madame's business. She called on me to draw up a memorial for her that has nothing in common with justice or finance."

"Ah! that's so," said Cérizet, "she came about the petition on the day when Dutocq met her—the day, you know, before the famous dinner at the Rocher de Cancale, when you played the Roman."

Then, as if he attached no significance to this reminiscence:

"Well, my worthy Madame Lambert," said he, "I'll get my patron to speak to the justice, but I give you warning that he is not on your side."

Mme. Lambert made her exit with numerous curtseys and protestations of gratitude.

"Well," said la Peyrade, when they were alone, "what about this du Portail?"

"Just this: he is a little old man as clear as amber," replied Cérizet, "and who, it seems to me, has the devil's own credit. Go and see him. It costs nothing, as they say."

As he finished speaking Dutocq came in, accompanied by his assistant clerk.

"Halloo!" said he, seeing la Peyrade and Cérizet together, "see the reconstituted trinity; but the object of the alliance, the *casus fœderis*, is gone down the stream. What have you done, my dear la Peyrade, to that good Brigitte? She hates you with a mortal hatred."

"And Thuillier?" asked the barrister.

It was the scene in Molière upside down; Tartuffe asking for news of Orgon.

"Thuillier in the beginning was not so hostile; but it appears that the business of the seizure is not so bad after all. As he needs you less he swims the more in the wake of his sister. If it is decided that there is no case against him, you will be only fit for hanging, in his opinion."

"I am well out of that mess," said la Peyrade, "and when

I get caught again in such another festival—— Farewell, my dears," he added.

When la Peyrade got into the courtyard, he was accosted by Mme. Lambert, who was awaiting him.

"Monsieur," said she, with unction, "I hope you do not doubt that I came by my money from my uncle in England; and that monsieur does not believe the horrible things Monsieur Cérizet said before you?"

"That's all very well," said la Peyrade, "but you must understand that, with all the yarns circulated by your master's relatives, there is little chance of your getting the prize for virtue."

"If it be the will of God that I should not obtain it——"

"You must see, too, how important it is to keep your secret to yourself as to the service I rendered you. On the first indiscretion the cash will be returned."

"Oh! monsieur may rest easy about that."

"Well, then, farewell, my dear," said la Peyrade, in a patronizing voice.

Brigitte had so strong an instinct of despotism that it was not only without regret but with secret joy that she saw the disappearance of Mme. de Godollo. That woman was in a crushing manner her superior; this added much to the good ordering of the house, but made her feel ill at ease. Brigitte felt when she had gone like those kings who for a long time had been dominated by capable ministers, and who rejoice when death steps in to remove the tyrant whose services and rival influences he has had to endure.

Thuillier felt much the same about it; but la Peyrade was a different thing, he felt the lack of his assistance. The councilor was called upon to draw up an official report. After having written such a pamphlet, it was impossible he should decline the task. But it was in vain that he shut himself up in his study, gorged himself with black coffee, mended his pens times without number, to write: "A Report to the Gentlemen, the Members of the Municipal Council of the City of Paris," time after time. Then, after starting off on another sheet: "Gentlemen," he would rush madly from the room, complaining of the terrible racket which had stopped his ideas, when some one had opened a closet door or moved a chair. This did not advance the business, nor even begin it.

But here Rabourdin came to the rescue. He wished some little alterations in his rooms. This Thuillier willingly allowed, and spoke to him of the difficulty of his task. Rabourdin, with his constant practice in official matters, gave an explanation, but when he had concluded he perceived plainly that Thuillier did not understand. He then informed him that he had an old report on a similar subject, and lent him the manuscript, from which he extracted more than enough for a capable, if inept, report. This report when read at the council was a great success, and Thuillier came home beaming with the compliments lavished upon him. Up to his death he spoke of "that report I had the honor of laying before the Municipal Council of the Seine." La Peyrade had sunk in his estimation—he could do without him.

A parliamentary crisis was impending; advantage was taken of this by the ministry to relax the stringent laws against the press and to extend clemency to political suspects, with the idea of disarming opposition. Thuillier was included in this hypocritical amnesty.

Then Dutocq's prophesy was realized. With this load taken off his back, Thuillier insolently swaggered over the dismissal of the case, and, with Brigitte chanting in chorus, spoke of la Peyrade as a sneak whom he had fed, who owed him considerable sums, and who had behaved with the worst ingratitude. Orgon was in full revolt, and, like Dorine, was ready to cry:

"A pauper who came without wearing shoes,
In old, draggled clothes that no beggar would choose."

Dutocq faithfully reported all this to Cérizet, but he had no opportunity of retailing them to la Peyrade, for they had not met since the interview in the justice's office. La Peyrade found it out himself. It happened in this wise:

Constantly pursued by thoughts of the handsome Hungarian and not waiting to know what Cérizet could learn, he scoured Paris in every direction. He might have been taken for the most indifferent of strollers. He was to be seen in the most crowded places; his heart ever telling him that sooner or later he would encounter the object of his ardent search.

One evening, it was about the middle of October, the fall, as often happens in Paris, was magnificent, and outdoors was as bustling as at midsummer. On the Boulevard des Italiens, once known as the Boulevard de Gaud, as he wandered past the long line of chairs in front of the Café de Paris, where, in the midst of some women of the Chausée d' Antin, accompanied by their husbands and children, may be seen in the evening an espalier of beautiful night flowers waiting only the gloved hand to pluck them, la Peyrade was struck to the heart; in the distance he fancied he saw his adored countess.

She was alone, in a splendid toilette which seemed rather out of place, taken in connection with her isolation; before her, mounted on a chair, trembled a white lap-dog which she caressed with her hands. After assuring himself that he was not mistaken la Peyrade was about to dart upon that so celestial vision, when he was forestalled by a *lion* of the most distinguished type; without throwing aside his cigar, without even putting his hand to his hat, this handsome young man entered into conversation with his ideal. When she saw the Provençal, pale and disposed to address her, the siren doubtless became alarmed, for she rose and took the arm of the man who was talking to her.

"Is your carriage here, Émile?" said she. "This is the

evening for the closing of the Mabile. I should like to go."

As thrown in the teeth of the unhappy barrister, the name of this disreputable place instead of causing a wound was a real charity, for it saved him from a silly action, that of addressing on the arm of her cavalier the unworthy creature of whom a few moments earlier he had thought of with a treasure of tenderness.

"She is not worthy an insult," he said to himself.

But as lovers are a people not easily driven to raise a siege when they have begun it, the Provençal was not as yet convinced that he had got to the bottom of the affair. Not far away sat another woman near the place whence the Hungarian had gone; but this one, ripe in years, feathers on her bonnet, showed beneath the folds of a colored shawl the sad relics of departed splendor. Her aspect was not imposing; it was the contrary. La Peyrade seated himself near and addressed her:

"Do you know, madame," he asked, without ceremony, "who the woman is that went away leaning on the arm of a gentleman?"

"Certainly, monsieur, I know all the *ladies* who come here."

"And her name is?"

"Madame Komorn."

"Is she as impregnable as the fortress by that name?"

"Is it that monsieur has an idea of making her acquaintance?"

"I don't know," said the Provençal, "but she is a woman who makes people think of her."

"And who is a very dangerous woman, monsieur," replied the matron, "a dreadful spendthrift, but one who makes little return in favors for what may be done for her. I am able to speak as to that; when she arrived here from Berlin, six months ago, she was warmly introduced to me."

"Ah!" exclaimed la Peyrade.

"Yes, at that time, in the neighborhood of the Ville d'Avray—a pretty little place with a park, covert, and fish-lakes—and being dull there and all alone, and had not the fortune necessary to lead the life of a castle, a number of gentlemen and ladies suggested that I should organize parties on the line of picnics. 'Madame Louchard,' says they——"

"Madame Louchard!" repeated la Peyrade. "Are you then any relation to Monsieur Louchard of the commercial police?"

"His wife, monsieur, but with a legal separation. He's a terror of a man who wants me to go back to him; but I, though willing to forgive most things, I can't stand a lack of respect. Why, one day he raised his hand to strike me——"

"In fact," said la Peyrade, interrupting her to call up the subject again, "you arranged these picnics and Madame de Godo—I mean Madame Komorn——?"

"Was one of the first in my home. She there picked up with an Italian, a fine man, rich, and a political refugee, but high and mighty. You can quite understand that it did not suit my purpose that intrigues should be carried on in my house; still the man was so much in love, and so unhappy because he couldn't get Madame Komorn to care for him, that it ended in my being interested in his love affairs. It brought lots of grist to madame's mill, for she managed to get heaps of money out of that Italian. Well, would you credit it? being just then in need of a little help, when I asked her to advance me a little cash, she absolutely refused and left my house, taking her lover along with her. He can't be very thankful for the connection though, poor man."

"Why, what came of him?" asked la Peyrade.

"Why it happened that this serpent knew every European language—she is smart to her finger ends, but more intriguing than smart—so being, as it seemed, employed by the police in some capacity, she turned over to the government a lot of correspondence which the Italian had inadvertently left laying around, so he was expelled France."

"And after the departure of the Italian, this Madame Komorn——?"

"Had a number of adventures and broke up some fine fortunes; I thought she had left Paris. For two months past she has not been seen. I believed she had totally disappeared, but the other day she turned up again more brilliant than ever. My advice to monsieur would be to leave her alone; but monsieur is a Southerner, he has the passion of the Southerners, perhaps what I have said may only serve to fire you up. However, she's a very fascinating creature—oh! very fascinating. Although we parted bad friends she came up to me and asked my address and said that she would call upon me sometime."

"Well, madame, I'll think about it," said la Peyrade, rising and making a bow to his informant.

It was a cold salutation, and his abrupt departure indicated that the man was not *serious* in his attentions.

The investment of the Thuilliers, prepared with such care by la Peyrade, at the price of such sacrifice of pride, was entirely useless. Flavie well avenged for the odious farce he had played with her, his position worse than when he was rescued by Cérizet and Dutocq, his heart filled with vengeful projects against the woman who had so easily beaten him out like a stupid sheep, the memory of what he had been subject to in his self-abasement—these were the thoughts and emotions of his sleepless night, except the few moments shaken by hideous dreams.

On the next day la Peyrade was a prey to fever, the symptoms became most alarming, the physician took every means to forfend brain fever; bleeding, cupping, ice on the head—this was the agreeable finale to his dream of love. But it must be said he arose cured, mentally as well as physically; he retained no other sentiment than cold contempt for the

Y

treacherous Hungarian, a sentiment that did not even rise to a desire for vengeance.

Once more on his feet he reckoned with his future; he asked himself whether he should attempt the reconquest of the Thuilliers, or whether he should fall back upon the crazy girl who had riches where the others had brains. Great commotions of the soul are like storms that purify the atmosphere; they induce good counsel and generous resolve. The bar was open to him; that was a broad path which was able to lead him to the acme of his ambition. Like Figaro, who showed more science and ability in order to live, than statesmen had shown in a thousand years in the government of Spain, he, in order to establish himself in the Thuillier household, to marry the daughter of a clarionet and a flirt, had expended more art, more wit, more dishonesty than would have made him successful in an honorable career.

"Enough," said he, "of such acquaintances as Dutocq and Cérizet; enough of the nauseating atmosphere breathed by the Minards, Phellions, Collevilles *et al.* Living in Paris," added he, "I'll shake off this provincial life, a thousand times more ridiculous and paltry than the provincialism of the country; that with all its narrowness has its individuality and customs, a *sui generis* dignity; they are frankly what they profess themselves, the antipodes of the Parisian; this other is only a parody."

With this determination la Peyrade called upon two or three attorneys who had offered to introduce him to the courts by giving him a few minor cases to plead. He accepted; he was no longer the advocate of the poor, but a recognized pleader.

He had become comparatively successful when one morning he received a letter from the president of the association of barristers asking him to call upon him, as he had somewhat of importance to speak of. At once la Peyrade thought of the Madeleine house transaction—this must have come to the knowledge of the Board of Discipline. It might be that du Portail had been told the whole story by Cérizet. It was plain that this man would stop at nothing, as witness his employment of the Hungarian. Was it that this virulent man whom he had never seen, seeing that he was becoming successful in his career, had determined to blight it by informing upon him? The barrister remained in cruel suspense for the hour when he might learn the truth. While he ruminated over his breakfast, Mme. Coffinet, who had the honor of being his housekeeper, entered to say that a Monsieur Étienne Lousteau wished to see him.

"Show him into my office," said he to the portress.

A moment later he met his visitor, whom he seemed to have a faint recollection of having seen before.

"Monsieur," said la Peyrade's guest, "I had the honor of once breakfasting with you at M. Véfour's; I was invited to that meeting, which was afterward somewhat troubled, by Monsieur Thuillier, your friend."

"Ah! very good," said the barrister, pushing a chair toward him, "you are attached to the staff of some newspaper?"

"Editor-in-chief of the 'Écho de la Bièvre;' it is on that matter I wish to speak to you. You know what has happened?"

"No," said la Peyrade.

"What, are you ignorant that the ministry met a frightful reverse yesterday. But instead of resigning they are going to throw themselves upon the country; so the Chamber is dissolved."

"I did not know that; I've not read the morning papers."

"All aspirants for a nomination as deputy are now in the field; I believe that Monsieur Thuillier intends to offer himself for the twelfth arrondissement."

"I believe such is his thought."

"Well, I am willing, monsieur, to place at his disposal an organ of which I think you will not fail to estimate the value,

The 'Écho de la Bièvre,' a trade paper, can have a decisive influence in that quarter on the election."

"And are you seriously disposed," asked the barrister, "to make that journal support Thuillier's candidature?"

"Better than that," replied Lousteau, "I am here to propose to Monsieur Thuillier that he purchase the organ; should he become the owner he could use it as he wished."

"But in the first place," answered la Peyrade, "what is the present condition of the enterprise? Being a trade journal, as you just called it, I have seen it but seldom; it would be unknown to me only for the remarkable article you were so kind as to devote to Thuillier's defense when the pamphlet was seized."

Lousteau bowed his thanks, and replied:

"The position of the paper is excellent; we can sell on easy terms, for we were about giving up its publication."

"That is strange with a journal that is prosperous," said the barrister.

"Nothing more natural, on the contrary," replied Lousteau; "the founders having gained the ends for which it was established, the 'Écho de la Bièvere' has thus become an effect without a cause."

"I should have thought, however," said la Peyrade, insistingly, "that a journal would be a lever that depended for its force on the number of its subscribers."

"Not for such as have a definite aim," replied Lousteau, dogmatically. "In such a case subscribers are an embarrassment, for you have to cater to and amuse them; and, during this time, the real object must be neglected. A paper which has but a circumscribed orbit should be like the stroke of that pendulum which, always striking steadily on one spot, fires at the right moment the cannon at the Palais-Royal."

"Well, what price do you put upon this publication, which may not even pay its expenses and is devoted to an utterly different purpose?"

"Before answering, I beg to ask you another question: Have you any intention of buying?"

"That depends upon circumstances," said the barrister; "I should naturally have to first present the matter to Thuillier, whom, I may remark, knows absolutely less than nothing of a newspaper and its workings. So that if you ask an alarming price I can inform you here and now that it would be useless for me to mention it to him; he certainly would not touch it."

"No," replied Lousteau, "I told you we should be reasonable; these gentlemen have given me a free hand; only I wish to remark that we have several propositions and I crave an early answer. The proposition is made to Monsieur Thuillier to pay him a particular courtesy. When may I hope for your reply?"

"To-morrow, most likely," answered la Peyrade, bowing out his visitor.

By the manner in which the Provençal had received the proposition to become the intermediary with Thuillier, the reader will see that a sudden change had taken place in his ideas. Evidently his "good friend" would have to come back to him; Thuillier's eager desire to be elected would hand him over tied hand and foot. Was not this the right moment to renew the affair of his marriage with Céleste? Moreover, if he received, as he dreaded, one of these censures which would ruin his future at the bar, it was the Thuilliers, the ones who profited by the cause of his fall, that his instinct claimed should afford him an asylum. Thinking thus, la Peyrade went to see the president of the barristers' association.

It was just as he had guessed; in a clear and very circumstantial report the matter of the buying of the house had been laid before the notice of his peers; the highest dignitary of the order admitted that an anonymous communication must always be regarded with distrust, but that he was ready to hear any explanations he might wish to make. La Peyrade dare not intrench himself in an absolute denial; the hand which had delivered the blow, as he thought, was far too determined and adroit to not hold the proof as well. But while admitting the facts in general, he gave them a pleasing color. He saw that he had not succeeded, when the president said:

"As soon as the next vacation is ended I shall send a report to the Council of our order of the charges made and the explanations you have given. The Council only can pronounce on a matter of such importance."

Thus dismissed, la Peyrade felt that his future at the bar was imperiled, but at least he had a respite. He put on his gown and went to the fifth court, where he had to plead a case. As he left the court, carrying a bundle of papers tied up with a strip of cotton webbing, and carried by the forearm being pressed against the chest, la Peyrade paced the Salle des Pas Perdues, with that worried look which distinguishes the overworked barrister; he perspired and mopped his brow as he walked, when, in the distance he saw Thuillier, who had just caught sight of him in that vast hall.

He was not surprised at meeting him. On leaving home he had informed Mme. Coffinet that he was going to the Palais and should be there until three o'clock, and she might send any person there who came to ask for him.

He had no wish to make his accosting by Thuillier a too easy matter, so he turned abruptly and took his way to one of the benches, as if he had changed his purpose, and there seated himself, taking a paper from the bundle and seemingly absorbed in its contents. During this time he watched Thuillier out of the corner of his eye; so Thuillier, thinking he was engaged on some serious matter, doubted whether to address him. After some backings and fillings the municipal councilor made up his mind and sailed straight before the wind, heading for the spot for which during the past fifteen minutes he had been steering.

"Halloo! Théodose," he exclaimed. "Then do you often come to the Palais now?"

"Well, to me it seems that barristers in the Palais are like Turks in Constantinople, where a friend of mine assures me that plenty are to be seen. It is I that should be astonished at seeing you here."

"Not at all," replied Thuillier, carelessly; "I'm here about that cursed pamphlet. Is there ever any end to your justice? I was summoned here this morning, but I don't regret it, as I have had the pleasure of meeting you."

"The same by myself," said la Peyrade. "I am enchanted to see you, but I must leave you. I have an appointment. You, too, have to go on the floor."

"I've been," said Thuillier.

"Your intimate enemy is in that court, Olivier Vinet. Did you speak to him?" asked la Peyrade.

"No, I didn't see him," and he named another judge.

"*Tiens!* that's queer," said the barrister. "He's held court there since morning; he has just given a decision in a case I pleaded."

Thuillier colored, and, making the best of his blunder:

"By the Virgin," said he, "I cannot tell one of you gentlemen of the robe from the other."

La Peyrade shrugged his shoulders, and said to himself aloud:

"Always the same man! Cunning, wriggling, never going straightforward."

"Of whom do you speak?" asked Thuillier, rather nonplussed.

"Why of you, my dear; do you take me for an idiot? As if I and everybody else did not know that your pamphlet affair tumbled overhead two weeks ago. Why then should you be summoned on the floor?"

"Well, it was something about fees—it's all Greek to me," said Thuillier.

"And they choose the precise day that the 'Moniteur' tells of the resignation of the ministry, that made you think of the twelfth arrondissement, eh?"

"And why not?" answered Thuillier, "what has paying my fees to do with my candidacy?"

"I'll tell you why," said la Peyrade, drily. "The court is essentially amiable and complaisant. '*Tiens*,' it said to itself, 'here is the good Thuillier a candidate for the lower Chamber; how hampered he is with the attitude his ex-friend la Peyrade has assumed; he wishes now that he hadn't quarreled with him; let us summons him for the fees he doesn't owe; that will bring him to the Palais where la Peyrade comes daily, thus he can meet him by chance, and avoid taking a step which would bruise his self-love.'"

"Well, that's just where you are wrong," replied Thuillier, breaking the ice; "I used so little cunning, as you call it, as to go to your house, and your porter told me you were here."

"Ah! that's better," said la Peyrade. "I can get along with folk who play straight. Have you come to talk about your election? I've already begun to work on it."

"Truly?" said Thuillier. "How?"

"Here," said la Peyrade, feeling under his robe for a pocket and bringing forth a paper, "read this; it's what I scribbled while the barrister on the other side was arguing."

The paper read thus:

ESTIMATE FOR A PAPER, QUARTO SIZE, AT THIRTY FRANCS A YEAR.

Calculating the edition at five thousand, the costs per month are:

|  | Francs. |
|---|---|
| Paper, five reams at 12 fr. | 1860 |
| Composition | 2400 |
| Printing | 450 |
| Editor | 250 |
| One clerk | 100 |
| Amount carried forward | 5060 |

|   | Francs. |
|---|---|
| Amount brought forward............... | 5060 |
| Managing editor, also cashier................. | 200 |
| Delivery clerk ............................ | 100 |
| Folders ............... ..................... | 120 |
| Office boy .................................. | 80 |
| Wrappers and office expenses................. | 150 |
| Rent ........................................ | 100 |
| License stamps and postage .................. | 7500 |
| Editing and reporting ....................... | 1800 |
| Total per month ........................... | 15,110 |
| "      "   annum ........................... | 181,320 |

"Do you want to start a paper?" asked Thuillier in dismay.

"I," said la Peyrade, "I want nothing at all; it is you that ask to be made a deputy."

"Undoubtedly; but consider, my dear fellow, one hundred and eighty-one thousand three hundred and twenty francs to plank down. Have I fortune large enough to meet the demand?"

"Yes," said la Peyrade, "seeing the end you have in view. In England they make far greater sacrifice to get a seat in Parliament, but some of the cost could be altogether cut off. You don't need a manager—you are an old accountant, I am an old journalist, we can well manage that—rent we needn't reckon; your old room, still vacant, in the Rue Saint-Dominique would make a fine office."

"But does a newspaper seem to you to be essential?"

"So much so that unless we have that power in our hands I won't have anything to do with the election. You do not live in the quarter any more, your election could be balked by one word—the one the English call *absenteeism*. This makes a hard game of it."

"I admit that," said Thuillier, "but the paper needs a name, and——"

"You don't suppose that I intend we should start a new

paper, not much. Here is one ready made, the 'Écho de la Bièvre,' a treasure for a man standing in the twelfth arrondissement. Only say the word and I place it in your hands."

"How?" asked Thuillier.

"*Parbleu!* by buying it; it can be had for a song."

"See there, now," said Thuillier, "you never counted in the cost of purchase."

"That's nothing," said la Peyrade, with a shrug of his shoulders; "there are other difficulties to solve."

"Other difficulties!" echoed Thuillier.

"Why, do you for one moment imagine," exclaimed la Peyrade, "that, after all that has taken place between us, I should boldly go in for your election without knowing exactly what I am to get for my services?"

"But," said Thuillier, somewhat astonished, "I thought friendship was a full exchange for services."

"Certainly; but when the exchange always consists in one side giving all and the other side nothing, friendship is inclined to grow stale. It asks for a rather more equitable settlement."

"But, my dear fellow, what then can I offer that you have not refused?"

"I refused because the offer was not frankly and heartily made, beside being seasoned with Mademoiselle Brigitte's special brand of vinegar; any self-respecting man would have played the same part that I did. You cannot give a thing and keep it is an axiom in law, but you persisted in trying so to do."

"I think you were unreasonable, but I have always treated you in good faith. What guarantees do you want?"

"I ask that it shall be Céleste's husband that manages your election, and not Théodose de la Peyrade."

"Well, hurry as we might," said Thuillier, "as Brigitte said, it would take fifteen days, and just think two weeks wasted out of the eight we have before us."

"The banns can be published the day after to-morrow, for the first time in the mayor's office; then, though the banns is not a step from which there is no retreat, it is at least a pledge before the public and a stride in the right direction; then your notary can draw the contract immediately. In addition, if you buy the paper, that will be another reason why you wouldn't go back on me, for the gun will be too heavy for you to handle for me to be afraid of your trying to fire it alone."

"Very good, my dear," said Thuillier. "Look properly after my interests. If the paper is all right, we'll buy it."

"Then I, on my part, will do everything for you as if it were for myself, which, by-the-by, is not altogether an hypothesis; I have even now received suggestions touching my own candidacy; if I were vindictive——"

"Certainly," said Thuillier, with humility, "you would make a better deputy than I. But you, it seems to me, are not of legal age."

"There is a much better reason than that—you are my friend; I find you again what you had been before. As for the election, I would rather hear: 'He makes deputies, but will not be made one.' Now I must leave you to keep my appointment; come to my office to-morrow and see me."

Who that has ever been a newspaper-man will ever be one: that horoscope is as sure as that of drunkards.

Whoever has tasted of that feverish occupation and relative idleness and independence; whoever has exercised that sovereignty which criticises intellect, art, genius, glory, virtue, absurdity, and even truth itself; whoever has ascended the tribune erected by his own hands, fulfilled for only one short hour the functions of that censorship to which he is self-appointed, that proxy of the public's opinion, looks upon himself when retired to private life as royalty did at Cherbourg—in lonely exile; the moment a chance offers he thrusts forth a hand eager to again clutch the crown.

For the reason that la Peyrade had once been a journalist, when Lousteau placed within his grasp the weapon known as the "Écho de la Bièvre," all his instincts as a newspaper-man were revived, notwithstanding the inferior quality of the blade. The paper had failed; la Peyrade was sure he could revivify it. The barrister threatened with being disbarred had at once a certain situation; he could hold it as a detached fort and compel his enemies to reckon with him. The Thuilliers would be bound to him by ties of self-interest, for their capital would be involved in the business; therefore, he need not fear their caprices or ingratitude. The cost of the purchase was absolutely low; a bank-bill for five hundred francs, for which Étienne Lousteau never satisfactorily accounted to the shareholders, put Thuillier in full ownership of the title, property, furniture, and good-will of the paper, which they at once proceeded to reorganize.

During the operation of this regeneration Cérizet one morning called upon du Portail, with whom more than ever la Peyrade was determined to hold no communication.

"Well," said the little old man, "what effect had the news we gave the president of the association on our man?"

"Phew!" said Cérizet, whose frequent intercourse with du Portail had made him more familiar; "there's no more any question of that now; the eel has slipped away again; neither gentleness nor violence has any effect on that devil of a man; he has quarreled with the association, but is thicker than ever with the Thuilliers. 'Necessity,' says Figaro, 'annihilates distance.' Thuillier needs him for his candidature in the St. James' quarter, so they kissed and made friends."

"Doubtless the marriage is arranged for an early date?" asked du Portail.

"Quite so," said Cérizet; "and then there's another machine to work; that crazy fellow has induced Thuillier to buy a newspaper; he'll let them in for forty thousand francs. When Thuillier once gets fairly involved he'll want to get his money back, so I expect to see them stick together for the rest of their lives."

"What paper is it?" asked du Portail, indifferently.

"A cabbage leaf called the 'Écho de la Bièvre,' a journal," said Cérizet, scornfully, "that an old journalist set up by the help of a lot of tanners in the Mouffetard quarter— the location of that trade."

"Well, for a local service it is not such a bad venture," said du Portail. "La Peyrade is talented, active, and has a bright intellect; he may make the 'Écho' resound. Under what banner does Messire Thuillier present himself?"

"Thuillier!" replied the banker of the poor; "he has no more opinion than an oyster. Until he published his pamphlet he was like all the rest of those bourgeois, a conservative; but since its seizure he has gone over to the Opposition. Self-interest for these people is the mainspring of their convictions."

"*Peste!*" said du Portail; "this combination of our barrister may rise to the importance of becoming a political danger from my view, which is conservative and governmental. I believe," said he, after a reflective pause, "that you worked on a newspaper once upon a time; you, 'Cérizet the Brave.'"

"Yes, and finely la Peyrade and I got paid for it," replied the usurer.

"Well," said du Portail, "why don't you go into journalism again?"

Cérizet regarded du Portail with dumb amazement.

"*Ah çà!*" said he at last. "Are you the devil, monsieur the gentleman, that nothing remains hidden from you?"

"Yes," said du Portail, "I know a few things. But what is arranged between you and la Peyrade?"

"Just this; he remembered my experience in the business, and, not knowing whom else to employ, offered me the management of the paper."

"I did not know that, but I thought it very likely," said du Portail. "Did you accept?"

"Conditionally. I asked time for reflection. I wished to know what you thought of the offer."

"*Parbleu!* I think that out of evil good may come, especially when it cannot be avoided. I had rather see you inside than outside that concern."

"Very good, but to get in there's this difficulty: La Peyrade is well aware that I have debts; he won't help me with the security for thirty-three thousand francs which must be posted in my name. I haven't got that amount, and if I had I should not care for it to be known and thus expose myself to my creditors."

"You have still a good part of that twenty-five thousand francs left that la Peyrade paid you not more than two months ago; is it not so?"

"Just two thousand two hundred francs and fifty centimes," replied Cérizet; "I cast it up last night. The remainder went to pay off pressing debts."

"But if you have paid your debts you can't have creditors."

"Yes, those I paid I don't owe; but those I didn't pay I still owe," said Cérizet.

"You don't mean to tell me that you owed more than twenty-five thousand francs?" said du Portail, incredulously.

"Would a man go into bankruptcy for less?" asked he, as though stating an axiom.

"I see I've got to stand the money myself," said du Portail, with some anger; "but the question is: whether your presence in the job is worth to me the interest represented by three hundred and thirty thousand three hundred and thirty-three francs and thirty-three centimes?"

"*Dame!*" said Cérizet; "if I were only installed there I would very soon have la Peyrade and Thuillier at loggerheads.

In the business of running a newspaper there are constant disagreements arising; now by taking the side of the ninny against the clever man you increase the conceit of the one and wound that of the other that it soon becomes impossible for them to work together. Beside, if, as you just now intimated, a shove now and again in the direction of political danger would assist——"

"'There's some truth in that," said du Portail; "la Peyrade's defeat is the aim."

"I've another gun to fire which would help to demolish him in the Thuilliers' estimation."

"Speak out then and let me know what it is," said du Portail, irritably; "you beat about the bush the same as if I were a man that could be finessed."

"You remember," said Cérizet, "that some time ago we wondered where la Peyrade obtained the twenty-five thousand francs with which he paid Dutocq off?"

"Ha!" said the gentleman, eagerly; "have you discovered the origin of that very improbable sum in the hands of the barrister?"

"Here it is," said Cérizet.

Then he related the whole details of Mme. Lambert's affair, but he acknowledged that all the sharp cross-questions of Dutocq and himself had failed to elicit a confession from her; but that both were convinced by her manner of the correctness of their suspicions.

Du Portail took the address of Mme. Lambert and told Cérizet to come and see him again on the morrow, adding:

"Accept la Peyrade's offer, but ask for a delay of twenty-four hours in which to obtain your security; if I find it to my interest I will furnish it—if not, you can get out of it by breaking your promise; you can't be sent to the court of assize for that."

Independently of an inexplicable kind of fascination that he exercised over his agent, du Portail never missed an occasion to remind him of the very shady commencement of their intercourse.

The next day, when Cérizet was again with the gentleman:

"You guessed rightly," said du Portail; "compelled to hide the existence of her booty, the woman, Lambert, who desired to draw some interest out of it, formed the idea of placing it in la Peyrade's hands; his devotional exterior may have suggested this to her; she most probably gave him the money without taking any receipt. In what kind of money was Dutocq paid?"

"In nineteen bills of one thousand francs each, and twelve of five hundred francs."

"That's it, exactly," said du Portail; "there is no longer room for doubt. Now how do you intend to use this information to bear upon Thuillier?"

"I shall tell him that la Peyrade borrows enormous secret loans; that he means to gnaw the profits of the newspaper to the bone; that the position of a man before the public must be compromised when it is known what manner of person his right hand is," said Cérizet.

"That's all right," said du Portail, "but Thuillier has not as yet learned who prompted that seizure of his pamphlet, has he?"

"Yes, he has," replied Cérizet; "la Peyrade was telling me yesterday, when he was explaining Thuillier's simplicity, that he gave him a silly humbugging, informing him that the seizure was instigated by Olivier Vinet's father, because that young man had once aspired to Mademoiselle Colleville's hand and been refused."

"Better and better," said du Portail; "well, to-morrow he shall receive a sharp note from Monsieur Vinet denying in full any such abuse of power—this will do as a basis for your other versions."

"Yes?" asked Cérizet, inquisitively.

"Another explanation must be given," continued du Portail; "you can assure Thuillier that he is the victim of the machinations of the police. You know that that is all the police are good for—machinations?"

"Perfectly," said the usurer; "I have sworn to that twenty times when I worked on a Republican newspaper and——"

"When you were the 'brave Cérizet,'" interrupted du Portail. "But for the present machination here it is: The government was much annoyed to see Thuillier elected to the Council without ministerial influence; it did not care to see an independent and patriotic citizen, who showed he could do without its aid; it further learned that this distinguished citizen was writing a pamphlet on finance, always a delicate subject, so what then did this corrupt government do, why it suborned a man in whom it was thought Thuillier had every confidence and for the sum of twenty-five thousand francs—a mere bagatelle to the police—this treacherous friend agreed to insert a few dangerous phrases which should expose it to seizure and cause the arrest of its author. Then clinch it by telling him that the very next day la Peyrade, whom Thuillier knows had not a sou, paid Dutocq that said amount of twenty-five thousand francs."

"The devil!" said Cérizet. "That's a good trick. All Thuillier's species believe anything that's said about the police."

"Well, he did you out of the lease and you are aiming at his happiness, so you need have no compunctions about what you do in this matter," said du Portail.

"It is a fact," said the wily usurer," that such an event will absolve me. Yes, I'll do as you wish; I follow the road you have pointed out. Still there's another thing: I cannot in my first appearance step up and make my revelation; that will need some time, but the security must be paid at once."

"Listen, Monsieur Cérizet," said du Portail; "if the

marriage of la Peyrade with my ward takes place it is my intention to reward your services with thirty thousand francs; now that amount on one side and twenty-five thousand on the other, you will get in all fifty-five thousand francs out of your friend la Peyrade's matrimonial combinations. Now if you risk your own money you will be eager to do the best for my cause; if on the contrary my money is at stake, you won't be nearly so ingenious in your dealings; if you are successful you will gain about a hundred per cent. That's my last word, I don't enter into any argument."

Cérizet had no time to make any, for at this moment the door of the office opened and a fair, slender woman, whose features showed angelic sweetness, came hastily into the room.

On her arm, wrapped in long, beautiful clothes, lay the form of an infant.

"There," said she, "that wicked Katt; she told me that you were not the doctor; I knew better; yes, I saw you come in. Well, doctor," she went on, addressing Cérizet, "I am not at all satisfied with the baby's condition; she is pale, she has grown so thin. I think it must be her teeth."

Du Portail made a sign to Cérizet to take up the rôle so suddenly thrust upon him, and which in some sense reminded him of the part he had assigned himself in connection with Mme. Cardinal.

"Evidently," replied he, "it is the teeth; children always grow pallid at such times; but there's nothing, madame, that need make you anxious."

"You really think so, doctor," answered the crazed girl—whom the reader, without a doubt, will guess to be Lydie, du Portail's ward—"but see her poor arms, look how thin they have become, they have dwindled to nothing."

Then taking out the pins that held the outer wrappings, she showed Cérizet a bundle of rags which, to her poor intellect, represented a sweet red and white baby.

"But no, no," said Cérizet; "she is a little thin, perhaps, but the flesh is clear and firm and color excellent."

"Poor darling!" said Lydie, kissing her dream lovingly. "What had I better give her, doctor? She won't take pap and soup disgusts her."

"Does she like sweet things?"

"Oh! immensely," said the crazy girl, brightening up, "she loves them; is chocolate good for her?"

"Certainly," said Cérizet, "but without vanilla; vanilla is heating."

"Then I'll get health chocolate," said Lydie, with all the intonations of a mother who listens to the assurances of the doctor as to the voice of a god. "Uncle," said she, addressing du Portail, "ring for Bruno and tell him to fetch some pounds from Marquis."

"Bruno has just gone out," he replied, "but there is no hurry; later in the day will do."

"See now," said Cérizet, "she has gone to sleep," for he was anxious, hardened as he was, to put an end to this painful scene.

"True," said Lydie, as she replaced the bandages; "I'll put her to bed. Farewell, doctor; if you doctors knew what good you can do a poor anxious mother, you would come more frequently. Oh! she is crying."

"She is so sleepy," said Cérizet; "she'll be much better in her cradle."

"Yes, and I'll play her that sonato that my dear papa used to like—the one from Beethoven; it is very charming. Farewell, doctor," and she threw him a kiss from the threshold of the door.

Cérizet was quite overcome.

"You see," said du Portail, "she is an angel, always the same, never the least ill-temper, nor a cross word; sometimes sad, but ever with a motherly solicitude. This it is that first gave the doctors an idea that if the reality replaced the hallucination, she might recover her reason. Well, this is the girl that ass of a la Peyrade refused, with the accompaniment of a handsome *dot*. But it has got to come to pass or I perjure my name. Listen!" he added, as the tones of a piano were heard; "hark! what talent! A mad woman! why there are a hundred thousand sane women who are not to be compared to her except on the surface."

When the sound of the playing ceased, Cérizet heard a woman's voice which was not that of Lydie.

"Is he in his office, the dear commander?" said a voice with a foreign accent.

"Yes, madame; but enter the salon, monsieur is not alone; I will inform him you are here."

And this last was the voice of Katt, the old Dutch housekeeper.

"Here—this way out," said du Portail to Cérizet with sharpness. And he opened a hidden door which led through a dark passage and on to the stairs.

The salutatory article by which new editors of every newspaper lay their "profession of faith" before the public is always a laborious and difficult case of child-birth. In this case it was necessary that Thuillier's candidature should be hinted at at least. The terms of this manifesto, after la Peyrade had drawn a rough draft of it, had resulted in a long discussion. This debate took place before Cérizet, who had accepted the management but postponed the payment of the security through the days of grace allowed in all changes of proprietorship, such as is allowed to the new officials.

The discussion was assisted by the facile master-knave who had constituted himself Thuillier's flatterer from the start; it more than once grew stormy, then bitter, but as the deed of partnership left all decision as to the editing to la Peyrade, he finally closed the matter by sending the manifesto to the printer exactly as he had first written it.

Thuillier was furious at what he called an abuse of power,

and on the following day, finding himself alone with Cérizet, he hastened to pour his woes and grievances into the bosom of his faithful manager; this gave a natural chance to insinuate the calumnious revelations already plotted with the man in the Rue Honoré-Chevalier.

This insinuation was presented with such art, with such skill and moderation, that it would have duped a much shrewder soul than Thuillier's. Cérizet appeared alarmed at having been entrapped into the betrayal of a secret, wrung from him by the ardor of his zeal and a sympathy which had been commanded by "the lofty mind and character which from the first had struck him about Monsieur Thuillier." The latter reassured the traitor that he should never be brought into the inquiry, which must of necessity follow such an alarming statement; he would say that other parties had informed him; if necessary he would throw suspicion upon Dutocq.

The scene had taken place at the newspaper office. Since he had concluded the purchase Thuillier came to the office two hours before it was necessary; he spent his day there and wore everybody out with his ardent activity. Now, being filled with this terrible revelation, he could not keep it to himself, he wished to unburden himself to some one. He sent for a hack and half an hour after had confided the whole story to his Egeria.

Brigitte from the first had vehemently opposed any further relations with la Peyrade, not even for the purpose of Thuillier's election would she make up with him. In the first place she had treated him badly, a good reason for disliking him; then she feared that if he married Céleste she would lose much of her authority, for her second-sight showed her some of the depths of his nature. So up to the present she had met her brother with fierce opposition in all matters relating to the newspaper:

"Ruin yourself, my dear," said she to Thuillier, "you are

your own master and can do as you like; what comes in by the flute goes out by the drum."

When, therefore, her brother related his confidences she did not reproach him, but gave a crow of triumph in honor of her own perceptions.

"So much the better," she exclaimed; "it is as well to know at last that he is a spy. I always thought so, a mean sneak. Throw him out of doors without any explanation. *We* don't need him, we can run the paper without him. That Monsieur Cérizet, who, from what you say, is after all a right good fellow, can easily find us somebody in his place."

"How fast you go," said Thuillier. "La Peyrade, my dear, has only been accused, he must be granted a hearing; beside a deed binds us."

"Oh! very well," said Brigitte, "I see the whole thing; you'll let that man twist you round his finger; a deed with a spy; as if deeds would stand with such fellows."

"Come, come, be calm, my dear Brigitte," replied Thuillier, "we must not act too hastily; if a justification, clear, categorical, and convincing, is not forthcoming, I shall break with him; I'll prove that I am not a plucked chicken. Cérizet himself is not certain; they are only his deductions; why I came to you was to see what you thought about demanding an explanation."

"Certainly, and if you don't get to the bottom of this affair I'll cast you off as my brother."

"That is sufficient," said Thuillier, solemnly; "you will find that we have one mind in such matters."

Thuillier found la Peyrade at his post as editor-in-chief; but during the last quarter of an hour he had found himself in a position of much embarrassment, caused by his high-handed assumption of being the sole selector of articles and contributors. Phellion pressed by his family, and as a consequence of being on the reading committee of the Odéon, had come to offer himself as dramatic critic.

"My dear, sir," said he, addressing la Peyrade, after having asked Thuillier as to his health, "I was a good student of the theatre in my youth; the play and its scenery have during my life had an especial attraction for me; the white hairs which now crown my brow do not seem any obstacle to me giving you some very profitable and interesting studies from my experience. As a member of the reading committee of the Odéon, I am also familiar with the modern drama; and, being sure of your discretion, I may confidentially inform you that among my papers it would not be impossible for me to find a certain tragedy entitled 'Sapor,' which in my younger days gave me some celebrity when read in drawing-rooms."

"Well," said la Peyrade, trying to gild the inevitable refusal, "why not try and have it placed on the stage? We might be able to assist you on that line."

"Certainly," said Thuillier, "the director of any theatre to whom we should introduce——"

"No," replied Phellion. "In the first place, as a member of the reading committee of the Odéon, having to sit in judgment on others, it would ill become me to enter the arena myself. I am an old athlete; my part is now to judge of the blows I can no longer deliver. In this sense criticism is within my sphere, the more so as I have some quite new ideas on the correct manner in which theatrical articles should be done. *Castigat ridendo mores*, by my humble lights, ought to be the great law, I might even say, the only law of the stage. Therefore I should show myself merciless in dealing with works of pure imagination in which morality plays no part, and which the ever-unerring discretion of the mothers of families——"

"Pardon me," said la Peyrade, "for interrupting you, but before allowing you to take the trouble to develop your poetical theories, I ought to inform you that our arrangements for the dramatic criticisms are already completed."

"Ah! that is different," said Phellion, "an honest man must keep his word."

"Yes," said Thuillier, "we have our dramatic critic, it was far beyond our hopes that you would offer your valuable collaboration."

"Well," said Phellion, grown somewhat cunning—for there is something in the newspaper atmosphere that flies to the head, especially a middle-class head—"as you think that my pen might be susceptible of giving you good service, a series of detached articles, perhaps, on divers subjects, which I should venture to entitle 'varieties,' might be of an interesting nature."

"Yes," said la Peyrade, with a maliciousness that was entirely lost upon Phellion, "thoughts, something in the style of Rochefoucauld or de la Bruyère, these might do—what say you, Thuillier?"

He intended leaving the matter of refusals, as far as possible, with the proprietor.

"But I should imagine," said Thuillier, "that detached thoughts would be rather wanting in connection."

"Obviously," replied Phellion, "when I say detached thoughts I imply the idea of a great range of subjects over which an author allows his pen to stray without presenting them as a whole."

"Of course you would sign every communication?" queried la Peyrade.

"Oh, no! messieurs," replied Phellion, dismayed. "I could not under any circumstances place myself on exhibition in that manner."

"Your modesty, which I fully comprehend and approve," said la Peyrade, "settles the matter. Thoughts are individuals, they require personifying by a name. Of this you yourself must be well aware. 'Sundry Thoughts, by M. Three-Stars,' means nothing to the public."

Seeing that Phellion was about returning to the charge,

Thuillier, who was in a hurry to get his hands in la Peyrade's hair, cut him off rather curtly:

"My dear Phellion," said he, "I ask your excuses for being compelled to say that I cannot longer be able to enjoy your conversation, but la Peyrade and myself have to consult on a matter of much importance; in a newspaper office—the time flies devilishly fast. If you wish, we will postpone the matter till a later day. Madame Phellion and Félix are well, I trust?"

"Perfectly," replied the great citizen, rising and not seeming to resent his dismissal. "When does the first number come out?" he added. "It is eagerly awaited in the arrondissement."

"To-morrow, I think," said Thuillier, conducting him to the door, "our profession of faith will make its appearance. You will have a copy sent you, my dear friend; come and see us again and bring that manuscript; la Peyrade's point of view is not absolute here."

This balm shed on the wound, and Phellion gone, Thuillier rang for the office boy.

"You would recognize that gentleman again who just went out?" said the own brother of Brigitte.

"Yes, m'sieu; anybody would remember that funny ball of a head; and, beside, it's M'sieu Phellion; I've opened the door for him hundreds of times."

"Well, whenever he comes here again, neither I nor Monsieur la Peyrade are ever in. Don't you forget the prescription; now leave us."

"The devil!" said la Peyrade, when they were alone, "how you manage bores. But lookout; sometimes electors may be among the number; you were right in promising Phellion a copy of the paper; he possesses influence in the quarter."

"Well, he's gone. Now be seated; I have something very serious to say to you," said Thuillier.

"Do you know, my dear fellow," answered la Peyrade, laughing, "that journalism is making you preternaturally solemn? 'Be seated, Cinna'—Cæsar Augustus would have said it no differently."

"Cinnas are, unfortunately, more numerous than people think," said Thuillier.

He still felt Brigitte's prod and he intended being cuttingly ironical; the top still rotated under the lashing it had received from the old maid's whip. The Provençal was seated and yet Thuillier did not commence; he went to the door, which stood ajar, intending to close it, but he first called to the office boy:

"Not in to anybody," he cried. "Now, my dear fellow," added he, addressing la Peyrade, "we can talk. My dear," said Thuillier, starting with sarcasm—for he had heard that this was a good way to nonplus an adversary—"I have learned something that will please you: I now know why the pamphlet was seized."

And he looked fixedly at la Peyrade.

"*Parbleu!*" said the latter in a natural tone of voice, "it was seized because they wanted to seize it. They sought and found, as you may always expect them to find the things they desire, known by the King's adherents as 'subversive doctrines.'"

"No, you are wrong," replied Thuillier; "the seizure was arranged for, concocted, and planned beforehand."

"Between whom?" asked la Peyrade.

"Between those who desired the death of the pamphlet and the miscreants who pledged themselves to betray it," said Thuillier.

"In any case those who bought," said la Peyrade, "got but a poor bargain; for, persecuted though it was, I don't see that it made much noise."

"But what about the vendors?" said the more than ever ironical Thuillier.

"Those who sold were the smartest, undoubtedly," said la Peyrade.

"Oh! I know you have a great esteem for smartness; but permit me to inform you that the police, whose hand is apparent in all this, is not apt to throw its money away."

And he stared anew at la Peyrade.

"So," replied the barrister, without blinking, "you have discovered that the police plotted in advance to smother your pamphlet?"

"Yes, my dear friend, and I know for a fact to whom the money was paid and the precise amount that honorable person received."

"The person," said la Peyrade; "I might guess the person, but as to the amount that is beyond me."

"Well, I can tell you that: twenty-five thousand francs," said Thuillier, emphasizing each word; "that was the sum paid to Judas."

"Allow me, my dear, twenty-five thousand francs is a lot of money. I won't deny that you are a most important man; nevertheless, you are not such a bugbear to the government as to cause them to make such a sacrifice. Twenty-five thousand francs is as much as they would give for the suppression of some celebrated pamphlet against the administration of the civil list; but our lucubration on finance was not bad like that, and such a sum taken from the secret service fund merely to plague you seems to me fabulously great."

"Apparently," replied Thuillier, with bitterness, "the honest intermediary may have exaggerated my value; one thing is certain, this monsieur had a debt of twenty-five thousand francs which was a great worry to him; and a short time before the seizure this same monsieur all at once found means to pay; unless you can tell me whence he obtained that money, I don't believe it is very hard to draw the inference."

In his turn la Peyrade gazed fixedly at Thuillier.

"Monsieur Thuillier," said he, raising his voice, "let us get out of generalities and enigmas; this person—will you do me the favor to name him?"

"Well, no," said Thuillier, striking the table; "I shall not name him because of the sentiments of affection which at one time united us; but you have understood me, Monsieur de la Peyrade."

"It is a fact, I should have understood," said the Provençal, in a voice broken with emotion, "that in introducing a serpent here it would not be long before I should be soiled by its venom. Poor fool, you! don't you see that this is one of Cérizet's calumnies, of which you have made yourself the echo."

"Cérizet has nothing whatever to do with it; on the contrary, he has nothing but good to say of you; how was it that you, not having a sou the night before (and I have cause to know this), that you were able to pay Dutocq the round sum of twenty-five thousand francs the next day, paid in bills of a known denomination?"

La Peyrade reflected a moment.

"No," said he, "Dutocq did not tell you; he is not the man who dare tackle me unless it would be of great benefit to him. The infamous calumniator is Cérizet, from whose hands I wrung your house on the Madeleine—Cérizet whom, in my kindness, I sought on his own dunghill to place him in an honorable position; that is the wretch to whom a benefit is only an encouragement to further treachery. *Tiens!* if I should tell you what manner of man that is, I should fill your heart with loathing; in the sphere of infamy he has discovered new worlds——"

Thuillier this time made an apt reply.

"I know nothing about Cérizet except through you," said he; "you it was who offered him the management, giving every assurance that he was reliable; but, by making him blacker than the devil, and even allowing that this communication comes from him, I don't see, my boy, that it makes you any the whiter."

"I was, without doubt, to blame in bringing him, but he understands the newspaper business; I thought he had reformed, that he was a man of straw, but I find him as he ever was, a man of mud."

"That's all well and good," said Thuillier, "but the twenty-five thousand francs which came so opportunely into your hands, whence came they? That is what you fail to explain."

"But use a bit of commonsense," replied la Peyrade; "a man in my position in the pay of the police, and yet so poor that I could not throw in the face of that harpy, your sister, the ten thousand francs she so insolently demanded of me."

"To end it all," said Thuillier, "if the origin of the money is honest, as I am most anxious to believe, what prevents you telling me who gave it to you?"

"That I cannot do," replied the barrister, "the source of that cash is a professional secret."

"See now, you told me yourself that the rules of your order prevented your entering into business of any description."

"It would be strange, if I had done something not quite in the regular course, that you should reproach me after doing what I did for you in the matter of the house."

"My poor friend, you are trying to put the hounds off the scent, but you can't put me off the track; I am the master of my confidence and esteem, and, if I pay you the amount stipulated in the deed, I take the paper into my own hands."

"So you mean to turn me out!" exclaimed la Peyrade. "The money you have put into this business, your chances of election, all sacrificed on one calumny brought by a Cérizet."

"In the first place," answered Thuillier, "a new editor-in-chief can soon be found to replace you, my dear; they said long ago that no man is indispensable. As to the election, I would sooner not win it than owe it to the help of one who——"

"Go ahead!" said la Peyrade, seeing that Thuillier hesitated, "or, no, rather be silent, for in less than an hour you will blush at your suspicions and ask my pardon on your knees."

The Provençal saw that without a confession he would have the newly recovered future cut from beneath his feet. He resumed his speech with great gravity.

"You will remember, my friend," said he, "that you were absolutely without pity, and that by subjecting me to a kind of moral torture you compelled me to reveal a secret which is not my own."

"Go on, all the same," replied Thuillier, "I'll take the whole responsibility; make me see the light in all this darkness, and I will be the first to recognize that I was wrong."

"Well," said la Peyrade, "those twenty-five thousand francs are the savings of a domestic who came with them to me asking me to pay her interest on them."

"A domestic who has saved twenty-five thousand francs! Strike me! it seems to me she must have lived in a bully house."

"On the contrary, she is the housekeeper of an old, infirm savant; it was for this reason of the discrepancy that you suggest that she wished to put the cash in my hands as a kind of fiduciary agent."

"By my faith, my friend," said Thuillier, in a flippant voice, "you said we needed a romancist, but with your talent we can rest quite easy. Here's imagination!"

"How's that?" said la Peyrade, angrily; "you don't believe me?"

"No, I don't believe you; twenty-five thousand francs of savings made in the service of an old professor; why, that's about as credible as that captain of the White Lady buying a castle out of his pay."

"But if I prove the truth of my explanation—if I let you put your finger in the wound?"

"In that case, like Saint-Thomas, I shall lower my flag before the evidence; but you must permit me to wait until you give that proof."

Thuillier thought himself superb.

"I would have given two louis," said he to himself, "if Brigitte were only here to see how I did it."

"Come then," said la Peyrade, "suppose that without going outside this office, and by means of a note which shall pass before your eyes, I bring before you the person from whom I received the money; if she confirms my statement, shall you believe then?"

This proposition and the assurance with which it was made staggered Thuillier.

"Then, of course," replied he, changing his tune. "But this must be done before the seance is over, eh?"

"Without going out from here, I said; it seems to me that is clear enough."

"And who will carry your note when you have written it?" asked Thuillier. He thought he displayed much acumen by looking after each detail.

"Who will carry it?" said la Peyrade. "*Parbleu!* your office boy; you can send him yourself."

"Write it then," said Thuillier, determined to push him to the wall.

La Peyrade took a sheet of paper with the letter-head and wrote, reading aloud, as follows:

<blockquote>
Mme. Lambert is requested to come immediately on urgent business to the office of the "Écho de la Bièvre," Rue Saint-Dominique-d'Enfer, whither the bearer will conduct her. She is impatiently awaited by her devoted servant,

Théodose de la Peyrade.
</blockquote>

"Well, will that suit?" said the barrister, passing it to Thuillier.

"Perfectly," said he, at the same time taking the precaution to fold the paper and to seal it himself. "Now add the address," he added.

Thuillier rang for Coffinet.

"You will go," said he, "to that address with this note, and the person will return with you."

When they were alone, la Peyrade took up a paper and appeared to be absorbed in its contents.

Thuillier by this time was somewhat uneasy.

"I ought not to have carried the matter so far," said he to himself; "I should have torn up the note." Then trying to show that he reinstated la Peyrade in the position from which he had threatened to dismiss him:

"Oh," said he, "I have just come from the printer; the new type has arrived; we can, I guess, make our appearance to-morrow."

La Peyrade made no reply, but got up and read his paper nearer the window.

"He is vexed," said Thuillier to himself; "well, if he is innocent, he is like to be; but why, after all, should he have brought such a man as Cérizet here?"

La Peyrade returned to the table, took up some paper and with feverish rapidity wrote like a man who is violently agitated, making the pen fairly fly across the paper.

Thuillier from the corner of his eye tried hard to see what la Peyrade was writing; he noticed it was arranged in numbered paragraphs:

"Halloo!" said he, "are you drafting a new law?"

"Yes," answered la Peyrade coldly, "the law of the vanquished."

Soon after the boy opened the door and introduced Mme. Lambert, who arrived looking rather afraid and minus much of her unctuous suavity.

"You are Madame Lambert?" asked Thuillier, in the tone of a magistrate.

"Yes, monsieur," replied the pious woman, in an anxious voice.

Requesting her to be seated and noticing that the office boy remained as if expecting further orders:

"That will do," said Thuillier, "go; and admit no one."

The gravity and lordly tone of Thuillier deeply impressed Mme. Lambert; moreover, the scene took place in a newspaper office, and we all know that, particularly in the eyes of the pious, everything that has to do with the press savors of the infernal and diabolical.

"Well, my dear fellow," said Thuillier to the barrister, "it seems to me that nothing hinders your explaining to madame why you have sent for her."

"We wish to ask you, madame," said la Peyrade *ex abrupto*, "if it is not true that about two and a half months ago you placed in my hands, subject to interest, the sum of twenty-five thousand francs?"

Madame Lambert could not restrain a start, though she felt the eyes of both were fixed upon her.

"Our Lord above!" she exclaimed, "and where should I get such a sum as that?"

La Peyrade showed no sign of the uneasiness he might have been supposed to experience.

As for Jérôme Thuillier, who now glanced at him with commiseration:

"You see, my dear fellow——" said he.

"So," went on the Provençal, "you are quite certain, madame, that you did not place in my hands the sum of twenty-five thousand francs; you declare it? You would swear to this?"

"Why, monsieur, is it at all likely that twenty-five thousand francs would knock at the door of such a poor woman as myself? Even the little I had has gone to help the housekeeping of that poor, dear gentleman whose servant I have been for twenty years."

"This," said the pompous Thuillier, "seems unanswerable."

La Peyrade showed no sign of annoyance; on the contrary, he seemed to have an air of playing into the hand of Thuillier:

"You hear, my dear," said he to him, "and if necessary I shall call upon you to so testify, that madame here never had twenty-five thousand francs; consequently she could not have given that amount to me; and as the notary Dupuis, with whom I fancied I had placed them, left Paris this morning for Brussels, carrying with him all his clients' money, I have a clear account with madame, and the flight of the notary Dupuis——"

"The notary Dupuis has absconded!" cried Mme. Lambert, carried away by this dreadful news out of her usual dulcet tones and Christian resignation; "the wretch, the villain, when only this morning he took the communion at St. Jacques du Haut-Pas."

"That was doubtless to pray for a safe journey," replied la Peyrade.

"Monsieur can talk lightly enough about it," continued Mme. Lambert, "but that brigand has carried off all my savings; but I gave them to monsieur, and monsieur, of course, is responsible for them; he is the only one I know in the matter."

"*Hein!*" said la Peyrade to Thuillier, pointing to Mme. Lambert, whose demeanor had something of a she-wolf who has had her whelps ravished from her; "is that nature? tell me, have we gotten up this comedy?"

"I am speechless," replied Thuillier, "at the audacity of that Cérizet; struck dumb by my own stupidity, I can but surrender at discretion."

"Madame," said la Peyrade gayly, "will please excuse me for alarming her, it was an absolute necessity. The notary Dupuis remains a pious gentleman, and incapable of injuring his clients. Your secret is as safe with him as me, so far as this gentleman is concerned."

"Very good, monsieur," said Mme. Lambert, "then you have nothing more to say to me?"

"No, my dear madame, except to beg your pardon for the slight fright we caused you."

But as Mme. Lambert went out she intimated that she would need the money very soon as she had "heard of a little property she meant to purchase." She was reassured by la Peyrade, who explained that she could get it any time by giving notice, and she then bade him adieu.

"You see, my dear," said Théodose, when he and Thuillier were alone, "into what a scrape your sick imagination has brought me. The debt was dormant, you have awakened it. Now she will press for it."

"I am desolate, my dear friend, for my silly credulity; but don't be uneasy about that matter, we can arrange all that, even if I have to go your security or make an advance on the wedding *dot*."

"For the rest, my excellent friend," said la Peyrade, "we will begin by taking stock of our mutual relationship; I have no appetite for being haled up every morning and interrogated as to my conduct; just now while we awaited that woman I drew up a little memorandum which we will talk over and sign, by your leave, before we issue the first number."

"But our deed of partnership," said Thuillier, "seems to me a chart——"

"That by a paltry forfeit of five thousand francs, as by clause 14," interrupted Théodose, "you can, when you wish, put me in the soup. Thanks! we will have something rather more definite."

At this moment entered Cérizet bubbling over with vainglory.

"My masters," said he, "I have brought the capital and in an hour the security can be perfected."

But seeing that the news was received with marked frigidity:
"Well," said he, "what's up now?"

"It is this," said Thuillier, "that I refuse to associate with double-faced men and calumniators; we have use for neither you nor your money, and I beg you to no longer honor these premises with your company."

"Dear, oh me!" said Cérizet, "so Daddy Thuillier has allowed himself to be caught again."

"Go away," said Thuillier, "we have no use for you."

"My boy," said Cérizet to la Peyrade, "it seems that you've twisted the good bourgeois round your finger again. Well, he's not the inventor of the printing press; and as for you, we have seen the kind of work you can turn out. Well, it doesn't matter, but all the same you were wrong in not calling upon du Portail, I shall tell him——"

"Will you go away, monsieur?" cried Thuillier, threateningly.

"After all, my dear sir," continued the usurer, "it was not I that looked you up. I was doing well enough before you sent for me, and I shall do quite as well after. Only you try and avoid paying that twenty-five thousand francs out of your own pocket, for that's hanging to your nose—I know all about it."

As he said this Cérizet replaced his pocket-book containing the cash in his breast-pocket, and, after smoothing his hat on his coat sleeve, went out.

Thuillier had been led by listening to Cérizet into a most disastrous campaign. Become the humble servant of de la Peyrade, he was compelled to bow to his conditions: five hundred francs a month for the barrister's services on the paper; his editorship of the journal to be paid for at the rate of fifty francs per column—an enormous sum, taking into account the small size of the sheet; a pledge to issue the paper for at least six months, this under a forfeit of fifteen thousand francs; the most absolute omnipotence as editor-in-chief, being free to insert, alter, or reject any article without being compelled to explain his reasons therefor; these were the stipulations signed in duplicate by both parties in "good faith."

But, in virtue of another private agreement, Thuillier gave security for the payment of the sum of twenty-five thousand francs for which la Peyrade was accountable to the pious one, "the said Maître la Peyrade," binding himself, in case the repayment was required before his marriage with Mlle. Colleville could take place, to acknowledge the said sum as being an advance on account of the *dot*. In this ingenious manner, the crafty Provençal got around the law which provides against such forestalling of the consideration mentioned in the marriage-contract.

Matters being thus arranged and everything being accepted by the candidate who, if he lost la Peyrade, could see no chance of his election, Thuillier had a happy thought. He went to the Cirque-Olympique, where he remembered in the box-office a former employé of his in his bureau—a man named Fleury, to whom he proposed the post as manager. An old soldier, a good shot and capital swordsman, Fleury would be properly respected in a newspaper office. Not less clever in the art of "leading his creditors a dance," he was the first clerk in the Bureau of Finance to hit on the ingenious idea of inventing spurious suits against his salary, thus preventing the collection of any legal attachments that might be taken. He took the same proceedings to preserve from his creditors the three thousand three hundred and thirty-three francs thirty-three centimes, which were required by the law to be deposited in his name. The working staff being thus constituted, the first number was launched.

Thuillier now recommenced his explorations about Paris as we previously saw on the publication of his pamphlet. Walking into a reading-room or café, he asked for the "Écho de la Bièvre," and when, as was unfortunately too often the case, he was told they did not know of such a paper:

"This is incredible!" he would exclaim, "that a place with any pretensions to respect does not take such a popular paper."

Then he would depart in disdain, without seeing that in many places where this drummer's dodge was quite understood they were laughing under his nose.

The evening of the day of the salutatory article, Brigitte, although it was not Sunday, had her salon thronged. Reconciled with la Peyrade, the old maid went so far as to say that his leading editorial was a "hit." The remainder of the company said the public was enchanted with the first number. The public! everybody knows what that is; the man who has launched a few lines in print upon a trusting world has his public in five or six intimates, who, from a desire to avoid a quarrel with the author, make some favorable comment upon his lucubrations.

"As for myself," said Colleville, "I can say that it is the first political editorial that did not send me to sleep."

"It is certain," said Phellion, "that the editorial appears to me to be stamped with vigor combined with an attic style which we may search in vain for in the columns of the ordinary public prints."

The next day Thuillier was early at the office, to be the first to meet the formidable fire of the ministerial press. After looking through every paper he found that not one of them had even mentioned the "Écho de la Bièvre," no more than if it did not exist. When la Peyrade arrived he found his unhappy friend in despair.

"That is nothing to be surprised at," said la Peyrade, tranquilly. "I let you enjoy yourself yesterday in the hope of a hot encounter with the press; but I well knew that it was most unlikely that any mention of us would appear in the morning papers. Is not every paper, brought out with any brilliancy, bound to be met with a conspiracy of silence?"

"A conspiracy of silence!" echoed Thuillier, admiringly.

He did not understand what this meant, but the words had a grand sound and appealed to the imagination. Then la Peyrade explained that by agreement no new journal was mentioned by the others lest it might serve to advertise the bantling. The explanation was not so good as the phrase. The middle-class is ever thus; words are coins which pass without question. For a word he becomes exalted or abased, will insult or applaud. With a word he can be brought to make a revolution and overthrow the government he has chosen.

But the journal was a means to an end. In a few days a letter from several electors appeared thanking the "Écho" for its firm stand and their delegate in the Council for looking after the welfare of his district. "This attitude," said the letter, "had brought down upon him the persecution of the government, which, towed in the wake of foreign powers, had sacrificed Poland and sold itself to England. The arrondissement needed such a man to represent it in the Chamber" —and so on.

This trial balloon had the happiest effect; the ten or twelve names thus pressed to the front were those who (supposedly) represented the will of the electors and were called " the voice of the quarter." Thus from the start Thuillier's candidature had made such a sprint on the way that Minard hesitated about putting his own claims in rivalry.

Brigitte was delighted with the course of events; she now urged that it was high time the marriage was arranged. A thorough explanation took place between the Provençal and the old maid. She told him of her apprehensions as to his taking the lead in the household, and further said that unless they could agree it were better that he should have his own home, adding: "We should not be the less friends for that."

La Peyrade replied by telling her that nothing was further from his thoughts, nothing in the world could induce him to consent to such an arrangement; he should feel the greatest security if only Brigitte would continue to exercise equally good management when he became one of the family, as she had done in the past. In short, he so completely reassured her that she urged upon him that immediate steps be taken for the publication of the banns and the signing of the marriage-contract. She, herself, was to mention the subject to Céleste.

"My dear child," said she one morning, "I think you have given up all thoughts of becoming Félix Phellion's wife. In the first place, he is more an atheist than ever, and, on the the other, you must have noticed yourself that his mind is unhinged. At Madame Minard's you have seen that Madame Marmus, who married a professor, an officer of the Legion of Honor and a member of the Institute. There could be no more unhappy woman; her husband has taken her to live at the rear of the Luxembourg, near the Rue Notre-Dame des Champs, in the Rue Duguay-Trouin, a small street that is neither paved nor lighted. When he goes out he does not know which way he is walking; he finds himself in the Champ de Mars when he meant going to the faubourg Poissonnière; he is incapable of even giving his address to a hack-driver; and he is so absent-minded that he doesn't know whether or not he has had his dinner. You can imagine what kind of a time a wife must have with a man who has always got his nose in a glass and snuffing at stars."

"But Félix," said Céleste, "is not as absent-minded as all that."

"Of course not; he's much younger; but by the time he gets that age both his absence of mind and his atheism will increase; we are all of one accord that he is not a suitable husband for you: your mother, your father, Thuillier, and myself—everybody that has any commonsense—we have decided, therefore, that you shall take la Peyrade, who will put your godfather in the Chamber, and will make his own way beside. We shall give you a much larger *dot* than we intended giving any other husband. So it must be considered as settled. The banns will be published and a week from to-day the contract will be signed. We shall give a big dinner and your trousseau and *corbeille* will be shown. Now don't be a baby, but accept it nicely."

"But, Aunt Brigitte," began Céleste, timidly.

"There's no 'but' about it, nor 'ifs' either," replied the old maid, imperiously. "It's all laid out and will be carried through unless, mademoiselle, you think you know more than your relatives."

"I will do as you wish, my aunt," answered Céleste, who felt as though a cloud had burst above her head; she knew only too well that she had not the strength to struggle against the iron will that had just pronounced her doom. She went and sought her godmother, but Mme. Thuillier advised resignation and patience; the poor child saw there was not even a passive resistance to be looked for in that quarter; her sacrifice was virtually accomplished.

The dinner was ordered from Chabot and Potel, not from Chevet; for by doing thus Brigitte set her initiative and proved her emancipation from Mme. de Godollo. When the time came to take their places at table three guests were missing— two Minards, father and son, and the notary Dupuis. The latter had written saying that it was impossible to be at the dinner, but that he would arrive with the contract at nine o'clock. Julian Minard, said his mother, was suffering with a sore-throat; Minard senior's absence was unexplained by Mme. Minard, but she begged them not to wait for him as he would assuredly come later. Brigitte on this ordered the soup to be kept hot for him, for among the middle-class code of manners a dinner without soup is not a dinner at all.

The meal was anything but cheerful, the fare was better, but the life and animation which had graced the famous nomination banquet was sadly missing. The absence of three of the guests may have been one cause; then Flavie was very glum, she had had an interview with la Peyrade at her own house which had ended in tears; Céleste, even had she been happy in her choice, could not well, as a matter of propriety, have shown too much joy on her countenance; she made no attempt to brighten a sorrowful face, and dared not look at her godmother, whose appearance looked, so to speak, like one long bleat. The poor girl, seeing this, feared to exchange a look with her, lest she might bring tears to her eyes. Thuillier had now become of such importance that he was stiff and pompous; while Brigitte seemed uneasy, awkward, and constrained.

Colleville tried a few of his facetious remarks to raise the temperature of the assembly, but the coarse flavor of his artist-jests, in the atmosphere in which they were produced, had an effect like a loud laugh in a sick chamber; a mute hint from Thuillier, la Peyrade, and his wife that he should behave himself effectually squelched his turbulence.

Singularly the person who succeeded, aided by Rabourdin, in warming the air was the gravest person of the party. The Abbé Gondrin, a man of cultivated and refined mind. He was the former vicar of St. Jacques de Haut-Pas, whose learning and gift of preaching had been the cause of the archbishop removing him from that poor quarter to that of the Madeleine. Since Mme. Thuillier and Céleste had again become his parishioners, the young abbé paid them occasional visits. Thuillier had explained to him the merits of the choice of la Peyrade and had culumniated the religious views of Félix Phellion, and had easily got him to contribute by his persuasive words to the resignation of the victim. He had just succeeded in getting off the frost when Minard came in.

After excusing himself on the ground of his official duties, he exchanged a significant look with his wife, which seemed to give an appearance that he had been detained by some private matter. La Peyrade and Thuillier caught this wink;

they had received an order for a box for the celebrated fairy burlesque of "Love's Telegraph," in which Olympe Cardinal was to make her début, and they were not altogether convinced of Julian Minard's indisposition; they therefore also exchanged significant glances, and wondered if the young gentleman's pot of roses had been discovered and whether the task of the elder one had not been that of learning the truth.

Being accustomed to pick up the thread of conversation wherever he found it, he tried to hide under a perfect freedom of spirit his parental anxieties:

"Gentlemen," said Minard, as soon as he had swallowed a few mouthfuls, "have you heard the great news?"

"What is that?" asked several voices at once.

"The Academy of Sciences has received to-day the particulars of an extraordinary discovery; the heavens have another star."

"*Tiens!*" said Colleville; "well, that will do to replace that one which Beranger thought had gone from its place, when, to the tune of 'Octavia,' he grieved over Chateaubriand's departure: 'Chateaubriand, why fly your land?'"

This quotation, which he sang, exasperated Flavie, and, if it had been the custom for wives to sit next their husbands at table, the old first clarionet of the Opera-Comique would not have got off with a mere "Colleville," which called him to order from the distance.

"What will give this meeting which I have the honor of addressing," said Minard, "a special interest in the great astronomical event is that the author lives in the twelfth arrondissement, which a number of you still inhabit or did inhabit for a long period of time. Indeed, everything connected with this great scientific fact is most remarkable. The Academy, on reading the communication which announced it, was so convinced of its existence, that a deputation was appointed to visit the domicile of this modern Galileo and compliment him on behalf of the whole body; and yet this star is not visible either to the eye even through the telescope; it is by the force of reasoning and calculation that its existence and the place it occupies are proved beyond all doubt. 'There must be an unknown star in that spot. I cannot see it, but I am sure of it.' That is what this savant said to the Academy, which he at once convinced by his deductions. And do you know, gentlemen, whom this Christopher Columbus is of the new celestial world? An old, purblind man, who has difficulty in seeing his way across the street."

"That is admirable! marvelous!" cried several guests, with one accord.

"What is the name of this savant?" asked several voices.

"Monsieur Picot, or, if you prefer, 'old' Picot, for that is the name everybody gives him in the Rue du Val-de-Grâce, where he lives; he is simply an old professor of mathematics, who, for the rest, has turned out some first-class pupils—by-the-by, Félix Phellion, whom we all know, he studied under him, it was he who, on the part of his old master, read the memorial to the Academy."

At the name of Félix, and remembering the promise to lift her to the sky, which when he said it seemed to savor of lunacy, Céleste looked at Mme. Thuillier, whose face had grown quite animated, and seemed to say to her:

"Courage, my child, all is not lost."

"My dear fellow," said Thuillier to la Peyrade, "Félix is coming here this evening, you try and corner him and obtain the communication; it would be a lucky scoop for our 'Écho' if we only could get it out first."

"Oh!" said Minard, volunteering a reply, "it would just be to the taste of a curious public, for it has made an immense sensation. The deputation, not finding Monsieur Picot at home, returned to the office of the minister of public instruction; at once the minister hastened off to the Tuileries, and the 'message,' which was issued early this evening, announces that Monsieur Picot is nominated a chevalier of the

Legion of Honor and is granted a pension of eighteen hundred francs from the fund for the encouragement of the sciences and letters."

"There," said Thuillier, "is a Cross well bestowed."

"I rather think," said la Peyrade, "that the worthy Monsieur Picot is not being well cared for; for just at this time his family, after failing to get a commission in lunacy, are trying to have trustees appointed. They claim that he is being robbed by a servant who lives with him. *Parbleu!* Thuillier, you know her; it is that woman who came the other day to the office, and who had been led to think that Dupuis, the notary, had gone off with some funds of hers."

"Yes, yes, very well," said Thuillier, significantly; "yes, you are right, I do know her."

"It's queer," said Brigitte, improving the occasion to emphasize the argument she had had with Céleste about Marmus', the mathematician, absence of mind, "that all these savants, outside their learning, are good for nothing, and that, when they are at home, they have to be cared for like children."

"That proves," said the Abbé Gondrin, "how greatly they are absorbed in their studies; but at the same time they possess an artlessness of nature which is most touching."

"When they are not as perverse as donkeys," replied Brigitte, testily. "As for me, Monsieur l'Abbé, I can tell you that, if ever I thought of marrying, a professor would not suit me. In the first place, what do they work at, these savants? At stupidities the most part of their time; for here you are all admiring the discovery of a star, and what good will that do any of us? For my part, I think we have plenty of stars already."

"Bravo!" Brigitte, said Colleville, again forgetting himself; "you are truth itself, my girl, and, like you, I think the man who can only discover a new dish would deserve better of mankind."

"Colleville," said Flavie, "I must say that your remarks are in the worst possible taste."

"My dear demoiselle," said the Abbé Gondrin, addressing Brigitte, "you might be right if man consisted of matter only, and if there were not bound to our body a soul having instincts and cravings that need to be satisfied. Now I think this sense of the infinite which dwells within us, and which each in his own way endeavors to satisfy, is wonderfully helped by the searchings of astronomy, that from time to time reveals to us new worlds which the hand of the Creator has strewn through space. The infinite within you finds another outlet; this passion for the welfare of those about you, this warm affection, so ardent, so devoted, which you feel for your brother, are at once the manifestations of the aspirations which have nothing of the material in them, which in seeking their end and object will never ask: 'What good is all this? What is the use of that?' Again, I must assure you that the stars are not without their uses, as you would seem to suppose; without these, navigators would be seriously impeded in their steering across the seas; they would be puzzled how to bring from distant lands the vanilla which has served to flavor this delicious cream that I am now eating. So, as observed by Monsieur Colleville, there is much affinity between a dish and a star; we should decry no person, be it an astronomer or a housekeeper."

The abbé was interrupted by a noise of loud altercation in the antechamber.

"I tell you I will go in," shouted a voice.

"No, monsieur, you shall not go in," replied the "male" domestic. "They are at table, I tell you; no one should force his way into a private house."

Thuillier turned pale; since the seizure of the pamphlet, he fancied all improvised visits betokened the advent of the police.

Among the various social dogmas laid down by Mme. de

Godollo for Brigitte's guidance, the one that had needed the oftenest repeating was never, as mistress of the house, to rise from the table unless it was intended as the signal for retiring; but present circumstances seemed to give amnesty to the injunction.

"I'll go and see what it all means," she said to Thuillier, quickly, as she noted his uneasiness. "What is it?" she asked the servant, when she reached the scene of the conflict.

"Here is a gentleman who is determined to come in; he says no one dines at eight o'clock."

"But who are you, monsieur?" said Brigitte to an old man, strangely attired, and whose eyes were protected by a green shade.

"Madame, I am neither a beggar nor a vagabond," replied the old man in a sonorous voice. "I am professor of mathematics, by name Picot."

"Rue du Val-de-Grâce?" asked Brigitte.

"Yes, madame, No. 9, next door to the fruit store."

"Come in, monsieur, come in, we are only too happy to receive you," cried Thuillier, who, hearing the name, had hurried out to meet the savant.

"He arrived like the 'Great Bear,'" said Colleville, deranging a proverb in Léon de Lora's style.

"*Hein!* scallawag," said the savant, turning to where the servant had been standing when he entered, but who had retired when he saw everything was amicably settled.

Père Picot was a tall, spare man, with a severe, angular face, which, in spite of the softening effect of a blonde wig with heavy curls, and the pacific green shade we previously spoke of, had a truculent and surly cast, and which hard study had ornamented with a surface of sickly pallor. He had given proof of his snappish, quarrelsome mind before entering the dining-room, where every one rose to receive him.

His costume consisted of an over-large frock-coat, something between an overcoat and a dressing-gown; under this was a big vest of iron-gray cloth, fastened from the throat to the pit of the stomach with a double row of buttons, huzzar style, and looking like a breast-plate. His trousers, though October was near its close, were of black thin serge, and gave testimony to long wear by dull-looking patches breaking the shining surface caused by wear, and a rough darn covered one knee. But, by daylight, his most striking feature was a pair of Patagonian feet, imprisoned in beaver cloth slippers, which, being moulded upon the mountainous excrescences of gigantic bunions, made one involuntarily think of a dromedary or an advanced case of elephantiasis.

When he was installed on the chair eagerly placed for him, and the company had resumed their seats at the table, amid the silence born of curiosity:

"Where is he," cried the old man, in a voice of thunder, "the villain, the scoundrel? Bring him forth, let me hear his voice."

"To whom do you refer, my dear sir?" asked Thuillier, in a conciliatory voice, in which was a slight tone of patronage.

"A scallawag whom I could not find at his residence, monsieur, and they informed me that he was at this house. I am, I believe, in the home of Monsieur Thuillier, member of Council, Place de la Madeleine, first floor above the entresol?"

"Precisely, monsieur," replied Thuillier, "and allow me to add, monsieur, that we are all your respectful sympathizers."

"And you will permit me, I hope," said Minard, "as the mayor of the adjoining arrondissement to that in which you reside, to congratulate myself in being present in the company of Monsieur Picot, the one who is without a doubt the discoverer of a star, and by this has immortalized his name."

"Yes, monsieur," replied the professor, raising once more the stentorian diapason of his voice, "I am Picot (Népomucène), the one you speak of, but I have discovered no star.

I am not such a faddist, my eyes are very weak; that insolent rascal is making me ridiculous with that hoax. I don't find him here; he is in hiding, the coward, and dare not sniffle a word before my face."

"Who is this person you are so annoyed with?" was asked the old man by a number of voices.

"An unnatural pupil," replied the old mathematician; "a good-for-nothing—a man of parts, though—his name is Félix Phellion."

This name was heard with amazement, as may be imagined. Finding the situation so funny, Colleville and la Peyrade shouted with laughter.

"You laugh, wretch," cried the irate old man rising from his seat; "just come and laugh within the length of my arm."

And he brandished an enormous, heavy stick with a China knob, which he used as a guiding cane, thereby nearly knocking over a heavy candelabrum on the table on to Mme. Minard's head.

"You are mistaken, monsieur," said Brigitte, seizing his arm in the nick of time, "Monsieur Félix Phellion is not here. He will most likely be here at our reception, somewhat later, but he has not yet arrived."

"They don't begin very early, your *soirées*," said the old man, "it is past eight o'clock. However, as Monsieur Félix will come later, you will permit me to wait for him. You were eating dinner, I think; pray don't allow me to disturb you."

And he quietly sat down.

"May I offer you anything?" asked Brigitte; "a glass of champagne and a biscuit?"

"As you are so kind, madame," replied the old man, "one never refuses champagne, and I can always eat between meals; you dine very late, though."

A place was found for him at the table between Colleville

and Mme. Minard; the musician filled the glass of his new neighbor, before whom was placed a dish of little cakes.

"Monsieur," said la Peyrade, in a wheedling voice, "you must have seen how surprised we were to hear you complain of Monsieur Félix Phellion, a so gentle young man, so inoffensive. What has he really done that your indignation is so great?"

His mouth full of pastry, which he was consuming at a rate which caused Brigitte much agitation, the professor signed that he would give an answer presently. Then, mistaking his glass and gulping down the contents of Colleville's:

"What has that insolent done?" he replied. "The miserable thing—and not for the first time, either. He knows that I cannot suffer stars, and with good cause. In 1807, being attached to the Bureau of Longitudes, I took part in a scientific expedition that was sent to Spain under the direction of my friend and colleague, Jean-Baptiste Biot, to determine the arc of the meridian from Barcelona to the Belearic Isles. I was just observing a star, perhaps the very star my rogue of a pupil has discovered, when suddenly, war in the meantime having broken out between France and Spain, the peasants, seeing me perched with a telescope at the top of Mont Galazzo, figured it out that I was signaling to the enemy. An infuriated rabble smashed my instruments and talked of stringing me up; I was go—gone up only that the captain of a ship took me prisoner and thrust me into the citadel of Belver, where I spent three years in dire captivity. Since that time, as you may well believe, I have let the whole celestial system alone; though I was, without being aware of the fact, the first to observe the famous comet of 1811; but I should have been careful to have said nothing about it only that Monsieur Flauguergues was so foolish as to publish it. Like all my pupils, Phellion knows my declared aversion to the stars, and he knew right well that the best trick that he could play upon me would be to saddle one on my back. So that deputation that went through the farce of coming to compliment me was more than lucky in not finding me at home, for, if they had, the respected gentlemen the academicians, and all the Academy included, would have passed a bad quarter of an hour."

Everybody found the greatest pleasure in this singular monomania of the old mathematician. Only la Peyrade was beginning to understand the part played by Félix, and he was vexed that he had insisted on the explanation.

"Still, Monsieur Picot," said Minard, "if Félix Phellion is only culpable by crediting you with this discovery, it seems to me that his indiscretion has been compensated to some extent; the cross of the Legion of Honor, a pension, and the glory that will accrue to your name."

"The Cross and the pension I take," said the old man, emptying his glass, which to the great horror of Brigitte he replaced upon the table with such force as to break the stem. "For twenty years the government has owed me them, not for discovering stars, either (things that I have always scorned), but for my celebrated treatise on 'Differential Logarithms,' which Kepler thought proper to term monologarithms, a sequel to Napier's tables; for my 'Postulatum' of Euclid, which I was the first to solve; but, above all, for my theory of 'Perpetual Motion,' four volumes, octavo, with plates: Paris, 1825. You can thus see, monsieur, that to give me glory is to pour water into the river. I had so little need of Monsieur Phellion to make me a position in the scientific world, that a long time ago I turned him out of my house in disgrace."

"Then this is not the first star that he has thrust upon you for a joke?" asked Colleville, flippantly.

"He did worse than that," cried the old man; "he has tarnished my fame. My theory of 'Perpetual Motion,' the printing of which cost me my all, when it ought to have been printed at the Royal Printery, was enough to have made my fortune and render me immortal. Well, that wretch of a

Félix hindered it all. From time to time, pretending that he knew my publisher: 'Father Picot,' he would say (the young sycophant), 'here are five hundred francs, or fifteen crowns, or, as it was one time, two thousand francs, which the publisher gave me for you, for your book is selling finely.' This went on for years, and my publisher, who was in the conspiracy, would say to me when I went to his place: 'Oh! yes, it is not doing so badly, it fairly *bubbles*, we shall soon get through the first edition.' I didn't suspect anything, and of course pocketed the money; I thought to myself: 'My book is to their taste, the idea will make its way; from day to day I may expect that some capitalist will come forward and propose to apply my system to——'"

"The 'Absorption of Liquids?'" asked Colleville, who had been constantly engaged in filling the old lunatic's glass.

"No, monsieur, my theory of 'Perpetual Motion,' 4 vols. in 4to, with plates: Paris, 1825. But, bah! days passed along and nobody ever came; so, thinking my publisher was not energetic enough, I tried to arrange for a second edition with another publisher. This it was, monsieur, that allowed me to discover the whole plot, and I turned the serpent out of doors. In six years there had been only nine copies sold; kept lulled in false security, I had done nothing to push my book, which had been left to take care of itself; thus was I the victim of jealousy and the blackest malice, and was unjustly despoiled of the value of my labors."

"But," said Minard, who had constituted himself the mouthpiece of the company, "may we not regard this as an act equally delicate and ingenious to——"

"To give me alms, is that what you mean?" interrupted the old man with a roar that made Mlle. Minard jump in her chair; "to humiliate me, dishonor me—me, his old tutor; is it that I need the succor of charity? Has Picot—I, Népomucène—to whom his wife brought a dowry of one hundred thousand francs, ever held his hand out to anybody? But nowadays nothing is respected; old fellows, as they call us, our religion, our good faith is taken advantage of, so that the younger generation may say to the public: 'These old dotards, can't you see plainly that they are good for nothing? it needs us, the modern men, us, Young France, to step in and bring them up by hand.' You, hobbledehoy, you try to feed me! But these old dotards have more knowledge in their little finger than you have in your whole brain; you will never be worth as much as us, miserable little intriguers as you are. As for that matter, I can wait for my revenge; that young Phellion is bound to come to a bad end; that which he did to-day, reading before the full board at the Academy a statement in my name, was nothing less than forgery, and the law punishes forgery with the galleys."

"Quite true," said Colleville, "the forgery of a public star."*

Brigitte trembled for her glassware, and her nerves tingled at the slaughter of cakes and pastry, so she gave the signal to return to the salon, where a number of guests had already assembled. Colleville politely offered his arm to the professor.

"No, monsieur," said he, "permit me to stay here. I am not dressed for a *soirée*, and, beside, a strong light injures my eyes. Then, I have no fancy to make an exhibition of myself; it will be best that the explanation between myself and my pupil should take place between 'four eyes,' as the saying goes."

No one insisted; the old man, all unconsciously, had uncrowned himself in the opinion of the guests. But the thrifty housewife, before leaving him, removed everything of a fragile nature from within his reach; then, by way of a slight recompense:

"Will you take coffee?" she asked.

"I'll take it, madame," replied old Picot, "and some cognac, too."

* It is impossible to produce the pun in English.

"Bless my life! he takes everything," said Brigitte to the "male" domestic.

When Brigitte reëntered the salon she found the Abbé Gondrin the centre of a great circle; as she approached she heard him say:

"I thank heaven for having granted me such happiness. Never have I felt such an emotion as that aroused by the scene in which we have just participated; even the somewhat burlesque form of the confidence, certainly very artless, for it was wholly involuntary, but adds to the glory of the astounding generosity revealed to us. Placed by my sacred calling in the way of learning of many charities, often also either the witness or intermediary of kindly actions, I think that never in my life before have I met with a so touching or more ingenious devotion. Keeping the left hand in ignorance of the doings of the right is a great step in Christianity; but to go so far as to rob one's self of one's own fame to benefit another under such singular circumstances, with every risk of being told he lied, is the gospel applied in its highest precepts; it is being more than a sister of charity, it is worthy the apostle of benevolence. I would that I knew this noble young man, that I might shake him by the hand."

Her arm passed through that of her godmother, Céleste was standing near the priest. Her ear heard every word, and as he talked of and analyzed Félix's generous conduct, she clung more closely to Mme. Thuillier's arm, saying in a low voice:

"You hear, godmother, you hear!"

To crush the inevitable effect which this eulogy would have on Céleste:

"Unfortunately, Monsieur l'Abbé," said Thuillier, "this young man on whom you have made such a 'grand oration' is not unknown to you. I have had before now occasion to speak of him to you, regretting that we had found it impossible to carry out certain plans we had arranged in connection with him; I allude to the very compromising attitude he affects in his religious opinions."

"Oh! is that the young man?" said the abbé; "you surprise me greatly; I must say that I should not have formed such an idea."

"You will see him presently, Monsieur l'Abbé," said la Peyrade, "and if you question him on certain points you will have no difficulty in discovering the ravages that the pride of science can exercise in the most happily tempered souls."

"I am afraid I shall not see him," said the abbé, "as my black robe would be out of place in the midst of the fashionable splendor that will soon fill this drawing-room. But you, Monsieur la Peyrade, are a man of sincere religious convictions, and as you doubtless feel an interest in that young man's welfare, as I do myself, I just say to you in parting: Do not be uneasy about him; soon or late such souls always come back to us, and, if the return of these prodigals may be long delayed, I should not despair of seeing them going to God, or that His infinite mercy would fail them."

As he spoke the abbé looked around for his hat, intending to slip quietly away; just as he thought it possible to be done unnoticed, he was accosted by Minard:

"Monsieur," said the Mayor of the Eleventh, "permit me to press your hand and thank you for the felicitous words of tolerance that have fallen from your lips. Oh! if all priests were like you, religion would soon be victorious. I am in domestic trouble and have to decide on a line of conduct about which I should be glad of your advice."

"Whenever you please, monsieur," replied the abbé; "Rue de la Madeleine, No. 8, in rear of the Cité Berryer; after six o'clock mass, I am generally in the whole morning."

As soon as the abbé had gone, taking Mme. Minard aside:

"Well, it is true," said Minard, "and the anonymous letter does not misinform us. Monsieur Julian is keeping an actress from Bobino's; it was to be present at her début at the Folies-

Dramatiques that he made a pretense of his throat being sore. The porter's wife is on bad terms with the creature's mother, an old fish-hawker, and for a hundred sous crown-piece she gave me the full account. This evening I shall have a serious explanation with monsieur, my son."

"My friend," said Mme. Minard, theatrically, "I implore you, be not violent."

"Lookout," said Minard; "everybody can see us. I have just asked the Abbé Gondrin to give us the benefit of his advice; we may scout the priests when all goes well, but when trouble comes——"

"But, my friend, you take the matter too seriously; he is but young."

"Yes," said Minard, "but there are things that cannot be overlooked. The son of a family in the hands of women like her; it is disreputable; it is the ruin of his family. You don't know, Zélie, what this dangerous class of actresses are—Phryne, Laïs, all. They say that our money earned in trade is but stolen; that it is gained by adulteration and trickery; they empty our pockets, as they claim, to make us disgorge—they mean to, and do, use every means to effect our ruin."

All at once a terrific uproar put a stopper on this conjugal aside. Into the dining-room rushed Brigitte, whence came the sound of falling furniture and crashing glass; there she found Colleville engaged in rearranging his cravat and assuring himself that his coat, crumpled and dragged out of shape, had not one or more rents in it.

"What's the matter?" asked Brigitte.

"Why this old fool," said Colleville, "is gone crazy. I came here to take my coffee in his company, and, at a little joke I made, he flew into so violent a passion that he seized me by the collar, dragged me over two or three chairs and a tray of glasses, because Joséphine was not able to get out of his way in time."

"It's all because you've been teasing him," said Brigitte,

crossly; "you would have done better to have stayed in the salon instead of coming in here to play your jokes, as you call it, eh? You always think that you are in the orchestra of the Opera-Comique."

With this sharp speech, Brigitte, resolute woman that she was, felt that she must get rid of this ferocious old man who threatened her household with fire and blood. She approached old Picot, who was tranquilly amusing himself by burning brandy in his saucer.

"Monsieur," she cried at the top of her voice, as if she was speaking to a deaf person (she evidently thought a blind one needed the same treatment); "I am here to tell you something which you will not like. Monsieur and Madame Phellion are now here and inform us that Monsieur Félix, their son, is not coming. He has a sore-throat."

"Which he got by reading *that* paper," cried the old professor, joyfully. "Well, that is justice. Madame, where do you purchase your brandy?"

"From my grocer, of course," said Brigitte, taken aback at the question.

"Well, madame, I think you ought to know that in a house where one can get such excellent champagne, which reminds me of that we used to quaff at de Fontane's table, grandmaster of the University, it is shameful to keep such brandy. With the same frankness I put into everything, I tell you plainly that it is only fit to wash your horse's feet in; if I had not the chance to burn it——"

"He must be the devil in person," said Brigitte; "not a word to excuse himself about all that glass, and now jaws about my brandy! Monsieur," said she, in the same raised diapason, "Monsieur Félix is not coming; I think your family will be anxious at your long absence, eh?"

"Family, madame; I have no family, as they want to make me out to be a lunatic; however, I have a housekeeper, Madame Lambert; I think she will be surprised at my being so long away. I think I had better go; but I must confess that I am not sure I can find my way in this strange quarter."

"Then take a hack."

"A hack to go, a hack to come; this would be an excellent chance for my relatives to say I am a spendthrift," said the testy old fellow.

"I have an important message to send into your quarter," said Brigitte, who found it was necessary to bear the cost; "my porter is about taking a hack there—if you would care to take advantage of that——"

"I take it, madame," said the old professor, rising; "if it comes to the worst you can testify for me that I was too niggardly to pay for hack hire."

"Henri," said Brigitte to her domestic, "take monsieur down to the janitor and tell him to do the errand I told him about; also to take monsieur to his own door and be careful of him."

"Be careful! be careful!" said the old man, refusing the arm of the servant; "what do you take me for, madame, a trunk or a piece of cracked china?"

Seeing that she had got her man fairly to the door, Brigitte gave her mind free vent:

"What I said, monsieur, is for your own good, and permit me to remark that you are not of the most agreeable disposition."

"Be careful!" repeated the old man; "but you, perhaps, don't know, madame, that it is words like that that brings a commission in lunacy? However, I won't be too rude in return for your hospitality, the more so that I have been able to put Monsieur Félix, who has purposely missed me, in his right place."

"Get out, you old brute; get out," said Brigitte, shutting the door behind him.

The restraint she had placed upon herself compelled her to drink a whole glass of water before returning to the salon;

this obstreperous guest had given her "quite a turn," by her own expression.

The next morning Minard was shown into Phellion's study. The great citizen and his son Félix were absorbed in an interesting conversation.

"My dear Félix," said the Mayor of the Eleventh, shaking hands heartily with the young professor, "it is you that brings me here this morning; I come to offer you my congratulations."

"What has happened, then?" asked Phellion; "the Thuilliers, have they at last——"

"It has nothing to do with the Thuilliers," interrupted the mayor. "But," he added, looking at Félix, "you don't mean to tell me that that sly-boots has kept the matter even from you?"

"I do not think," said the great citizen, "that my son has ever hidden aught from me."

"So, then, the sublime astronomical discovery which he has communicated to the Academy of Sciences, you know all about?"

"Your kindly feeling for me, Monsieur le Maire," said Félix, quickly, "has misled you; I was but the reader, not the author, of the paper."

"Oh! be quiet!" said Minard, "the reader only! all is known."

"But see," said Félix, offering Minard the "Constitutionnel," "here's the newspaper, which announces the discoverer to be Monsieur Picot; not only so, but it mentions the rewards, without the loss of a moment, that have been bestowed upon him by the government."

"Félix is right," said Phellion, "that is a faithful journal; I think the government has acted in this with commendable promptitude."

"But, my dear commander, I repeat that the secret is

blown; your son is shown to be a most admirable fellow. Placing to the account of his old professor his own discovery so as to obtain for him the favors of the authorities, I certainly do not know of any finer trait in all antiquity."

"Félix," said Phellion, testifying some emotion, "the immense labor to which you have devoted yourself so persistently, those never-ceasing visits to the Observatory——"

"But, my father, Monsieur Minard has been misinformed."

"Misinformed!" repeated Minard, "when the whole business was made known by Monsieur Picot himself."

At this statement, made in such a way as to preclude all doubt, the truth began to dawn upon Phellion.

"Félix, my son," he cried, rising to embrace his son.

But he was compelled to sit down again; his legs refused to support him, he became pale, and his nature, usually so impassible, seemed ready to give way under this sudden happy shock.

"*Mon Dieu!*" said Félix, alarmed, "he is ill; ring for help, I beg you, Monsieur Minard."

He rushed to the old man, rapidly loosened his cravat and collar, and slapped his hands. But this faintness was only temporary, he was soon himself again; Phellion pressed his son to his breast and there held him for some time; then, in a voice broken with emotion:

"Félix, my noble son," said he, "so large of heart, so great in mind."

The bell had meanwhile been given a resounding peal by the magisterial hand; the whole household was on its feet.

"It is nothing, nothing," said Phellion, dismissing the servants, who had rushed in. But at the same moment he caught sight of his wife, who had entered with the others, and resumed his habitual pomposity:

"Madame Phellion," said he, pointing to Félix, "how many years is it since you brought that young man into the world?"

Mme. Phellion, bewildered by the question, hesitated for a moment before replying:

"Twenty-five years next January."

"Have you not thought," continued Phellion, "up to now that God has amply gratified your maternal longings by making this child of your womb an honest man, a dutiful son, and one gifted as a mathematician, the science of sciences?"

"Undoubtedly," said Mme. Phellion, understanding less and less at what her husband was driving.

"Well," went on Phellion, "you owe heaven an additional meed of thanks for granting that you should become mother of a genius; those toils, which so lately we condemned and from which we feared the loss of our boy's reason, formed the rough and steep path by which men attain fame."

"*Ah çà!*" said Mme. Phellion, "don't you think it would be as well if you would explain yourself?"

"Monsieur, your son," said Minard, being more cautious this time in administering the happiness he was about to bestow, and fearing another new fainting-fit of joy, "has just made an important astronomical discovery."

"Truly?" said Mme. Phellion, going up to Félix and taking him by both hands quite lovingly.

"When I say important," continued Minard, "I only try to spare your maternal emotions; it is a great, a bewildering discovery, as I said. He is but twenty-five, yet his name is already immortal."

"And this is the man," said Mme. Phellion, effusively embracing her son Félix, "to whom that la Peyrade is preferred!"

"They do not prefer him, madame," said Minard, "for the Thuilliers are not the dupe of that intriguer; but he has become necessary to them. Thuillier thinks that by his means he can become a deputy. The election is not yet won; they are sacrificing Céleste in gaining it."

"But that is atrocious," said Mme. Phellion, "to consider ambition before a child's happiness."

"Ah!" said Minard, "Céleste is not their child; she is their adopted daughter."

"Yes, on Brigitte's side," said Mme. Phellion; "but on the side of Handsome Thuillier——"

"My dear," said Phellion, "no recriminations; the good God has sent us much comfort. Beside, that marriage, about which I regret to see Félix does not behave with his customary philosophy, may still not take place."

Félix shook his head incredulously.

"Yes," said Minard, observing this, "the commander is right. Last evening, when the contract was to be signed, a hitch occurred. You were not present, by-the-by; your absence was remarked."

"We were invited," said Phellion, "but at the last moment we felt that we should be placed in an equivocal position, and then Félix was overcome with excitement and fatigue —which is now apparent as having been caused by his essay read before the Academy. It would have been bad form to go without him, so we absented ourselves."

The vicinage of the man whom he had come to pronounce immortal did not prevent Minard, when the chance was thus presented, of rolling under his tongue that most tender morsel of the middle-classes—gossip.

"Figure to yourself," said he, "the most extraordinary things that occurred at the Thuilliers last night, one succeeding the other." Then he started off with the funny episode of old Picot's visit, following this by the warm approval given to Félix by the Abbé Gondrin and the desire expressed by the young preacher of meeting him.

"I'll call on him," said Félix; "do you know where he resides?"

"Rue de la Madeleine, No. 8," replied Minard; "I have just this minute left him. I saw him on a most delicate matter, and his advice was shrewd and charitable. But that was not the great event of the evening. Every one was present to hear the contract read; they waited in expectation of the notary for a full hour, but he never came."

"Then the contract was not signed," said Félix eagerly.

"Nor even read, my friend. All at once some one came in to say that the notary had started for Brussels."

"Undoubtedly on more urgent business," said Phellion, innocently.

"Much more urgent," replied Minard, "a little bankruptcy of five hundred thousand francs, which the gentleman skipped."

"But whom is this public officer," demanded Phellion, "so recreant to his trust, as, in this scandalous manner, to forego the sacred duties of his calling?"

"Think now! your neighbor, on the Rue St. Jacques, the notary Dupius."

"What!" said Mme. Phellion, "so pious a man as he? Why he is the parish churchwarden."

"Ah! madame," said Minard, "it is just those very people who go it; he is not the only one."

"Tell us all about it," said Mme. Phellion, with animation.

"Well, it seems," Minard went on, "that this canting swindler had the savings of a number of servants placed in his hands, and that Monsieur la Peyrade—you see they are all in a clique, these pious folk—was charged with the duty of recruiting clients for him among that class."

"I always said he was no good, that Provençal," said Mme. Phellion.

"Just recently," replied the mayor, "he had placed with Dupuis the savings of an old housekeeper, herself one of the pious, amounting to quite a nice little sum; my faith! it was worth a care—twenty-five thousand francs, if you please; this housekeeper, named Madame Lambert——"

"Madame Lambert," interrupted Félix, in his turn; "but

that is M. Picot's housekeeper—scrimpy-cap, a pale, thin face, shows no hair, always speaks with lowered eyes?"

"That's the very woman, a true picture of a hypocrite," said Minard.

"Twenty-five thousand francs of savings!" said Félix; "I am no longer astonished that poor old Picot is always pinched."

"So that some one had to meddle with the sale of his books," said Minard, slyly. "Well, however that may be, you can imagine that she was in a dreadful state when she heard of the notary's flight. First, she went to la Peyrade's lodgings—out, but dining at the Thuilliers; to the Thuilliers then, arriving there at ten o'clock, when all the gaping company sat wondering what next to do, neither Brigitte nor Thuillier having sense enough to redeem such an awkward position; I can tell you we all missed the finesse of Madame de Godollo and the talent of Madame Phellion——"

"You are too polite, Monsieur le Maire," said Mme. Phellion, primly.

"Well, as I said, there she was in the vestibule and asking for la Peyrade, of course being greatly excited."

"Quite naturally," said Phellion, "he was the intermediary, the woman had the right to question him."

"You should just have seen the Tartuffe," continued Minard. "He had scarcely left the room when he returned with the news. As everybody was anxious to be going, there was a general stampede. Then what does our man do? He goes back to Madame Lambert, who never ceased crying she was ruined! she was lost!—which, of course, may have been true, but might also merely have been a scene carefully arranged between them—before all the guests in the antechamber. 'Reassure yourself, my worthy woman,' said the editor-in-chief of the 'Écho de la Bièvre,' 'the investment was made at your own request; consequently, I owe you nothing; but it is sufficient that as the money passed through my hands my conscience tells me that I am responsible; if the assignees of the notary do not realize enough, I will pay you in full.'"

"Yes, just what I should have done and said," put in Phellion. "Such upright conduct cannot be termed jesuitism."

"You! why, certainly you would have acted the same, so should I," said Minard; "but we should not have performed it to the sound of a brass band, but have paid it quietly, like gentlemen. But this election manipulator, with what can he pay? Out of the *dot!*"

At this moment entered the little servant-boy, who handed a letter to Phellion junior—recognizing it as from M. Picot, and written by Mme. Lambert. Obtaining permission to peruse it, and informing them whom it was from, he passed it to his father:

"You may read it aloud, if you wish," said he.

"He rakes your hair nicely, I guess," said Minard. "I never saw anything so comical as his fury last night."

Phellion took the letter and in a pompous voice and manner:

"My dear Félix," began the great citizen, "I have just received your note; it arrived in the nick of time, for they tell me that I was in a rage with you. You say that in being culpable in abusing my confidence (about which I proposed giving you a good whipping), in order to give a knockout blow to my family by showing that a man who was capable of making the elaborate calculations necessary for this discovery you have made was not by any means the man to be accounted a lunatic, and to have his affairs controlled by others. This argument pleases me, it is such an excellent answer to the infamous proceedings taken against me by my relations; I must commend you for thinking of it. But you sold that idea pretty dear when you placed it in juxtaposition with a star, making me, me! its philosopher and friend. It is not at my age and when I have solved the great problem of 'perpetual motion' that a man should trouble himself about such trumpery rubbish; all right for such gabies and sucking-scientists as yourself; that is just what I said to the Minister of Instruction this morning, by whom I must acknowledge I was received with great urbanity. I asked him whether, as he had made a mistake and sent them to the wrong address, he had perhaps better take back his Cross and his pension, though I certainly deserved them for other things.

"'The government,' answered the minister, 'is not in the habit of making mistakes; what it does, it always does well; it never annuls an ordinance given under the hand of his majesty; your excellent work has well merited the two favors granted by the King; it is an old debt, I am only too pleased to pay it off in his name.'

"'But Félix?' I said; 'for after all, for a young man, it was not such a bad discovery.'

"'Monsieur Félix Phellion,' the minister replied, 'will to-day receive his appointment as chevalier of the Legion of Honor; the King will sign the order this morning; it happens, too, that just now there is a vacancy in the Academy of Sciences, and if you are not a candidate——'

"'I in the Academy!' I interrupted, with the frankness of speech you know so well, 'I execrate all the academies; they are wet blankets, assemblies of slothfulness, stores with fine signs and nothing to sell.'

"'Well,' said the minister, smiling, 'I think at the forthcoming election M. Félix Phellion has every chance of being elected, the influence of the government will be at his back, which I account a potent factor.'

"There, my poor boy, this is all that I have been able to do to-day to reward you for your good intentions and to prove that I no longer bear malice. I think my relations will pull a rather long face. Come and talk it over with me as soon as possible, say about four o'clock—for I don't dine after bedtime, as I saw a lot of folk doing last night in a house where I took occasion to speak of your talent in a manner much to your advantage. Mme. Lambert, who can handle a pan better than a pen, will distinguish herself, although it is Friday, and you know she never lets me off on a fast day; but she promises me a dinner for an archbishop, with a half-bottle of champagne, which if required can be doubled, to redden the ribbon.
"Your old professor and friend,
"PICOT,
"Chevalier of the Legion of Honor.

"P. S.—Is it possible to obtain from your worthy mother a little flask of that excellent old cognac that you once gave me? Not a drop is left, and yesterday I was compelled to drink some that wasn't good enough to wash a horse's feet in; I did not hesitate to so inform the charming Hebe who served me."

"Certainly, yes, he shall have some," said Mme. Phellion; "and not a flask only, but a *litre.*"

"And I," said Minard, "who pique myself on mine, will also send him a few bottles; but pray don't let him know from whom it came—be my sponsor—for there is no saying how he would take it."

"Wife," said Phellion, "bring me a white cravat and a black coat. Monsieur the Mayor will excuse me, if I leave him."

"I must be going myself," said Minard, "for I have a little affair on with monsieur, my son, who has *not* discovered a star."

Phellion, not saying whither he was going, though anxiously questioned by his wife, sent for a hack, and half-an-hour after found himself in the presence of Brigitte, who was superintending the careful putting away of the china, glass, and silver used the previous night.

"Well, Papa Phellion," said the old maid, they had proceeded into the salon, "you gave us the slip yesterday; you had a keener nose than the others. Do you know the trick the notary played us?"

"I know all," said Phellion, "and the unexpected check you have received in the execution of your projects is what I shall take as my text for the important conversation which I wish to have with you. At times it seems as though Providence took pleasure in counteracting our best-devised plans; sometimes it seems also to intimate that we tend too much to the right or left, and the obstacles it raises in our path are apparently meant to give us a pause that we may reflect upon our way."

"Providence! Providence!" said the strong-minded Brigitte, "it seems to me has something else to do than look after us."

"That is one opinion," replied Phellion, "but I have often seen its decrees in the little as in the great things of life; and certainly if it had permitted the fulfillment of your arrangements with M. de la Peyrade to have been begun as intended, you would not have seen me here."

"Then," said Brigitte, "you think that the notary having defaulted, the marriage will not take place, eh? But for lack of a monk the abbey did not close."

"My dear lady," said the great citizen, "you will do me the justice to acknowledge that neither my wife nor myself have attempted at any time to influence your decision; we have allowed the young people to love each other without troubling ourselves as to where such attachment might lead and——"

"To upsetting their minds," interrupted Brigitte; "that is just what love does, and that is why I deprived myself of it."

"What you remark is indeed true as regards my unhappy son," replied Phellion; "for, notwithstanding the lofty occupations by which he has tried to distract his thoughts, he is so overcome this morning, despite the glorious success he has attained, that he is talking of circumnavigating the globe—an undertaking which would mean his absence from home for three years, if, indeed he escaped the dangers of a voyage so prolonged."

"Well," said Brigitte, "it is not such a bad idea; he would return consoled, especially if he discovered two or three or more stars."

"His present discovery satisfies us," replied Phellion, with double his usual solemnity. "It is under the auspices of that triumph which has raised his name so high in the world of science that I have the assurance to say to you point-blank: I come, mademoiselle, to ask you, on behalf of my son, Félix Phellion, who loves and is beloved, for the hand of Mademoiselle Céleste Colleville."

"But, my little father," replied Brigitte, "you are too late; remember that we are *diametrically* engaged to la Peyrade."

"It is never too late to do well, they say; yesterday, in my idea, would have been too soon to have presented myself.

My son, having no compensation to offer for the disparity in fortune, could not then have said: 'If Céleste by your generosity has a *dot* which mine is far from equaling, I have the honor of being a member of the royal order of the Legion of Honor, and shall soon, to all appearance, be a member of the Academy of Sciences, one of the five branches of the Institute.'"

"Certainly," said Brigitte, "Félix is becoming a very pretty match, but our word is passed to la Peyrade; his name has been put up with Céleste's at the mayor's office, and only for an extraordinary accident the contract would have been signed; he is engaged in Thuillier's election, which he has put in good shape; we have capital invested with him in this newspaper business; it would be impossible for us to go back on our promise even if we so desired."

"So," said Phellion, "in one of those rare occasions in which reason and inclination point the same way, you think you must be only guided by the question of interest? Céleste, we all know, has no inclination for la Peyrade. Brought up with Félix——"

"Brought up with Félix!" interrupted Brigitte, "she was given a certain length of time to choose between Monsieur de la Peyrade and monsieur, your son, that's how we coerce her, and she would have nothing to say to Monsieur Félix, whose atheism is well known."

"You are mistaken, mademoiselle, my son is not an atheist; for Voltaire himself doubted if there could be atheists; no later than yesterday, in this very house, an ecclesiastic, as celebrated for his talent as for his virtue, after making an eulogistic speech in favor of my son, expressed the desire of becoming known to him."

"*Parbleu!* to convert him," said Brigitte; "but as for this business of the marriage, I am sorry to tell you that the mustard is mixed too late for the dinner; never will Thuillier give up his la Peyrade."

"Mademoiselle," said Phellion, rising, "I feel no humiliation in having taken this useless step; I do not even request you to keep it secret, for I shall be the first to talk of it to all our acquaintances and friends."

"Talk away, my good man, to whoever you wish," said Brigitte, bitterly. "Just because your son has discovered a star, if, indeed, he did really discover it, and not that old man whom the government has decorated, do you think that he can marry one of the daughters of the King of the French?"

"Enough," said Phellion, "we will say no more; without wishing to depreciate the Thuilliers, I might reply that the Orleans family seems to me the more distinguished of the two. But I do not wish to introduce ascerbity into our conversation, and, therefore, begging you to receive the assurance of my humble respects, I will retire."

This said he made a majestic exit, leaving Brigitte under the sting of his comparison, discharged after the manner of the Parthian's* arrow *in extremis*, and she in a rage all the more savage because the evening before Mme. Thuillier, after the guests had gone, had had the incredible audacity to say something in favor of Félix. It is needless to say that the helot was brutally snubbed and told to mind her own business. But this attempt at showing a will of her own on the part of her sister-in-law had already put the old maid in a vile humor, and Phellion, speaking on the same subject, had further exasperated her.

Joséphine the cook and the "male" domestic received the full force of the after-clap resulting from this scene. Brigitte found that in her absence everything had been wrongly done, so "turning to" herself, at the risk of her neck, she clambered on a chair to reach the topmost shelves of the closet in which she kept her choicest china under lock and key.

* Fighting only on horseback, they were noted archers.

This day, which for Brigitte had opened so badly, was to turn out one of the busiest and stormiest of all this story.

As an exact historian we must go back and begin the day at six o'clock in the morning, when we see Mme. Thuillier on her way to the Madeleine to hear the mass which the Abbé Gondrin celebrated at that hour, and afterward to approach that holy table, a viaticum which pious souls never fail to fortify themselves with when it is in their minds to accomplish some great resolution.

At eight o'clock, as we have learned, Minard had called upon the young vicar by virtue of his appointment. The Abbé Gondrin gently blamed him for training his son to a profession which, while it seems to lead to a life of hard work and study, really tempts a youth to every folly: barristers without briefs and doctors without patients, when impecunious, are the nursery grounds of revolution and mischief; so, when they are rich, they ape the youthful aristocracy, which, bereft of all its privileges but the *dolce far niente*, devotes the leisure of an idle and useless life to training horses for the course or women for the stage.

In this particular instance the strong proceedings contemplated by the Mayor of the Eleventh were purely chimerical. There is no longer a Saint-Lazare for the accommodation of wild youth, and Manon Lescauts are no longer kidnapped to America. The abbé suggested that the father should suffer some pecuniary sacrifice; the siren should be paid off and married out of the way; thus would morality triumph in two ways. As the girl had a mother, the better plan would be for Minard to send for and treat with her.

About mid-day the Abbé Gondrin had a visit paid him by Mme. Thuillier and Céleste. The poor child wanted some further explanation of the words by which the priest, in Brigitte's salon, had vouched for Félix Phellion's salvation. It seemed strange to this young theologian that without practicing religion a soul could be admitted to mercy by Divine justice, for surely the anathema is explicit: "Out of the church there is no salvation."

"My dear child," said the Abbé Gondrin, "you must learn to better understand those words which seem so inexorable. It is spoken more to the glorification of those who have the happiness to dwell within the pale of our holy mother the church than a malediction on those who are so unfortunate as to be separated from it. God sees the depths of all hearts and knows His elect; and so great is the treasure of His loving-kindness that it has been given to none to limit its generosity and abundance. Who shall dare to say to God, the Omnipotent: 'Thus far Thou shalt be generous and munificent.' Jesus Christ forgave the woman taken in adultery; on the cross He promised paradise to the repentant thief; these show us that His wisdom and mercy and not man's judgments shall be supreme. He who thinks himself a Christian may in the eyes of God be but an idolater; another who may be thought to be a pagan may, by his feelings and actions, and unknown to himself, be a Christian. Our holy religion has this that is divine about it—all generosity, all grandeur, all heroism, are but the practice of its precepts. As I said yesterday to Monsieur de la Peyrade, pure souls must always be won over in the end; we have but to give them time; it is most important to give them due credit, a confidence which returns great dividends; beside all, charity commends it."

"Oh! my God!" cried Céleste, "to see this too late; I who could have chosen between Félix and la Peyrade, and dared not follow the dictates of my heart. Oh! monsieur, could you not speak to my mother? She always listens to your words."

"That is impossible, my child," replied the vicar; "if I had the direction of the conscience of Madame Colleville I might perhaps say a word, but we are too often accused of imprudently intermeddling in family affairs. Believe me, my intervention would be more like to do harm than good. It is for yourself and those who love you," he added, glancing at Mme. Thuillier, " to see if the already so advanced arrangements could not be changed in the direction of your wishes."

It was written that the poor child was to drink to the dregs the cup of her own intolerance; as the abbé finished speaking his housekeeper came in to ask if he would receive M. Félix Phellion. Thus, like the charter of 1830, Mme. de Godollo's officious mendacity had become a truth.

"Pass out this way," said the vicar hastily, showing out his two penitents by a private passage.

Life has such strange encounters that it does at times happen that the same form of proceeding must be used by a courtesan as a man of God.

"Monsieur l'Abbé," said Félix, " I have heard of the very kind manner in which you spoke of me yesterday in Monsieur Thuillier's salon; I should have hastened to call upon you to express my thanks even if another interest had not brought me hither."

The Abbé Gondrin hastily passed over the compliments, being anxious to learn in what manner his services might be useful.

"With thoughts which I believe to be charitable," said the young professor, "you were spoken to yesterday about the state of my soul. Those who read it so fluently are able to know far more about my inner being; for during the past few days I have experienced strange, inexplicable feelings. I have never denied God; but face to face with that infinitude in which he has permitted my mind to follow the traces of His work, I seem to have gathered a less vague sense of Him, and one more immediate; this has led me to ask whether an honest, upright life is the only homage His omnipotence expects of me. And yet there are numberless objections which arise in my mind against the worship of which you are a minister, and, while sensible of the beauty of the exterior form, in many of its precepts and practices I find myself deterred by my reason. I may pay dearly, perhaps the happiness of my whole life, for the indifference and delay which I have shown in seeking the solution of my doubts. It is now that I have decided to search them to the bottom. None better than yourself, Monsieur l'Abbé, can solve my doubts. It is a cruelly afflicted soul that appeals to you. Is this not a good preparation for receiving the seed of your word? By what studies can I pursue the search for light?"

The abbé protested his joy which, notwithstanding his insufficiency, he would endeavor to reply to the scruples advanced by the young professor. After inviting him to often call upon him, and begging Félix to accept him as his friend, he asked him to read as a first step the "Thoughts" of Pascal. A natural affinity in their talent for geometry might be found to exist between them.

While this scene was passing, another one of sharp and bitter discord, that chronic malady of middle-class households, where the pettiness of mind and deep passion leaves an open door by which it enters, was raging in the Thuillier house.

Mounted on her chair, her hair in disarray, her hands and face disfigured by dust and dirt, Brigitte, feather-duster in hand, was cleaning the shelves of the closet in which she was replacing her library of plates, dishes, and sauce-boats, when Flavie came in.

"Brigitte," said she, "when you have finished what you are about you had better come and see us, or else I will send Céleste to you, it seems to me she intends giving us some of her nonsense."

"In what way?" asked Brigitte, going on with her dusting.

"Yes, I think she and Madame Thuillier went this morning to see the Abbé Gondrin, for she has given me a fine setting-to about Félix Phellion, talking of him as if he were a god; you can easily understand that to refuse la Peyrade is but another step."

"Those cursed skull-caps," said Brigitte, "they are all the time meddling in something. I didn't want to invite him, but you would insist."

"But it was only proper."

"What do I care for what is proper?" replied the old maid. "He is a maker of long speeches, who puts his foot into it. Send Céleste to me. I'll fix her——"

At this instant the servant announced the arrival of the head-clerk of the notary, chosen in default of Dupuis, to draw up the contract. Not giving a thought to her disordered appearance, Brigitte ordered him to be shown in. However, she had the decency to come down from her perch to talk to him.

"Monsieur Thuillier," said the clerk, "came to our office this morning and explained the clauses of the contract he is so good as to intrust to us. But before writing out the stipulations of the marriage, we usually obtain from the mouth of each donor a direct expression of their intentions. Monsieur informed us that he intended giving the bride, at his death, the reversion of the house he inhabits, which, I presume, is this one."

"Yes," said Brigitte. "As for me, I give three thousand francs per year in the Three-per-cents, capital and interest; but the bride is married under the dotal system."

"That is so," said the clerk, consulting his notes. "Now there is Madame Céleste Thuillier, wife of Louis-Jérôme Thuillier, who gives six thousand in the Three-per-cents, with six thousand more at her death."

"That," said Brigitte, "is as safe as if the notary had seen her; however, if it is usual for you to see them, my sister-in-law is here; they will conduct you to her."

And the old maid told the servant to take the clerk to Mme. Thuillier. A moment later the clerk returned, saying there was evidently some misunderstanding, for Mme. Thuillier said she had no intention of making any settlement whatever in the contract.

"Here's a pretty go," said Brigitte; "come with me, monsieur."

And like a cyclone she rushed into Mme. Thuillier's chamber. She was pale and trembling.

"What is this you have told monsieur, that you give nothing toward Céleste's *dot*?"

"Yes," said the slave, declaring insurrection, but in a shaking voice; "my intention is to do nothing."

"Your intentions!" said Brigitte, scarlet with rage; "that's something new."

"They are my intentions," said the mutineer.

"At least you will give your reason why?"

"The marriage does not suit me."

"Ah! since when?"

"It is useless that monsieur should listen to our discussion," said Mme. Thuillier, "it will not appear in the contract."

"You do well to be ashamed of yourself," said Brigitte, "for you don't appear in a very favorable light—— Monsieur," said she, turning to the clerk, "it is easier to mark out things in a contract than to add them, eh?"

The clerk nodded in the affirmative.

"Then draw it up as originally told; later, if madame still persists, you can strike it out."

The clerk bowed and left the room. When the two sisters-in-law were alone:

"So you've lost your head, have you?" asked Brigitte. "What freak is this you have taken?"

"It is a not a freak; it is a solid idea."

"For which we have to thank your Abbé Gondrin; you dare not deny that you went with Céleste to see him?" said Brigitte.

"Yes, Céleste and I did call this morning upon our confessor, but I did not open my mouth about what I intended."

"So, then, it sprouted out of your empty head?"

"I told you yesterday that a more suitable marriage could be arranged for Céleste than this; I don't see that I should despoil myself in favor of a marriage that I do not approve."

"That *you* approve! Upon my word, we must begin and ask madame's advice."

"I know well enough that I have been a nobody in the house," said Mme. Thuillier. "But I don't care for myself; I do, though, care for the happiness of a child, which I look upon as if she were my own——"

"You were never smart enough to have one," cried Brigitte; 'for certainly Thuillier——"

"Sister," said Mme. Thuillier, with dignity, "I took the communion this morning; those are things that I cannot listen to."

"There's just our good sacrament-eaters," cried Brigitte, "acting the holy hypocrite and bringing trouble into the household. And you think it will end here, do you? Thuillier will be here soon; he'll shake you up——"

By calling on the marital authority, Brigitte made confession of her weakness before the unexpected resistance made to her inveterate tyranny. Mme. Thuillier became calmer as Brigitte waxed more wroth; she could return nothing but insolence:

"A drawl," she shrieked, "a lazy, good-for-nothing, incapable of even picking up her handkerchief—this wants to be mistress of the house!"

"That I don't wish to be, but I will be mistress of my own property, and I shall keep it to use as I think best."

"Good dog, there!" said Brigitte, ironically, "*her* property?"

"Mine, yes, that which I had from my father and my mother, which I brought as my *dot* to Monsieur Thuillier."

"And who was it then that turned it over—this money, and made it bring in twelve thousand francs a year?"

"I have asked account of nothing," replied Mme. Thuillier, gently; "if it had been lost in the uses you made of it you would not have heard a word of complaint from me, as it has prospered it is only fair I should reap the benefit. I do not reserve it for myself."

"That's how it may happen if you give yourself such airs; it is not so sure that you and I will long pass in and out by the same door."

"You think, perhaps, that Monsieur Thuillier will cast me off? He must have cause, thank God, before he can do that. I have been a wife without reproach."

"Viper! hypocrite! heartless!" cried Brigitte, at the end of her arguments.

"My sister," said Mme. Thuillier, "you are in my apartments."

"Get out then, dish-rag," yelled the old maid, in a paroxysm of fury. "If I didn't restrain myself——"

And she made a gesture of insulting menace.

Mme. Thuillier rose to leave the room.

"No, you don't," cried Brigitte, pushing her down again, "and until Thuillier returns and decides what is to be done with you, I shall leave you locked up where you are."

When Brigitte, her face aflame, returned to Mme. Colleville, she found her brother, whose early return she had predicted. He was radiant.

"My dear," said he, not noticing the state she was in, "all goes well; the conspiracy of silence is at an end; two papers, the 'National' and a Carlist journal, have this morning reproduced two of our articles, and there's a little attack in a ministerial paper."

"All is not going well here, though," replied Brigitte, "and if things continue as they are I shall leave the barracks."

"What has upset you?" asked Thuillier.

"Your insolent wife, who has made quite a scene; it has caused me to tremble all over."

"Céleste made a scene!" said Thuillier; "then it's the first time in her life."

"Everything has a beginning, and if you don't bring her to order——"

"But what is it all about—this scene?"

"About Madame Thuillier not agreeing that la Peyrade should have her goddaughter; she says she will give nothing in the contract."

"Come, compose yourself," said Thuillier, whom the admission of the "Écho" into the field polemic had made into another Pangloss: "I'll soon settle all this."

"You," said Brigitte to Flavie, "had better return home and tell Céleste not to see me; I don't like conspiracies, and I might box her ears. You can tell her that if she doesn't want to see her *dot* reduced to less than a bank messenger can carry in his eye—which is as much as you are able to give her —that she——"

"But, my dear Brigitte," interrupted Flavie, turning restive under such impertinence, "you may dispense with reminding us of our poverty; for after all we have never asked you for anything and we pay our rent punctually, and beside all Monsieur Félix Phellion would gladly take Céleste even if she had no more *dot* than a bank messenger could carry in a *bag*."

And she did not forget to accent this word as she pronounced it.

"Oh! so you are going to meddle, too," cried Brigitte; "eh, well, go and get your Félix. I know very well, my little mother, that this marriage doesn't suit you; it is disagreeable to be nothing more than mother-in-law to your son-in-law."

At this moment Thuillier returned; his beatific air was flown.

"My dear Brigitte," said he, "you have a most excellent heart, but at times you seem apt to be violent——"

"The deuce!" cried the old maid; "I am tackled on that side, too."

"But, my dear friend, to raise your hand against your sister."

"I lift my hand against that ninny? That's a good 'un."

"And then," continued Thuillier, "a woman of Céleste's age cannot be made a prisoner."

"Your wife; have I put her in prison?"

"You can't dispute my word, for I found the door double-locked."

"*Parbleu!* that's because in my anger at the infamous things she vomited at me that I turned the key without thinking."

"Come, come," said Thuillier; "these are not proper things for people of our class to do."

"Oh! after twenty years of devotion to be treated like the scum of the earth," replied Brigitte.

And rushing to the door, which she violently slammed after her, she went away.

Thuillier stayed behind with Flavie and commenced to expatiate to her on the great political and literary good luck of the morning when he was again interrupted, this time by Joséphine, the cook:

"Monsieur," said she, "will you tell me where I can find the key of the great chest?"

"What for?" asked Thuillier.

"For mademoiselle, who told me to take it to her room."

"What is she going to do with it?"

"Mademoiselle is doubtless going a journey; she is getting her linen out of the drawers, and all her dresses are on the bed."

"I don't know anything about it," said Thuillier; "go and tell her it is lost."

"Oh! yes," said Joséphine, "I should like to see myself doing that."

Just then the door-bell rang.

"That is la Peyrade, I guess," said Thuillier in a tone of satisfaction. In fact, the Provençal was admitted.

"Faith, my friend," said Thuillier, "you come just in the nick of time, for the house, all on your account, is turned upside down; it needs your silvery tongue to restore it to peace and propriety."

Then he told the barrister the cause of the declaration of this civil war.

Addressing Mme. Colleville:

"Under the circumstances," said Théodose, "I may, I think, without impropriety be allowed a few moments' interview with Mademoiselle Colleville."

Here the Provençal showed his usual acumen; he grasped the idea at once, that the key to the situation was Mademoiselle Céleste—by her means alone could pacification be accomplished.

"I will send for her and leave you alone together," said Flavie.

"My dear Thuillier," said la Peyrade, "you must, without being harsh, let Céleste understand that she must give her consent without further delay. After that leave her to me; I will do the rest."

When Céleste came in to her godfather:

"My child," said Thuillier, "your mother has told us things that have astonished us; can it really be true that, with the contract all but signed, you have not yet decided to accept the marriage arranged for you?"

"My godfather," replied Céleste, rather surprised at the abrupt interrogation, "it seems to me that I never said this to my mamma."

"Did you not just now speak of Monsieur Félix Phellion in terms of extravagant praise?"

"I spoke of Monsieur Phellion as every one else is speaking of him."

"Come, now," said Thuillier, authoritatively, "let us have no more equivocation; do you—yes or no—refuse to marry Monsieur de la Peyrade?"

"My good friend," said the Provençal, intervening, "your way of putting the case is too crude and rough, and, with me present, it seems altogether out of place. I should like, if mademoiselle will permit me, I am sure Madame Colleville will not object; there can be nothing in my request for an interview to alarm her maternal prudence."

"So be it," said Mme. Colleville; "you account yourself very smart, but if you let that child get the better of you, so much the worse for yourself. Come, Thuillier, it seems we are in the way here."

As soon as the two designed for each other were left alone:

"Mademoiselle," said la Peyrade, placing a chair for Céleste and taking one himself, "you will admit, I think, that I have not pestered you with my attentions. I have known both the impulse of your heart and the repugnance of your conscience; I hoped that after a time I should have made an agreeable refuge for those two currents of sentiments, but we have now reached a point where I think it is not impertinent or indiscreet to beg you to let me know upon what course you have decided."

"Monsieur," said Céleste, "as you speak so frankly and kindly to me, I will tell you, what you already know, that, brought up as I was with Monsieur Félix Phellion, knowing him longer by far than I have known you, the idea of marriage was less repugnant in regard to him than it would be to others."

"At one time," remarked Théodose, "you were allowed a choice——"

"True, but at that time religious difficulties beset the way."

"And to-day those difficulties have disappeared?"

"Nearly," answered Céleste. "I am in the habit of subordinating my opinion to that of others who are wiser than myself, monsieur, and yesterday you heard the manner in which the Abbé Gondrin spoke of Monsieur Phellion. And this morning he went to see him."

"Oh!" said la Peyrade, with a touch of irony, "it seems he must certainly have seen Father Anselme, then? But, admitting that he has become all you wish on the religious side, have you reflected on the great event which has just taken place in his life?"

"Most certainly, but that is not a reason for thinking less of him."

"No, but it is a reason why he should think more of himself. His present modesty, and the humility, once the chief charm of his character, may be replaced by great assumption. He has discovered one world, mademoiselle; will he not strive to discover two? Your rival will be the whole firmament."

"You plead your cause most intelligently," said Céleste, smiling, "so that I can fancy you the barrister fully as troublesome as a husband as would be M. Phellion the astronomer."

"Mademoiselle," said la Peyrade, "let us speak seriously, I am confident of your extreme delicacy. But do you know what is happening to M. Félix Phellion? He has not lost anything by his devotion to his old master; his pious fraud is known to all, the discovery has been granted as his, and Monsieur Minard says that he is to be made chevalier of the Legion of Honor and a member of the Academy of Sciences. Now, if I were a woman, I own that I should be distressed if, at the very time I had decided to take a man into favor, such an avalanche of good things should fall upon him; I should dread lest the world should say I adored the rising sun."

"Oh! monsieur," said Céleste, quickly, "you cannot believe me capable of such baseness."

"I, no," said the Provençal; "I should affirm precisely the contrary; but the world is rash and unjust and perverse in its judgments."

He saw that he had caused inquietude and a sense of dismay in the young girl, who made no reply.

"Now," continued la Peyrade, "to speak of a much worse aspect of your situation, one which is not merely personal, a question, one may say, between you and yourself: are you aware that at this moment you are the cause in this very house of terrible and most regrettable scenes?"

"I, monsieur?" said Céleste, with surprise not unmingled with dread.

"Yes; concerning your godmother; by the extreme affection that she bears you she seems to have become an entirely different woman; for the first time in her life she shows a will of her own. She declares that she will not make her proposed liberal gift to you; I need not inform you, of course, whom the person is that this rigor is directed against."

"But, monsieur, I assure you that this idea of my godmother's was quite unknown to me."

"I know that," said la Peyrade; "it would also be a matter of minor importance but for the fact that Brigitte takes your godmother's attitude as an insult to herself. Painful explanations have taken place. Thuillier, between the hammer and the anvil, could do nothing; indeed, he further imbittered matters, till now Mademoiselle Brigitte is packing up to leave the house."

"Monsieur! what is this you are saying?" exclaimed Céleste, horrified. "I cannot be the cause of such terrible harm."

"You did not intend to be, but the harm is done; I pray heaven it may not be irremediable."

"But what can I do, my God?" said Céleste, wringing her hands.

"I should reply, unhesitatingly, sacrifice yourself, if it were not that in the present circumstances I should have to play the ignoble part of victimizer."

"Monsieur," said Céleste, "you do not interpret me aright; I have certainly had a preference, but I never considered myself a victim; whatever may be necessary to restore peace to this house I will most willingly do."

"That for me," said la Peyrade, with much humility, "would be more than I dare ask for myself; but for all our sakes I must say that something further is needed. It is necessary that Madame Thuillier should hear this from your own lips. She will never, after what has occurred, take the word of another. Let it seem that you accede to my suit with eagerness—of course assumed, but sufficiently so for her to fully believe it."

"So be it," said Céleste. "I shall know how to seem smiling and happy. My godmother, monsieur, has been to me a mother; and for such a mother what would I not undergo?"

The position was so pathetic, and Céleste had so artlessly betrayed the depth and, at the same time, her determination to make the sacrifice, that, if la Peyrade had possessed any heart at all, he must have loathed his part; but to him Céleste was but a rung, and, provided the ladder can hold and raise you, who would bother to ask whether it cared or not? Therefore it was decided that Céleste should go to her godmother and prove to her that it was all a mistake to suppose she had expressed objection to la Peyrade. Then la Peyrade was to take upon himself the task of making peace between the two sisters-in-law; and it may be supposed that he was not wanting in words to promise the innocent girl a life in the future, when, by his unfailing respect, affection, and devotion, he would spare her every regret for the necessity under which she had accepted him.

When Céleste went to her godmother she found it but a slight task to convince her. The tension of will necessary for her late rebellion was almost superhuman, for she was acting against her every instinct. She was thus an easy dupe to the comedy played for la Peyrade's benefit in Céleste's tender heart. The tempest calmed on this side, la Peyrade had no difficulty in showing Brigitte that she had gone rather too far in her attempt at suppressing the revolt against her authority. That authority being no longer disputed, Brigitte was no longer incensed against her sister-in-law whom she had been on the point of slapping, so the quarrel was settled with a few pleasant words and a kiss, poor Céleste paying the war indemnity.

After dinner, which was only a family meal, the notary having the contract in hand made a call with a "fair copy;" he came to submit it before having it engrossed. This attention was not surprising in a man just entering into business relations with so important a person as a municipal councilor, whom it was to his interest firmly to hook as a regular client. La Peyrade was too shrewd to object to any of the clauses in the contract as it was read. A few of Brigitte's changes gave the new notary a high opinion of the business capacity of the old maid, and showed la Peyrade that more precautions were inserted against him than were altogether in good taste; but he raised no difficulties, he knew the meshes of no contract could be so closely drawn that a determined and smart man could not in some way edge through them. The appointment was made for the contract to be signed at two o'clock next day, at the notary's office.

During the rest of the evening, taking advantage of Céleste's promise to seem smiling and happy, la Peyrade played, as it were, the poor child, forcing her to respond to him in a manner far from the real feeling of her heart, now wholly filled by Félix. Flavie, seeing the Provençal putting forth all his fascinations, remembered how, not so long ago, he had used the same seductive manner to entangle her. "The monster!" she said in a hissing mutter; but she was forced to mask the torture beneath a smiling face. La Peyrade was approved of all, but he was to be shown a hero in a past service he had done the house of Thuillier.

Minard was announced.

"My dear friends," said he, as he came in, "I have come to make a little revelation to you which will cause much surprise. It will, I think, be a lesson to all of us when the question of receiving foreigners in our houses comes to the fore."

"How is that?" said Brigitte, inquisitively.

"That Hungarian woman with whom you were so delighted, that Madame Torna, Comtesse de Godollo——"

"Well?" said the old maid.

"Well," Minard went on, "she is no better than she should be; for two months you petted in your house one of the most impudent of kept women."

"Who crammed you with that yarn?" said Brigitte, not willing to admit that she had been made a dupe of.

"It is no yarn," replied the mayor; "I know the facts myself *de visu*."

"Humph! then you associate with kept women, eh?" said Brigitte, assuming the offensive. "A nice state of affairs, and suppose Zélie knew?"

"It is not he," said Thuillier, knowingly, "who keeps such company, but monsieur his son; we have heard about it."

"Well, yes," said Minard, quite provoked at the manner in which his communication had been received; "and since that impudent rascal has had the impudence to introduce his trumpery actress to you so that she might be written up in your paltry sheet—for I know about this—I cannot conceal it. It was in her company that I met *your friend*, Madame de Godollo. It seems to me I speak plainly enough."

"Perhaps it may be plain enough to you," replied Brigitte, "but unless you are one of those worthy men, fathers whom their sons introduce to their mistresses, I should like to know how you, you, found yourself in company of Monsieur Julian's 'fair?'"

"Ah! you play yourself," said Minard, in a fury; "do you suppose that I am the man to lend a hand to my son's profligacy?"

"I suppose nothing," retorted Brigitte; "you said: 'I found myself in her company——'"

"I said nothing of the kind," interrupted Minard; "I did say that I had seen Madame de Godollo, whose real name is Komorn, and is no more a countess than you or Madame Colleville are, in the company of an unworthy creature with whom my son wastes his money and time. Now, perhaps you would like me to explain the how and why of the meeting."

"Why, yes," said Brigitte, incredulously; "the explanation does not seem unnecessary."

"To show the manner in which I shut my eyes on my son's misconduct, when I was warned by an anonymous letter telling of his debaucheries, I took steps to have the evidence of my own eyes; for I know how far an anonymous letter is to be relied on."

"By-the-by," said Brigitte, in a parenthesis, and turning to la Peyrade, "it's funny we have had none about you."

"If you don't care to listen," said Minard, nettled at being interrupted, "it is useless to ask for particulars."

"That's so," replied Brigitte, "we are listening. You wished to see with your own eyes——"

"Yes," said Minard, "and on the day of your dinner, when I came in so late, I had been to the Folies-Dramatiques, the scene of Julian's dissipations, where this creature was to make her début. I wanted to see if that young scoundrel was really there; it is funny how these actresses will cause such a lunatic to make excuses—you know he said he was too ill to come here."

"Was he there?" said Brigitte, showing little sympathy for the woes of M. the Mayor.

"Yes, but not in the audience; he was on the stage talking to a fireman; he was so far forward as to interrupt the view of some one in the theatre, who shouted: 'Turn out that cocoa-nut.' Judge how my paternal heart must have rejoiced on hearing this agreeable admonition."

"It is because you have spoiled him, your dear Julian."

"Spoiled him, far from that; I should have handled him without gloves only for having taken the advice of the Abbé Gondrin, who counseled tolerance."

"Just as if priests understood anything?" said Brigitte, in great disdain.

"Well, anyway, it was by his advice that I was successful in arranging with the creature's mother. I further told her that I should cut off the supplies. She said a good round sum was just the thing, as there was a copying clerk in the twelfth arrondissement who had his eye on Olympe, and would take her at once."

"This copying clerk," said la Peyrade, "did she mention his name?"

"I think not," said Minard; "at any rate, if she did I have forgotten it; I settled everything in a moment with the mother, who seems to me a pretty good sort of woman."

"But in all this I see no Madame de Godollo," said Brigitte.

"Hold yourself in patience," said Minard. "'The only thing I fear,' said the mother of the actress, 'is the bad advice which may be given by a Polish woman, one named Madame *Cramone*, who has my girl by the hair and does as she likes with; perhaps if you saw her and hinted at some little perquisite for herself, she might help to play our game. Shall I call her? I won't name no names, I'll just tell her: "Here's a gentleman as wants to see you."' The lady was brought in; you can imagine how astounded I was when I found myself face to face with your Madame Godollo, who ran off, laughing, as soon as she saw me."

"And you are sure of it being her?" asked Brigitte. "If you only saw her——"

The wily Provençal was not the man to let such an occasion as this slip, beside retaliating on the Hungarian's practical joke.

"Monsieur le Maire is not mistaken," said he with authority.

"Oh, so you know her too," said Mlle. Thuillier, "and you allowed vermin like this to consort with us?"

"On the contrary," said la Peyrade, "it was I who without any fuss or scandal, and without informing any person, rid your house of her company. You remember how suddenly the woman went away; it was I, who, having discovered what she was, gave her two days in which to clear out, threatening unless she did so to discover the whole truth to you."

"My dear fellow," said Thuillier, seizing the hand of the barrister, "you acted with great prudence and determination. This is but another obligation you have placed us under."

"You see, mademoiselle," said la Peyrade, addressing Céleste, "the strange protectress a friend of yours had."

"Thank God!" replied Mme. Thuillier, "Félix Phellion is above all such vile things."

"Oh! there, Papa Minard," said Brigitte, "we'll all keep mum as to this. Our mouths shall be kept locked about Monsieur Julian's escapades. You will take a cup of tea?"

"Willingly," replied Minard.

"Céleste," said the old maid, "ring for Henri and have him put the large kettle on the fire."

The next day Brigitte, to quote Thuillier, got on the "rampage" early in the morning, although the visit to the notary was not to be made until two in the afternoon. She prevented Thuillier going to the office; she worried Joséphine the cook about hurrying on the breakfast, and, notwithstanding the results of the previous day, with difficulty restrained herself from nagging at Mme. Thuillier. Then she went in to the Collevilles and made the same disturbance; Flavie was too elegant; Céleste was not wearing the hat and dress in which she wished her to appear; Colleville, who could not be detained from his office, must go in his dress suit and had to set his watch by hers that he might have no excuse for being tardy. The most amusing thing of it all was that Brigitte, looking so much after the others, was very nearly late herself.

At half-past one la Peyrade, Thuillier, Colleville, Mme. Thuillier, and Céleste were assembled in the salon. Flavie joined them soon after, fastening her bracelets as she came to disarm any squabbling; she was relieved to find that she was ready before Brigitte. As for her, already furious at finding herself late, she found another cause for vexation. The event seemed to require the wearing of a corset, a refinement in which she seldom indulged. Now, the unhappy maid, who was at that time engaged in lacing her, tried to discover just how tight she wanted them drawn; she alone knew the storms and terrors of a corset-day.

"I had rather," said the girl, "lace the obelisk; I believe it would turn out a better shape; I know, at any rate, it couldn't use its mouth as much."

While those in the salon were laughing and talking, under their breaths, at the flagrant breach of punctuality in which Queen Elizabeth was caught, the porter came in and gave a sealed package to Thuillier, addressed to "M. Thuillier, proprietor of the 'Écho de la Bièvre'—Urgent."

Opening the envelope he found it contained a copy of a ministerial paper which had hitherto shown itself discourteous and hostile, refusing to "exchange," a thing usually made willingly between all newspapers.

Puzzled at this being sent to his house instead of the office of the "Écho," he hastily unfolded the sheet and read with an emotion that may be imagined the following article, recommended to his especial notice by a circle in red ink:

An obscure organ was about expiring in its darkness, when a person of recent ambition bethought himself of galvanizing it. His object was to make it a stepping-stone to climb from his municipal functions to the envied one of a deputy. By good fortune this intrigue has floated to the surface. The electors will certainly not be caught by such a cunning manner of advancing one's own interests; when the proper time arrives, if ridicule has not already done justice by routing this absurd candidate, we shall ourselves prove to the nincompoop that for a man to attain to the honor of representing the country, something more is required than having the money with which to buy a paper and to hire a whitewasher to put the horrid jargon of his articles and pamphlets into decent French. We confine ourselves to-day to this brief notice, but our readers may rely on us keeping them fully posted as to the progress of this electoral farce, if such be the case that the thing is courageously continued.

Thuillier twice read this declaration of war, which left him anything but calm and impassive; then, taking la Peyrade aside:

"See this," said he; "it looks serious."

"Well?" said he.

"How—well?" asked Thuillier.

"Yes, what is there particularly serious in this?"

"What is there that is serious? Why, the article is injurious to me."

"You cannot doubt," said la Peyrade, "that some virtuous Cérizet is doing it in a spirit of revenge by throwing this fire-cracker between your legs."

"Cérizet or anybody else who wrote this diatribe is an insolent fellow," said Thuillier, getting excited, "and the matter shall not rest here."

"As for me," said la Peyrade, "I should make no rejoinder. You are not named, though the attack is aimed at you; we should let the enemy more openly declare himself, then when we discover him—rap his knuckles."

"Not at all," said Thuillier; "it is impossible that I should rest under such an insult."

"The devil!" said the barrister; "what a thin skin you

have. You must bear in mind, my dear boy, that you are a journalist, and a candidate; you must harden yourself to the like of this."

"I, my friend; I make it a principle of mine that I allow no one to tread on my toes. They announce, beside, that they will keep it up. So I am going to cut off these impertinences."

"Well," said la Peyrade, "in journalism, as in being a candidate, a hot temper has its benefits; it makes a man respected; it stops attacks——"

"*Certainly*," said Thuillier, "*principiis obsta*. Not to-day, for we haven't the time, but to-morrow, I shall lay this article before the court."

"The court!" exclaimed the Provençal; "go to law about such a matter as this? But there is no case; neither you nor the paper is named; beside, a lawsuit is a pitiable business; you'll look like a boy who has been fighting and got licked running to complain to his mammy or his schoolmaster. Now, if you said that you would allow Fleury to be put into the question, I could understand it, though even then it would be difficult to do, for this is so entirely personal, it would seem."

"Pshaw!" said Thuillier, "do you imagine, for example, that I am going to commit myself with a Cérizet or any other newspaper knocker-out? I pique myself, my dear, on possessing civic courage which does not give in to prejudice; and which, instead of taking the law into its own hands, has recourse to that means of defense provided by law. Beside, the new law against dueling may be enforced; I have no desire to spend one or two years in prison."

"We can discuss all this later," said la Peyrade; "here is your sister; she would think all was lost if it reached her ears."

Seeing Brigitte come in, Colleville shouted: "Standing room only," and sang the refrain of "la Parisienne."

"God's sake! Colleville, how vulgar you are," said the tardy one, hastening to throw a stone into the other's garden before one could be thrown into hers.

"Well, are we all ready?" she added, arranging her cloak before the glass. "What time is it? It won't do to be there before time like country people."

"One fifty," said Colleville; "I go by the Tuileries."

"We are just right, then," said Brigitte; "it will take about that much time to get to the Rue Caumartin. Joséphine," she cried, going to the door of the drawing-room, "we dine at six; therefore, be sure to put the turkey to roast at the right time, and just don't let it burn, like the last one. Gracious! what's that?" and with a hasty movement she closed the door she had been holding open. "What a nuisance! I hope Henri will have sense enough to say we are out."

Not at all; Henri came in to say that an aged gentleman, wearing decorations, very genteel, had asked to be received on urgent business.

"Why didn't you say we were out, Mister Orator?"

"I should have done so, if mademoiselle had not opened the door of the salon so that the gentleman could see all the family assembled."

"Of course; you're never in the wrong, are you?"

"What answer shall I make him?" asked the servant.

"Say," replied Thuillier, "that we are exceedingly sorry that we are unable to receive monsieur, but that we are expected at the notary's to sign a marriage-contract, and that if he will return in two hours——"

"I have already told him all that," said Henri, "but he says the matter is more important to yourself than him."

"Then show him into my study," said Thuillier; and, opening a door from the salon, he went in first to receive his guest.

Instantly Brigitte's eye was at the keyhole:

"What an imbecile that Thuillier is; he has given him a seat at the farther end of the room so it is impossible that I can hear what they are saying."

La Peyrade covered an inward agitation by an outward air of indifference; he approached the three ladies and greeted Céleste most graciously, who responded with the smiling, happy satisfaction that her part consisted in. As for Colleville, he was composing an anagram on these six words: *le journal l'"Écho de la Bièvre,"* and had arrived at the following combination of letters, little reassuring, as far as it went, to the future of that paper: *O d'Écho, jarni! la bévue réel*——; but a final E was lacking to complete—O but the Écho's a blunder: this, of course, was an imperfect finish.

"He takes a lot of snuff," said the peeping Brigitte, her eye glued to the keyhole; "his gold snuff-box is larger than Minard's; I never saw one so large; perhaps, though," said she, as a running comment, "it's only silver-gilt. He's doing the talking and Thuillier sits listening like a dunderhead. Pretty soon I shall go in and tell them they can't keep ladies waiting like this."

Just as she had put her hand on the lock she heard Thuillier raise his voice, and that made her take another squint through the keyhole.

"He's standing up; he's evidently going away," said she, with satisfaction.

A moment later she saw she was mistaken, for the little old man had only left his chair to amble up and down the room to continue the conversation with greater freedom.

"By my faith! I'm going in," said she, "to tell Thuillier we are going without him; he can follow us."

So saying the old maid gave two imperious sharp raps on the door, and then resolutely entered the study.

La Peyrade, goaded by anxiety, had the bad taste to look through the keyhole; he thought he recognized the "commander" who had waited upon Mme. de Godollo. Then he saw Thuillier addressing his sister with gestures of authority very unlike his usual style of deference and submission.

"Thuillier finds some interest in that creature's talk," said Brigitte, reëntering the salon. "He told us to wait until he is through, ordering me very bluntly to leave them. Really it seems to me that since he has begun to make newspapers that I don't know him; one would think he led the world with a wand."

"I am afraid he is being entangled by some adventurer," said la Peyrade. "That old man I think I saw with Madame Komorn on the day I told her to clear out; he must belong to the same crowd."

"Why, you ought to have told me this!" said Brigitte; "I should mighty soon have asked after the countess, and let him know what we think of his Hungarian."

Soon Thuillier entered the room, his face clouded with care, his manner exceedingly grave.

"My dear la Peyrade," said he, "you did not inform me that another proposal of marriage had been seriously considered by you?"

"Indeed I did; I told you that I had been offered a very wealthy heiress, but that my heart was here; I did not choose to go further into the matter, and so nothing came of it."

"My friend, the conversation I have just had has been most instructive to me; when you know what I know, with many other things personal to yourself, of which I shall inform you privately, I believe you will enter into my ideas. One thing is positive, we shall not go to the notary's to-day. Were I in your place I should at once go and see Monsieur du Portail."

"Again that name! it pursues me like remorse," cried la Peyrade.

"But, my poor boy," said Brigitte to Thuillier, "you have been bamboozled by a rascal; this man belongs to the Godollo clique."

"Madame de Godollo," replied Thuillier, "is not at all

what you suppose her to be; the best thing this house can do is never to say anything about her, good or evil. As to la Peyrade, as this is not the first invitation he has received, I cannot for the life of me see why he hesitates to go and see Monsieur du Portail."

"The deuce is in it if that old fellow has not completely fooled you," said Brigitte.

"I tell you this, that that old man is all that his exterior shows. He has seven crosses, he drives a handsome equipage, and he has told me things that have absolutely astounded me."

"Well, perhaps he's a fortune-teller, like Madame Fontaine."

"Well, if he is not a magician, he has a very long arm," said Thuillier, "and no good can be had by neglecting his advice. Why, he only caught one glance at you, Brigitte, and he said you were a master-woman and born to command."

"The fact is," replied Brigitte, licking her chops after this compliment like a cat lapping cream, "he has a well-bred air, this little old man. Listen to me, my dear boy," added she, turning to and addressing la Peyrade, "when such a bigwig wants to see you, why go and see him—them's my advice. Go and see this du Portail. I don't see that it would commit you to anything."

"Most certainly," said Colleville; "were I but you I would pay thirty calls on du Portail, or all the Porta*ls*,\* or Port*ers*, or Port*ents*, or Port*wines* on earth, if I should only be asked."

The scene was beginning to be very like that in the "Barbier de Séville," when everybody tells Basil to go to bed, till he feels in quite a fever. La Peyrade took up his hat in a huff and went whither his destiny called him: *Quo sua fata vocabant.*

\* A pun impossible to translate.

On arriving at the Rue Honoré-Chevalier, la Peyrade felt a doubt; the dilapidated appearance of the house where he was to call made him think he had mistaken the number. How could a person of M. du Portail's importance live in such a place! But when he introduced himself, the deportment of Bruno, the old valet, the appearance of the furniture and the other appurtenances made him think he had come aright. His surprise was great when he found himself in the presence of the commander, so-called by Mme. de Godollo, the very man whom he had so recently seen at Thuillier's.

"At last," said du Portail, rising and drawing forward a chair, "we meet my recalcitrant gentleman; your ear has taken some pulling, though."

"May I know, monsieur," said la Peyrade, haughtily, and not taking the seat offered him, "what interest you can possibly have in meddling in my affairs? I do not know you, but I may add that the place in which I once happened to see you did not create an absolutely unconquerable desire to make your acquaintance."

"Where did you see me?" asked du Portail.

"In the lodging of a kind of street-walker, who went by the name of Madame la Comtesse de Godollo."

"Where monsieur himself was presumably calling, with a less disinterested reason than my own," said the little old man.

"I am not here," said Théodose, "to bandy wit. I have the right, monsieur, to demand an explanation of your proceedings in reference to myself. Do not, I beg you, delay them with a facetiousness that I shall be far from appreciating."

"Then, my dear fellow," said du Portail, "do sit down; I am not in the humor to dislocate my neck by talking to such a great height as you are at."

This was a reasonable intimation, and was given in such a manner as to convey the fact that lordly airs would not alarm the old gentleman. La Peyrade, as offensively as might be, therefore deferred to his host's wishes.

"Monsieur Cérizet," said du Portail, "a man of exceedingly high position in the world, and who has the honor to be one of your friends——"

"I no longer see the man," said la Peyrade, tartly, understanding the old man's malicious insinuation.

"But the time has been," replied du Portail, "when you did occasionally see him, as, for example, when you paid for his dinner at the Rocher de Cancale—I was about to say that I requested the virtuous Monsieur Cérizet to sound you as to a marriage——"

"Which I refused," interrupted Théodose, "and which I still refuse, with more energy than ever."

"Precisely," replied the gentleman, "that is the question ; it is to talk of that business that I have waited so long a time to meet you. I think, too, that you will accept it."

"But this crazy girl that you are flinging at my head," said la Peyrade, "who is she? She is not your daughter, nor a relative, I suppose, for in such a case you would show more decency in chasing a husband for her."

"This girl," said du Portail, "is the daughter of one of my friends; she lost her father some ten years ago, since which time she has been living with me; I have given her every care demanded by her sad condition. Her fortune, to which I have greatly added, in addition to my own which I intend leaving her, will make her a very wealthy heiress. I know that you have no aversion to handsome *dots*, for you have sought for them in even the lowest ranks, in the Thuilliers' house, for instance; or, to use your own words, in that of a street-walker whom you hardly knew; I could therefore figure on your being willing to accept at my hands a very rich young woman, especially as her infirmity is pronounced curable by the best physicians; whereas you can never cure Monsieur and Mademoiselle Thuillier—the one of being a fool, the other of being a termagant—any more than you could cure Madame Komorn of being extremely giddy and of an easy virtue."

"It might suit my convenience," replied la Peyrade, "to marry the goddaughter of a fool and vixen if I choose her myself, or I might become the husband of a coquette, if the passion so seized me; but the Queen of Sheba, if imposed upon me, neither you, monsieur, nor the most able or powerful man living could force me to accept."

"So for that very reason I address myself to your good sense and intelligence; but in order to speak to people we have to come face to face with them. Just let us see what your position is. Don't get angry if, like a surgeon who wishes to save his patient, I place my hands mercilessly on the wounds of a life up to now so laborious and tempest-tossed. The first point to make is that the Céleste Colleville affair is ended for you."

"Why so?" asked la Peyrade.

"Because I have just seen Thuillier and terrified him with a picture of all the disasters he has already incurred, and those he will further incur if he persists in the thought of giving you his goddaughter in marriage. He knows that it was I who annulled Madame du Bruel's kindness in the matter of the Cross; that it was I who had his pamphlet seized; that I sent that Hungarian into his house to play you all so neatly; that it has been my care to see that the ministerial journals have commenced a fire which will grow fiercer with each succeeding day—not to mention other machinery which will be set in motion to oppose his candidacy. So you see, my dear sir, not only will you lose the credit of being the great help of his election, but that you are actually the stumbling-block to Thuillier's ambition. This is enough to prove to you that the side by which you imposed yourself upon that family, who never liked you at the bottom, is now quite reduced and dismantled."

"But you that flatter yourself that you have done all this," said la Peyrade, "who are you?"

"I won't reply that you are very inquisitive, for I intend later to answer your question; but with your permission, for the present at least, we will continue your life's autopsy— now a dead life, but to which I propose to give a glorious resurrection. You are twenty-eight; you have barely started on the career in which I forbid you taking another step. Some few days hence the Barristers' Association will meet and will censure you, more or less severely, for the manner in which you placed that property in the Thuilliers' possession. Have no illusions. Censure—I mention only your least peril —for a lawyer is not like a hack-driver whom the disapproval of the court does not prevent his driving his coach; if you are but mildly censured, you might as well have your name stricken off the roll."

"And it is to your benevolence, doubtless, that I shall owe this precious result," said la Peyrade.

"I am proud to believe so," answered du Portail; "for in order to tow you back into port it was necessary to cut away your rigging; unless this had been done, you would always have been trying to navigate under your own sails among the shoals of the middle-classes."

Seeing that he had to play against a strong hand, the adroit Provençal took a more respectful manner:

"Permit me to await further explanations before making my acknowledgments," said he.

"Here you stand then," said du Portail. "Twenty-eight, without a sou, without a profession, with antecedents that are —well—very mediocre; with associates like Dutocq and the 'brave! Cérizet;' owing Mademoiselle Thuillier ten thousand francs, which your pretty conscience urges you to pay (even if your still prettier vanity did not insist); to Madame Lambert twenty-five thousand francs more, which you of course will be only too glad to replace in her hands; and as an end-all, this marriage, your last hope, your plank of safety, has just been rendered an impossibility. Between ourselves, if I make any reasonable proposition, do you not think you had better place yourself at my disposal?"

"I cannot form any resolution until your designs are more fully explained," said la Peyrade.

"At my instigation you were spoken to in reference to a marriage," said du Portail; "that marriage is, at least in my idea, closely connected with a past existence by which a kind of hereditary duty devolves upon you. That uncle of yours in Paris, to whom you applied in 1829, whom in your family was thought to be a millionaire, what was he? He died suddenly, almost a pauper; he did not leave enough money with which to bury him; this was his end."

"Then you knew him?"

"He was my oldest, my best friend," replied du Portail.

"But," said la Peyrade, eagerly, "a sum of one hundred louis, which in my first days in Paris came to me from an unknown source——"

"Was sent by me," replied the gentleman; "unfortunately at that time I was overwhelmed with a rush of business, so I could not follow your fortunes closely; this will explain why I left you on the straw in a garret, to ripen, like medlars, to that maturity of poverty which brought you into the meshes of a Dutocq and a Cérizet."

"I am not the less grateful, monsieur; if I had known or by any means discovered my benefactor, I should have hastened——"

"A truce to compliments," said du Portail. "Your uncle was an agent of that occult power which forms the theme of so many absurd fables and is the object of such silly prejudices."

"I cannot grasp your meaning, may I beg you to be more explicit."

"If your uncle were living to-day," said du Portail, "and

should say: 'You seek fortune and influence, you wish to rise above the multitude, you wish to play your part in the events of the epoch, you want to employ an active mind, resourceful, with a trend to intrigue; in short, an opportunity to exert in a higher, more elegant sphere that strength of will and subtlety now utterly wasted in grappling with that most barren, hide-bound animal on earth—a bourgeois. Well, nephew mine, lower your head, creep in after me through that little door which I will open to you; it gives entrance to a great house, of not much repute, but far above its reputation. Statesmen, kings even, will give you their most inmost thoughts; none of the joys that money and the highest power can bestow upon a man will be lacking to you.'"

"But, monsieur, while not understanding you, I might remark that my uncle died so poor that, as you inform me, he was buried at the expense of public charity."

"Yes; he was a man of rare talent, but he had a weak side; he was eager for pleasure, a spendthrift, without a thought for the future; he wanted to taste those joys intended for the common order of men, but which in great vocations are snares and impediments—the joys of family life. He had a daughter, whom he madly loved; through her his terrible business prepared the awful catastrope which ended his life."

"And this you think is an encouragement for me to tread the path in which he would have bidden me follow him?"

"But if I should offer to guide you?" said du Portail.

"You, monsieur!" said la Peyrade, in amazement.

"Yes, I, who was first your uncle's pupil and afterward his protector and providence; I, whose influence for a half-century has had a daily increase; I, to whom all governments, falling over each other like houses of cards, come to ask for safety and for the power with which to build their future; I, who am the manager of a great theatre of marionettes, which includes in its cast Columbines of the style of Madame de

Godollo; I, who to-morrow, if it became necessary to the success of one of my burlesques or dramas, might present myself before your eyes the wearer of the grand cordon of the Legion of Honor, the Golden Fleece, or the Garter. Would you know why neither you nor I will die by poison? Why it is that I, happier than my contemporary kings, can transmit my sceptre to whom I choose? It is because I, like you, my young friend, in spite of your Southern complexion, have been cool and calculating, never tempted to waste my time trifling on the threshold; because my ardor, when circumstances compelled me to use it, never lay deeper than the surface. It is more than likely that you have heard of me; well, for your benefit I will open a window in my darkness; look closely upon me, observe me well; I have not a cloven hoof nor a tail at the base of my spine; on the contrary, I seem to be the most inoffensive of gentlemen in the St. Sulpice quarter; in that quarter where I have enjoyed for five-and-twenty years, I may say, the esteem of all; I am known as du Portail, but to you, by your permission, I shall call myself— CORENTIN."

"Corentin!" exclaimed la Peyrade, with dismay and astonishment.

"Yes, monsieur, and as you must see, by revealing my secret to you I lay my hand upon you and you are enlisted. Corentin, 'the greatest man in the police of modern times,' as the author of an article in the 'Biographies of Living Men' has said of me—though I ought, to do him justice, to remark that he doesn't know the least thing about my life."

"Monsieur, I can assure you that I shall keep your secret; but as to the police; to be in your employ——"

"That makes you uneasy," said Corentin. "But why? Are you afraid to encounter the terrible prejudice that it brands on the brow?"

"It is certainly a necessary institution," said la Peyrade; "I don't know that it is always calumniated. If it is an honorable business, why do those who pursue it conceal themselves?"

"Because all that threatens society," replied Corentin, "and which the mission of the police is to suppress, is plotted and arranged in the shadow. Do thieves and conspirators wear on their hats: 'I am Guillot, the shepherd of this flock;' or ought we when we go to search for them to be preceded by a clanging bell to let them know we are coming—like as the health-officer does on his rounds every morning to see that the janitors sweep in front of each door?"

"Monsieur," said la Peyrade, "when a sentiment is universal it ceases to be a prejudice, it becomes an opinion; this same opinion should be a law to every man who desires his own esteem and that of others."

"And when you despoiled that bankrupt notary," exclaimed Corentin, "you stripped a corpse to enrich the Thuilliers to your own advantage; this, I suppose, you will pretend was in keeping with your esteem, but did it hold that of the barristers? Now, I have done naught of which I need feel ashamed. My care of the daughter of my old friend, Peyrade, has not been a path strewn with roses. As I feel the years advance, I offer you my position, to fit you to take my place, a bride with two heaping bags of money——"

"What!" cried la Peyrade, "is that girl my uncle's daughter?"

"Yes; the girl I wish you to marry is the daughter of your Uncle Peyrade,* for he democratized his name, or, if you like it better, she was the daughter of Father Canquoëlle, a name taken from the estate on which your father starves with eleven children. You turn your nose up at the police, but, as the common folk have it, you owe the best of your nose to the police. Your uncle was born in the purple; the King, Louis XVIII., delighted in his conversation. The question now before us is that of succeeding me—me, Corentin. Do

* See "The Harlot's Progress."

you think you can escape this by any foolish considerations of a bourgeois vanity?"

Corentin arose; he saw that la Peyrade was smiling, showing that at heart he was not so opposed to the proposal as his words would imply.

"The police!" said Corentin, pacing the room as he spoke, "it might be said of the police, as Basile said of calumny to Bartholo: 'The police, monsieur, you know not what you despise.' And in fact," he went on, after a pause, "who are they that despise it? Idiots, who know no better than to insult the power which protects them. Suppress the police, you destroy civilization. Do the police ask the respect of these people? It seeks but to impress them with one sentiment—fear—that great lever which moves mankind; an impure race, whose horrible instincts God, hell, the executioner, and the gendarme can scarcely restrain."

Stopping in front of la Peyrade, looking at him with a disdainful smile:

"And you are one of those simpletons," continued the panegyrist, "who see in the police nothing but a horde of spies and informers? And you have never suspected the statesmen, the diplomatists, the Richelieus it has produced? But Mercury, monsieur, Mercury, the most intellectual of pagan gods, what then was he but the police incarnate? It is true that he was also the god of thieves. We are better than he, for so far we have not doubled the parts."

"And yet," said la Peyrade, "Vautrin, the famous chief of the detective police——"

"Eh! yes, in the lower grades," replied Corentin, resuming his march, "there is always some mud; still, don't make any mistake, Vautrin is a genius, but his passions, like those of your uncle, dragged him astray. But mounting higher (for the gist of the whole question, to wit, the finding of the rung of the ladder on which a man must perch) is the whole thing: The prefect of police, a minister, honored, respected, flattered—is he a spy? Well, I, monsieur, I am the prefect of the occult police of diplomacy—of the highest statesmanship; and you hesitate to mount the throne which I, Charles V., in my old age think of abdicating? To appear small and yet do great things; to live in a comfortable den like this, and command the light; to have ever at your hand an invisible army always ready, always devoted, always submissive; to know the other side of everything; never to be the dupe of any wire-puller, for you hold all the wires yourself; to peer through every partition; to penetrate all secrets; search all hearts, all consciences; these are the things you fear! And yet you were not afraid to wallow in the foul, dark bog of a Thuillier's household; you, a thoroughbred, allowed yourself to be harnessed to a hack, to the ignoble career of an election agent, and of a paper run by a rich bourgeois."

"One must do what first turns up," replied la Peyrade.

"It is most remarkable," Corentin went on, taking up again his former line of thought, "the language has done us more justice than opinion, for it made the word 'police' the synonym of civilization and the antipodes of savage life when it wrote: *l'État policé*.\* I can assure you that we care little for the prejudice that tries to injure us; none can understand men as we know them; to know them is to scorn their contempt, as we have contempt for their esteem."

"There is certainly much of truth in what you have advanced with so much warmth," said la Peyrade.

"Much truth!" replied Corentin, going back to his chair, "say rather it is all true, and nothing but the truth; but enough for to-day, monsieur. To be my successor in these functions and to marry your cousin with a *dot* that will not be less than five hundred thousand francs, that is my offer. I do not ask you for an answer now. I should have no confidence in a decision not seriously reflected upon. To-morrow I

\* From the Greek πολιτεία—policy: hence policy of State.—[TRANSLATOR.]

shall be here all the morning; I shall hope that my conviction may have convinced you."

Dismissing his visitor with a curt little bow, he added: "I do not say adieu, but *au revoir*, Monsieur de la Peyrade."

Fatality seemed lavish in the offer of inducements for him to succumb. Mme. Lambert, now become an importunate creditor, had at length been promised repayment the day after to-morrow, this being the 31st of October; November 2d was the day on which the courts would reopen. To the summons to give an account of his transactions before his peers, he replied that he did not recognize the right of the Board to question him on his private affairs. This was some kind of an answer, certainly. It meant most inevitably that his name would be stricken from the rolls, but seemed in a measure to have an air of dignity and saved his self-love.

Finally he wrote Thuillier, in which he informed him that his visit to du Portail had resulted in his being obliged to make another marriage. All this was curtly said, without the slightest expression of regret for the marriage he renounced. A postscript read: "We shall be obliged to meet and discuss my position on the newspaper," hinting that he might also withdraw from that, too. He was careful to make a copy of this letter, so, when later in Corentin's study he was asked as to his night's reflections, he simply presented for all answer the matrimonial renunciation he had written out.

"That is good," said Corentin, "but your position on the paper you had better retain for a little while; that fool's candidacy ruffles the government, we must in some manner trip up the heels of this municipal councilor; as editor-in-chief, you may turn a trick on him; I really don't think you would kick much at the ordeal."

"Certainly not," said la Peyrade; "the remembrance of the humiliations to which he has so long exposed me will give a keen relish to the lash I should apply to that middle-class brood."

"Be cautious," said Corentin, "you are but young, you must guard against vengeful feelings. In our austere profession we love nothing, hate nothing. Now let us speak of your cousin, whom I should imagine you have some curiosity to know."

La Peyrade was not obliged to pretend eagerness; the feeling was genuine.

"Lydie de la Peyrade," said Corentin, "is nearly thirty, but her innocence, joined to a gentle form of mania, has kept her apart from all those passions, ideas, and impressions which rise up in life, and has embalmed her, as one might say, in a kind of perpetual youth. She always carries in her arms a bundle of linen which she nurses and fondles as a sick baby. She thinks that all other men than myself and Bruno are doctors; she consults them about her child, and listens to them as to oracles. A crisis which occurred some little time ago has convinced Horace Bianchon, that prince of science, that, if the reality were substituted for this long illusion of motherhood, her reason would be soon completely restored. Is it not a worthy task to bring back light to a soul that is barely clouded? Does it not strike you that the bond of relationship between you makes it more than ever your part to be the means of effecting that cure? Now I will take you to Lydie's presence; remember to play the rôle of doctor; for the refusal to enter into her notion is the only thing that upsets her serenity."

After passing through several rooms, Corentin was on the point of taking la Peyrade into the one usually occupied by Lydie, when they were arrested by the sound of two or three chords struck by the hand of a master on the piano.

"What is that?" asked la Peyrade.

"That is Lydie," said Corentin, with what might be termed a sort of paternal pride; "she is an admirable musician; she was an excellent composer, but lately has not written anything, though she improvises, and in a manner that moves me to the soul—the soul of Corentin," added the little old man, smiling at the thought.

La Peyrade was amazed as he listened; his impressionable nature was deeply stirred by this inspiration and science.

To a very quick *scherzo* the player added the first notes of an *adagio*. After a few measures of a *ritornella* in *arpeggio*, a vibrant voice was heard which seemed to stir the Provençal to the depths of his being.

"How the music moves you!" said Corentin. "You most undoubtedly were made for each other."

"Oh, my God! the same air! the same voice!"

"Have you, do you mean, ever met Lydie before?" asked the great master of the police.

"I don't know. I—I think not," answered la Peyrade, in a stammering manner; "and yet in any case it must have been long ago—— But that air! That voice! It seems to me——"

"Enter," said Corentin, suddenly pushing open the door and pulling the young man after him into the room.

Lydie, sitting with her back to the door, and prevented by the sound of the piano from hearing them, did not notice their entrance. La Peyrade advanced a step. No sooner had he seen the face of the crazy girl than:

"It is she!" he cried, wildly clasping his hands over his head.

"Silence," cried Corentin.

But Lydie had heard Théodose's exclamation, and turning round she fixed her attention on Corentin.

"How naughty and troublesome you are to come and bother me," said she. "I don't like being listened to. Oh! you have brought the doctor; that's right, I was going to send for him."

Then she arose and ran for what she called her child in a corner of the room. So she went toward la Peyrade, carrying her precious bundle in one hand, arranging its little cap

"BUT LOOK AT THE DOCTOR," SHE CRIED.

with the other, but as she neared him, pale, trembling, with a glassy eye, Théodose now fully recognized Mlle. de la Peyrade. He retired in evident terror, not pausing until a chair behind him stopped his progress; losing his equilibrium, he fell into it.

So strong a man as Corentin, knowing as he did every incident in the tragedy by which Lydie had lost her reason, had already guessed the truth.

"Look, doctor," said Lydie, presenting the bundle, "does she not grow thinner and thinner?"

La Peyrade was unable to reply. He buried his face in his handkerchief; his breath came so fast that he was incapable of uttering a word.

Then in a gesture of feverish impatience, to which her mental state predisposed her:

"But look at the doctor," she cried, pulling his arm violently and thus compelling him to show his features. "My God!" said she, when she saw the face of the Provençal.

And, dropping the bundle of linen, she started back; her eyes grew haggard; she passed her clammy hands through her hair and over her forehead, and seemed to be making a frantic effort to revive some dormant memory to her mind. Then like a frightened filly who comes to smell an object that has alarmed it, she slowly neared the Provençal, stooping to look into his face, which he kept lowered, and amid a profound silence examined him for a few seconds. Suddenly a terrible cry escaped her throat, she sought refuge in the arms of Corentin, and, pressing against him with all her strength:

"Save me! Save me!" she shrieked. "It is he; the wretch, the villain! That is he who did it all!"

And with her finger extended she seemed to nail the miserable object of her aversion to the spot.

After this explosion she grew limp, and Corentin laid her on the couch, insensible.

"Do not stay here, monsieur," said Corentin. "Go into my study; I will join you presently."

Shortly after, when he had summoned help and sent for Dr. Bianchon, Corentin rejoined la Peyrade.

"You see," said he, with solemnity, "that while following up this marriage with a sort of passionate zeal, I was doing the will of God."

"Monsieur," said la Peyrade, with compunction, "I should, indeed, confess to you——"

"It is useless," interrupted Corentin, "you can tell me nothing I do not already know; on the contrary, there is much I can tell you. Old Peyrade, your uncle, in trying to earn a *dot* for his idolized daughter, entered into a dangerous private enterprise; a thing I would advise you to always avoid. He encountered Vautrin on his way. Your uncle, clever as he was, could not cope with that man, who rejected no aid to success—neither murder, poison, nor rape. To paralyze your uncle's efforts, Lydie was enticed to a seemingly respectable house; there she was kept concealed for ten days. She was told this was done at her father's wish, so, not being alarmed, she spent her time—well, you remember how she can sing."

"Oh!" ejaculated la Peyrade, covering his face with his hands.

"Held as a hostage," continued Corentin, "the unfortunate young girl, in case her father did not do as was required of him within ten days, was reserved for a most horrible fate. A narcotic and a man were to play the executioner with the daughter of Sejanus——"

"Monsieur, monsieur; have mercy," groaned la Peyrade.

"I told you yesterday that you might have more on your conscience than that house of the Thuilliers'; but you were young then. Without experience, bringing with you the brutality of your country, you had that frenzied Southern blood, which on occasion flings itself blindly on. Then your relationship was known to those who were plotting the ruin of this new Clarissa Harlowe; fortunately Providence has permitted, in this appalling history, that there is nothing irreparable in it. The same poison, as it may be employed, gives death or health."

"But, monsieur, shall I not always be an object of horror to her?"

"The doctor, monsieur," said Katt, opening the door.

"How is Mademoiselle Lydie?" asked la Peyrade, eagerly.

"Quite calm," answered Katt; "and just now when we persuaded her to go to bed—though she did not want to go, saying she was not ill—I took her the bundle of rags: 'What do you suppose I want with that, my poor Katt?' said she with a puzzled air; 'if you want me to play with a doll, get me one that is made with more care and turned out in better shape than that one.'"

"You see," said Corentin to the Provençal, "you have become the lance of Achiles."

Then he left the room to receive Dr. Bianchon. Soon after the door opened and Cérizet was ushered in.

"Ha! ha! I knew it," cried the copying clerk. "I knew you would see du Portail in the end. And the marriage—how is it coming on?"

"It is of yours we expect news," said la Peyrade.

"The deuce! then you have heard of it? My faith! yes, my dear. All things must have an end, after a long voyage on storm-swept seas. You know the bride, do you?"

"Yes, a young actress, Olympe Cardinal, a protege of the Minards, who are to give her thirty thousand francs for setting her up."

"And that," said Cérizet, "added to thirty thousand promised by du Portail and the twenty-five I got out of your marriage which didn't come to pass, makes up a total capital of eighty-five thousand francs; with that and a pretty wife a man must be forsaken of heaven if he cannot succeed in a few speculations. But du Portail sent me to see if we could not arrange some scheme to prevent Thuillier's election. Can you suggest any scheme?"

"No;" replied la Peyrade, "and I don't feel any way imaginative either."

"Well, here is how the thing stands: the government is afraid that Thuillier might get elected; Minard, afraid of his popularity, mopes in a corner and takes no steps. Pompous idiots like Thuillier are embarrassing when in the Opposition; they are pitchers without handles, you cannot tell how to hold them."

"You seem well informed as to the government's intentions," said la Peyrade, curious to learn how far he had been admitted to Corentin's confidence.

"Oh, no, indeed; I only tell you what Monsieur du Portail instructed me."

"So!" said la Peyrade, lowering his voice; "who is this du Portail? You appear to have been intimate with him for some time. A man so penetrative as yourself should have gauged the depths of this person who, between you and I, seems to partake somewhat of the mysterious order."

"My friend," said Cérizet, "is a deuced strong man. He's a downy old boy and has had, I fancy, some post in the administration; I think he may have been employed in some department suppressed with the Empire."

"Yes?——" said la Peyrade.

"There, I guess," said Cérizet, "is where he made his roll, and, being an ingenious kind of a fellow, and having a natural daughter to marry, he has concocted this philanthropic yarn of her being the daughter of an old friend named Peyrade; your name being the same suggested, I suppose, the idea of fastening upon you."

"That may be so," replied la Peyrade, "but explain his connection with the government and his interest in the elections."

"That's easy. Du Portail is a man who loves money, and likes to finger it; he has done some little service to Rastignac, that great manipulator of elections, a compatriot of his; in return he gives the other hints in his stock-gambling on the Bourse."

"Did he give you all this confidential information?" asked la Peyrade.

"What do you take me for?" replied Cérizet; "with this worthy man, who has already promised me thirty thousand francs, as you see, I play the simpleton, but I make Bruno talk; you may ally yourself to this family without fear; why, my dear boy, this du Portail is enormously wealthy; he can get you made a sub-prefect, from whence to a prefecture and a fortune it is but a step."

"Thanks," said la Peyrade. "But how came you to know him?"

"Oh! that is quite a history; by my intervention he was able to recover a lot of diamonds that had been stolen."

At this moment Corentin appeared:

"All is going well," said he to la Peyrade. "There are signs of returning reason. Bianchon would like to talk to you, so Monsieur Cérizet will excuse us until this evening."

On the day following Thuillier was discussing with Brigittte Théodose's letter renouncing Céleste's hand, particularly dwelling on the postscript which intimated that la Peyrade might not continue as editor of the "Écho de la Bièvre." At this moment Henri, his servant, came in to ask if he would receive M. Cérizet.

Thuillier's first impulse was to deny himself. Then, thinking better of it, he reflected that Cérizet might prove a resource if he were left in the lurch. Cérizet presented himself without the least embarrassment.

"Well, my dear sir," said he to Thuillier, "you are beginning, I suppose, to get posted as to the Sieur la Peyrade?"

"What do you mean by that?" asked the old beau.

"Well, I should think a man who for a long time has been intriguing to marry your goddaughter abruptly breaks off the marriage, as he will sometime also do about the contract he made you sign about his editorship, cannot be the object of the blind confidence you formerly reposed in him."

"So," said Thuillier, quickly, "you know something then of his intentions to leave the paper?"

"No," said the banker of the poor, "we are not now on such terms as that I should be given his confidence. I draw my inference from what I know of his character."

"You have had some former dealings with him then?"

"Yes, indeed," replied Cérizet. "That business of your house; I started the hare in that. He was to put me in communication with you and make me the first lessee; but the unfortunate event of the bidding-in gave him the opportunity to swindle me and to keep all the profits himself."

"Profits!" exclaimed Thuillier. "I can't see that he got anything out of that beyond the marriage that he refused."

"What!" said the usurer, "ten thousand francs for the Cross which you never received; the twenty-five thousand due Madame Lambert, which you went surety for, which, like a good boy, you are apt to have to pay."

"What's this I hear!" cried Brigitte, bounding out of her chair; "twenty-five thousand francs you stand security for?"

"Yes, mademoiselle," replied Cérizet, "behind the sum that woman was said to have lent him there was some mystery, but la Peyrade was smart enough not only to whitewash himself before your brother, but also to get him to secure——"

"But," interrupted Thuillier, "if you have not seen him, how did you learn that I had become his surety?"

"From the servant herself, monsieur, who tells the whole story now she is sure of being paid."

"Monsieur Cérizet," said Thuillier, holding himself on his reserve, "as I once told la Peyrade, no man is indispensable;

now, if the editorship of my paper becomes vacant, I can readily find persons eager to proffer their services to me."

"Is it for my benefit you speak like that?" asked Cérizet. "You make a bad mistake if it is, for I have no desire to offer mine. For a long time I have been disgusted with journalism. I let la Peyrade jolly me into it, why I don't know, but I have now abjured it for ever. I came to see you about another thing."

"Ah!" said Thuillier.

"Yes," replied Cérizet; "remembering the handsome manner in which you acted in the business of this house, in which you do me the honor of receiving me, it occurred to me that I could not do better than to call your attention to a similar case I have in hand. It is a purely business transaction and I expect to make my profit on it. Now, as the subletting of this house must be a terrible humbug to mademoiselle, for I notice that all the stores still remain unlet, it would suit me to become the principal tenant—I think that might be calculated as part of the profits."

"But this affair?" said Brigitte, "that is the first thing to know."

"It is exactly," said Cérizet, "the contrary to that transaction you had with la Peyrade. You got this house for next to nothing, but were worried by a higher bidder. Now, this is a farm, in Beauce, which has just been sold for a crumb of bread, as they say; it has been placed in my hands to resell at a small advance; you could get it at a fabulously low price."

Then Cérizet set forth the details which had more fascination for Brigitte than it would be like to have for the reader. The statement was precise and interested Thuillier in spite of himself; it was a good speculation.

"Only," said Brigitte, "we must see the farm."

"Nothing is easier," said Cérizet. "I want to see it myself, and intended making an excursion there to-day. If you say so, I'll take you down, calling at your door for you this afternoon with a chaise; we shall be there early to-morrow morning, examine the farm, have breakfast, and return in time for dinner."

"A post-chaise," said Brigitte, "is very lordly. The diligence seems to me——"

"They are too uncertain," said Cérizet. "But you need not think of the expense, for I shall have to go, and otherwise it would be alone; I am only too happy to offer you two seats in my carriage."

To the avaricous little gains often determine great events; after a little resistance, *pro forma*, Brigitte accepted, and that day the three set out on the road to Chartres, Cérizet advising Thuillier not to send word to la Peyrade lest he might play "some dirty trick" on him.

The next evening by five o'clock the trio had returned; and the brother and sister, who kept their opinions to themselves in Cérizet's presence, were both of one mind, that the purchase was a good thing, and this idea of becoming the mistress of rural property seemed to Brigitte the final consecration of opulence.

"Minard," said she, "has nothing but his town-house and invested capital, whereas we shall not only have those but a country place beside. One can't be really rich without that."

Thuillier was not sufficiently charmed by this dream to forget the paper and his candidacy. He no sooner got back than he asked for the "Écho" issued that morning.

"It has not yet been delivered," replied the servant.

"That's a pretty delivery," said Thuillier peevishly, "when even the owner cannot get served."

Although it was late and he was tired, he ordered a hack and drove to the office of the "Écho." There a new disappointment awaited him; the new issue was made up and all the employes had left, even la Peyrade. Coffinet was not at his post as office boy, he had "gone of a arrand," said his wife, and had taken the key of the closet in which the remaining copies of the paper were locked up. It was impossible to get a copy of the journal which the unhappy proprietor had come so far to procure.

To paint Thuillier's indignation is impossible. He marched about the room, talking aloud to himself, as people often do under great excitement.

"I'll turn them all out!" he cried. We are compelled to omit his further objurgations.

While he fulminated his anathema there was a knock at the door.

"Come in," thundered Thuillier, in a voice of wrath and frantic impatience.

Minard appeared, who precipitated himself into his arms.

"My good, my excellent friend," began the Mayor of the Eleventh, his embrace ending in an earnest handshaking.

"Why? what is it?" said Thuillier, understanding nothing of this vehement demonstration.

"Ah! my dear friend," continued Minard, "such an admirable proceeding, one may say really chivalrous, most disinterested! The effect throughout the arrondissement is enormous."

"But what? again I ask," exclaimed Thuillier, impatiently.

"The article, the new departure," said Minard, "all so noble, so elevated."

"But what article? What departure?" said the owner of the "Écho," beside himself with irritation.

"The article of this morning," said Minard.

"The article of this morning?"

"Come, you didn't write it while you slept, or are you like Monsieur Jourdain writing prose, heroical without knowing it?"

"I! I have written no article," cried Thuillier. "I have been absent from Paris since yesterday. I don't even know what is in the paper this morning, and there is no office boy here to give me a copy."

"I have one," said Minard, pulling the much-desired number from his pocket. "If the editorial is not yours, you must have inspired it, and, in any case, the deed is done."

Thuillier had snatched the sheet that Minard held out to him, and devoured, rather than read, the following :

For a long time the owner of this regenerated journal submitted, without complaint or reply, to the cowardly insinuations with which a venal press insults all citizens who, strong in their convictions, refuse to pass under the Caudine Forks of power. So during this long time, a man, who has given proof of his devotion and abnegation in the important functions of an ædile of Paris, has endured the imputation of being nothing but an ambitious intriguer. M. Jérôme Thuillier, strong in his dignity, has suffered these coarse attacks to pass with his scorn, but, encouraged by this contemptuous silence, the stipendiaries of the press have dared to state that this journal, an outcome of intense conviction and disinterested patriotism, was but the stepping-stone of a man, the speculation of a seeker after an election. M. Jérôme Thuillier, in his high dignity, has held himself immovable before these shameless imputations because truth and justice are patient, and he wished to crush the reptile with a blow. The day of execution has arrived.

"A devil of a la Peyrade!" said Thuillier, stopping short at that phrase. "How he hits it off."

"It is magnificent," said Minard.

Reading aloud, Thuillier went on :

All the world, enemies and friends, can testify that M. Jérôme Thuillier has done nothing to seek a candidacy which was spontaneously offered him.

"That's evident," said Thuillier, interrupting himself. Then he continued :

But seeing his sentiments have been so shamefully misrepresented, his intentions so foully travestied, M. Thuillier owes it to himself, and, above all, to the great national party in which he is but the humblest soldier, to give an example which shall confound the vile sycophants of power.

"Truly, la Peyrade gives me full credit," said Thuillier, pausing again in his reading. "I see now why he didn't send me the paper; he wanted to enjoy my surprise: 'Confound the vile sycophants of power,'" repeated he, after rolling it in his mind:

M. Thuillier was so far from founding a paper in opposition to the dynasty to support and promote his election, that at the very time when his election seems to be assured, and most disheartening for his rivals, he here publicly declares, and in the most formal, absolute, and irrevocable terms, that he RENOUNCES HIS CANDIDACY.

"What? How?" cried Thuillier, thinking he had misread or misunderstood.

"Go on," said the Mayor of the Eleventh.

And as Thuillier, with a bewildered manner, seemed indisposed to continue his reading, Minard took the paper in his hands and read, in his stead:

He withdraws from the contest and requests the electors to transfer to M. Minard, mayor of the eleventh arrondissement, and his friend and colleague in his municipal functions, all the votes they seemed disposed to honor him with.

"But this is infamous!" cried Thuillier, recovering his speech, "you have bought that jesuit, la Peyrade."

"So," said Minard, stupefied by Thuillier's attitude, "the article was not arranged between you?"

"The wretch has profited by my absence to slip it in the paper; this explains why he prevented a copy reaching me."

"My dear fellow," said Minard, "what you are saying will seem incredible to the public."

"But I tell you it is treason, a beastly trick. Renounce my candidature—why should I renounce it?"

"You will fully understand, my friend," said Minard, "that if this is an abuse of confidence, I am made desolate; but I have issued my electoral circular, and, by my faith! luck to the lucky."

"Leave me," said Thuillier, pointing to the door, "you have paid for this hoax."

"Monsieur Thuillier," said Minard, in a threatening tone, "I would advise you not to repeat those words unless you intend giving me your reason."

Happily for the "civic courage" of Thuillier he was re-relieved from a reply by Coffinet, who opened the door of the editorial sanctum, announcing:

"The gentlemen electors of the twelfth arrondissement."

This consisted of a deputation of six, an apothecary being the president, who, addressing Thuillier, said they had read the article of that morning and wished to clearly understand what it meant. He was told that a candidate does not belong to himself, but to the electors who have supported him. "But," he finished up, casting his eye on Minard, "the presence in these precincts of the candidate for whom you have gone out of your way to recommend to us, indicates a connivance between you."

"No, gentlemen, no," said Thuillier, "I have not renounced my candidacy; that editorial was written unknown to me and without my consent. To-morrow the denial will appear in the same paper; you will learn, too, that the infamous wretch who betrayed me has been dismissed the editorship."

"Then," said the orator, "you are still a candidate and will support the Opposition?"

"Yes, gentlemen, to the death," said Thuillier.

"Good! Very good!" cried the deputation.

Then, after a cordial handshake all round, Thuillier conducted them to the outer door.

He had barely reëntered the room when:

"Gentlemen the electors of the eleventh arrondissement," said Coffinet, opening the door.

This time the arrondissement consisted of seven persons. A dry-goods man was the president, his little speech ran:

"Monsieur, it is with a sincere admiration that we were apprised this morning that the great art of public virtue, which has greatly touched us all, is not lost. You have proved, by thus retiring, a disinterestedness far from the ordinary, and the esteem of your fellow-citizens——"

"Permit me," said Thuillier, interrupting him, "I cannot allow you to continue; the article upon which you congratulate me was inserted by mistake."

"What!" said the dry-goods man, "do you mean to say that you don't retire from the contest? It will be a great pity if you lose this chance to place yourself in the eyes of your fellow-citizens by the side of Washington and other famous men of antiquity."

"I will to-morrow make all clear to you," said Thuillier. "I trust when you know the whole truth I shall not suffer in your esteem."

"This seems a funny sort of a game," shouted an elector.

"Yes," growled another, "it seems like they were making fools of us."

Whereupon the deputation retired.

It is hardly probable that Thuillier would have gone further with them than the office door, but if he had so intended it was prevented by the entrance of la Peyrade.

"I have just come from your house, my dear fellow," said the Provençal, "they told me I should find you here."

"And you came, doubtless, to explain to me the strange editorial you allowed yourself to insert in my name?"

"Exactly," said la Peyrade. "The man of whom you know, and whose far-reaching influence you have already felt, confided in me yesterday, to the interest both of yourself and the government, and I saw it was inevitable that you would be defeated. I therefore arranged a dignified and honorable retreat for you."

"Very good, monsieur," said Thuillier, "but you will understand that from the present you are no longer the editor of this paper."

"That is what I came to tell you."

"And doubtless also to settle up the little account we have together."

"Gentlemen," said Minard, "I see you have business to attend, I make you my bow."

Minard gone:

"Here are ten thousand francs," said la Peyrade, "which I beg you to hand to Mademoiselle Brigitte; here, also, is the bond by which you secured to Madame Lambert the payment of twenty-five thousand francs, to which is attached her receipt in full."

"Quite right, monsieur," said Thuillier.

La Peyrade bowed and went out.

"Serpent!" said Thuillier, watching him out.

"Cérizet struck the right word," said la Peyrade, "he is a pompous idiot."

The blow struck at Thuillier's candidacy was mortal, but Minard did not profit thereby. While they disputed for the suffrages of the electors, a "castle-man," an aide-de-camp of the King, arrived on the scene, his hands full of tobacco licenses and other the like electioneering small change, and, like the third thief, he stole in between the two candidates who were busy eating each other. It goes without saying that Brigitte did not get her farm at Beauce; this was only a mirage, by the help of which Thuillier was enticed from Paris to enable la Peyrade to deliver his knock-out blow. A service rendered the government, and which was at the same time a full revenge for the humiliations the Provençal had suffered.

Thuillier had some general suspicions as to Cérizet's complicity, but that gentleman justified himself, and, by engineering the sale of the "Écho de la Bièvre," which had become a nightmare to its unfortunate proprietor, he made himself as white as snow. Bought out by Corentin, the poor sheet of the Opposition became a "canard" sold on Sundays in the taverns after being concocted in the den of the police.

About a month after the scene in which la Peyrade had been shown that through a crime in the past his future was irrevocably settled, he had married his victim, who now had long intervals of lucidity, though the full return of her reason could not be counted upon until the time and conditions previously indicated by the physicians had become fulfilled. One morning Corentin was closeted with his successor. Taking part in his labors, and serving his apprenticeship for the delicate and arduous duties of his office, Théodose did not bring that acumen and spirit into the work that Corentin desired. He saw that his pupil had cherished a feeling of degradation; time would heal the wound, but the callus was as yet unformed.

Opening a number of sealed envelopes containing his agents' reports, most of which were contemptuously pitched into the waste-paper basket, to be afterward burnt, the great man gave particular attention to one he came across; as he read it he slightly smiled once or twice, and when he had finished:

"Here," said he to la Peyrade, passing the manuscript over, "this will interest you; it shows that our profession, which at present seems to you unpleasantly tragic, does at times dabble in comedy, in addition. Read it aloud, it will amuse us."

Before la Peyrade had commenced to read:

"I ought to let you know," added Corentin, "that this report is from a man named Henri, whom Madame Komorn placed in service with the Thuilliers."

"So," said la Peyrade, "you have servants to your hand; is that one of your methods?"

"Sometimes," replied Corentin, "to know all, all means must be utilized; but, on this subject, many lies are spoken about us. It is not true that the police make a regular system of this. But I wanted an eye and ear in the Thuillier household, so I let the Godollo loose upon it; she in turn installed one of our men there, quite an intelligent fellow, as you will learn. But suppose another servant came and said he was willing to sell me the secrets of his master, I should have him arrested and let a warning be sent to the family to distrust the other servants."

Monsieur the Chief of the Secret Police, I did not stay long with the little baron; he is a man wholly absorbed in frivolous pleasures; there was nothing to gather worthy of a report. I have another situation though where I have seen a number of things which have a bearing on the mission intrusted to me by Mme. de Godollo; I take the liberty of acquainting you with them. The household in which I am now in *service* is that of an old professor, M. Picot, who lives on a first floor, Place de la Madeleine, in the suite and house lately occupied by my former masters, the Thuilliers.

"What!" cried la Peyrade, interrupting himself, "Old Picot, that ruined old lunatic, occupying such splendid apartments?"

"Go on, go on!" cried Corentin; "life is full of stranger things than that; you will find the explanation lower; our correspondents—it's one of their defects—are too fond of drawing facts in detail; they are always over careful in dotting their *i*'s."

The man Henri went on:

The Thuilliers, some time ago, left here to return to their Latin quarter. Mlle. Brigitte never really liked our sphere; her total lack of education made her uncomfortable. Because I spoke correctly she dubbed me "the orator," and her porter she disliked, because, being sexton at the Madeleine church, he has some manners; she even complained of the market-people in the market at the rear of the church, and said they gave themselves "capable" airs, only for that they are not so coarse-tongued as those of the Halle, and laughed when she tried to beat down their prices. She has let her house now to an ugly man with only half a nose, one Cérizet, who pays a rent of fifty-five thousand francs. This leaseholder seems to know his road about; he has just married an actress at a minor theatre and was about to occupy this floor, using it also as offices for a company issuing policies for marriage-portions, when M. Picot, arriving from England with his wife, a very wealthy Englishwoman, saw the suite of rooms and offered so large a rental that M. Cérizet felt constrained to accept it. It was then that being introduced by M. Pascal, the janitor, I took service with M. Picot.

"M. Picot, married to a very rich Englishwoman," said la Peyrade, again interrupting himself; "it is inconceivable!"
"Read on," said Corentin; "you will comprehend later."

The fortune of my new master is quite a history, and Mme. de Godollo was mixed up with the marriage of a pupil of his—a M. Félix Phellion, the inventor of a star—who in despair at not being able to marry that demoiselle whom they wanted to give to M. la Peyrade, of whom Mme. de Godollo made such an ass——

"Scoundrel!" said the Provençal, in a parenthesis; "is that how he speaks of me? He doesn't know yet with whom he has to deal."
Corentin laughed heartily and told his pupil to go ahead.

and who in despair at not being allowed to marry her had gone off to England, whence he was to set off on a journey round the world; just a lover's notion. Hearing of this departure, M. Picot, his old professor, went after him to prevent this nonsense, which was not a difficult matter. The English are naturally very jealous about discoveries, and when they saw M. Phellion about to embark with their own professors they asked him if he had an order from the Admiralty; not being provided with this, they laughed in his face and would not permit him on board at all; they feared he would prove more learned than they.

"He seems to think a great deal of the *entente cordiale*, your M. Henri," said la Peyrade, jokingly.

"Yes," replied Corentin, "you will be struck in the reports of our agents with this general and continued spirit of calumniation. But what can be done! we cannot expect angels to take up the trade of spies."

Left upon the shore, Telemachus and Mentor thought best to return to France; they were about doing so when M. Picot received a letter such as none but an Englishwoman could have written. It said that the writer had read his theory of "Perpetual Motion," and had also heard of the wonderful discovery of a star; she regarded him as a genius next only to Newton; if the hand of her who addressed him, joined to eighty thousand pounds, or two million francs, suited his convenience, she was at his disposal. M. Picot liked the offer; he met the English lady, a woman of forty at the least, with a red nose, long teeth, and spectacles. He had intended offering her his pupil, but he saw that this was out of the question, so he told her that he was old, half-blind, had not discovered the star, and did not possess a son. She replied that Milton was not a young man and was stone-blind; as for the star, she did not care much about that; that the author of "Perpetual Motion" was, and had been for ten years past, the man of her dreams; and she again offered herself with a *dot* of eighty thousand pounds sterling; beside, he only had a cataract on his eyes; she was the daughter of a noted oculist and knew this. M. Picot made answer that if his sight were restored and she would consent to live in Paris, for he hated England, he would permit himself to be married. The operation was successfully performed, and, at the end of three weeks, the newly wedded couple arrived in the capital. All these details I learned from madame's maid with whom I am on intimate terms.

"You see, conceited puppy!" said Corentin laughing.

But the remainder of what I have to inform M. the Chief are facts of which I speak *de visu*. When the Picots were comfortably installed they gave invitations to a dinner to all the guests, and a few others, who had attended a dinner at which M. Picot had had a funny encounter with Mlle. Thuillier. The whole company were on hand at the time named, but M. Picot did not appear. The guests were received by Madame, who does not speak French and could only say: "My husband will soon be here;" at last M. Picot arrived, and they were stupefied on seeing, instead of a shabby, blind old man, a handsome, hale, young old man, carrying his years jauntily, like M. Ferville, of the Gymnase, and saying:

"I beg your pardon, ladies, for not being here when you arrived, but I was at the Academy of Sciences, awaiting the result of an election—that of Monsieur Félix Phellion, who was unanimously elected less three votes."

The news seemed to be well received by the company.

"I must also ask your pardon, ladies, for my rather peculiar behavior in this very place, a few weeks ago. My excuses are my late infirmity, the annoyances of a law-suit, and an old housekeeper who robbed and plagued me in a thousand ways and of whom I have the happiness of being now delivered. To-day you see me rejuvenated, married to an amiable spouse, and with only one cloud to obscure my happiness—that of my young friend who has been crowned by the Academy; all here are more or less guilty toward him; I, for my ingratitude, when he turned over to me the benefits of his discovery and the reward of his immortal labors; that young lady I see there with tears in her eyes, for having foolishly accused him of atheism; that other stern-looking one, for replying with harshness to his proposals made by his worthy father, whose white hairs she should rather have honored; M. Thuillier, for having sacrificed him to ambition; M. Colleville, for not having done his part as a father, and choosing the most worthy man; M. Minard, for giving in to his jealousy and trying to foist his son in his place. There are but two present who have done him common justice—Madame Thuillier and M. the Abbé Gondrin. I shall now ask that man of God whether we may not almost doubt Divine justice, when we see this generous young man, the victim of all of us, tossed at the mercy of the waves and tempest, to which for three long years he is consigned before he returns?"

"Providence is mighty, monsieur," said the abbé; "God will protect M. Félix Phellion in the midst of peril; in three years let us have the firm hope that he will be safely restored to us."

"But three years," said M. Picot. "Will it still be time? Mlle. Colleville, will she wait for him?"

"Yes, I swear it," cried the young girl, carried away by an uncontrollable impulse.

"And you, Mlle. Thuillier," continued Picot, "and you, Mme. Colleville, will you allow this?"

"Yes, yes," cried everybody; for M. Picot's voice, full and sonorous, had tears in it.

"It is time, then," said M. Picot, "to grant an amnesty to Providence." Then rushing to the door where my ear was glued to the keyhole—by George! he nearly caught me:

"Announce," said he to me, "M. Félix Phellion and family."

Thereupon a door opened and five or six persons came out, who were led by M. Picot into the salon.

At the sight of her lover Mlle. Colleville fell in a faint, but the spell was soon over, and, seeing M. Félix at her feet, she threw herself, weeping, into Mme. Thuillier's arms, crying:

"Godmother, you always told me to hope."

Mlle. Thuillier, who, as I have always thought, despite her harsh nature and lack of education, is a very remarkable woman, had a happy inspiration:

"One moment," she said, for they were just starting for the dining-room. "Monsieur Phellion," she said, going up to him, "monsieur and old friend, I ask for the hand of M. Félix Phellion for our adopted daughter, Mlle. Colleville."

"Bravo, bravo!" cried all in chorus.

"My God!" said M. Félix Phellion, tearfully, "what have I done to deserve so great a happiness!"

"You have been an honest man and a Christian without knowing it," replied the Abbé Gondrin.

Here la Peyrade flung down the letter.

"Well! you haven't finished it?" said Corentin, picking it up. "But there's not much more; M. Henri just informs me that he was 'moved'—*him!* no, wait," added Corentin, "here's another detail of some importance:"

The Englishwoman made it known during dinner that, having no heirs, her fortune after the deaths of herself and husband, will go to Félix, who, as a consequence, will become enormously wealthy.

La Peyrade had risen and was striding rapidly about the room.

"Well, what's the matter?" asked Corentin.

"Nothing," answered the Provençal.

"Yes, there is," replied the detective; "I think you are a little jealous of that young man's good fortune. My dear fellow, allow me to suggest to you that if you wished such a conclusion for yourself, you should have acted as he has done.

When I sent you one hundred louis to study law, I did not then intend you as my successor; I expected you to labor at the oars of your own galley, to have the courage for obscure and hard toil; your day must have come. But you choose to violate Fate."

"Monsieur!" said la Peyrade.

"I mean, hastened it—cutting the hay while yet green. You took a fling at journalism; you made acquaintances of Cérizet and Dutocq; and, frankly, I think you very fortunate in reaching the port in which you have now found a refuge. Beside, you are not of a nature sufficiently simple-hearted to enjoy such bliss as is reserved for Félix Phellion and——"

"These middle-classes," said la Peyrade, quickly; "I know them now, to my cost. They have great absurdities, great vices even; but they have their virtues, or, at the least, very estimable qualities; in them lies the vital force of our corrupt society."

"*Your* society!" said Corentin, smiling; "you speak as if you were still in the ranks. You are struck off the roll, my dear, and you must learn to be more content with your lot; governments pass; societies perish or dwindle; but we—we dominate all things; and the Police is eternal."

www.ingramcontent.com/pod-product-compliance
Lightning Source LLC
Chambersburg PA
CBHW022057300426
44117CB00007B/489